The Road to Luxury

The Road to Luxury

The Evolution, Markets, and Strategies of Luxury Brand Management

Ashok Som
Christian Blanckaert

WILEY

Cover image: iStock.com/Emilia_Szymanek
Cover design: Wiley

Published by John Wiley & Sons Singapore Pte. Ltd.
1 Fusionopolis Walk, #07-01, Solaris South Tower, Singapore 138628

Other Wiley Editorial Offices

John Wiley & Sons, 111 River Street, Hoboken, NJ 07030, USA
John Wiley & Sons, The Atrium, Southern Gate, Chichester, West Sussex, P019 8SQ,
United Kingdom
John Wiley & Sons (Canada) Ltd., 5353 Dundas Street West, Suite 400, Toronto, Ontario,
M9B 6HB, Canada
John Wiley & Sons Australia Ltd., 42 McDougall Street, Milton, Queensland 4064,
Australia
Wiley-VCH, Boschstrasse 12, D-69469 Weinheim, Germany

Library of Congress Cataloging-in-Publication Data is Available

ISBN 978-0-470-83002-4 (Hardcover)
ISBN 978-0-470-83004-8 (ePDF)
ISBN 978-0-470-83005-5 (ePub)
ISBN 978-1-118-81432-1 (oBook)

Typeset in 11.5/14pt Bembo by Laserwords Private Limited, Chennai, India

Printed in Singapore by C. O. S. Printers Pte Ltd

10 9 8 7 6 5 4 3 2 1

We dedicate this book to
Elliot, Ines, Valentin, Victor, and Zoya

Contents

Acknowledgments   xi
About the Authors   xiii
Prologue: The Pink Bag   1

Chapter 1: Introduction: Definition and Crisis of Luxury   5
                Issues of Defining Luxury   6
                Crisis   8
                The Luxury Industry   10
                Reaction to the Crisis of Global Markets   12
                Effect of Crisis on the Luxury Industry   18
                Strategic Response to Crisis   20
                Conclusion   25
Chapter 2: Evolution of the Global Luxury Market   29
                Evolution   32
                How Has It Changed?   38
                Luxury Industry Trends   40
                Conclusion   44

Chapter 3:   Who's Who of Luxury   47
                 The Consumers   48
                 The Actors   50
                 Conclusion   88
Chapter 4:   Branding   89
                 Luxury Marketing: Highly Creative and
                     Selective   92
                 Cobranding: Does It Enhance Branding or
                     Selling?   107
                 Brand Extensions   109
                 Pricing   112
                 Storytelling: Culture, Event, and
                     Communication   115
                 Digital Marketing   119
                 Discussion   129
                 Conclusion   130
Chapter 5:   Brand Identity, Clients, and Ethos   133
                 Brand Identity   134
                 Ethos   140
                 Clients   144
                 Discussion   149
                 Conclusion   153
Chapter 6:   Family Houses, Corporatization, and New
                 Entrants   155
                 What Is a Family Business?   158
                 Family Business during Crisis   177
                 Family Businesses of the Future:
                     Corporatization   178
                 Changes during Transition from Family
                     Business to Corporation   182
                 Entrepreneurs and New Entrants   186
                 Trends and Discussion   190
                 Conclusion   193
Chapter 7:   Management Styles in the Luxury Industry   195
                 Path Dependency: Management Styles   197
                 Managing Paradoxes   202
                 Examples of Styles   210

	Analysis	227
	Conclusion	230
Chapter 8:	Skills	235
	Historical Craftsmanship	238
	Entrepreneurial Designers	240
	The Sales Team	243
	The Professional Managers	244
	Skills Required	245
	Managing Talent	248
	Conclusion	261
Chapter 9:	Services: The Point of Sale	265
	Issues in Point-of-Sale	268
	The Customer Dimension	269
	The Service Dimension	277
	Conclusion	280
Chapter 10:	Systems and Operations in the Luxury Business	285
	The Challenge	286
	Global Supply Chain	290
	Customer Relationship Management	295
	Information Technology	301
	Conclusion	302
Chapter 11:	Retail, Distribution, and E-Commerce	307
	Channels of Distribution	309
	Travel Retail and Duty-Free Stores	324
	Strategic Decisions in Geographic Expansion	328
	Online Distribution and E-Commerce	331
	Conclusion	335
Chapter 12:	Intellectual Property Rights and Counterfeiting	337
	Counterfeiting: Issues for Luxury Brands	340
	The Issue of Legality	344
	Is It an Emerging Market Phenomenon?	346
	Effect on a Brand	347
	Examples of Responses to Counterfeiting	350
	What to Do to Prevent Counterfeiting?	353
	Gray Market	362
	Conclusion	364

Chapter 13: Emerging Markets and Emerging Market Luxury
Brands   367
Brazil   369
Russia   381
India   386
China   395
Strategic Actions   404
Conclusion   409
Chapter 14: The Future and Questions to Ponder   411

Research Design, Methodology, and Data Collection   421
Bibliography   427
Index   433

Acknowledgments

I taught the course on strategy in the program of MBA in International Luxury Brand Management from 2004 to 2012 at ESSEC Business School. The idea of the book crystallized during my interactions with the participants of the program. Prompted by my students, I started to create assignments such as case studies, which the students from the program wrote under my supervision. Those teaching materials were used in the program with great success and were adapted worldwide in other universities and business schools. I am grateful to the participants in this program for their insights and feedback. My work environment in a French *grande ecole* provided and sustained my interest in French and Italian luxury businesses. I appreciate the efforts of my colleague Simon Nyeck to involve me in the program and my friend Michel Phan to discuss and debate the world of fashion and luxury trends. My sincere thanks to Esther Boinville, Anthea Davis, Armelle Leduc, Denis Morisset and other members of the team managing the MBA in International Luxury Brand Management program for the last two decades.

I acknowledge the support of all my students, especially Yu Cao, Arushi Chopra, Sushanta Das, Rashi Gupta, Hannes Gurzki, Naja Pape, Shiva Pappu, and Milan Rabold who supported me in my research while writing this book. My sincere thanks to my students, Manuela Brische, Lilly Liu, Deepak Yachamaneni, Boris Gbahoué, Geraldine Carter, Stephanie Masson, Misha Gupta, Karyn Bell, Anna Nolting, Fernanda Harger, Nora Kato, Raghavendra Sheshamurthy, Nonika Vyas, Tina Huang, Sid Shetty, Priscilla Mark, Mario Sanz del Castillo, Lynn Chou, Lan Wu, Leonardo Banegas, Pajaree Kasemsant, Salman Bukhari who spend their time revising and integrating my comments multiple times to make their work publishable. Also my appreciation goes to Ruchi Shangari Dsouza, Debjani Roy, Daniel Tobar-Richter, Clara Gonzalez Goicoechea, Valerie Flexor, Jisook Anh, Mo Cheng, Wenjing Wang, Meng Li, Erik Lobatom Kanika Holloway, Sophia Redford, Alessandro Cannata, Hui Xu and many others worked diligently in my course on Managing the Global Corporation. My most sincere appreciation goes to Nathalie Delforge for administration and logistics, to our Department assistants Christiane, Alexandra & Nathalie, and to my editor Tracy Donhardt, who helped me shape the manuscript.

I unhesitatingly acknowledge the support and encouragement of Françoise Rey, who motivated me to try new concepts and creative ways of managing programs. I express my sincere thanks to Jean-Michel Blanquer, Vincenzo Esposito Vinzi, Radu Vranceanu, Marie-Laure Djelic, Gilles van Wijk, and all my colleagues who supported me in this endeavor.

I acknowledge the companies such as Bavaria; British American Tobacco; BMW; DFS; Ganjam; the Leela Palaces, Hotels, and Resorts; Van Cleef and Arpels; Chaumet; Pernod Ricard; Krug; Baccarat: Raketa and many others who enhanced our knowledge about the different sectors of the luxury business. I acknowledge the strong support of Piyush Kumar Sinha from IIM Ahmedabad, India, who codirected the Advanced Management Program in Luxury for the past four years.

Despite the best efforts of the contributors, I remain responsible for any shortcomings. Finally, I would like to acknowledge the efforts of my seven-year-old daughter, Mekhala-Zoya, who regularly reminded me not to waste my time on browsing Facebook but to complete my part of the chapters before the ever-extending deadlines.

Ashok Som

About the Authors

ASHOK SOM is Professor of Management Department at ESSEC Business School. Professor Som is one of the pioneering thought leaders in designing organizations and an expert in Global Strategy. His books *Organization: Redesign and Innovative HRM* was published by Oxford University Press (2008) and *International Management: Managing the Global Corporation* was published by McGrawHill, UK (2009). At ESSEC, he was the Founding Associate Dean of the full-time, one-year post experience, Global MBA program; the founder of the India Research Centre; and the founder and Director of the Global Management Programs on Luxury and Retail Management (in partnership with Indian Institute of Management [IIM] Ahmedabad). He received his PhD from IIM Ahmedabad; M.Sc and M.Tech from the Indian Institute of Technology, Kharagpur; and bachelor's degree from Presidency College, Calcutta, India. He is passionate about case-based research and teaching. He was the winner of the EFMD Case Writing Competition 2008 in the Indian Management category. He won the Case Centre Award 2014 in the Entrepreneurship category. He is Adjunct Faculty at IIM Ahmedabad (India) and Mannheim Business School (Germany), and Visiting Professor at IIM Calcutta (India), Auckland University of Technology (New Zealand), Graduate School of Business, Keio University (Tokyo), and Tamkang University (Taiwan). His current research is on creative industries, focusing on luxury industry. He is a regular speaker in international conferences and consults with European and Indian multinationals.

CHRISTIAN BLANCKAERT's resume establishes him as a global leader in luxury. He is currently the nonexecutive Chairman of Petit-Bateau and Advisor to the Chairman of EPI Group (J.M. Weston, Alain Figaret, Bonpoint, Champagne Piper-Heidseick and Charles Heidseick), the family holding Descours. He is also Senior Advisor of Eurazeo and a board member of Moncler. From 1996 to 2009, Blanckaert was the Chairman and CEO of Hermès Sellier and Executive Vice President of Hermès International. From 1988 to 1996 he was President of Comité Colbert (a French organization that represents 70 French luxury companies). During his career, Christian has been a consultant with the Boston-based consulting firm Harbridge House. He was Managing Director of the do-it-yourself chain Bricorama, Chairman and CEO of Thomson-Distribution, and Managing Director of the SCAC group. Christian was also for many years Chairman of the Board of the French National School of Decorative Arts (ENSAD). Blanckaert was Mayor of Varengeville-sur-Mer for 21 years and is the author of six books: *Les Chemins du luxe* (Grasset, 1996), *Portraits en Clair-Obscur* (Balland, 2001), a biography of Roger Salengro (Balland, 2004), *Luxe* (Editions du Cherche-Midi, 2007), *Luxe Trotter* (2012 Editions du Cherche–Midi, 2012), and *Les 100 mots du Luxe* (Les Presses Universitaires de France PUF, 2012). He is a visiting professor at ESCP-PARIS. Blanckaert graduated from the Institut d'Etudes Politiques de Paris, the Faculty of Law of Paris, and has an MBA from INSEAD.

Prologue

The Pink Bag

I t had been sitting there, on the shelf, for ages.

Two years, three years —nobody knew exactly, but it was surely a "depreciated asset," as a slick city banker might say.

They could have hidden it away at the back of a store cupboard, but that would have been too sad, too harsh. The bag had become a fixture, a familiar friend of the store, and it sat there, doggedly, fixedly—probably for a long time.

This bag had personality. It was pink. Pink crocodile leather with a diamond clasp. Worth a small fortune. Yet still on the shelf.

From time to time, someone would move it to another spot.

It would be showcased, at the entrance, or to one side, or right in the middle, or at the back of the store.

It had attracted plenty of dust, watched thousands of customers pass by, as it waited in vain to catch someone's eye.

1

The pink crocodile bag filled the sales assistants with despair, but it was no use to think about it. They kept it, convinced that one day there would be a new turn of fate.

The pink bag had aged a little, the candy pink had begun to fade slightly, and the diamonds, which were polished every day, had lost some of their sparkle.

"We should take it off the shelf," said the leather section manager. "We can't keep it on sale," said the head sales manager. In short, the pink bag was a nuisance; its continual presence was annoying and it was beginning to stand out like a sore thumb.

The bag felt ashamed. What could be the reason for its failure? Its price, its color, its skin?

The sales assistants resorted to making jokes and calling it "unsellable," which is of course the worst insult for a handbag.

One Monday morning, a customer came across the bag, high up on its perch. The bag seemed rather aloof, almost condescending, as it looked down on the crowd of customers.

"May I have a look at it?" inquired the lady.

Excited, the sales assistant took down the bag, taking care to don her white gloves, so as not to scratch the crocodile leather. She announced the price, one hundred and ten thousand francs, and said rather clumsily, almost apologetically: "Madam, just look at the magnificent diamonds." The customer replied, "No, I think the bag itself is beautiful. The color is unique. I've never seen a pink quite like it." Gilberte, the sales assistant, couldn't believe her ears when the lady added, "I'll take it."

With a wave of her arms, a hand in the air, Gilberte did all she could to alert her colleagues.

"The pink bag has been sold!"

The news spread through the store like wildfire.

At the checkout, the bag was ready and waiting, all polished and packaged, magnificent in its superb orange box.

The sales assistant accompanied the customer to the checkout.

"How would you like to pay?" she asked.

"American Express," replied the lady, confidently.

Normally, the transaction is accepted at the first try. But this time, the machine tried once, twice, three times … before the harassed cashier was obliged to announce, in hushed tones, "I'm sorry Madam, your card is refused."

"The swine!" cried the customer. "It's my husband's doing, we're divorcing and he's blocked the account. I'll come back tomorrow and pay cash."

A few shrugs and gesticulations later and the whole store heard the message that something was wrong.

The bag remained calmly in its box while its would-be owner stormed out.

Gilberte slowly removed the packaging, took the bag out of the orange box, and placed it back on the shelf.

At closing time, the bag was still there, shrouded in disappointment and surrounded by the sales team, who were muttering, "It's because of the color," and "It will never sell." In the end, the manager said, "We'll take it off sale tomorrow."

The story of the pink bag should have ended there.

The next day, around 11 a.m., a man stopped at the store, asked to see the bag, examined it lovingly, and bought it.

This time, the American Express card was accepted, the bag was sold; a victory for candy pink and a relief for Gilberte. The pessimists and the gigglers were both left speechless.

The story of the pink bag should have ended there. It had been purchased by its very own knight in shining armor.

That afternoon, something extraordinary happened.

Nobody had believed the lady when she said she would come back for the bag and pay cash. They had sold it without as much as a second thought for her.

And who was going to believe that divorce story, anyway?

Well, she turned up, all happy and smiling, and proudly placed 110,000 francs in notes on the desk.

"I've come to pick up my dream," she said.

The reactions among the sales assistants ranged from unease to sheer horror.

This was not going to be easy to explain. What could they say?

It was Gilberte who took the plunge. She explained the situation and promised to remedy it. And so a second and last bag was made, identical to the first.

They say crocodiles will wait a long time to catch their prey.

Chapter 1

Introduction

Definition and Crisis of Luxury

uxury has a long and fascinating history. It is apparent in artifacts from the Egyptian period of lavishness, from 1550 to 1070 B.C. Another great wave of luxurious lifestyle occurred during the Italian Renaissance, an era of great painters, sculptors, and architects during the fourteenth through sixteenth centuries A.D. This was followed by the reign of King Louis XIV of France (1638–1715), whose reign expressed an authentic French lifestyle. Then came Charles Frederick Worth (1825–1895) of Great Britain, a designer who created the concept of haute couture. Worth moved to Paris in 1846 to perfect and then commercialize his craft, holding the first fashion shows and launching the use of fashion labels. Coco Chanel (1883–1971) and Christian Dior (1905–1957) gave birth to modern fashions and ideals, marked by the rise of New York City as a luxury capital. The 1960s and 1970s then experienced the second Italian luxury revolution. Gucci and

Bernard Arnault started applying the principles of strategic management to modern luxury by building the first multibrand conglomerate, Louis Vuitton Moët Hennessey (LVMH) group. The latest chapter to this fascinating tale of luxury and high fashion is the information technology revolution, in which news about a new product spreads like wildfire and opinions on brands, products, and companies are shared at the click of a button. The story of the evolution of luxury is really about the evolution of society.

Countries evolve through various phases of luxury consumption. The first stage is deprivation, in which a country is crushed by poverty, which builds in the populace the desire to consume. As soon as the country manages to free itself from the shackles of deprivation and witness economic progress, its citizens are lured into buying luxuries that have high functional utilities, like washing machines, cars, and practical appliances. Then the wealthy and elite start buying luxury products. The third stage of development is marked by the desire of citizens to show their wealth: Mere possession is insufficient when luxury goods become a symbol of social status and bestow their owners with an aura of divinity. Then comes a stage in which most people in the nation are well-off and have sufficient resources; however, they have a need to fit in with their group. If someone is not carrying or wearing an appropriate social marker, they might find it hard to fit in with a particular group. Finally, luxury becomes a way of life. When people become used to this lifestyle, it becomes difficult for them to go back to their previous habits. Here luxury is more and more associated with personal tastes and pleasure, and not necessarily with wealth or status.

Issues of Defining Luxury

It is important to understand why certain brands are called luxury brands and what justifies the superior positioning they command. Luxury empires are not built by selling tasteful products at an exorbitant price. Luxury brands have been carefully crafted through meticulous strategies in marketing and brand building, making their mark in the consumer's subconscious and having the following main characteristics: brand strength, differentiation, exclusivity, innovation, product craftsmanship and precision, premium pricing, and high quality.

It is the differentiated quality of the material, design, and performance of a Patek Philippe watch that merits a 1,000-percent premium over a normal watch picked up from a general store. It is the craftsmanship that goes into the Kelly bag made by Hermès that justifies its exceptionally high price tag. It is only the brand strength of Louis Vuitton that can entice customers to preorder bags months in advance. It is attention to craftsmanship and nuances of details that help differentiate a luxury product.

Many misconceptions exist that surround the luxury industry: (1) Do luxury and fashion mean the same thing? (2) Does a high price imply a luxury product? and (3) Does luxury imply perfection?

Luxury and fashion do not mean the same thing; they can coexist, but that's not always the case. Until the nineteenth century, only the very privileged few could afford to keep up with changing trends. So only those who could bear the cost of luxury could afford to make and follow fashion. However, the twenty-first century consumer doesn't need to be wealthy to be fashionable; being trendy no longer needs to be costly. For example, streetwear brands produced by H&M and Zara are fashionable and affordable. Haute couture is still the trendsetter but is not the only reference anymore. Luxury products used to be seen as investments, which are not replaced that often, but now they have become more of a lifestyle choice. Many luxury houses try to release fashionable products along with their traditional luxury goods. For instance, Chanel offers fashionable products in order to keep up with the times and renew interest in their classic items.

If one pays a high price for an item, that does not mean that the product is a luxury good. Everyday products could trade up and charge a higher price. All luxury products are expensive, but not all expensive products are luxurious. This means that it is difficult to sell premium products as luxury goods—a phenomenon known as "premiumization" or "trading-up." Similarly, it is unwise to reposition a luxury brand as a premium product to extend its market. Automobile companies have tried to reposition products both ways and have failed, such as Mercedes with both the launch of the Smart car and its acquisition of Chrysler. It had to launch Maybach. In the meantime, BMW traded-up to the 6 and 7 series together with trading-down to the BMW 1-series. Toyota and Nissan, on the other hand, launched the Lexus and the Infiniti from the very beginning. Porsche gained a significant market share with the launch of Cayenne in 2002, but in the meantime it suffered a lot of complaints from its loyal customers about the degrading of the brand image. When one pays a tidy sum to procure a luxury brand, what does he or she pay for? Perfection? Not necessarily. In some ways, what defines the luxury brands are the creators and not the consumers. A luxurious product may thus be far from perfect. However, would these characteristics be questioned in times of a recession, when consumers become more cautious, have a limited budget, and spend less?

Crisis

Bling is over. Red carpetry covered with rhinestones is out. I call it the new modesty.

—Karl Lagerfeld

There were several economic crises during 1970s to 2014, starting with the oil crises in 1973 and 1979, the stock market crash in 1987, the 1992 Black Wednesday crash, and 1997's Asian financial crisis. The first 10 years of the twenty-first century also saw many crises. The stock markets collapsed in early 2000, following the dot-com bubble of the late 1990s. In 2001 the world watched as the terrorist attacks in New York and Washington took place, followed by the war in Afghanistan in 2001 and the invasion of Iraq in 2003. The early 2000s also saw a recession in many countries of the world, aggravated by the outbreak of SARS in Asia in 2003. In 2004, the tsunami in Asia killed hundreds of thousands. Finally, in 2007 the subprime mortgage crisis that began in the United States housing market spread all over the world and caused, among many other things, the collapse of Lehman Brothers and the European debt crisis of 2011, which continues to have effects such as the Cyprus bailout and political turmoil in Russia and Italy.

Crisis can essentially be of four forms: (1) endogenous (inner), such as economic and financial crises; (2) exogenous (outer), such as a political crisis; (3) natural disasters; and (4) mixed characteristics. An *economic crisis*

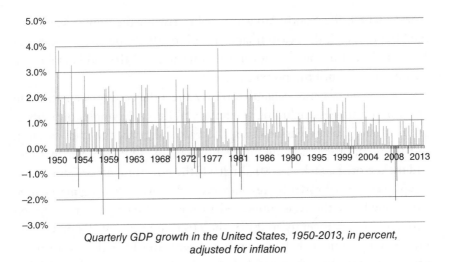

Quarterly GDP growth in the United States, 1950-2013, in percent,
adjusted for inflation

Figure 1.1 Quarterly GDP Growth in the United States, 1950–2013 (in percent adjusted for inflation)

is one where the real economy, of one country or worldwide, experiences a significant slowdown. The gross domestic product consumption stagnates or shrinks, along with investments, capacity utilization, household incomes, company profits, and inflation, while bankruptcies and unemployment rates rise. Figure 1.1 shows periods of shrinking GDP between 1950 and 2013 using the example of the world's biggest economy, the United States.

On the other hand a *financial crisis* is a sudden devaluation of assets, such as stocks or currencies, which may or may not have an effect on the real economy. In itself, a financial crisis only leads to the destruction of paper wealth. It has been observed that there is a reciprocal relationship with other types of crises, such as economic crises and political crises, which is the reason why financial crises generally lead to increased levels of caution within politics and the real economy. Examples of such financial crisis are the burst of the dot-com bubble, together with the September 11, 2001 terrorist attacks, the subprime crisis of 2007, and the ongoing Eurozone debt crisis facing the world, transforming from the private debt property bubble of 2008–2009 into the sovereign debt crisis of major banks and economies of Europe, in which the Dow Jones lost about 50 percent of its value. Other such crises that affected the world include the South American debt crisis of the 1980s, known as the "lost decade"; the Asian financial crisis of 1997; the Russian crisis of 1998; and the European debt crisis that started in 2010 and has taken an enormous toll until the present moment.

Like financial crisis, *political crisis* may affect the economy and have an effect on industries, including the luxury industry. Examples of political crises are the Cuban Missile crisis, the Falkland crisis, the Iraqi invasion of Kuwait and the following intervention by the United States in 1990, and the terrorist attack in 2001. In 2011, the governments of Tunisia and Egypt were overthrown by revolutions and Libya saw a regime change after a civil war that was supported mainly by France and the United Kingdom. More recently in 2013, the election results of Beppe Grillo's Five Star movement in Italy combined with the EU's decision on tax issues in Cyprus have fueled disbelief in the democratic problem-solving capacity of the EU and its members.

Natural disasters such as the tsunami in Asia in 2004, the Tōhoku earthquake and tsunami that caused a meltdown at the Fukushima nuclear plant in Japan in 2011, and the typhoon Bhopa in the Philippines in 2012 had devastating effects on the local economies.

The Luxury Industry

Past crises have had different impacts on varied groups (be it luxury conglomerates or independent luxury houses) at different times; this could be attributed to the exogenous and endogenous characters of the economic cycles. Nonetheless, the 2009 financial crisis was global in nature; it ultimately evolved into the Eurozone crisis and in 2014 is still continuing to affect the major countries in both Europe and America.

To understand the effect of crisis in the luxury industry, luxury must first be divided into (1) hard luxury, such as watches and jewelry; and (2) soft luxury, such as fashion. A more comprehensive definition of the luxury industry includes products and services such as wine and spirits, food, travel, hotels and spas, technology, and cars. Among the most well-known luxury brands are Louis Vuitton, Hermès, Gucci, Cartier, Porsche, Ralph Lauren, Rolex, Tiffany, Armani, Burberry, and Ferrari. In 2012 the worldwide market for luxury grew more than 4 percent over 2011 to a massive €212 billion. In 2013 the worldwide market for luxury grew over 2 percent over 2012 to a massive €217 billion.[1]

During 2009–2013, this industry felt the impact of the crises. Luxury consumers changed, and so did the industry, with the rise of luxury multibrand conglomerates such as LVMH of Bernard Arnault, Kering of Francois Pinault, and Richemont of Johann Rupert, which were formed by the acquisitions of traditional family-run brands. Other luxury brands (usually family-owned) that resisted being taken over by the aforementioned conglomerates also grew alongside the conglomerates. The family brands protected their brand heritage and DNA; in addition, they purchased their suppliers and integrated vertically. They focused on brand equity, investing heavily in international expansion while repurchasing franchises and licenses to gain more control over their retail operations. Figure 1.2 depicts conglomerates that have a portfolio of brands selling

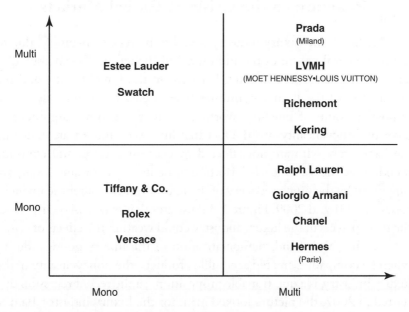

Figure 1.2   Where Conglomerates Fall in Different Brand and Product Categories

---

[1] Compared to the size of the luxury industry in 2014, no formal industry existed even during the 1980s. The luxury industry was an island where a happy few dwelled, unaffected by the worries of life.

different product categories (LVMH), conglomerates with many brands on one product category (Estée Lauder), companies with one brand and only one product category (Rolex), and houses with one brand with many product categories (Chanel).

Due to the oligopolistic nature of the luxury industry, there arose intense competition among the handful of competitors. The most important driver for luxury brands to succeed was, thus, dependent on the disposal income of its clientele, which translated to consumer buying power. The disposable income of high-net-worth individuals had increased during the preceding 10 years. As society become relatively more affluent, consumers with disposal income were "created" through advertising to create an artificial demand for products beyond the individual's basic needs.

Reaction to the Crisis of Global Markets

On one hand, the luxury industry is said to be recession-proof[2] due to the noncyclical nature of the industry. This belief may be attributed in part to the change of consumer behavior in the United States and the broadening of the luxury consumer base, fueled by an increase in the disposal income of high-net-worth consumers. Another argument in favor of noncyclicality was the fact that luxury customers are generally the happy few who are not affected by economic crises and continue spending at the same levels.[3] Both arguments, to a certain extent, are supported by the quick recovery of the luxury industry after the financial crises of 2001 and 2009. Figure 1.3 illustrates that over a 14-year period, the main players in the luxury industry could weather the effects of crises.

On the other hand, democratization of the luxury goods industry whereby companies created accessible products, the noncyclicality of the luxury industry, is a questionable proposition. In the recent recession that started in 2007, the picture looked grim for the luxury industry. Bain & Company estimated that the sector lost 10 percent of its revenues in

---

[2]Jean-Marc Bellaiche, Antonella Mei-Pochtler, and Dorit Hanisch, 2010, 1; Jean-Noel Kapferer and Olivier Tabatoni, 2010, 11.
[3]Forbes, "Luxury Is in Crisis, Yet Luxury Brands, Tiffany's, LVHM Still Report Sales Growth," 2011.

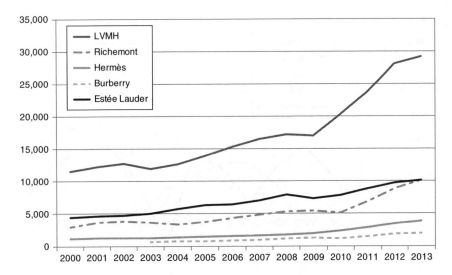

Figure 1.3 Revenues of the Main Players of the Luxury Industry, 2000–2013

2009. Reports from Bain & Company and Italian luxury goods traders Altagamma after a close watch indicated that luxury sales slumped to 5 percent in 2013 as compared to 13 percent in 2011 due to the debt crisis, which has currently gripped Europe since 2010. The growth of foreign tourism shopping in Europe slowed down to 18 percent in 2013, compared to 28 percent in 2012. Figure 1.4 depicts the effects of these two recessions, showing that the luxury firms are not immune to the slowdown in growth and revenue that follow each crisis.

The economic crisis had deeply affected the luxury world, but in a way that was somewhat predictable. For many years, the luxury brands were undergoing constant growth, and no one thought they could be affected by a world financial crisis. They thought quite the opposite, in fact. The general opinion was that these losses would soon be overshadowed by the perennial story of growth and profitability.

The sales figures from countries across the globe were interesting to observe in the light of the above discussion. In fact, the crises of 2009 and 2010–2013 helped us to better understand the luxury world. Most interesting was the behavior of consumers. Countries that were considered to be the homes and strongholds of the luxury planet were affected.

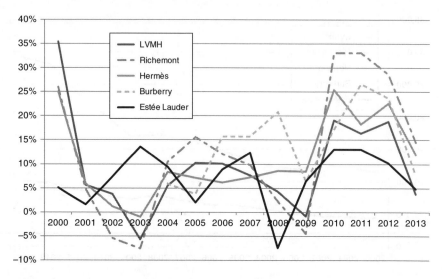

Figure 1.4   Revenues of the Main Players of the Luxury Industry as a Percentage of the Previous Year, 2000–2013

Japan

Japan was a star of luxury for 25 years, beginning in the 1980s. It represented 30 percent of sales for Hermès in 2005, at least 35–40 percent for Louis Vuitton, and up to 41 percent of the worldwide luxury goods market. Japan had been always a place where luxury shopping was considered to be an occasion. At the time of the global financial crisis, Japan represented about 50 percent of the clients of all key luxury brands. Up until 2005, luxury companies forged their futures with Japanese consumers in mind. For example, 94 percent of Japanese women in their twenties owned a Louis Vuitton handbag; 92 percent owned products from Gucci; more than 58 percent owned a Prada item, and over 51 percent possessed a product with a Chanel label on it. Traditionally, this market had been impervious to recession. Most major companies like LVMH, Hermès, Richemont, Kering, and Coach made supernormal profits in Japan until 2009. Two local crises hit the Japanese economy: the earthquake and resulting tsunami and the Fukushima nuclear meltdown.[4] Since Japan accounted for a significant share of global luxury

---

[4]Kelly Wetherille, 2011.

sales, the shares of LVMH, Hermès, and Burberry tumbled when the crisis hit.[5] Overall, the Japanese market retreated between 20 percent and 30 percent. LVMH witnessed declining sales by 6 percent. Salvatore Ferragamo reduced prices of its 42 items by 7 to 10 percent for the first time since it began operations in Japan. Chanel held a sale of clothes and other items. Distributors such as Seibu and Sogo merged to form Millenium, Isetan merged with Mitsukoshi, Takashimaya merged with Hankyu, and Daimaru merged with Matsuzakaya to survive. Clearly, Japan became a nightmare for most luxury brands, as consumers saw the stock market at a five-year low and hoped to reduce their consumption to prepare for rainy days in the future. For the first time in history, 2009 showed the decline of the luxury market in Japan. Given the aftermath of the tsunami and nuclear disaster that rocked Japan, it is not surprising that people did not feel like shopping.

In 2014, Japan registered between 5 to 16 percent of luxury sales. Chinese customers now account for about 15 percent of former Japanese sales. Does that mean that Japan has become a nightmare? It does not seem so. It is still, more than ever, a key market: stable, mature, and full of promise. Based on an interview about sales outlook, done by McKinsey & Co., on 20 CEOs of luxury companies who were based in Japan, 75 percent were optimistic about the future prospects of Japan's luxury market. It would have been a mistake to consider that the market was lost. For brands like Van Cleef & Arpels, Cartier, Bottega Veneta, Hermès, Prada, Chanel, and others, Japan remains a strong and vital market. It is still the world's third-largest luxury market outside Europe, after the United States and China.

Europe

During the global financial crisis, Europe—the birthplace of luxury goods—surprised everybody. Europe had witnessed 40 percent or more of all luxury sales, but after the crisis it showed its resilience, with an average decline of only 5 percent. Compared to Europe, Asia-Pacific, mainly due to China, showed a growth of 20 percent. The luxury

---

[5]James Topham, 2011

market in France in particular did not decline. Old Europe was again a market to cultivate during the period of financial turmoil. Brands that were present in small European cities reaped the benefit of their regional strategies. Hermès, Chanel, Louis Vuitton, Armani, and Tod's were among the companies who were not significantly affected due to their sales in Europe. This proved that Europe has been and still is the most important market for luxury, and may continue to remain so, for two reasons. First, the cultural heritage of Europe is linked to luxury. Europeans love luxury goods and have the buying power to be the most stable luxury goods consumers of the world. Second, Europe remains the number-one destination for tourists, France in particular. It meant that though the luxury business was going through the global financial crisis, the continuous flow of tourists who spend a considerable proportion of their budget buying luxury goods offset the effect of the crisis. For example, the Chinese spent nearly 1,500 euros per person annually. At the Galeries Lafayette, 60 percent of the total business came from tourists, and within this 60 percent, between 60 and 80 percent are Chinese tourists.

China

Asia overall, including Russia, China, India, Hong Kong, South Korea, and the Middle East, came to the rescue of most luxury brands after the global financial meltdown. During the recession phase, China became the winning horse that reported a growth of 20–30 percent for most luxury brands. Richemont was one brand that relied heavily on Asia Pacific consumers to help buttress its sales. The same held true for Hermès, which also sold heavily in Asia. They were saved, although the crisis affected all the actors in the luxury sector, at each level. China alone during this period could show the difference it made to the top line of a luxury company. When the distributors in the United States and Japan nearly collapsed, when Neiman Marcus reported a 20 percent decline in sales, stores in Beijing and Shanghai were reporting sales growth of up to 30 percent. Businesses in mainland China, Hong Kong, and Macau were flourishing.

China emerged as the luxury market in which to have a presence, a market that didn't exist 10 years before in 2003. China saved many brands from sliding into the red. During this period, Kering witnessed double-digit growth in China. Richemont and Zegna, which were otherwise losing money, enjoyed healthy growth in China. Brands like YSL regretted not maintaining showrooms in mainland China. The Ferragamo family trusted Chinese women to continue demanding statement handbags, which they continued distributing despite an otherwise gloomy environment. Some brands, on the other hand, were apprehensive about the Chinese miracle. Patek Philippe was cautious with China, as it felt that the country could impose sudden import duties or levy taxes, which could destroy the business instantaneously. Despite the deepening of the European debt crisis and the slowdown of China's economic growth in 2013, China represented around a quarter of global luxury purchases.

United States

The American market represents a great untapped potential for European luxury brands, as only 17 percent of the luxury goods sold in the United States are personal luxury goods, compared to 47 percent in Italy, 25 percent in Japan, and 25 percent in China. However, it is worth noticing that the U.S. market alone drives 70 percent of Ralph Lauren's and 55 percent of Tiffany & Co.'s worldwide sales, whereas this market accounts for only 15–25 percent of the worldwide sales of most European brands such as Hermès. Moreover, it can be observed that luxury sales are high in areas with a large Latin American population due to this group's appreciation of personal luxury goods. Thus, the American market offers a promising outlook for European brands if they manage to exploit the potential.

The U.S. market over the years was always open to brands that had the capacity to invest, to persevere, and to face conflicts. It remained a difficult market that required a lot of time, energy, and resources. Luxury brands suffered in the United States. For example, Dior went in the wrong direction, running after licenses, opening everywhere, and lost money. Fred Segal, which opened in Los Angeles, could not meet its overhead costs and was acquired by LVMH. But the U.S. market has strong potential in the long run in many cities besides expensive centers such as New York, Los Angeles, and Miami. This is the reason why luxury brands should ask the question, "To be or not to be in the

United States"—Leonard Fashion answered "Not to be." They were right. Hermès, LV, Cartier, and Chanel succeeded in the United States, competing with Coach, Ralph Lauren, and Tiffany & Co. The U.S. brands had hundreds of stores, a very different tactic from the European shopping experience. Americans do not yet have the taste for luxury; they have a long way to go, and apart from two or three main cities, the interior of America is not ready to understand the French or the Italian luxury world. It will take time and effort to develop a customer base. It is, however, a market full of promise. All the factors to succeed in the United States are there. It is a stable and rich country, and the only country where a great number of women are millionaires.

Africa

The Northern African market also experienced crises. The most notable local crisis was the Egyptian revolution in 2011 and the Arab Spring. Burberry and Ferragamo stores were closed permanently, while the companies that remained open watched as sales declined up to 70 percent. One reason was that wealthy customers were the first to leave Northern Africa during the unrest. This was corroborated by the fact that the occupancy in luxury hotels such as the Four Seasons, Kempinski, Hyatt, and Sofitel dropped by 30 percent. However, due to democratization of the luxury industry, perfume sales in Africa were increasing at a rate of 25 percent, due to licenses from Gucci and Dolce & Gabbana. It has also been predicted that distributor sales for perfume will reach $100 million in the coming decade. Niche brands have started to make their mark in Africa. For example, Vlisco, a luxury textile brand from Holland engaged in textile wax, has long been successful in Ghana. Soon the entire continent of Africa will be a promising market for luxury brands.

Effect of Crisis on the Luxury Industry

The luxury world was a place where no one expected to perish. And then suddenly Christian Lacroix rang its bell—investors collapsed in the face of the coming of Louis Vuitton and Céline and were obliged to leave the company when the shareholders of Escada refused to inject the fresh capital required to turn around the company.

On the other hand, consider the resurrection of the legendary Italian haute couture house Schiaparelli, known for the introduction in the 1920s of women's shorts, colored zip fastenings, and catwalk shows. After being shut down since World War II, it was repurchased in 2009 by Diego Della Valle and relaunched in 2012. Diego Della Valle, the chairman of Tod's Group who also revived the famous brand Roger Vivier, has brought Schiaparelli back on the stage of the fashion business after more than 60 years. This is not the only case in the luxury world. The almost immortal vitality and endless potential of a luxury brand can never be compared to any other normal brands.

The crisis was a wake-up call for the luxury industry. All *métiers* were hit by the 2009 recession but not at the same level. The métiers reacted in different ways. Watches were showing the most profound weakness, decreasing in all markets to the tune of 20 percent, which scared the Swiss and most other brands. Jewelry followed with a decrease of 15 to 20 percent. *Arts de la table* fell at least 20 percent or much more. Ready-to-wear for women and men fell 10 to 20 percent depending on the brands, and even perfumes fell between 7 to 15 percent. It affected L'Oréal, Estée Lauder, Clarins, and their competitors. The most resilient were leather goods, which explains the consistency of Louis Vuitton, Goyard, Hermès, and, within the brands, Chanel, Gucci, and Dior bags and other leather goods.

Overall, the watches and jewelry segment faced a mixed reaction. While the recession was known to hit the watch industry the worst, some people still invested in the Rolex brand in times of crashing stock markets and devaluing currency. Luxury houses like LVMH were known to have fared better than the likes of Richemont, because LVMH, through TAG Heuer, invested in hard luxury versus Richemont, which focused on soft luxury. Brands like Hermès, Swatch, Chopard, Hublot, and De Beers faced declining profits, whereas Dior fared well in the watches and jewelry sector. However, industry figures depicted a decline of 31.9 percent in June 2009 and a slowdown in the summer of 2013 due to unfavorable economic climate in Europe and in China. Swiss exports of watches declined, indicating that it was an industry-wide phenomenon.

For the wines and spirits sector, brands like Diageo, Moët & Chandon, Pernod Ricard, and Rémy Martin all reported a significant decline in profits. Diageo, which was more exposed in Ireland and Greece at the time they were saddled by the debt crisis, was the worst hit of all, indicating a strong negative impact on sales.

Luxury cosmetic and fragrance brands were hit by the recession, too. Estée Lauder and L'Oréal slid into the red, and undertook significant cost-cutting operations. The recession hit this segment in part because women tend to stock beauty products and perfumes. During times of recession, they usually fall back on the stock they have built over the years. However, some companies managed to stay profitable, including Sephora, Revlon, and Sally Beauty.

The crisis was affecting other brands, especially in the field of *arts de la table*. In 2009, Lalique, Daum, Baccarat, Cristalleries de Saint Louis, and many others suffered a great deal. On the other hand, 2009 was a very interesting period that tested the strengths and weaknesses of the sector. The conglomerates showed poor figures compared to the bright numbers posted year after year for the previous 10 years. Sales of brands such as Burberry, Armani, and Cartier—including the whole Richemont Group—suffered. Hermès, Louis Vuitton, and Prada were probably the most successful survivors; in fact they were winners in terms of announcing positive figures of sales.

The crisis was for real as far as the luxury world was concerned. The response of the luxury sector revealed to the analysts, researchers, investors, and other stakeholders that luxury was sensitive to the economic situation of the global world, just like every other sector. In fact, no one could pretend that luxury was invincible, and rich investors realized that the niche aspect of luxury was fading away. This was in fact the consequence of the evolution of the luxury world. Not only big and financially strong conglomerates with millions of customers faced the crisis—it was also faced by small family-owned players in the luxury business. They were all affected by the crisis and the stock market.

Strategic Response to Crisis

The strategic response to the crisis was not easy. It showed that the evolution of the luxury sector was still wide open. Transformations were taking place. Luxury could not be defined as it had been before. Brands had to reposition themselves during the crisis, adopting starkly opposing strategies.

The response to the 2009 crisis was varied. A change in consumer behavior was observed during the recession, wherein consumers spent a lot more time comparing prices of various fashion brands. Thus, the conversion of a potential customer into an actual customer required more time and resources. Before, a consumer bought 10 products, but now he or she buys just one, and only after careful deliberation.

The broad strategies adopted by players during and postrecession involved two fundamental orientations: internal and external. Internal strategies, as the name suggests, were internal to the company and were those that were not visible to the consumers, whereas external strategies were those that were undertaken to gain the consumer's attention and buy-in. The internal strategies included cost-cutting, greater focus on the product quality, financial restructuring, and downsizing. Bernard Arnault described it thus: "a natural tendency of companies during a crisis such as the one we are in now is to cut costs, drop prices, and stop expanding, because it has the most immediate impact on numbers."[6]

The external strategies included expansion in terms of both product offering and geography, repositioning, upscaling of the brand to tap the richer among the super-rich, or downscaling to recruit a larger customer group.

In response to the crisis, as a knee-jerk reaction, some luxury brands tried hiring freezes, reducing the number and the size of the collections, rationalizing media spending, and reducing headcounts. It was felt that dropping prices and cutting costs were the last resorts. The press referred to it as cost containment. For example, Dolce & Gabbana slashed its prices by 10–20 percent. At the same time the company began a search for alternative low-cost stitching techniques and reduced spending on advertising (returning to low rates of 20 years before). Stella McCartney closed its boutique in Moscow just 18 months after it was opened. Richemont closed 62 stores, mainly in the United States, while Burberry absorbed heavy charges on its Spanish stores. In November 2009, Burberry unveiled a cost-cutting program, which resulted in the

---

[6]Vanessa Friedman, 2009.

closure of the Thomas Burberry collection. It hoped to generate infrastructure efficiencies by shutting down six stores and reducing headcount by more than 1,000 people. All this cost Burberry $6.7 million in the period, with the hope the company would generate savings of $77.8 million. In response to the slowdown of Asia, their key market, Burberry announced in September 2012 that it would freeze hiring, lower travel expenditures, cut marketing spending, and defer IT projects. Estée Lauder followed a four-pronged strategy with layoffs of about 2,000 employees, freezes in pay, discontinuations of non-profit-making brands, and cuts in discretionary capital expenditures of 25 percent.

Contrary to the cost containment approach, Bernard Arnault stated, "What we have learned in the many crises we have been through is that this (cutting costs) is a mistake, especially when it comes to luxury.... If you don't put your products on sale, consumers feel they are buying something that retains its value.... Even during tough times we can continue to invest and during the crises I went through in the past 20 years, we always gained in market share."[7]

Different companies tried a different set of strategies to reposition their brands. Christian Dior exited its logo and accessory product business as it pursued an upscaling drive, in the hopes that the super-rich would not be affected by the crisis. Coach, which happened to be in the heart of the subprime crisis in the United States, felt that "normal" buying behavior among consumers had experienced a shift and consumer spending levels would never return to what they had been precrisis. Thus, an internal change in the company itself was required. Coach explored lower price options for the consumer, providing them with a larger range of accessible products. Driven by a similar thought process, Swatch and Ralph Lauren also launched products at lower price points. To reduce costs, some brands took their manufacturing operations to low-cost regions of the world. Prada and Burberry shifted their manufacturing base to China for certain products. Louis Vuitton considered building a shoe factory in India.

Armani suffered a 41.4 percent drop in its net profits in 2008–2009. Dior experienced almost flat sales through the recession, and Burberry,

---

[7] Vanessa Friedman, 2009.

which opened stores in India, the Middle East, Macau, and China, posted a loss of $8.8 million in 2009 compared to a profit of $232.5 million in 2008. Some companies, on the other hand scaled down their operations. For instance, Dolce & Gabbana scaled back their operations in Japan. As an LVMH executive summarized, "Before the crisis, we were putting a lot of energy into beautiful stores, but now we care a bit less about expanding our network and even more about design and price."[8]

However, some companies decided not to compromise on such factors. One of the major winners from the crisis, Bottega Veneta, had a very different strategy: The company decided to not change its positioning at all. Bottega Veneta continued to manufacture its products in Italy and invested in its artisans to ensure that they continued to produce traditional, quality output. The idea was to ensure that their product was exclusive enough to merit the premium price they intended to demand. It held steady and stuck to what it was best at—finely crafted products with clean, classic lines. This ensured that the brand was two steps ahead of its panic-stricken competitors. IWC also practiced this philosophy. It utilized handmade craftsmanship, limited distribution, and impeccable service. Hermès manufactured its leather goods and silk products in France and Italy and did not resort to production in China. Not only did some companies try to deliver unmatched service quality, but they also standardized this service quality across continents. This ensured that the consumer walking into an outlet in New Delhi would not get a different experience from one walking into an outlet on Rodeo Drive or the Champs-Élysées. Ritz-Carlton and HFS were brands that worked on the parameter of service excellence.

Continuing with varied strategic response, some brands saw the crisis as an opportunity and expanded through (1) widening or spreading to new geographies, and/or (2) launching new products. Notable among those companies that expanded geographically (or widened its base) were Prada, Hermès, Bottega Veneta, and Christian Dior Couture.

Prada, in 2008–2009, undertook its most aggressive investment plan. It hoped to get out of the crisis with a very strong distribution network. Having seen earnings slide by 22 percent in 2008, the company saw

---

[8] *The Economist*, "LVMH in the Recession: The Substance of Style," 2009.

heavy increases in revenues and profits from 2009 onward. Hermès, like Prada, expanded during the crisis. Hermès opened stores in Manchester in England, Las Vegas, Japan, India, Wuxi in China, and Busan in South Korea during that period. Hermès was known for weathering the crisis rather gracefully.

During the recession some brands launched new and special products while simultaneously trimming their overall product lines. This resulted in fewer offerings and simultaneous price increases on both existing and new products, stimulating consumer demand and generating market interest, discontinuing low-margin products, and increasing prices in some product categories. Some companies ventured into new products and product lines (deepening), whereas others consolidated their brands under one umbrella. Burberry ventured into a new product line with a stand-alone children's store in Hong Kong, Bottega Veneta ventured into watches, and Versace launched a new fragrance, Gianni Versace Couture. Brioni reacted to the crisis by including more accessible items in its product range of suits such as T-shirts. Coach kept the prices of its regular lines stable, but introduced new lines, such as the Poppy handbags, to cater to a less affluent segment. Estée Lauder moved away from a strategy that fostered competition among various brands. It believed in following a more synergistic and coordinated policy of brand interdependence rather than competition. Its aim was probably to make the consumer feel that its brands were complementary in nature rather than supplementary. By maintaining or increasing prices for example, these brands resegmented their consumers and were more likely to pick up market share after the recession. Francois-Henri Pinault, CEO of Kering, was of the opinion that "There's a new perception of luxury, a more discrete sophisticated luxury where notions of heritage and craft play a big role."[9]

During this period many consumers had to cut back on their purchases, and many sensed that it was not appropriate to show off with obviously expensive products. It was something that only traditional, artisanal, and legitimate houses could uphold. Brands did not act at all but kept true to their values and their traditional offerings. These included Hermès, Harry Winston, IWC, Chanel, and Patek Philippe.

---

[9]Dominique Ageorges, 2010.

Some brands explored new channels to deliver their products to the customer. Gucci and Ralph Lauren adopted the QR code. This was an image that shoppers could scan and download through their camera phone to obtain more information about the product or make purchases via their phone. Cartier adopted advertising through mobile phones. Companies like LVMH and Gucci also adopted online retail as an option for selling their products. This was quick to gain acceptance in Japan, where 20 percent of consumers make their purchases online.

Some brands diversified during the recession to strategic but complementary businesses or acquired greater control of their current businesses. From 2000 onwards, most if not all luxury brands, be it multibrand conglomerates or family houses, expanded horizontally into different traditional luxury categories. For example, Louis Vuitton expanded into fashion, high jewelry, and watches. Montblanc expanded into watches and jewelry. Chanel diversified into high jewelry. Salvatore Ferragamo expanded into fragrances and accessories. During the recession, Louis Vuitton, Bulgari, Armani, Missoni, and Trussardi diversified into a nontraditional luxury goods category with the opening of luxury hotels. Moreover, brands acquired greater control of their core businesses to integrate vertically, purchased key suppliers, and bought back licenses and franchises to increase efficiency, control their brand image, and generate superior margins.

Some companies tried to understand changing customer needs during the recession. For instance, Diageo noticed that people reduced their consumption of alcohol outside their homes. Thus it launched premixed cocktails such as Smirnoff Tuscan Lemonade for home consumption. Ritz-Carlton coined Mystique, its CRM system, to keep a closer tab on the consumers' pulse. Taking this flexibility a step ahead, some companies let the consumer guide the company, rather than the other way a round (which has been the norm in luxury branding). For instance, Nordstrom was lauded for its policy of refunding money to dissatisfied customers.

Conclusion

In conclusion, different brands adopted different strategies as a response to the crisis. None of the brands adopted a single universal strategy. They

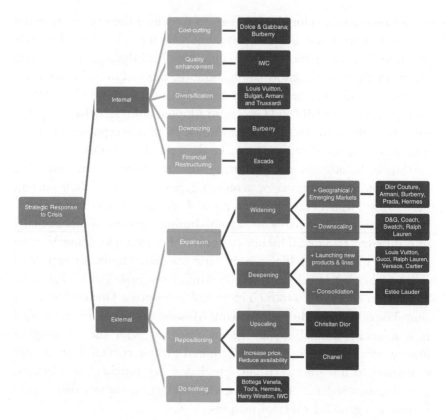

Figure 1.5   Luxury Brands and Their Crisis Management Strategies

remained creative in their responses. Some succeeded, some did not. As the industry rebounded, they adjusted. The bouquets of responses were meant to encompass different type of customers from different cultures and geographies. A global brand strategy was needed to convince several segments of clients—so different and interested by so many various luxury sectors. With crisis it was seen that luxury loses its definition, the market remained totally open, and goods varied from premium, super-premium, and ultimate luxury.

Formerly accessible to a few, the luxury industry democratized from 1985 onwards—three decades—with brand extensions such as perfumes and eyewear attracting more numerous (and younger) consumers. The future of luxury would therefore be built on the capacity of brands to understand the scope of potential customers, fixing a strategy based on a specific language. There was no universal response, nor any universal language. Chanel speaks Chanel, Hermès speaks Hermès, and Gucci has its own vocabulary—the challenge is to keep the dream going, for everyone, after the crisis.

Figure 1.5 summarizes the different strategic responses of luxury brands to the global financial crisis.

Chapter 2

Evolution of the Global Luxury Market

Luxury is the opposite of vulgarity. Luxury is the opposite of status. It is the ability to make a living by being oneself. It is the freedom to refuse to live by habit. Luxury is liberty. Luxury is elegance. True elegance is refusal.

—Coco Chanel

The term *luxury goods* was popularized by Wall Street analysts who needed a term to describe companies such as LVMH, Richemont, and Gucci, which had become public companies. Prior to the popularizing of the term *luxury goods*, these companies were not really known as luxury goods companies but instead were known for their specific areas of expertise and the global reputation they had garnered.

Luxury is about exception and exclusivity, whether it comes to products, or services. A luxury product/service is unique, and not only because of its outstanding quality. It tells more than what it is. Beyond the usefulness or the wellness it brings, it tells a story, it reflects a style and a spirit that contribute to the dream. Luxury is about a product but also a brand, a universe.

—Eric Vallat, ex-Bonpoint

It is an association with a compelling and binding meaning in terms of emotional connectivity, personal harmony, spiritual connection or a connection to the world of the inherently beautiful, the greater the marginal value of the object to the seller.

—James Taylor, Harrison Group LLC

Luxury used to be "ordinary goods for exceptional people" but now can be defined as "exceptional goods for ordinary people." It had to do with an object, its use, five senses, it was an offering, attraction, a product, a niche and serendipity. Today it is about marketing push, process, synergy, volume and efficiency.

—Wilfried Guerrand, Hermès

Luxury is a state-of-mind. It is about a bridge between dream and daily routine, a way of appreciating one's time and life, a statement of being oneself.

—Franka Holtmann, Le Meurice, Paris, and Feng Gao, ex-Bottega Veneta, China

The language of value in the world of *objet de luxe* is modest in inverse proportion to the price, value, and authenticity of the item. Value might connote a different meaning in the world of luxury.

The value of luxury products is shaped by meaning content, not design; even clumsy design can be valued, collected, and treasured.

—James Taylor, Harrison Group, LLC

The Boston Consulting Group defined luxury goods as "Items, products, and services that deliver higher levels of quality, taste, and aspiration than conventional ones."

Luxury is also about brands. Bernard Arnault's famous definition notes that "Star brands should be timeless, modern, fast-growing, and highly profitable.... There are fewer than 10 star brands in the luxury world, because it is very hard to balance all four characteristics at once—after all, fast growth is often at odds with high profitability—but that is what makes them stars. If you have a star brand, then basically you can be sure you have mastered a paradox."

Buyers in this segment are not only interested in the product but also with its associated values in terms of class-consciousness, emotional and artistic appeal, a unique design, and a cultured and refined taste. Yves Carcelle, former chief executive of Louis Vuitton, said "It's about reliability, quality, style, innovation, and authenticity."

Luxury products offer self-reflexive connections to a person's sense of self-esteem, competence, and personal value. It is said to be characterized by: "Inherent scarcity, sincerity, consistency, transitivity, emotional connectivity, mastery of excellence, service—elegance."

Definition of Luxury is dialectic. Luxury is a break, a deviation from what is ordinary and what is necessary. And it is the variations between the ordinary and the necessary during different times, societies, and cultures that will lend themselves to major developments in luxury. Sacred in origin, secular when it becomes an instrument of worldly power (Louis XIV), reduced to a minimum for the emerging bourgeoisie (a comfort-based and necessity-based luxury), subject to market laws since the French revolution, a superfluous necessity of today. The dialectic is based on a double movement—on one hand, a human need to create a special moment, objects, practices, and behaviours discordant with the ordinary and necessary and on the other, a movement of integration for these gaps in the regular course of society. It is vital for human beings as they search for more, for better, for beautiful.... It is nothing other than humanity forever separated from a world governed by the order of our needs, into an ideal world, where one shall desire what is good for him or her. Nothing more, nothing less. Hence the moral dimension is always attached to luxury.

—Emmanuelle Sidem, Connex Consulting

Evolution

In the context of the historical perspective of luxury, as a snapshot, it is important to trace the evolution that might point out some empirical truths about luxury and whether such an industry can stand the test of time and whether new brands can survive in such an environment.

Has the luxury industry itself changed over time? Contextually, in every era luxury is about selling a dream; it is aspirational. The term *luxus* or *excess* was coined in Rome. To understand how luxury and luxury items are able to sell such a dream factor one has to look at what dream is being sold. It is a dream of being special, of feeling like you belong to a special set of people. That hasn't changed since time immemorial. The Roman baths were exclusive and only the elite were allowed. Only the elite could wear certain materials and participate in certain activities. The *Sumptuariae Leges* of Ancient Rome[1] were various laws passed to prevent inordinate expense in banquets and dresses, such as the use of expensive Tyrian purple dye.[2] Individual garments were also regulated: ordinary male citizens were allowed to wear the *toga virilis* only upon reaching the age of political majority. In the early years of the Empire, men were forbidden to wear silk,[3] and details of clothing including the number of stripes on the tunic were regulated according to social rank.

While in modern times there are no such laws, it nevertheless amounts to the same thing when some things are more expensive than others, thus making them affordable only for a selected few. The more unaffordable they are, the more desirable they become. If we look at when the Romans traded with the Britons, there was internal trade between the Celtic tribes of Britain, especially in metals and pottery. The Romans and Celts shipped pottery, glass, bronze and iron objects, and wine to Scotland. In return they received slaves, cattle, hides and furs, animals, and possibly wool. The Romans increased production of minerals, particularly lead, but also silver, gold, and tin. Also, British woolen products were considered the best in the Empire and were much sought after as fashionable goods. In every country, precious

---

[1] Rebeiro, *Dress and Morality*, 22.
[2] Jacoby, "Silk in Western Byzantium before the Fourth Crusade."
[3] "Silk: History," *Columbia Encyclopedia*.

metals and gemstones and good cloth were considered luxury. Consider the Egyptians, who also admired luxury and even buried their kings with enough, if not too much, luxury goods so the journey after life could be more comfortable. In the Renaissance or Restoration periods, luxury was still being able to afford jewelry, fine clothes, and better transport, better living conditions, and better food. And it is from supplying this need that companies such as Cartier, Louis Vuitton, and Hermès were able to be as successful as they were. Luxury is as relevant in today's society as it always has been.

Traditionally, Europe has always looked toward the East for gems, silk, and spices. Traders used the Silk Route to travel east. The route grew during the rise of the Roman Empire because the Chinese initially gave silk to the Roman-Asian governments as gifts.[4]

Originally, the Chinese traded silk internally, within the empire. Caravans from the empire's interior would carry silk to the western edges of the region. Often small Central Asian tribes would attack these caravans, hoping to capture the traders' valuable commodities. As a result, the Han Dynasty extended its military defenses further into Central Asia from 135 to 90 B.C. in order to protect these caravans. Chan Ch'ien, the first known Chinese traveler to make contact with the Central Asian tribes, later came up with the idea to expand the silk trade to include these lesser tribes and therefore forge alliances with these Central Asian nomads. Because of this idea, the Silk Road was born.

Northwestern Indians who lived near the Ganges River played prominent roles as middlemen in the China-Mediterranean silk trade because as early as the third century A.D., they understood that silk was a lucrative product of the Chinese Empire. The trading relationship between the Chinese and the Indians grew stronger with increased Han expansion into Central Asia. The Chinese would trade their silk[5] with the Indians for precious stones and metals such as jade, gold, and silver, and the Indians would trade the silk with the Roman Empire. Silk proved to be an expensive import for the Roman Empire since its trade across Indian and Central Asia was heavily controlled by the Parthian Empire.

---

[4]"The Romans in Britain: Trade and Travel." http://h2g2.com/dna/h2g2/A3473967.
[5]Garthwaite, *The Persians*, 78.

While the Chinese silk trade played a minor role in the Chinese economy, it did increase the number of foreign merchants present in China under the Han Dynasty, exposing both the Chinese and the foreign visitors to different cultures and religions.

And this is one of the first evidences of globalization in luxury. It was an intricate and long-drawn-out pattern, but the goods exchanged and the cultural exchanges had enough value to endure the lengthy and uncomfortable process. What makes it luxury is that the items being traded were not actually part of daily living. What was being traded were things that people did not actually need to survive but desired anyway. This is the true essence of luxury: Demand for something for which there is no need.

But it did decline eventually and become specific to certain areas, such as the silk–fur trade with the Russians, north of the original Silk Route—as means of transport were not the most convenient. It revived under the Song Dynasty in the eleventh and twelfth centuries when China became largely dependent on its silk trade. In addition, trade to Central and Western Asia as well as Europe recovered for a period of time from 1276–1368 under the Yuan Dynasty when the Mongols controlled China. As overland trade became increasingly dangerous, and overseas trade became more popular, trade along the Silk Road declined. By the end of the fourteenth century, trade and travel along the road had decreased.

This is somewhat reminiscent of what is happening today, though only in terms of the importance of China and what China has to offer. China is an important factor in today's luxury economy. As a part of the growth of globalization and the emergence of new markets, it's one of the most important countries. Again, this is not new. Historically there were explorers such as Marco Polo forging Sino–Italian/European ties. This is also one of the first examples of globalization and looking eastward. In the mid-thirteenth century, Marco Polo spent 17 years in China fulfilling a wide variety of tasks in Kublai Khan's administration. He was in effect a member of an occupying force, speaking Mongolian but not Chinese, so his understanding of the people was limited. But he traveled a great deal, often trading on his own as well as serving the emperor. Figure 2.1 gives a snapshot of the evolution of the luxury industry.

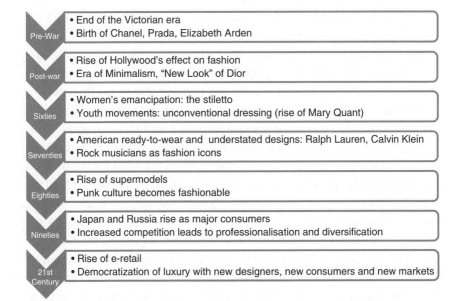

Figure 2.1   The Evolution of the Luxury Industry

The twentieth century was when the best-known luxury brands of today came to prominence. Though these brands may have been established earlier, the 1900s saw them gain the distinct identity that they still possess. While the first half of the century generally saw fashion relegated to the background in favor of robust economic development, the second half saw the luxury economy grow to become a major contributor to the modern-day economy. Through the course of this chapter, we intend to look at the major milestones in the evolution of luxury in the twentieth century.

Several luxury and prestige brands such as Louis Vuitton, Burberry, and Chanel were launched in the nineteenth and early twentieth centuries, when a strict social class system defined society and royalty and aristocracy reigned supreme. During this period, designers like Christian Dior, Yves Saint Laurent, and Guccio Gucci designed clothes and leather goods exclusively for the noble men and women of society. Their work was an art form that took several weeks and sometimes months to produce, and this was all a part of the "luxury and prestige" experience. During this period, it was the norm to literally dress in one brand from head-to-toe.

In the present twenty-first century environment, the story is differ-ent. The luxury market is no longer reserved for the elite. It has tran-scended boundaries. At the beginning of the century, luxury consumers were a small segment of the population who all looked the same. First, a class of wealthy people have emerged the world over. In the last three to four decades however, a vast amount of wealth has been accumulated by individuals due to several economic, social, and technological break-throughs. Second, there has emerged a sea of luxury brands, and this has affected the high entry barrier that the industry guarded for centuries. It has also given luxury consumers more choice than ever before. Third, the rapid growth of digital information and communications technology has given consumers more variety in luxury product offerings, easier access to view the choices, and lower switching costs, especially on the Inter-net. This has empowered the consumers to become more individualistic, experimental, and bold enough to mix luxury and high-street fashion in one outfit; something that their mothers and grandmothers would have considered a taboo in the past.

The result of this change is the phenomenon of trading-up and trading-down. The new wealthy class that is enjoying its ability to acquire luxury products practices "trading-up." "Trading-down" is the practice of mixing the use of luxury items with fashion brands. This practice is also popularly called "the democratization of luxury." Therefore it is no longer a surprise to find a wealthy celebrity wearing jeans from H&M, earrings from Chanel, shoes from Coach, a shirt from Zara, and a bag from Louis Vuitton.

In 2013, companies and even luxury companies are seeing China as the land of opportunities. The other way of looking at luxury from a historical point of view is to review the actual evolution of the brands and companies and evaluate if there is any difference in their success depending on their structure and business model. Traditionally, the lux-ury sector was highly fragmented, characterized by a large number of family-owned and medium-sized enterprises. In the past two decades, it has been increasingly dominated by multibrand luxury conglomerates. Some small niche brands do survive as independent companies, such as Goyard, but they are in some danger of being acquired. Acquisitions occur for a few different reasons. As in the case of LVMH, a company may be trying to gain market share and control as much of the industry as possible, or as in the case of Hermès, a company may be seeking vertical integration to be in control of their own production and supply chains. The industry is now dominated by conglomerates. The day of the family-owned business is over unless it is financed by a private wealthy family such as Tiffany, Chanel, Armani, Ralph Lauren, or a number of others.

Luxury has evolved over time from family businesses to conglomerates, from old luxury to new luxury, from uber luxury to affordable luxury. Figure 2.2 denotes the evolution of family businesses to multibrand corporations in the luxury industry. The connections and validations have to be made by royalty—whether it is as old as the Roman Period, when the Emperor was given silks as gifts, or the modern era, when brands give celebrities gifts that they wear or use in public to legitimize the products. The main evolution has occurred in the way that luxury has been promoted during the years. We have discovered that desire or the dream factor of luxury has always been the same and will probably always remain the same. As long as consumers aspire to own the things they cannot afford and the same things are always more rare, more beautiful, or more coveted, then the concept of luxury will remain the same.

The cycle continues—Europe will look East either to benefit from acquiring new and exotic products such as silk and gemstones and ivory

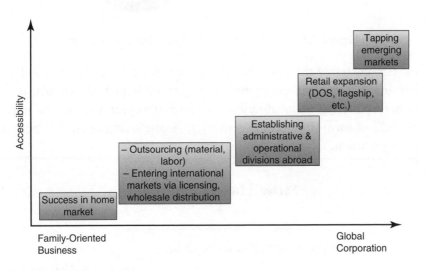

Figure 2.2   From Family Business to Multibrand Corporation

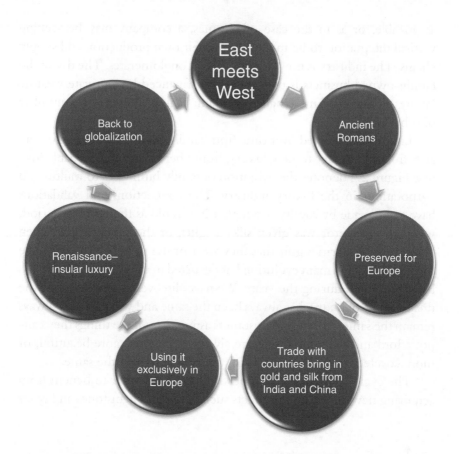

Figure 2.3 The Circular Path of the Heritage of Luxury

or, as is currently the case, they will look toward expanding to the East because that is where the growth is. Figure 2.3 depicts the circular path of luxury heritage. Globalization is an eternal subject, with maybe some changes of form through the centuries. As the saying goes, the more it changes, the more it remains the same.

How Has It Changed?

Plus ça change, plus c'est la même chose.

—Jean-Baptiste Alphonse Karr

Two decades ago, the luxury industry model was almost completely dominated by the family businesses. However, the winds of change were felt in the 1990s, especially by one man—Bernard Arnault. The ensuing rivalry between Bernard Arnault, the owner of Dior Group, and Henry Racamier, husband of Mademoiselle Vuitton, owner of Louis Vuitton, created a historic structural shift within the industry as each selfishly fought for market control through growth and acquisition. Until then, luxury was about fashion. Within this struggle, Bernard Arnault came out the winner and went ahead for consolidation to create the luxury empire of today. He transformed the fashion into a business. Buying and selling companies with intricate financial maneuvers, he conquered the luxury space by making Louis Vuitton Moët Hennessy (LVMH) the largest luxury conglomerate in the world. The interesting point to note about this conglomerate is that each brand was allowed to carry on its own culture and know-how and to be managed separately. However, if it was felt that the brand needed a push, Arnault stood right behind it. Furthermore, he created the famous notion of "star brands" that were timeless, modern, fast-growing, and highly profitable. He would find new brands and mix and match a suitable designer and an apt management team for the brand. He would revamp the production, control, storage, distribution, to offer a completely new and unique package to the customer. Thus, it led to the development of the counterintuitive idea of "constrained freedom," wherein the brands were allowed latitude; however, the latitude was limited to the lines that Arnault drew.

Some French companies, such as Hermès, which was owned by the families of Dumas, Puech, and Guerrand, and Chanel, which was owned by the Weirthemer family, could stay partially and fully independent. Hermès, the legendary leather-goods fashion house established in 1837, remained family owned. The Wertheimer family has owned Chanel since 1954. They never introduced Chanel to the stock market. The house is showing longevity in its independence, which is rare in the sector. Not listed on the stock market, the Maison Chanel continues to meticulously keep their financial data a top secret. Its aura of mystery is cultivated by the owners, Alain and Gérard Wertheimer, who drive the company firmly and discreetly.

In France, the Comité Colbert, founded in 1954 by Jean-Jacques Guerlain, consists today of 75 houses of French luxury that have different histories, cultures, sizes, and management. However, they share common governance rules and are willing to promote their values and know-how. The term "houses," as opposed to the luxury company members of the Comité Colbert, illustrates their respective stories, the transmission of their know-how from one generation to another, which keeps their creation secrets. Indeed, most of the members or familial business, and the family CEOs of the Comité Colbert, call each other "chef de Maison."

In Italy, Altagamma (Italian Association of Industries of Alta Gamma), founded in 1992, is an association whose purpose is to promote the work of several Italian companies on an international level and encourage their development. Currently the Foundation Altagamma brings together 76 Italian companies operating in the fields of fashion, design, transport, jewelry, shoes, perfume, and hospitality.

Despite these tectonic shifts in this industry, the family business remained a paramount and dominating factor in the Italian luxury enterprise until the last decade. Slowly but steadily some famous brands were acquired by the three multibrand conglomerates—LVMH, Richemont, and Kering Group. LVMH, after acquiring more than 60 luxury brands, acquired two of the largest Italian groups, Bulgari and Loro Piana, in 2011 and 2013 respectively. Gucci, Brioni, Bottega Veneta, and others were acquired by Kering in Italy and in France. The more recent crisis has spurred a desperate fight for survival, pushing the luxury industry further away from its historic structure as the key factors of success become finance instead of family, and the focus shifts from the small artisan businesses to the colossal conglomerates.

Luxury Industry Trends

Luxury is a cyclical industry. Given the continuing deterioration of the macroeconomic backdrop and the cyclical nature of the luxury market, 2009 was a very low year for luxury spending globally, though spending then peaked in 2010. However, spending in 2011 went back down to close to where it was in 2009. The 2012 Luxury Report by Unity Marketing reported that luxury spending grew by only 1.3 percent between 2009 and 2011. During this time, the highest spending was witnessed in luxury travel (up 40.8 percent), kitchenware and cooks' tools (up 37.5 percent), entertainment (up 33.6 percent), dining (up 26.5 percent), and fashion accessories (up 23.4 percent). The categories falling most from 2009 to 2011 were kitchen appliances (down 23.9 percent), watches (down 20.1 percent), jewelry (10.2 percent), and furniture, lamps, and floor coverings (down 7.3 percent). Analysts expect luxury goods markets will slow down in sequence, as the ripple effects from the global recession travel around the world. Pam Danzinger, president of Unity Marketing, noted, "Last year we were looking for the return of the HENRYs (high-earning, not rich yet) back into the luxury market and this year we can say they have returned and are more positive about spending in the future. For example, in 2009 only 18 percent of the luxury consumers surveyed expected to spend more on luxury in the next 12 months; by comparison 26 percent in 2011 predict greater spending on luxury throughout 2012."[6]

Despite global macroeconomic headwinds, worldwide sales of personal luxury goods grew an estimated 10 percent in 2012 to 212 billion euros, led by an estimated 16 percent increase in the leather goods category. By region, sales rose an estimated 18 percent in Asia-Pacific, 13 percent in the Americas, 8 percent in Japan, and 5 percent in Europe. Bain & Company projects worldwide luxury goods sales to reach between 250 billion and 350 billion euros by 2015, supported by 4 percent to 6 percent annual growth.

Hard luxury players are expected to be particularly under pressure in this environment, as their underlying demand disadvantage is compounded by dependence on the wholesale channel. Big-ticket-item purchases like mechanical watches are likely to be delayed, especially by men, and retailers will be de-stocking.

There is no hiding place in the high end. The notion that the luxury market high-end segment may be immune to the cycle appears to be an investment myth, as it is not supported by evidence and analysis. In the current context, emerging markets exposure is seen to be the key short-term factor limiting adverse trends in more mature markets. In addition to better momentum in the future, markets like China

---

[6]Unity Marketing, *Luxury Report 2014*, April 2013. www.unitymarketingonline.com /catalog/product_detail.php/pid=72~subid=230/index.html.

will provide superior long-term structural growth opportunities. This will give a key advantage to first movers with the necessary resources to "make it big" in emerging markets.

In difficult times, investors should go back to fundamentals: mega brands. Scale rules in an industry where fixed costs have increasing importance. It is argued that "mega brands" will continue to dominate the luxury and fashion industry, enjoying faster top-line growth and superior profitability.

Scale pays, as mega brands can lead the advertising expenditure league, while committing a smaller portion of their sales. Besides, scale allows superior downstream integration into retail. Various data confirm that there exists a direct relationship between sales per square meter and advertising expenditures. Direct retail operations are essential to luxury goods brands: Luxury mega-brands have an interest in "escalating the race" for direct-retail operations, in order to further leverage their scale advantage. Escalating into larger, richer, more prominent and ultimately more expensive directly operated stores (DOS) allows mega brands to awe consumers even more and to extend the distance in consumers' minds between the mega brands and everything else. Downstream integration into profitable DOS allows mega brands to push the envelope on entry price points and to lead the way in globalization.

The luxury goods industry is currently estimated to be valued at around US$320 billion, which includes jewelry, watches, leather goods, wines and spirits, perfumes, and apparel. The recent trend shows that luxury consumers are looking for brands that will help them to develop themselves through a unique and sensual experience and provide them with an emotional state of mind. These consumers wish to own something authentic, with a heritage and with personalized style. Luxury items must combine historical quality with the trendiest designs, which would also be a means of self-expression. For example, Bulgari is known for its classical chic design sensibilities, with jewelry pieces of voluminous precious stones for traditional clients and a modern, simpler, trendier line for younger clientele.

In general, luxury wines and spirits account for the largest part of luxury sales at approximately 30 percent, fashion and clothing accessories account for 20 percent, and premium fragrances and cosmetics account for 18 percent, followed by the watches and jewelry sector at 15 percent and premium handbags and travel goods at 6 percent.

One of the major trends facing the luxury goods industry was that of consolidation. Many of the major players in the industry have, since the 1980s, been transformed from small family-owned businesses into global powerhouses. This has resulted in a profound shift in the way in which many luxury companies are managed today. Such luxury conglomerates are driven by the bottom line, and the companies who dominate are able to exploit synergies across brands and product categories.

The power of the conglomerates is underscored by the struggling small independent brands, the fashion doyennes of yesteryear, such as Pierre Balmain, who filed for bankruptcy, and Ungaro, which was sold in 2005. Nevertheless, consolidation has not always been successful even for the large companies such as LVMH, whose earnings from Louis Vuitton are often eroded by the losses from the less-than-successful brands.

In the wake of September 11 and the Iraq war, the luxury goods industry faced one of the worst downturns for three decades, finally rebounding in 2004 when many companies in the industry posted a 10 to 15 percent increase, finally returning to the black. Since then, other major events such as the subprime mortgage crisis, Japanese earthquake, and Eurozone financial crisis have occurred, though the luxury market had been relatively untouched. The future outlook for the industry remains relatively positive while Mintel forecasts that the luxury goods industry will see market growth of 10 percent for 2012, although it expects growth rates to slow in the following two years to nearer 6 percent. Similarly, Bain is forecasting growth for the world market of 4–6 percent from 2013–2015 at constant exchange rates, bringing the total value of the luxury industry to US$320 billion by the middle of the decade.[7]

Developed Markets

The largest market for luxury goods is in Europe, which accounts for 33.7 percent of the world's expenditure, followed by Japan with

---

[7]Bain & Company press release, October 12, 2012. www.bain.com/about/press/press -releases/bain-projects-global-luxury-goods-market-will-grow-ten-percent-in-2012.aspx.

28.4 percent and North America with 24.6 percent. Yet, the Asia Pacific region accounts for the largest sales of leather goods. Although these nations are strategically important, these markets are becoming increasingly mature.

Emerging Markets

Changing conditions in the world's two most populous nations, India and China, followed by the emergence of a market in Russia present renewed growth opportunities for luxury brands. It is estimated that within 10 years these three nations will account for 30 percent of the world market. The increasing liberalization of the Chinese and Russian economies has resulted in an increase in average consumer purchasing power and the number of high-net-worth individuals. In fact, the average spending per consumer in China is on a par with Japanese spending. This has important implications for luxury brands, as the large population base can translate into a significant increase not only in consumer numbers but in revenues as well. This was the case for the Chinese market in particular.

Conclusion

In conclusion, there is no single definition of luxury. The definition is in the mind of the connoisseur of luxury goods. The definition is dynamic. What is luxury today for some may not be luxury for others and, with time, may even not be considered as luxury. For this reason, luxury goods have prospered in time. The evolution of the luxury goods market has witnessed the shifting sands of time, from the Romans, Egyptians, Chinese, and Indians to the Italians and the French through the formation of the multibrand conglomerates. With globalization and the growth of emerging markets, the markets have gone East. Hong Kong, Shanghai, Singapore, Beijing, and Tokyo have the most sizeable concentrations of luxury and affordable luxury brands. This is a distinct trend that is here to stay. Consolidation of the luxury market is also here to stay. In addition, the rise of emerging market luxury brands will be a force to reckon with in the future. The luxury market is open to new definitions and new discoveries. The rise of affordable luxury brands both from the West and the East will open new possibilities and opportunities. New brands will emerge and new markets have emerged making the industry more enigmatic than ever.

Chapter 3

Who's Who of Luxury

The top six players in the luxury industry—LVMH, Richemont, Kering, Swatch, Tiffany, and Hermès—account for 30 percent of the industry turnover.

Moreover, luxury goods have traditionally been associated with France and Italy, with Italy producing one third of all of the world's luxury goods, making it the largest luxury-goods-producing nation. Italy was the birthplace of famous brands such as Armani, Moncler, Prada, Zegna, and Ferragamo, to name just a few.

The multibrand conglomerates with revenues in excess of US$1 billion are LVMH, Richemont, Kering, Swatch, Hermès, and L'Oréal.

Similarly, there exist star monobrand companies with revenues in excess of US$1 billion, for example, Burberry, Chanel, Tiffany, Armani, Ralph Lauren, and others. While many of these companies operate under only one brand name, they compete in a variety of product sectors. Table 3.1 gives the details of the mono- and multibrands.

Table 3.1　Leaders in the Multibrand and Monobrand Luxury Sector

Multibrands	**Monobrands**
L'Oréal	Tiffany
LVMH	Chanel
Richemont	Burberry
Kering (ex-PPR)	Armani
Swatch	Versace
Hermès	Salvatore Ferragamo
Prada	Valentino
	Ermenegildo Zegna

The Consumers

By 2005, luxury goods were no longer exclusive to high-net-worth individuals. Worldwide, 7.7 million people have the purchasing power to buy prestigious goods for themselves. Globally, women represent the largest purchasers of luxury goods; they account for 80 percent of cosmetics and 70 percent of fashion. The consumer profile is evolving. Men also are spending on luxury products that portray quality, service, prestige, and gracious style. The brands have given birth to a need that does not exist and created an image that can seduce. Middle-class consumers are increasingly seeking quality and designer clothes. For example, recent trends show luxury consumers are purchasing one Brioni suit for $3,000 rather than three ordinary suits at $1,000 each. These consumers are both quality- and price-conscious and weigh their options on pleasure and aesthetic.

The last few years have witnessed a shift from the traditional affluent target consumers to a broader and younger audience. This phenomenon was driven by the conspicuous consumption movement, influenced by celebrities' endorsements of luxury goods. This meant that younger consumers were accessing the luxury market by purchasing small price-point items like caps and key rings. Luxury goods companies were only too happy to oblige via downward extensions, making their brands accessible to consumers who could not otherwise afford to purchase a luxury product. For example, Tiffany sold silver bangles and Louis Vuitton produced cheaper synthetic versions of its super-expensive leather and crocodile-skin bags. Currently, low-ticket items comprise approximately 55 percent of all luxury sales.

What Creates Demand in the Luxury Industry?

Luxury goods are particularly sensitive to the effects of economic cycles and world events, since a large portion of the luxury goods industry was dependent on travelers. In 2003, the luxury goods industry was hit by three economic phenomena—the SARS epidemic, which impacted the Asia Pacific region; the Iraq war; and the strengthening of the euro versus U.S. currency, which not only reduced consumers' purchasing power in Europe but also impacted companies' bottom lines, as revenues were in weaker currencies and costs were in the much stronger euros.

In 2006, the luxury industry was hit by war in Lebanon and the bomb scare issued by the UK, which restricted the types and sizes of liquids that travelers could carry onboard the plane while traveling. Duty-free sales were estimated at $26 billion a year globally and $7 billion in the U.S. liquor sector, and perfume makes up anywhere from 20 percent to 50 percent of sales. The travel retail channel was lucrative and most major luxury firms, including LVMH, L'Oréal and Estée Lauder, produced fragrances and other beauty products that were exclusive to those shops.

Options to brace for this threat included stores delivering customers' items to the airline, which would stow them in the baggage hold and hand them over to passengers when they disembarked. Another option might be scanners capable of identifying dangerous liquids. During the wake of this sudden incident, Ed Brennan, chief executive of DFS, LVMH's duty-free operation, commented, "I believe we will be able to restore the ability to sell those product categories to departing passengers in a safe way again. We have a strong partnership with airports around the world, and we will work together to find a solution."

Surprisingly, while a major economic downturn occurred in 2008 and 2011, the luxury industry remained strong. Luxury sales in Europe increased by 16 percent, with an increase in sales of Hugo Boss to €2.06 billion and record sales of €2.8 billion of Hermès in 2011. This showed that in the face of the various economic cycles, the luxury industry remained resilient.

Why Are There Increasing Demands in This Business?

As competition intensified in the luxury goods industry, more and more brands increased their average advertising expenditure in an effort to stimulate demand for their product.

Luxury goods companies attempting to garner consumer awareness have begun investing more heavily in retail store networks. Many luxury goods companies viewed flagship stores in key capital cities such as Milan, Tokyo, Hong Kong, New York, and Paris as vehicles for advertising their brands and conveying their brand images. As witnessed, key luxury goods companies increasingly invested in larger and larger flagship stores.

The Actors

Listed here are profiles of eight of the top luxury brand companies.

LVMH—Louis Vuitton Möet Hennessey

LVMH, undeniably the world's largest luxury goods group with revenues of about US$29 billion, is often acknowledged as one of the most successful luxury goods groups in the world. LVMH boasts many of the industry's star brands, such as Louis Vuitton, Christian Dior, and Moët & Chandon. LVMH's brands span a variety of sectors from fashion to leather goods, cosmetics, watches and jewelry, and wines and spirits.

The genesis of LVMH can be traced back as far as 1854, when Louis Vuitton started manufacturing luggage and trunks for the traveling aristocracy. The company was founded on January 1, 1923. Subsequent generations of the Vuitton family, most notably Henry Racamier, transformed this business from a two-store operation into a billion-dollar giant by tapping into the lucrative Asian market.

This family business began its evolution into a luxury conglomerate when Moët & Chandon boss Alain Chevalier, fearing a stock-market takeover, formed a merger with Louis Vuitton in June 1987, forming LVMH. (The Moët and Hennessy brands had previously merged in 1971; this merger also owned the rights to Parfums Christian Dior.) The parent company owned 98 percent of Vuitton shares, but more importantly, this union gave the four families 51 percent of the voting stock, thus staving off a takeover.

At this stage, Bernard Arnault, LVMH's current chairman, had already obtained ownership of the failing Boussac empire in 1984, using $15 million of his own capital and $45 million from investors. Boussac owned the world-famous Christian Dior Haute Couture house, and in time Bernard Arnault returned Boussac to profitability through divestments and redundancies. He entered the LVMH picture when he was approached by Henry Racamier to invest in LVMH as an ally against Alain Chevalier, as the relationship between Louis Vuitton and Moët-Hennessey had quickly soured. Bernard Arnault, with the help of Guinness, initially purchased 24 percent of LVMH stock. It was Racamier's attempt to block Bernard Arnault from gaining control that pushed Arnault to purchase even more stock and subsequently increase his shareholding to 37.5 percent. Shortly thereafter, he increased his shareholding to 43.5 percent, assuring his control of LVMH. This merger between Bernard Arnault and LVMH allowed Arnault to finally reunite Parfums Christian Dior with Dior couture.

Bernard Arnault and his family owned 46.4 percent of LVMH as of 2013. As France's richest man, as of 2012 Bernard Arnault had an estimated personal fortune nearing $29 billion dollars.[1]

Group Companies   LVMH specializes in the production and distribution of various consumer goods, including fashion and leather goods, wines and spirits, perfumes and cosmetics, and watches and jewelry. The company's key products and services are depicted in Table 3.2.

Organizational and Financial Structure   The Arnault family and Foreign Institutional investors owned 46.4 percent and 29.8 percent shares of the company respectively. The rest of the company were owned by French Institutional investors (14.8 percent), the Bulgari family (2.5 percent), and treasury stock (1.6 percent).

Footprints/International Expansion   LVMH distributes its products through company-owned stores and licensed distributors across

---

[1]Miller and Newcomb, 2012.

Table 3.2 Brands under LVMH

Wine and Spirits	Fashion and Leather	Perfume and Cosmetics	Watches and Jewelry	Selective Retailing
Hennessy	Louis Vuitton	Parfums Christian Dior	TAG Heuer	DFS Galleria
Moët & Chandon	Fendi	Guerlain	Zenith	Sephora
Chateau Cheval Blanc	Donna Karan	Parfums Givenchy	Chaumet	Le Bon Marché Rive Gauche
Chateau d'Yquem	Céline	Makeup for Ever	Hublot	Starboard Cruise Services
Krug	Loewe	Acqua di Parma	Fred	
Dom Perignon	Givenchy	BeneFit Cosmetics	Bulgari	
Belvedere	Edun	Kenzo Parfums	De Beers	
Mercier	Kenzo	Fresh		
Glenmorangie	Nowness	Perfumes Loewe		
10 Cane	Thomas Pink	Fendi Perfumes		
Ruinart	Berluti	Nude		
Domaine Chandon California, Australia	Marc Jacobs			
Bodega Chandon, Argentina	Emilio Pucci			
Veuve Clicquot				
Ardbeg				
Cloudy Bay				
Cape Mentelle				
Newton Vineyard				
Cheval des Andes				
Terrazas des Los Andes				
Numanthia				
Wenjun				

Other Activities

Groupe Les Echos
Royal Van Lent
Cheval Blanc
Jardin d'Acclimatation
Samaritaine

various regions worldwide, including Asia, Western Europe, and the United States. The group has established strong presence in developed markets such as Europe, Japan, and the United States and is rapidly expanding into emerging economies of Asia, which provide a huge potential market. LVMH operates through more than 883 stores in Europe (excluding France), 621 stores each in the United States and Asia (excluding Japan), 390 stores in France, 360 stores in Japan, and 165 stores in other countries. Asia (excluding Japan), the group's largest geographical market, accounts for around 30 percent of the total. Furthermore, a revenue growth of around 28.8 percent from this region partially offset the declining revenues from other matured markets, indicating that the geographical positioning to a certain extent enabled the company to weather the decline experienced in its major markets.

Strategy   LVMH pursued both organic growth and growth by acquisition strategy. LVMH focused most of its acquisition efforts on brands within the luxury segment; however, these brands span a variety of diverse product segments.

The LVMH luxury goods group was organized into five different divisions: selective retailing, fashion and leather goods, perfumes and cosmetics, wines and spirits, and watches and jewelry. However, LVMH also had interests in economic, financial, and investment publications, as well as other companies such as the Jardin d'Acclimatation in Paris.

LVMH in its acquisition choice sought to purchase and restore French heritage brands, transform them into star brands that would evoke French heritage and its savoir faire, and uphold innovation and quality.

To achieve its organic growth objectives, LVMH focused on new product launches, expanding its retail network, and increasing its expenditures on communications.

Growth and Mergers and Acquisitions   After taking over as chairman of LVMH, Bernard Arnault pursued growth by acquisition in order to build a portfolio of the world's most revered luxury brands.

The growth spree started through the acquisition of Céline and Givenchy couture and eventually of Kenzo in 1993. Fashion and leather-goods brands such as Donna Karan and Kenzo were added to the stable, as well as watches and jewelry with TAG Heuer, Zenith, Chaumet, and Fred in the mid-1990s.

In 1997, Bernard Arnault entered into selective retailing with a 61 percent ownership of DFS. This was further expanded to include Sephora cosmetics stores, France's leading cosmetic retailer; Le Bon Marché Parisian department stores; and La Samaritaine.

The period from 1999 to 2000 marked a spending spree for Bernard Arnault, who spent an estimated $1.1 billion U.S. dollars on luxury-good brands from watches to edgy and trendy U.S. cosmetic brands such as Fresh and Benefit.

Not all acquisitions were successful. In January 1999, Bernard Arnault sought to gain a seat on the board of the famed Italian leather-goods house, Gucci. Gucci countered this move by issuing additional shares, and then offered PPR (today known as Kering) a 40 percent stake in Gucci for $2.9 billion. This forced Bernard Arnault to make a bid for 100 percent of Gucci for $4.9 billion. The takeover of Gucci sparked a bitter feud between PPR's boss, François Pinault, and Bernard Arnault, resulting in litigation before the Dutch courts. The courts ultimately ruled in favour of Kering (ex-PPR) and in the year 2000 Bernard Arnault finally sold his Gucci stock to François Pinault.

From 1999 to 2008, LVMH also undertook a series of divestments. In 2003, LVMH divested itself of some 50 unproductive brands, among which were Michael Kors; Bliss Spas; and Philips, de Pury, and Lux-embourg auction house. Most notably, in 2005 LVMH sold Christian Lacroix, the fashion house that Bernard Arnault helped to create in 1987.

History repeated itself in 2013, when Mr. Arnault attempted to take control of Hermés by gradually gaining hold of a 22.6 percent stake (valued at US$2 billion) of the company without making any declaration. It was called an "unfriendly attack" by Patrick Thomas, ex-CEO of Hermès. The dispute ended at this point with a symbolic US$10 million amount fine on LVMH by the Financial Markets Authority. This action resulted in a very courageous and strong family reaction to block any possibility for LVMH to control the family Maison by blocking more than 51 percent of the shares.

Nevertheless, this series of divestitures did not dampen the com-pany's growth by acquisition strategy. In 2004, LVMH purchased whiskey-maker Glenmorangie PLC for £300 million. In November

2011, LVMH acquired 100 percent of the shares of ArteCad, one of the leading Swiss manufacturers of watch dials. In October 2011, LVMH launched a public tender offer over all ordinary shares of Bulgari, after which LVMH held 98.09 percent of the share capital of Bulgari. This helped LVMH increase its presence in the watch and jewelry segment. Also, in October 2011, the company and the Koh family, the founders and controlling shareholders of Heng Long International, signed an agreement to jointly own and control Heng Long International. The partnership with the Koh family strategically complemented LVMH in the procurement of high quality crocodilian skins. Such strategic acquisitions helped the company to generate incremental revenues to contribute for future growth.

Key Success Factors   LVMH's success could be attributed to the way in which it managed brand independence and creativity. Bernard Arnault gave his designers a free rein to invent, as was evidenced by John Galliano's creations for Dior.

However, this costly creative process is counterbalanced by strong cost control measures in other areas, such as manufacturing, synergizing media and advertisement, renting of retail space, logistics, sourcing and inventory control, and other back-end operations.

Another key success factor of LVMH had been its stringent adherence to producing products of quality. LVMH was able to place such strict quality controls as it manufactures most of its products, with some limited outsourcing. This strong control over the brand was also mirrored in LVMH's tight control over its distribution network. In fact, Louis Vuitton is one of the few luxury goods companies that owns and operates 100 percent of its store network.

Part of LVMH's success can be attributed to the group's competence to partner with the right creative talent and the right brand, like John Galliano with Dior before, Marc Jacobs with Louis Vuitton, Michael Kors and later Phoebe Philo with Céline, and others, all of which have been highly successful.

Future Outlook   LVMH's future outlook was investment oriented. The group looked forward to continue its growth and seize new opportunities. A free cash flow of €2.5 billion enabled the company to invest in a substantial number of new acquisitions. The focus of the company was on innovation, expansion in new territories, and an increase in their production capabilities.

Kering (Previously Known as PPR)[2]

Kering (ex-PPR) was founded in 1963 by François Pinault as a building materials business trading in timber that then transformed itself into a specialized retail and luxury goods distribution company by the mid-1990s. PPR operated with three key divisions: Luxury, Sports & Lifestyle, and Fnac. The company's retail division marketed fashion, accessories, Beauté care products, home furnishings, cultural products, and household appliances. PPR marked a new stage in its development with the purchase of Gucci in 1999 and thereafter built a multibrand luxury goods division. PPR continued to grow and develop its businesses through strong and highly reputed brands through the 2000s. Since 2005, the group transformed itself from a diverse conglomerate into a cohesive, integrated group. In 2007, PPR seized a new growth opportunity with the purchase of a controlling stake in Puma, a world leader in sports and lifestyle, further establishing PPR as a leader in global brands. Following the demerger and proposed flotation of Fnac and the disposal of Redcats' businesses, in 2013 the group would withdraw completely from the mass distribution sector. In March 2013, the PPR name was changed to Kering. While this phonetically sounded like "caring," it was also a play on the Brittany origins of the business. In Breton, "Ker" means "home" or "place to live," explained François-Henri Pinault. It portrayed that the company took care of its businesses, its people, customers, and stakeholders—as well as the environment.

Group Companies   Diversified product and brand offerings helped the company cater to the various needs of its customer base. It offered cultural and technological products, including personal computers,

---

[2]On March 22, 2013, François-Henri Pinault announced that the group would change its name to "Kering." This new name was approved by shareholders at the Annual General Meeting on June 18, 2013.

photography, TV/video, software/games, office equipment, and tele-
phony, as well as operating book and music stores. The company was
also involved in retailing apparel, home furnishings and appliances, and
furniture. In addition, Kering produced athletic footwear, apparel, and
accessories under the Puma, Volcom, Cobra, Electric, and Tretorn brand
names; and luxury goods in the brands of Gucci, Bottega Veneta, Yves
Saint Laurent, Alexander McQueen, Balenciaga, Brioni, Christopher
Kane, Stella McCartney, Sergio Rossi, Boucheron, Girard-Perregaux,
Qeelinbrands, and others.

Organizational and Financial Structure   During the fiscal year
2013, Kering (then PPR) generated €9,748 million in revenue overall, 67 percent of which came from the luxury division and 33 percent
from the sports and lifestyle division. More specifically, the luxury division generated €6,470 million in revenue, with 55 percent coming from
Gucci, 16 percent from Bottega Veneta, 8 percent from Yves Saint Laurent, and 21 percent from other brands.

Footprints/International Expansion   Kering organized its luxury
division into five geographical regions: Western Europe, North America,
Japan, Asia Pacific, and other countries. During the fiscal year 2013,
the luxury division generated 33 percent of its revenue from Western
Europe, 19 percent from North America, 10 percent from Japan, 31
percent from Asia Pacific, and 7 percent from other countries.

Strategy   Kering's strategy had primarily been based on the organic
growth of its current (luxury and sports and lifestyle) brands: to expand
into new markets, reinforce their presence in mature markets, and
develop their distribution network and channels, including e-commerce.
Its strategy also included acquisitions of small to medium size, with
promising expansion prospects and meeting strict criteria, that would
strengthen and complement the brand portfolio.

Growth and Mergers and Acquisitions   In 2001, Gucci Group
bought Bottega Veneta and Balenciaga and signed partnership deals
with Stella McCartney and Alexander McQueen. Between 2001 and

2004, PPR reinforced its capital participation in Gucci Group. In 2003, PPR sold its company Pinault Bois et Matériaux to the British group Wolseley. After symbolizing the very first step of the group in the wood trade sector, and becoming a famous French retailer in wood material construction, import, and transformation, Pinault Bois was sold for €565 million. In 2004, PPR sold the electrical material manufacturer Rexel. After a public bid, Pinault-Printemps-Redoute increased its shares to 99.4 percent of Gucci Group's capital. In 2005, Pinault-Printemps-Redoute changed its name to become simply PPR. In 2007, it acquired a 27.1 percent controlling stake in Puma, followed by an increase in this stake to 62.1 percent on completion of a tender offer and acquisition by Redcats USA of United Retail Group. In 2011, it announced the acquisition of Brioni and Volcom, Inc. (Volcom and Electric brands). In December 2012, PPR SA bought a majority stake in Chinese jeweler Qeelin, which has four boutiques in Hong Kong and three in Europe, to enlarge its sales in the largest market for high-end goods. The acquisition price was undisclosed.[3] And it sold the Redcats USA business. In 2013, it acquired 51 percent of the luxury UK designer brand Christopher Kane and transformed itself to Kering.

Case Study: Gucci

Gucci, the world's third largest multibrand luxury group, hails back to Florence, Italy, when in 1921 Guccio Gucci first opened a leather-goods shop, creating products that sported a casual yet elegant style and catering to the wealthy.

Guccio's son, Aldo, became chairman of Gucci from 1953 to 1984. During the 1950s and 1960s, the company's intertwined "GG" logo became highly recognized first in the accessories business and later when Gucci expanded into fashion. Unfortunately, during the 1970s and 1980s Gucci's overlicensing

---

[3]Roberts and Chan, 2012.

negatively impacted on the company's image; the brand logo was licensed to over 10,000 products.

Guccio Gucci had bequeathed a 50 percent share of the company to each of his sons Rodolfo and Aldo. Upon the death of Rodolfo, his only son Maurizio Gucci inherited a half-share in the company. This marked the beginning of bitter family feuds between Maurizio and his Uncle Aldo, which also heralded a loss of direction for Gucci. This bickering culminated in Aldo being forced out from his position as chairman of the group in 1982, ceding the position to Maurizio. Investcorp, a Bahrain investment bank, then entered the picture, purchasing the half shares of Aldo and his son, Vasco.

Maurizio, understanding that the company name had become devalued, attempted to restore the brand image by reducing the number of products, points of sale, and repurchasing licensing agreements retaining only perfumes, watches and sunglass licenses. Unfortunately, Maurizio's zeal to restore Gucci to an up-market name coupled with an economic downturn, and poor production planning resulted in Gucci being unable to make up for lost sales from discontinued products. Maurizio's excessive spending further exacerbated Gucci's woes, plunging the company into debt and into potential bankruptcy.

This eventually culminated in Investcorp taking over Maurizio's share of Gucci in 1993 due to the violation of an agreement between Maurizio and Investcorp. Maurizio remained as consultant for Gucci until his untimely death in 1995 when Maurizio was murdered by his ex-wife Patrizia Reggiani.

In October 1995, Investcorp took Gucci public, eventually selling all of its shares in a secondary offering in March 1996 for over double the original asking price.

At this stage, Mr. Domenico De Sole, a native Roman and lawyer by profession who had presided as president-CEO of Gucci since 1984, set about to restore the brand image by reorganizing distribution and investing heavily in promotion and

(continued)

(*Continued*)

merchandising. These efforts were spurred by the arrival of Tom Ford, an American designer who infused the Gucci brand with a cocktail of racy advertising and sexy clothing. Although Gucci started out as an accessories company, its success hinged on its specific competency in fashion and on its reputation as the leading Italian luxury brand.

In 1999, PPR purchased a 40 percent stake in the Gucci group, resulting in the protracted LVMH/PPR battle for Gucci, with PPR eventually winning when the European commission approved the PPR/Gucci deal. A 100-percent stake in Gucci was finally completed in 2003.

Sanofi Beauté, which owned the Yves Saint Laurent brands, was purchased from Artémis, Francois Pinault's private holding company, thus establishing a new luxury conglomerate.

Finally, in 2003, the winning duo of Gucci CEO Domenico de Sole and creative director Tom Ford departed Gucci after they failed to reach an agreement over their contracts. This left many industry pundits questioning the future of Gucci. However, the brand continued to see success after Tom Ford left, with Frida Giannini becoming creative director of Gucci Women's ready-to-wear in 2005, and the sole creative director for the brand in 2006. Around the same time, Mr. Robert Polet, the former head of Unilever's ice-cream division was named as the CEO of the Gucci Group following de Sole's departure.

In 2011, a major restructuring took place, resulting in Polet leaving the company and François-Henri Pinault taking over management of the Gucci Group under his role as PPR CEO.

Analysis

The strength of Gucci was in its established, very strong brand image and international presence. Gucci had also the ability to control its distribution channels. This has been a part of Gucci's defensive strategy in the value-chain to capture the value added instead of giving it to middlemen such as suppliers and retailers.

Its aggressive strategy, accomplished through diversification and communication, was another of Gucci's strengths. Gucci changed its strategy of carrying a single brand to branching out to a multibrand group. This strategy was also adopted by other conglomerates such as Louis Vuitton and Prada. Some luxury companies, such as Armani, Ralph Lauren, and Versace, use the strategy of focusing on only one brand and adding other business segments. This strategy allows the positioning of the brand in the industry to differ depending on the number of brands and the number of business segments the company wants to compete in. This is the idea behind focus (monobrand) versus diversification (multibrand).

Key Success Factors   Kering had a dominant position in the luxury market as one of the world's leading multibrand luxury goods companies. Its products have been sold under Gucci, Bottega Veneta, and Yves Saint Laurent brands. Boucheron offers complementary expertise in segments like jewelry and watches. Balenciaga, Stella McCartney, Alexander McQueen, and Sergio Rossi are cutting-edge brands with high potential for long-term growth. Furthermore, Gucci also distributed eyewear, fragrances, cosmetics and skincare products. In addition, Gucci Group created and distributed high quality luxury goods, including ready-to-wear items, handbags, luggage, small leather goods, shoes, timepieces, jewelry, and ties. This vast range and the sharing of specific expertise among the various brands were the group's greatest assets. Thus Kering established its strong presence in the luxury goods market, which allowed the company to take advantage of the scale and benefit resulting from the growth of the market.

Future Outlook   The group's decision to change its name was in line with its transformation into an integrated and international group. Following the demerger and proposed flotation of Fnac and the disposal of Redcats' businesses, in a few months' time the group withdrew completely from the mass distribution sector.

Richemont

Richemont, controlled by the Rupert family, was the world's second largest luxury-goods player with an annual revenue of €10,150 million in 2013. Although the company had interests in leather goods, fashion, and pens, it predominantly owned jewelry and watch brands. Through its luxury goods subsidiary, the Vendôme luxury group, watch and jewelry sales account for 69 percent of Richemont's turnover.

Anton Rupert and his son Johann spun off Rembrandt's (a large South African tobacco and liquor giant) non–South African holdings, which included a 30 percent stake in Rothmans International. Rothmans had a controlling stake in Dunhill holdings (accessories and tobacco) as well as Cartier, which was acquired piecemeal throughout the 1970s and 1980s. The newly formed group was called the Compagnie Financière Richemont, which is based in Zug, Switzerland. Richemont went public in 1988. To avoid paying UK taxes, Richemont divided its assets into two publicly traded companies: Rothmans International (tobacco), which was subsequently sold to British Tobacco in 1999, and the Vendôme Luxury Group, which since 1997 was a wholly owned subsidiary of Richemont.

Organizational and Financial Structure   To grow its business, Richemont focused on allowing the companies to operate independently—the marketing, development, distribution, and so forth were all handled separately by each brand. In terms of their distribution network, Richemont maintained a mix of directly operated stores and franchise operations.

Their operations were global in nature, with the largest market being in Asia Pacific. As of March 31, 2013, 36 percent of their sales were generated within Europe, and 41 percent in Asia Pacific.

Their organization was structured with central support services, regional support services, and the Maisons. Its business activities in four operating divisions: (1) jewelry maisons with Cartier and Van Cleef & Arpels; (2) specialist watchmakers with A. Lange & Söhne, Baume & Mercier, IWC, Jaeger-LeCoultre, Officine Panerai, Piaget, Roger DuBuis, Vacheron Constantin, and the Ralph Lauren Watch & Jewelery Co.; (3) Montblanc Maison, and (4) other businesses with

Alfred Dunhill, Alaïa, Chloé, Lancel, the Net-a-Porter Group, James Purdey & Sons, and Shanghai Tang. Additionally, their shareholder structure consisted of the Rupert family maintaining a key stake in the Richemont group, with other shares dispersed into the public.

Footprints/International Expansion   Richemont, with a strong presence across the world, had operations in Europe, Asia, and the Americas. Asia, the company's largest market, generated 41 percent revenues in FY2013. Europe contributed sales of 36 percent, while the United States contributed 14 percent. The company's operations were well balanced across various geographical regions, which reflected its reduced dependency on any one market. Therefore, with its global presence, the company was positioned very strongly to face any economic mishaps. This helped the company compete strongly and maintain its position as market leader.

The focus on high-growth markets was evident from increased investment in mainland China with the expansion of its retail network to 323 stores. During the same period, the jeweler Cartier (Richemont) had 37 stores in China. Moreover, the company's strategy in China was to continue to develop its distribution network and offer its customers a high-quality shopping experience in keeping with the values of the Maisons. Given its presence in China, and its longstanding experience in luxury goods, Richemont was well placed to take advantage of the growing Chinese luxury market.

Strategy   Some of the world's leading luxury goods companies were under Richemont. All of these companies, or "maisons," were kept independent. The growth strategy of the Richemont group focused on creating innovative products and marketing them appropriately. Its diverse geographical operations were crucial for the group to gain a competitive advantage.

Growth and Mergers and Acquisitions   In recent history, Richemont did not have major watch-related mergers and acquisitions. It mainly used M&A to increase its production capabilities. Aside from Dunhill and Cartier, Richemont's stable of luxury brands included

80 percent ownership of Van Cleef & Arpels, Piaget, and Vacheron Constantin. In 2000, Richemont acquired Jaeger-LeCoultre, IWC, and A. Lange & Söhne for $1.8 billion against the bid by LVMH, enabling Richemont to gain a large stake in the high-end luxury watch market. By 2013, specialist watches increased to 27 percent of the group sales while the jewelry segment represents 51 percent of the total sales.

An overview of Richemont's M&A history is listed in Table 3.3.

Key Success Factors   The key success factors for Richemont were actually the mix of the companies under its portfolio. The brands were some of the most prestigious brands in the luxury industry and known for their exclusivity and status. For example, Van Cleef & Arpels had been the first jewelry house on Place Vendôme and was known to be one of the most exclusive brands within the industry of high jewelry.

Table 3.3   Richemont's Mergers and Acquisitions

Company	Description	Acquisition Date
Cartier	Jewelry and watches	1970s and 1980s
Piaget	Watches	1988
Officine Panerai	Watches	—
A. Lange & Söhne	Watches	2000
Alfred Dunhill	Menswear and accessories	1988
Baume & Mercier	Watches	1988
Chloé	Womenswear, jewelry, fragrances, and accessories	—
IWC	Watches	2000
Jaeger-LeCoulture	Watches	2000
Lancel	Leather goods	1997
Montblanc	Writing instruments	—
Purdey	Firearms	1994
Vacheron Constantin	Watches	1996
Van Cleef & Arpels	Jewelry and watches	1999 (60%) 2001 (40%)
Fabrique d'Horlogerie	Components and watches	2006
Minerva	High-end watches (20%)	2007
Greubel Forsey	Watch cases and bracelets	2008
Donze-Baume	High-end watches	2009
Roger Dubuis Rouages	Wheels and pinions	

Beyond the brand portfolio, Richemont's geographic reach was also a huge success factor. As Asia was the prime growth market for the luxury industry at this time, Richemont's presence was a huge asset. This was evident based on the financial results of Richemont within Asia Pacific. Further to simply their presence in the market, Richemont's focus on developing its distribution network was a huge asset. This ensured consistency within the retail experience for all consumers.

Future Outlook Richemont targeted Asia Pacific, which could compensate for slow growth in the European markets. But the group was unsure about the growth prospects in Asia Pacific as a result of slow wholesale goods growth. It was expected that the strong demands in China and the Middle East might offset the weakness in the markets in Japan and the United States.

Swatch

Swatch, the world's largest watchmaker, was formed from the merger of ASUAG (which was founded in 1931 and which owned many watch-making companies such as Rado and Longines) and SSIH (which was forged from the merger of Tissot and Omega in 1930).

By the 1970s, the Swiss watch-making industry was suffering due to the onslaught of cheap Japanese imports. Ironically, many of the popular Japanese watches employed quartz technology, which, although discovered by the Swiss, had been largely ignored by the industry.

As these Swiss watch-making companies faced bankruptcy, Nicolas Hayek was recruited as a consultant to provide recommendations on the future of the Swiss watch-making industry. Mr. Hayek suggested that SSIH and ASUAG merge and that they produce a low-cost watch that could be sold globally at a set price to compete at the lower end of the market, in which Swiss watch manufacturers had 0 percent market share at the time.

Thus in 1983 the two companies merged to form SMH (Société Suisse de Microélectronique & d'Horlogerie) with its headquarters located in Biel, Switzerland. Later that year, the Swatch watch was launched to become an international success and an icon.

Nicolas Hayek later purchased a 51 percent controlling stake in SMH and he became CEO in 1985. SMH changed its named to the Swatch group in 1998.

In 2002, Nicolas Hayek Sr. resigned as CEO, with the post now being occupied by his son, Nicolas Hayek, Jr.

Group Companies   The Swatch watch company is composed of several divisions, including watches (which accounted for 50 percent of Swatch's sales), jewelry, watch movements, watch components and microelectronics. Swatch also had interests in telecommunications and Internet.

Swatch owned the following brands: Breguet, Harry Winston, Blancpain, Glashütte Original, Jaquet Droz, Léon Hatot, Omega, Tiffany & Co., Longines, Rado, Union Glashütte, Tissot, CK watch & jewelry, Balmain, Certina, Mido, Hamilton, Swatch, Flik Flak, Endura, and Tourbillon. There were also a number of production companies under the Swatch Group.

Swatch, as a group, controlled 25 percent of the world's watch market and was a dominant player in the luxury Swiss watch market, controlling 30 percent, followed by Rolex with 22 percent and Richemont with 20 percent (see Table 3.4).

Organizational and Financial Structure   Swatch Group operated through three segments, namely Watches & Jewelry, Production, and Electronic Systems. The company's watches and jewelry business segment offered watches and jewelry, the production segment was involved

Table 3.4 Luxury Watches

Private Label	Mass	Mid	Prestige	Luxury
Endura	Flik Flak	Calvin Klein	Longines	Blancpain
	Swatch	Certina	Rado	Breguet
		Hamilton		Glashütte
		Mido		Jaquet-Droz
		Pierre Balmain		Léon Hatot
		Tissot		Omega
				Swatch Paparazzi

in manufacturing watches and chronological watch movements and jewelry, and the electronic systems segment engaged in the development and production of electronic components and systems related to watches. In addition, the company also followed forward integration with the establishment of direct distribution and/or retail channels. Its own retail channels included monobrand stores and a network of multibrand prestige watch and jewelry boutiques. Thus the company held an outstanding industrial position with a high degree of verticalization (forward and backward) in the sector of watch movements and components production as well as in the electronic systems sector.

Footprints/International Expansion The company had its operations in Europe, America, Middle East, Australia, South East Asia, Africa, and a few other regions. Swatch Group had subsidiaries in many countries, including Switzerland, Austria, Belgium, Denmark, Finland, Germany, Greece, Australia, China, Hong Kong, the United States, India, Brazil, Canada, Mexico, Panama, United Arab Emirates, and South Africa. Its production centers were located principally in France, Italy, Germany, Malaysia, Switzerland, Thailand, and China. Swatch Group operated more than 160 affiliated companies in more than 30 countries around the globe. For countries in which Swatch Group had no subsidiaries, it operated through local distributors. The company distributed its products through global distribution network or its own retail channels (monobrand stores and a network of multibrand prestige watch and jewelry boutiques). Its prestige and luxury brands were represented at its Tourbillon multibrand and monobrand boutiques located in the world's most prestigious shopping districts.[4] Further, at airports the company operated watch and jewelry boutiques through its Tech-Airport company.

Strategy

- **Growth strategy:** Historically, Swatch achieved a large portion of its growth through acquisition. In fact, all brands in the Swatch group

---

[4]Swatchgroup.com., www.swatchgroup.com/en/brands_and_companies/distribution.

have been acquired with the exception of Swatch itself, which was built from the bottom-up, a complete green-field venture. This series of acquisitions enabled Swatch to further entrench its position in all watch segments.

While Swatch's sales growth was boosted by increased demand in the luxury watch segment, Swatch has been quoted as saying that while its focus will continue to remain on organic growth, further expansion via acquisition has not been discounted.

- **Integration:** As a luxury goods company, Swatch's distinguishing feature was its highly integrated structure, which encompassed components suppliers, manufacturing and retail.

A key part of Swatch's strategy was to integrate backward by purchasing key suppliers of watch components. The purpose of integration was to control quality and costs in all of the watch segments. Swatch currently owns 160 production facilities located in Switzerland, Italy, France, Germany, United States, Virgin Islands, Thailand, Malaysia, and China.

While Swatch had some overseas production facilities, the bulk of Swatch's manufacturing remained in Switzerland, unlike many other manufacturers who have shifted their entire production to low-cost countries. The strategic rationale behind this decision was to leverage the renown of Swiss-made watches.

- **Technology:** However, backward integration was not the only strategy that Swatch pursued to reduce costs. New product techniques and technology such as radical innovation in product design, automation, and assembly also contributed to Swatch's competitiveness in the marketplace. Swatch also directed its efforts toward increasing efficiency in its supply chain, particularly between its component suppliers and the watch manufacturers.

- **Product:** The Swatch's group initial product strategy was to focus on producing fashionable collectible watches at an affordable price rather than a watch that is purchased as an heirloom. This emotional marketing strategy proved highly successful for Swatch and is the main point of differentiation with its competitors. Swatch has now moved into integrating technology into its watches, as evidenced by the 2004 launch of Swatch Paparazzi in collaboration with MSN (Microsoft)—a watch that can link to updated news and weather.

- **Distribution strategy:** Swatch's distribution strategy had always been to have one profitable, growing brand in each watch segment. While the mass watch segment was important for Swatch, the luxury watch segment with Omega was reputed to provide some 44 percent of Swatch's margin.

    Swatch's distribution strategy had always been marked by forward integration into fully owned stores, particularly in major capital cities such as Paris' Place Vendôme, New York's Time Square, and Tokyo's Ginza district. In addition, Swatch had diversified into new product groups such as its Dress Your Body line of jewelry.

    Furthermore, the Swatch group was one of the first luxury groups to enter into emerging markets. Swatch, which was present in India for some time, plans to open eight new Omega boutiques in India in nonmetro cities through multibrand stores in these markets.

- **Communication:** Finally, Swatch's communication strategies hinge upon sponsorship of events such as the Swatch Alternative Fashion week, targeted toward young consumers. Table 3.4 gives an overview of different watch brands owned by the premier luxury groups.

Growth and Mergers and Acquisitions   The company in 2009 renewed its agreement with the International Olympic Committee (IOC) for a long-term partnership in the areas of timing, scoring, and venue results services for the Olympic Games. It also foresaw the provision of similar services for the Paralympic Games. This renewal of the contract emphasized the longstanding successful relationship with IOC. Further, in 2009 the company's subsidiary, Tech-Airport Holding SAS, won the bid to operate watch and jewelry outlets at Geneva International Airport. In addition, it won the bid to operate watch and jewelry outlets at the Nice Cote d'Azur airport. Tech-Airport planned to introduce the Hour Passion concept in the airport boutiques at Nice Cote d'Azur and build a new exclusive point of sales in the business aviation terminal. Tech-Airport engaged in providing the retail activities of Swatch Group in airports. It operated 28 stores (nine at Roissy Charles de Gaulle, France; nine at Orly, France; five in Nice, France; one in Nantes, France, and another scheduled to open in Vienna, Austria). This renewal contract followed by the continuous expansion of its presence at different European airports underlined the quality of Tech-Airport as a multibrand retailer of jewelry and watches in an airport environment.

Strategic Acquisitions   The company in 2009 acquired the remaining 90 percent of its Swiss Precision Watches (Pty) Ltd, a watch distribution company located in Johannesburg, South Africa. Swiss Precision Watches was formed in 2003 together with the Moss Family for the distribution of watches produced by the group. It was subsequently renamed The Swatch Group (South Africa) (Pty) Ltd. This acquisition helped in controlling of a network of nine Swatch franchise stores that were operated by the distribution company. In March 2013, Swatch acquired the Canadian-owned watch and jewelry brand Harry Winston for US$1 billion.[5] The acquisition will help Swatch compete against Richemont in the high-end jewelry market, as well as for watches decorated with precious stones, after their previous collaboration with Tiffany & Co. fell into legal dispute in 2011.

Key Success Factors   Swatch's key strength is definitely in its man-ufacturing prowess and vertical integration; these are the factors that enabled Swatch to launch a high-quality mass product and produce it in a high-cost country like Switzerland. The highly vertically integrated model of Swatch enables it to maintain its strategic independence in the marketplace and better control over its brands.

This success was also been emphasized by the Swatch Group's strong brand portfolio with high-profile brands such as Omega. Each brand from a marketing perspective operated independently of the others, while from a manufacturing perspective coherence among the divisions is high. Finally, Swatch's presence in all areas of the market, spanning from mass to luxury, enabled it to achieve a critical mass that increased its competitiveness in the marketplace.

Future Outlook   The company had good growth in January, which made it optimistic about its prospects in 2015. There had been

---

[5]DeMarco, 2013.

an increase of 26 percent in the net income of the group in 2012. Swatch expected considerable growth from its Harry Winston group acquisition. The company's watches and jewelry division, which was also its production division, saw an increase in profits that resulted from new output methods. China was a promising growth market for Swatch, as the group derived 40 percent of its sales from there.

L'Oréal

L'Oréal, the world's largest cosmetics and fragrances manufacturer, was founded in 1909 by French Chemist Eugene Schueller, who in 1907 developed innovative hair dyes. In fact, since the company's inception, innovation in product technology has been the guiding principle at L'Oréal.

L'Oréal's activities were divided into three major areas: cosmetics, dermatology, and other. The cosmetics division, which accounts for 98 percent of L'Oréal's turnover, was divided into the professional, consumer, luxury, and active cosmetics product divisions.

The professional division offered specific hair care products for use by professional hairdressers; therefore, distribution of these products is limited to professional salons and outlets. The consumer division encompasses all of the products that are sold in the mass-market channels and accounts for approximately 50 percent of L'Oréal's cosmetics turnover. The active cosmetics division markets dermatological and cosmetic brands to pharmacy and Beauté outlets. Although a predominant portion of L'Oréal's cosmetics business is not luxury, L'Oréal's luxury business accounts for approximately 25 percent of its turnover, making the L'Oréal Luxury division a dominant player in the luxury perfumes and cosmetics industry.

The company generated 60 percent of its sales outside of France.

Group Companies   L'Oréal's global brand recognition, product quality, and marketing experience enabled it to create one of the strongest consumer brand franchises in the world. The company marketed its products under 27 international, diverse, and complementary brands.

Some of the well-known brands of L'Oréal included L'Oréal Paris, Lancôme, Vichy and L'Oréal Professionnel, Body Shop, Garnier,

Table 3.5   L'Oréal's Portfolio of Brands

Professional Products	Consumer Products	L'Oréal Luxe	Active Cosmetics
L'Oréal Professional Products Kerastase	Maybelline	Lancôme	La Roche Posay
Redken	Garnier	Helena Rubinstein Biotherm	Vichy
	L'Oréal	Kiehl's	SkinCeuticals Sanoflore
Matrix Mizani Keraskin Esthetics	Softsheen Carson	Giorgio Armani	Inneov Roger & Gallet
Shu Uemura Art of Hair	Club de Createurs de Beauté	Ralph Lauren	
Pureology	Essie	Cacharel Shu Uemura Yves Saint Laurent Clarisonic Diesel Victor & Rolf Yue Sai Stella McCartney Maison Martin Margiela	

Maybelline, Giorgio Armani Parfums, Yves Saint Laurent, Kerastase, Vichy and Redken (see Table 3.5).

Organizational and Financial Structure   L'Oréal, a publically listed company, marked by a very concentrated shareholding structure with the Bettencourt family, France's richest family (30.50 percent) and Nestlé (29.30 percent) collectively owned 59.8 percent of the stock.

The company registered revenue of €22.98 billion in 2013, which kept slight increasing over the past five years, recovering from the worldwide economic crisis. The company's operating profit also increased to €3.875 billion, with biggest growth in cosmetics of 17 percent.

Footprints/International Expansion   A strong global presence helped the company mitigate the various risks associated with overdependence on a particular region. L'Oréal was one of the largest cosmetics companies with a presence in 130 countries and more than 23 international brands with more than 674 patents. The company generated 35.1 percent of its total revenues from the Western European region, 25.1 percent from the North American region and 39.8 percent in New Markets (comprising Asia, Eastern Europe, Latin America, Africa, Middle East, Pacific). A wide geographical presence decreased the business risk of the company. This also facilitated smooth expansion of the company, as wider reach in terms of geography would mean reaping more benefits, improving profit margins, and attaining economies of scale and recognition on a worldwide basis.

Strategy

- **Growth strategy:** L'Oréal's evolution focused on a mix of both inorganic and organic growth strategy.

    In recent times, L'Oréal's growth through acquisition strategy focused particularly upon emerging markets, as is evidenced by the purchase of Mini-nurse and Yuesuai Chinese cosmetic brands in 2004, as well as Colorama, a Brazilian cosmetic brand, in 2001. These acquisitions not only enabled L'Oréal to gain a foothold in these markets but it also afforded L'Oréal the opportunity to exploit the channels built by these local brands to launch its key global brands such as Garnier and Maybelline.

    Much of L'Oréal's continuous strong sales result can be attributed to its growth strategy of focusing on emerging markets. It was touted that within the next five years, emerging markets will be responsible for potentially 30 percent of L'Oréal's sales. The importance of emerging markets to L'Oréal's business is underscored by an increasingly mature cosmetics and fragrance market in Western Europe.

- **Diversification strategy:** L'Oréal's overall strategy was to focus solely on cosmetic and beauté products, preferring instead to direct its diversification efforts in retail channels. L'Oréal is unique in that it is present across mass, luxury, niche and direct market channels. To date, L'Oréal was one of the few cosmetics and perfume groups to be successful in multiple distribution channels. As of 2013, L'Oréal also forward integrated into its own retail outlets with the opening of Kiehl's, Lancôme, and Biotherm boutiques. Other boutiques in the L'Oréal stable include shop-in-shops in London's Heathrow, New York's JFK, and Montreal's Trudeau airports.

- **Product strategy:** A cornerstone of L'Oréal's strategy is to continually produce products that are at the cutting edge of technology. As a result, L'Oréal invests heavily in research and development by allocating 3 percent of its annual turnover to R&D, one of the highest benchmarks in the cosmetics and perfume industry.

  Not surprisingly, L'Oréal's innovativeness pushed L'Oréal to enter new product categories such as men's cosmetics; the launch of Mizani, an ethnic hair care line; and the development of Inneov, a nutricosmetic (oral cosmetic), which was the result of a joint venture with Nestlé. L'Oréal continually focuses on strong product launches to drive sales, particularly in the luxury fragrance segment, which it supports with strong advertising and event sponsorship such as the biannual L'Oréal Toronto Fashion Week.

Growth and Mergers and Acquisitions　　In 2009, L'Oréal USA acquired Idaho Barber and Beauté Supply (IBB), a distributor of professional products to hair salons in the United States. The company had acquired a 50 percent stake in Club des Créateurs de Beauté and YSL Beauté, a luxury products company. It also acquired CollaGenex in the United States and expanded its operations into the area of dermatology. Further, in 2009, the company acquired three distributors in the United States, namely Idaho, Maly's Midwest, and Marshall Salon Services. These three distributors cover up to 80 percent of the United States under the Salon Centric brand. In April 2010, the company's subsidiary, L'Oréal USA, announced the acquisition of Essie Cosmetics, the nail color authority in the United States, sold mainly in American salons and spas. This acquisition enabled the company to increase its share in the nail color and care market. In November 2012, L'Oréal announced its purchase of the cosmetics brand Urban Decay, known for its young, edgy, and fashion-forward luxury image. With these acquisitions, the company increased opportunities to gain leadership position in the global luxury cosmetics market. On April 15, 2013, L'Oréal acquired the health and beauty business of Interconsumer Products Limited (ICP) in Kenya. This acquisition furthered L'Oréal's strategy of expanding in the African and Asian markets.

Key Success Factors   L'Oréal enjoyed an annual growth in pretax profits for the last 20 years with the final 10 years witnessing double-digit sales growth. A key factor behind this success was the synergies that L'Oréal had been able to exploit among the brands and the various channels.

First, through its wide stable of brands, L'Oréal was able to leverage R&D technology between brands, which other competitors in the mass and luxury channels cannot do. That is, L'Oréal used its innovation technology in its luxury products, eventually rolling them out to the mass products. This strategy enabled L'Oréal to both maximize sales and minimize cannibalization of its high-end brands from its mass brands.

Second, L'Oréal's broad channel strategy insulated L'Oréal from economic downturns in its various channels, in particular if consumers for economic reasons shift from purchasing in the luxury segment to the mass segment.

Another important driving force behind L'Oréal's success had been the strength of top management coupled with a unique and driven corporate culture. Mr. Owen Jones, the iconic former CEO of the L'Oréal group, had occupied this position for 20 years. The group's success has hinged on Mr. Owen Jones's consistent focus on the Beauté business as well as his deep knowledge of the industry, having spent his entire career in cosmetics.

With an innovative recruitment policy, the L'Oréal management hires young university graduates and offers them a lifelong career and training at L'Oréal. A recent employment technique was the "e-strat challenge," an online competition where students managed a virtual cosmetics company. This challenge provided L'Oréal with access to people across many countries and campuses that showed an aptitude for strategic thinking as well as financial and marketing skills.

At L'Oréal, a strong corporate culture fosters competitiveness among the different brands and encourages an internal drive to succeed.

The management style that this corporate culture engenders can be likened to that of coaching: responsibility was delegated to managers, although top management is involved in all major brand decisions. This management model served to mitigate the risk of a potential brand failure if a wrong decision were made.

Finally, L'Oréal enjoyed a premier position in the cosmetics and fragrance industry as it was not a technologically led organization, but rather marketing and technology carry an equal weight within the organization, conferring both marketing and a technological prowess on L'Oréal.

Future Outlook   The company's growth in future was driven by innovations in emerging markets. Along with the consumer division, the focus of the group was on professional (salon) and luxury segments.

Hermès

Hermès International SA, founded in 1837 by Thierry Hermès, is often touted as the luxury brand of the elite. The business began in saddlemaking, and its origins scan still be seen today in the Hermès trademark—a horse-drawn carriage.

Over time the business evolved into designing luggage, wallets, and most notably handbags. Today, Hermès International SA designs, produces, and markets leather goods (luggage, handbags, and belts), silk goods (ties, scarves, and accessories), perfumes, clothing, watches, shoes, tableware (china and crystal), accessories (jewelry, gloves, and hats), and art of living products.

Hermès is one of the few luxury goods houses that remains predominantly in the hands of family members. It was Emile-Maurice, Thierry's son, who began the evolution of Hermès into an international luxury house; he was the first to incorporate zippers into products. Succession then passed to son-in-law Robert Dumas, who brought Hermès to notoriety in the 1950s with the "Kelly" bag, named after actress Grace Kelly, which remains Hermès' iconic product.

Interestingly enough, Hermès did not see itself as a luxury brand but rather as a brand that designs quality products made by skilled craftsmen.

Organizational and Financial Structure   Hermès became a public company in 1993, yet the family retained the majority of the equity.

Footprints/International Expansion Geographically diverse operations helped the company mitigate the various risks associated with overdependence on a particular market. The company was engaged in the design, manufacturing, marketing, and retailing of luxury goods. The company had a strong market position in Europe, the Americas, and Asia Pacific. During the first quarter of the fiscal year 2013, the company generated 36 percent revenue from Europe (16 percent from France and 20 percent from the rest of Europe); 15.5 percent from the Americas; 47 percent from Asia Pacific (17 percent from Japan and 30 percent from the rest of Asia Pacific) and 1.5 percent from others.

Strategy   There had been a conscious effort on the part of Hermès to differentiate itself from its rivals, and this has never been more evident than in the strategies that Hermès pursued that were in contrast to its competitors.

First, Hermès targeted a more elite and exclusive clientele as opposed to the aspirational ones of its competitors, maintaining the highest level of quality and innovation.

Second, while Hermès has continually invested in expanding its store network like a plethora of other luxury goods houses, Hermès did not follow the industry trend of building "luxury cathedrals"; instead it directed most of its efforts toward renovating its current network of stores and controlling its growth with extreme care.

Third, unlike its competitors, Hermès' main focus was on achieving organic growth and to a much lesser extent growth by acquisition. Rather, Hermès acquisitions were made in a bid to both preserve luxury craftsmanship and to enhance Hermès own expertise. In fact, many of these companies, like the silver-maker Puiforcat, are small niche brands.

Nevertheless, as part of its strategy Hermès decided to employ the avant-garde fashion designer Jean Paul Gaultier to produce the ready-to-wear collection for Hermès in creating designs that maintain the codes of Hermès while incorporating Jean Paul Gaultier's own style into the mix.

Growth and Mergers and Acquisitions   Hermès' growth strategy had been dependent on its ability to open and operate new stores and the availability of suitable store locations on acceptable terms. The company's products were available worldwide through a network of around 300 exclusive stores, of which 165 are branches.

Beyond store expansion, Hermès also invested in brand extension. It rolled out a home collection in Paris. As of 2013, 20 boutiques dedicated areas presenting the home interior range of products, which included new contemporary furniture creations. In addition to its tableware and art of living collections, Hermès also developed a complete range for the home, including upholstery fabrics and wallpaper. This line was created in partnership with an established brand in the sector: the Italian fabric specialist Dedar.

Key Success Factors   Undoubtedly the cornerstone to Hermès' success is its strong brand franchise, which is fostered by the company's meticulous attention to impeccable craftsmanship. Such a strategy is possible given the strong family ownership structure. A strong focus on product innovation has been a competitive advantage for the company. Hermès for over 170 years has been creating and inventing a wide range of products. The company started designing new and innovative products from 1837 with the launch of its harnesses and saddlebags and never stopped its spirit of innovation. Thus, a strong focus on innovation has strengthened the company's product offerings and brand image. The company's new product development capabilities helped it to broaden its product portfolio and expand its market share.

Future Outlook   Hermès looks forward to expanding its network all over the world. It also looks forward to expanding its production capacities in France and in Europe. The focus of the group is also on innovation to give it a strategic advantage in the market of luxury goods.

Burberry

Burberry began when Thomas Burberry in 1856 founded an out-fitter store in Basingstoke, England. Burberry's rise to prominence occurred when in 1880, Thomas Burberry invented the breathable and waterproof gabardine. In 1901, Burberry was commissioned by the war office to design a new uniform for the British Offices and the "trench coat" was born. The trench coat's iconic status was bolstered by its popularity among famous actors such as Humphrey Bogart. The eponymous Burberry check, which was registered as a trademark in 1920, was soon added as a lining to the trench coats, and in 1967, this famous check, synonymous with Burberry, began to appear on accessories.

Unfortunately, with time, the cachet of the Burberry brand diminished as it was seen as an overly traditional and conservative English label. In fact, at the time when Rose Marie Bravo, the ex–chief executive of Saks Fifth Avenue, took the helm at Burberry's, major English department stores like Selfridges and Harvey Nichols would not stock Burberry's products and, like Gucci, Burberry suffered the fate of over-licensing. However, Rose Marie Bravo was credited with revitalizing the Burberry brand, taking sales from 250 million pounds in 1997 to 675 million pounds in 2003.

Burberry's was purchased by the Manchester-based Universal stores (GUS) in 1955 and in 2002, GUS floated approximately 25 percent of shares on the stock market, reducing GUS' ownership to 66 percent.

Burberry's products include men's, women's and children's apparel and footwear as well as fragrances, cosmetics, accessories, eyewear, and watches.

Burberry's performance since 2012, in particular at the retail level, confirmed the vitality and health of the brand even in a market under severe pressure. Product offer enhancement, democratic positioning within the luxury sector (helped by the weakness of the British pound), and the brand's iconic style increased its attractiveness in the eyes of final consumers searching for "value for money" investment pieces in times of budget constraints. The brand refreshment and repositioning of the past few years had successfully passed the test of the economic crisis.

Overall, Burberry was able to do the following quite convincingly:

1. **Brand momentum** improved dramatically due to product development and innovative communication. A specific mention must be made of the innovative use of the Internet (three-dimensional catwalk shows, the creation of an online campaign called "Art of the Trench" and dedicated to the trench coat, broadcasting of shows via the Web). Burberry has more than a million Facebook fans.
2. **Accessories** represented 33 percent of sales in 2013, showing that the brand expansions had been successful.
3. **Exposure to own retail** improved to 58 percent of sales and was set to improve further.
4. **Factory outlets** did not prevent the brand from selling full-priced items; rather, they helped to significantly reduce inventories (by almost £100 million).
5. **Reduced the iconic pattern** from all but 10 percent of the items produced. This not only helped in controlling the widespread counterfeiting but also helped Burberry reclaim its identity.

Organizational and Financial Structure   Burberry had consistently delivered an outstanding return on invested capital, historically 29–36 percent. Although retail investments and restructuring are expected to dilute the ROIC to 25–28 percent over the next couple of years, it will remain at best-in-class levels for the luxury-goods industry. The group achieved record financial results in 2013. Total revenue grew to £1,999 million, from which £1417 million was generated in retail network.

Burberry now has more than 206 mainline stores, 214 concessions, and 49 outlet stores, in addition to their digital store. Management is targeting additional new retail space of about 10 percent a year, with a specific focus on new markets and leveraging on brand segmentation and children's wear.

While the 469 directly operated stores registered 12 percent sales growth in 2013, the wholesale channel performance has been rather flat, with small increases in North American department stores and Asia Travel Retail franchises. Additionally, new franchise stores were opened in markets such as Croatia, Romania, South Africa, and Thailand. Income from global product licensees (in fragrance, eyewear, and timepieces) and the European wholesale children's wear licensee accounted for £109 million, more than 5 percent of the group's total revenue in 2012–2013. Though having a double-digital underlying growth in royalty income, Burberry purchased back its fragrance and beauty licensee from Interparfums in 2013 and is going to directly operate in Japan after the expiration of its Japan licensee in 2015. All these ambitious moves are coherent with its new global luxury brand strategy.

In addition to a return to a normal "organic" environment, Burberry still had the potential to expand further its wholesale presence: in children's wear, department stores (especially in the United States, where management believes it can double the business in the medium term), and in new markets, where initial moves are usually through franchised stores rather than DOS.

Leveraging on the Franchise: Brand Segmentation   Burberry's brand was segmented into three different lines: at the top of the pyramid, the Prorsum runway collection; in the middle, the London Collection, a line of office-style tailored apparel; at the bottom, the Brit lifestyle collections, which will be further developed with the strengthening of sports and denim lines. The Brit and London labels were first used in the Autumn/Winter 2009 advertising campaigns and were distributed starting with the Spring/Summer 2010 collections.

Footprints/International Expansion

- **Premium positioning in Japan:** Burberry's presence in Japan was through a longstanding license agreement with Sanyo Shokai and Mitsui & Co., which produced and distributed lines exclusively for the Japanese market and were positioned in the premium segment rather than in luxury. The retail turnover generated by the Burberry brand in Japan was in the region of £1 billion.
- **Emerging markets focus:** Another key growth area was emerging markets, which Burberry defined as China, the Middle East, Russia, and India.

Strategy   Upon her arrival in 1997, Rose Marie Bravo set about repositioning the Burberry brand, transforming it into a young and fashionable luxury brand while leveraging its classicism and heritage.

This repositioning strategy was coupled with a firm grip on production, marketing, and distribution, with Burberry repurchasing many licenses.

Burberry, however, has retained some licenses in Japan that were responsible for producing nearly all Burberry's clothing for distribution in that domestic market. Rose Marie Bravo was quick to point out that her approach to licensing was different in that it was more of a partnership approach in which the brand had input.

Burberry supported its strategy by featuring celebrities such as Kate Moss in its advertising campaign, and it adapted the trademark Burberry check in different variations. Perhaps Burberry's products became too accessible and too high profile; in the wake of soccer hooligans sporting the Burberry check, Burberry has scaled back the checks from 20 percent on clothing to just 5 percent. The check remains a prominent feature on handbags, which represent 70 percent of the collection. Burberry diversified its product range in 2004 when it launched an upscale ready-to-wear line, Prorsum.

Burberry's business model was such that it manufactured some of its clothing but it outsourced a large portion. Its products were distributed through its own stores and wholesale accounts, and like most other luxury houses it has entered emerging markets with its February 2004 store opening in Russia.

Angela Ahrendts joined Burberry as its new CEO in early 2006. Angela was the executive vice president responsible for women's and men's brands at Liz Claiborne, Inc., the U.S. apparel company. After a superb innings of eight years at Burberry, Angela joined Apple in mid-2014. Following that Christopher Bailey assumed the role of both creative director and CEO of Burberry.

Growth and Mergers and Acquisitions   In November 2008, the company set up a majority owned joint-venture in Japan, also with Sanyo Shokai and Mitsui & Co, with the aim of developing the distribution of Burberry's luxury nonapparel products in Japan. The JV became operational in 2009, with distribution having started from Spring 2010.

In October 2009, the apparel license with Sanyo was amended to give Burberry more favorable conditions. In particular, the expiration date of the agreement was brought forward to June 2015 from June 2020, and there was no right of renewal for the licensee. In addition, royalty payments terms had been recalculated. In the medium term, the new agreement would have the effect of significantly raising the royalty income generated by the Japanese apparel license, which started in December 2011. In September 2008, the company established the Burberry Middle East (BME) joint venture, which currently managed 11 stores, 2 of which were stand-alone children's wear stores. BME should contribute some 3 percent of group retail revenues in FY09/10. Another joint venture had been signed in India with Genesis Colours. It was estimated that Burberry generated about 7 percent of group revenues in Greater China, where the company managed 44 stores, and believed there is potential to open 100 stores in the future.

Future Outlook   The group tried for growth, in China which was a key market for the company. It also digitized the offerings. The group opened a new flagship store in Chicago. The emphasis was more on retail sales, since the wholesale sales were down by 3 percent in 2013.

Chanel

Chanel, a privately held company, is fully owned by the Wertheimer family. Although revenues were not officially disclosed it was estimated that worldwide sales of Chanel were to the tune of €4–5 billion in 2014.

Chanel began as a hat shop in Paris 1910. Gabrielle "Coco" Chanel was renowned for her revolutionary, innovative style. She freed women from the fettered corseted clothing of the times by designing free-flowing trousers, cardigans, and the famous little black dress in 1926. In 1924, Chanel was the first designer to launch a fragrance bearing her name: Chanel No. 5.

In 1924, Chanel, Pierre, and Paul Wertheimer worked together to create Parfum Chanel, in which Chanel herself possessed 10 percent of the capital and profits. In 1954 the Wertheimer family finally purchased Chanel.

In 1983, several years after Coco Chanel's death, the fashion house was revived with the entry of Karl Lagerfeld. Lagerfeld had been artful in his ability to rework some of Chanel's iconic products, such as the Chanel blazer, to keep them modern and relevant.

Strategy   Chanel's approach to the luxury-goods industry had been very consistent, and it could be argued that this was a result of the very stable family-owned ownership structure.

Chanel owns more than 100 boutiques worldwide where a single jacket may retail for as much as $5,000, but Chanel, like many other luxury houses, expanded its product lines in a limited way into less expensive accessories and bags, making them more accessible to a wider and younger consumer base. In fact, this strategy had been credited with the brand's success in Asian markets, particularly in Japan.

Key Success Factors   Product quality remained one of the main strengths of Chanel. Craftsmanship was the core value of the brand and it was perceived to be one of the best luxury brands. Some of the products like Chanel No. 5 have achieved an iconic status and have been able to connect with consumers across different generations because of their timeless appeal. Established since 1910, with a unique brand DNA and its heritage around Coco Chanel, Chanel always held its place as one of the famous luxury companies of the world. In the of Chanel, its traditional quality and its location at the Place de Vendôme assured its brand image.

By associating Chanel with Coco, who gave the company the rights to use her name as well as her style and image, customers perceived Chanel as "luxury." Coco Chanel, as a core personality of Chanel, was indeed the DNA of the brand Chanel and the company's greatest strength. The French chic style she presented and the "little black dress" she designed made her immortal. Her legendary lifestyle and the fact that she remained celebrated as an icon for generations shows the strong personality she had and the significance of her image to the brand. The brand understands very well her influence and launched a series of books and films around her stories. The mix of Coco's immorality and lady likeness gives Chanel an extravagant touch of deluxe by proving a consistency and relevance to current market needs.

- **Brand signatures—Camellia and double C logo and celebrity endorsements:** The brand has a rich heritage. Even some of the products have a long history. Chanel had been able to develop a couple of strong brand signatures that gave the brand instant recognition among consumers.

The change of image in the 1980s by Karl Lagerfeld turned out to be another great success. His uncanny ability to interpret Coco Chanel's work and translate it into the present made him an icon for Chanel and brought the label to the 18–25 age group. Through his designs, the luxury brand achieved a high level of exposure among its target customer audience of the twenty-first century.

Besides that, Chanel's strength lay in its celebrity endorsements by celebrities like Kate Moss, who was the main personality for Coco Mademoiselle from 2001 till 2005 and was succeeded by Keira Knightley in 2007, who remained coherent with the unique mix of boyish and ladylike charms of the brand. Chanel's policy of celebrity endorsement can be traced back to early 1952 when Marilyn Monroe said "I only wear Chanel No. 5 to bed."

- **Limited productions:** As just mentioned, Chanel was not seen as overly aggressive as far market share and turnover was concerned. The limited productions helped in establishing a super-premium luxury aura for the brand where waiting lists for a product became an accepted norm. In fact, for certain products, it was normal to have a brand waiting list as well as another waiting list to get onto the brand waiting list.

  Having a wait list and not being able to meet the entire demand, definitely affected its turnover. In certain cases, consumers who were no longer willing to wait moved on to other brands. In a way, one of Chanel's strengths was at the same time one of its weaknesses.

- **Unique marketing efforts to build visibility like the Mobile Art exhibition:** Chanel is credited with some innovative and unique marketing efforts to reach out to consumers. And in a post-recession era, these aspects become relevant not only to connect with new consumers but also to re-emphasize the brand's relevance with its existing consumers. Chanel was involved with certain initiatives in the arts world, and the Mobile Art exhibition was one of the projects that the brand undertook to showcase its commitment to this form of expression.

- **Strong competition in the Chinese markets:** Chanel did not have the first mover advantage in China, though it was extremely

Table 3.6 Brand Comparison of Some Major Labels

		LVMH	Kering (PPR)	Richemont	Swatch	L'Oréal	Hermès	Burberry	Chanel
Marketing Model									
Marketing Stratefy									
Marketing Strategy	Target Consumers	Aspirational	Aspirational	Elite	Mass to super-premium	Mass and elite	Elite	Aspirational	Aspirational Elite –Fashion
Channel Strategy	Store Network	Rapid expansion	Cautious	Slow	Rapid expansion	Rapid expansion	Slow expansion	Rapid also Digital media	Slow Expansion
	Store Structure	100 percent store network	Retail, wholesale, and franchise	Boutiques, franchise, third party	Fully owned stores	mixed	100 percent own store network	Own, JV, Licenses	Retail & Wholesale
Communication Strategy	Channel Strategy	Luxury only	Luxury only	Luxury only	All channels	All channels	Luxury only	All	All Channels
	Communication Strategy	Sponsorship of events that reflect travel heritage	Sponsorship reflecting new luxury	Events, celebrity placements	Sponsorship of events	Aggressive	Events that reflect equestrian heritage	Celebrity endorsements	Sponsorship reflecting old luxury
Product Strategy	Level of Accessibility	Entry-level products	Entry-level products	High-jewelry to entry-level	Fashionable, collectible watches	Mass and premium, R&D	Entry-level products	Entry-level sub-brand	Entry-level products
	Licensing	Minimal	Fragrances	Yes	None	None	None	Eyewear, Japan (to end in 2015)	Eyewear
	Origins	Accessories	Accessories			Cosmetics	Accessories	Outdoor Wear	Hats

Organizational Model								
Integration	Forward integration into selective retailing	Mixed	Independent maisons	Full vertical	Forward integration into retail	Backward and forward integration	Digital synchronizati-on	Full Vertical
Synergies	Excellent	Good	Not evident	Excellent, pure watch player	Good	Medium	Good	Low
Growth Strategy	Organic and acquisition	Organic and acquisition	Organic & inorganic	Organic	Mostly Organic	Mostly organic		Organic
Emerging Markets	Fast, pioneer	Slow expansion	Moderate	Fast, pioneer India	Strong Expansion	Cautious	Aggressive	Expansion Russia, India
Strongest Markets	Asia	Europe	Europe followed by China	Airport	Europe	Europe	China	Europe & Middle East
Heritage								
Iconic Product	LV Mono-gram	Gucci Loafers	High-jewelry	Irony; Paparazzi	Cosmetics	Kelly bag	Trench coat	Blazer, Quilted handbag
Founded in	1854	1923	1988	1931	1909	1837	1856	1910

successful in Europe, the United States, Asia, and Japan. Some brands like Burberry have had an early entry and have been able to entrench themselves quite strongly in the market. Moreover, initially China was a men's- and a gift-dominated market as far as the luxury sector was concerned and, thereby, the major brands that had been doing well had strong men's lines (such as Armani, Dunhill, and others). This highly competitive market of the fashion business presented a dangerous factor for the couture house. Chinese buyers, as they become more educated, no longer see luxury consumption as a one-time purchase. They are rapidly making luxury consumption as a lifestyle choice. They are also increasingly becoming committed to high-end niche products. Though Chanel was a late-entrant, Chanel became one of the favorite luxury brands, according to reports in 2013. It was the third most-sought-after luxury brand, after Audi and BMW and ahead of Louis Vuitton, Prada, Dior, Burberry, Giorgio Armani, and Versace.[6]

Future Outlook   In the case of Chanel, as observed, the double-C logo strategy worked well in China. Together with the bling strategy, its conservative strategy also worked well. Interestingly, the top-five luxury brands are publicly traded, while Chanel did not have to worry about the pressures of the stock market or any external or internal stakeholders. Its strategy of selective, trading-up by steadily increasing the prices of iconic brands, having a waitlist, and fewer innovations compared to the industry competition has served it well in one way; in another way it might be perceived that Chanel did not utilize the full potential of its classic brand.

Conclusion

It seemed that the luxury industry had become increasingly consolidated with many converging strategies (see Table 3.6 for a summary), but the quest to solve the industry paradox remains: How does a luxury brand retain its exclusivity and desirability while it democratizes and appeals to the masses?

---

[6] *World Luxury Index China 2013*, Digital Luxury Group.

Chapter 4

Branding

I n consumer electronics, aviation, and the automobile industry, evolution has been and will continue to be of a technological nature.
For example, when the first video recorder appeared, the choice
of standards was vital: Sony's Betamax, Philips's VCR, or JVC's VHS?
VHS won out in the end. The Airbus A380 is an aircraft capable of carrying 600 passengers, and in recent history the Concorde could fly to
New York in three hours and forty-five minutes. Technology is indeed
what alters the relationship with the customer: The DVD, iPhone, and
BlackBerry are a few examples.

In luxury, technology plays practically no role. Fragrances, materials, shapes, tastes, colors, decoration, and architecture are what have
been and will continue to be the driving forces behind new trends and
changes. This difference is essential!

In industrial companies, aviation, transportation, and energy, engineers are the drivers. In luxury, creators are the ones who lead, bring
along the company, and seduce the clientele, which is another characteristic of the luxury sector.

In actuality, one world is dominated by reason and rational logic whereas in the other, day-to-day emotions outweigh reason, and innovation on the supply side does not necessarily correspond to an analysis of the demand side.

In consumer electronics, the equipment penetration rates of households are examined and it becomes apparent that a household that has already purchased two televisions and two refrigerators is likely to stop there. That's saturation. The same applies to cars, of course.

Generally speaking, when it comes to luxury, marketing cannot be based on a market analysis because there is no limit or saturation of a market. There are no equipment penetration rates, either. A woman will never have too many pairs of shoes, can always try out a new perfume, and will be tempted by a new dress, gloves, belt, or gem. No one can truly say where the luxury product market begins or ends.

It is a world without limits, borders, or measures.

As a result, sales in the luxury sector all depend on creation, innovation, and a capacity for seduction. This is why we see enormous successes and incredible failures. The perfume expert Guerlain can also create a perfume like Champs Élysées, which completely missed the mark. Tom Ford, a celebrated designer, never managed to fit in well at YSL, but revived Gucci overnight.

The purveyors of famous names are all astonished when failure strikes and sometimes are just as surprised at their unpredictable successes! The marketing of luxury products is an improbable and uncertain endeavor.

The shape of a bottle can be tested, the contents subjected to trials, jewelry can be shown to female consumers, and men can be questioned about the colors and shapes they want and expect in a tie. Each has his own idea, his own "marketing," but ultimately no one really knows for sure.

Luxury marketing is something of an exercise in futility for market study companies that usually only introduce more uncertainty and unlikely leads in a pseudoscientific vocabulary that will make your head spin, and for good measure they say: "It's useful."

In reality, success in fashion or accessories has never been prepared, analyzed, or predicted by a study.

Neither the Kelly bag nor the Birkin bag by Hermès, nor the classic bag by Chanel, nor the trunk by Louis Vuitton were the results of market analysis.

Never did Yves Saint Laurent or Jean-Paul Gaultier read any market studies on women consumers to create a collection and show.

Marketing generally helps a company to gain an understanding of consumers' expectations, but in luxury the problem consists not in meeting needs, but in anticipating, suggesting, and persuading. It is a diametrically opposed approach that puts an emphasis on breaking with the past and least of all on the use of logic.

This is the pathway of the unexpected, of disorder. It can be thought of as the opposite of marketing.

The trick in luxury is to have the creative process—together with its right to mistakes and disorder, sometimes with dire consequences—exist alongside the necessary management function. This is what luxury marketing should be, a complex and subtle process that combines a knowledge of the whims of the day with a good understanding of customers' mores, trends, and habits, and at the same time an ability to outpace those trends and anticipate tastes and aspirations in order to give birth to products that are ahead of their time but right on target. If luxury is too out of touch with the times, it doesn't sell, which is precisely the point: finding the most appropriate expression that takes into account the times and comes out at exactly the right moment.

That kind of marketing is not based on merits. Appropriate creation proceeds from profound knowledge of the most diverse technologies, and a definition of that kind of marketing is also informed by extensive, documented experience rich with artistic history, contemporary art movements, and a blend of worldwide innovations.

When standing before an aircraft, when appreciating a landscape, and especially when encountering beauty in the streets, we breathe deeply and admire.

In a museum we discover a shape or a color; marketing is then a matter of taking information gleaned from here and there to create a fabric, an armchair, a dress, a bag, a bottle, a luxury object.

So, luxury marketing does exist, but it is peculiar, a kind of marketing that proceeds from a global approach, day and night, everywhere on the planet, at home, with others, in an effort to identify and discover some detail, make a connection to another detail elsewhere in another realm, and then innovate by assembling them.

Could carbon fiber, a material for aviation, be used to make an attaché case?

Hermès thought so.

And what if, one day, leather were no longer the only material to be used to make suitcases, bags, and belts?

Luxury marketing also means thinking about materials, possible substitutions, and incisive innovation.

Ultimately it means bridging the gap between customers and creations, always articulating what users think and taking their comments into consideration, not to start over but rather to move forward.

It cannot be said that marketing does not exist in luxury, but it is very specific, the polar opposite of the usual kind, and indeed this strange term and extreme luxury—name-based luxury—make for poor bedfellows. It is the natural companion of marketing luxury, but is such luxury *really* luxury?

Luxury Marketing: Highly Creative and Selective

We must always try to be a little bit against the current.
As the Chinese proverb goes—only a dead fish sails in the
direction of flow.
We do not do marketing. . . . We are in a group that creates.
The creation of our innovations is what creates the market and
not vice versa. . . . We create, invent, and from there, as our
inventions are quite successful, the market adheres.

—Bernard Arnault

The world of luxury branding is one of many paradoxes. It is an interesting paradox, as it challenges the notion of modern-day principles of marketing. For the marketing discipline, the world of luxury is a melting pot. The world of luxury holds a special place, as it has in some way taught marketers the principles of brand management. Though the modern discipline of brand management is officially accredited to Procter & Gamble and a memo written in 1931 by Neil McElroy, luxury brands have been practicing the art of branding long before McElroy was born, and even before P&G was founded. For example, almost a century ago, Gabrielle "Coco" Chanel did more than create products. She redefined the whole nature of the categories—the tweed suit, the little black dress, the cashmere cardigan, No. 5 perfume, costume jewelry, the total look, among others. Coco Chanel in passing commented "Fashion passes, style remains." Such was her power in branding Chanel with her own name that after one hundred years all of these inventions are part of the fashion legend. Thus luxury brand management is a place where tradition and creativity collide. It is a place where ancient founders, artisans, and youthful models meet and make mad magic together. It is a place where impoverished artisans make a brand with their names that remains for generations. Thus on one hand, luxury brands represent the origin of brand management, and on the other, they question the fundamentals of the marketing principles of building a brand.

Managers who worked in the luxury industry with multiple brands agree with the above notion. For example, Ashish Sensharma, former CEO of Vilebrequin luxury swimwear, commented, "I'm not a follower of the classic marketing techniques used by FMCG (fast-moving consumer goods) companies—my reasoning? They lack the emotion to convey the 'soul.' In luxury, the real sense of marketing is about creating and conveying the passion we have in creating the product—it is a real story, which the user can see and feel. There is no one better than the luxury brands to convey a story, provide a dream, and sell aspirations."

Emmanuelle Sidem, senior partner and founder of Connex Consulting in Paris, also agreed with the paradox of marketing and the universe of luxury branding. She commented, "Marketing is luxury's childhood disease. Like all childhood diseases, the best way to prevent it is vaccination. The vaccine strain is based in the cultivation of the maison's identity, its history, its values . . . ."

The concept of marketing is a misnomer in the luxury industry. The 8 Ps—product, price, place, promotion, people, process, physical evidence, and productivity—of marketing do not work the same way as for other industries. In simplistic terms, the classic marketing strategy proposes that a unique and differentiated brand positioning allows a brand to gain market share from its competitors and thereby define a strategy that is valuable, rare, and difficult to imitate, thus providing sustainable competitive advantage for a brand. Though the principles remain the same, for every principle there is a contrasting notion in the luxury industry.

- **Brand:** The consumer in the luxury industry is more conscious of the brand. The story of the brand is vital for the aspiration it creates. It is never about the functional needs of a product. For example, if someone desires a Ferrari, he is not satisfied with a Maserati or BMW or Mercedes. Any other brand is not in competition with his or her needs, even at a similar price-point. The need for a Ferrari has nothing to do with another substitute with the same utility. It has also nothing to do with the functionality of the car (fuel efficiency, seating capacity, design, and other factors). The luxury brand translates the essence of the product, the heritage, and the history into one's desire to own it.

- **Positioning:** Brand positioning identifies ways that a brand should choose a relevant way to be identified and differentiated in the consumer mind with respect to its competitors. Consumers use comparative methods to select a product, based on functional and emotional perceptions that the brand has managed to create in their minds. For example, in manufacturing industries, engineers innovate and invent the product while marketing managers pilot the position of the brand. The concept of brand positioning is in a way not applicable to the luxury market. Coco Chanel's comment that "luxury is a necessity that begins where necessity ends" in fact was positioning the luxury industry. The creators of goods that are not necessary are the marketers who imagine how to persuade the customers and organize the media. They are at the origin of the brand position. The purchase decision thus is "superlative" and not "comparative," and has nothing to do with needs or utility. Luxury shoppers choose the brand that best reflects who they are and how they want to be perceived by society. Each luxury brand offers a unique character, an identity that cannot be replicated or compared. Comparing two luxury brands is like comparing the work of two painters or two musicians. Who is a better painter, Monet or Manet? Who is a greater composer, Mozart or Beethoven? The comparison doesn't make sense. It also doesn't make sense to ask which bag is better, the one from Hermès, Chanel, Bottega Veneta, or Vuitton.

- **Product:** Marketing managers are responsible for identifying relevant consumer needs and trends. Once these needs are identified, the company designs and markets a product with those features that could be standardized and mass-produced. Mass production achieves economies of scale, thus reducing unit cost. As profit is a function of cost and price, keeping differentiation and service constant, greater profitability can be achieved with lowering of cost. In the luxury world, it is in effect just the opposite. Luxury brands are never mass-produced. Rather, their production is about craftsmanship, being handmade, and being uniquely personalized to an individual's taste and preferences. It is about the creation of the designer. It is the reflection of the creator's skills and his or her personality. It is not the result of consumer feedback. Consumers are advised, educated about the characteristics, unique history and merits of the brand. This will in turn increase authority and desirability.

- **Place:** In marketing strategy, place denotes how and where the goods are sold. It is about the distribution strategy. It is to get the product into the hands of as many people as possible. The underlying premise is that the goods have to be available readily. In a competitive environment, consumers are not willing to go out of their way to purchase it. In the luxury industry, exclusivity and inaccessibility is the way to go. The luxury good has to be earned, it is a journey toward excellence, an experience, and an initiation into a cult. It cannot be easy. The greater the inaccessibility, the greater the desire. The place for distribution has to be carefully selected, ideally directly managed stores where the brand message can be controlled and communicated properly. It is the place where educating the potential buyer about the privileges that come with owning the brand, and turning them into members of the selective brand club, is the key. It is of course the place to sell the luxury product, but that is not the goal in itself.

- **Price:** Pricing strategy in consumer brand management is about launching a product at a low enough price and then trading-up. When the segment becomes more competitive, brand managers often use price incentives to maintain or increase the demand. Contrary to the conventional wisdom, when the imagined price is higher than the actual price, it creates higher perceived value. Also in contrast to the tradition of pricing as a function of demand, luxury pricing is supply-based. In luxury, first the product is created and then the pricing is set. The more it is perceived by the client to be a luxury, the higher the price it can fetch. In a standard market model, when the price falls, demand rises. With luxury, the relationship is reversed. It means that with time, prices rise in order to increase demand and remain exclusive. For example, in the wine and champagne industry, selling great quantities is the norm. But the luxury segment has reversed this notion, selling fewer products, but at a higher price. This way the exclusivity remains while margins are higher. The growth and profits thus are more from the top-line products. For a very similar reason, as the LV monogram became accessible and overexposed, with time Bernard Arnault implemented with his daughter Delphine Arnault at Louis Vuitton a change of strategy. They stopped selling the €800 monogram hand-bags and concentrated on the Sophia Coppola line of €3,000 bags. The all too accessible €800 handbags were actually damaging their business and image.

- **Promotion:** Conventional wisdom suggests that advertising is done for brands using a mix of rational and emotional messages that entice clients to consider it. In the luxury world, the dream is what sells. There is no need for a rational reason to justify a purchase. Con-ventionally, even with the premium brands, people buy emotionally and justify rationally. In the world of luxury, products must be orig-inal or have a unique character. With this uniqueness there may be unique flaws, too. The unique flaws are also a way to increase desir-ability. For example, luxury mechanical watches are known to be less accurate at keeping time than quartz watches. A Ferrari uses "hot" technology rather than the meticulous "cold" technology of German cars.

    The exposure is never the priority. On the other hand, the con-tent is very important. Only high-quality advertisements will be found in a highly selective communication channel, all consistent with the brand's image. Every brand generates its own story, which is told through different channels. No brand can imitate the marketing of another: What works for Hermès will not work for Louis Vuitton and vice versa. Promotion in luxury is linked to a deep understand-ing of the DNA of the brand, and it is essential to stay faithful to the brand's assets. Every luxury brand has its own DNA, and suc-cess cannot be duplicated. Graphically, a luxury brand advertisement promotion almost always uses suggestive imagery with a minimum number of words, if any at all. Ford's management of the Jaguar and Land Rover brands is an example of applying the classical principles of marketing to luxury products. Both brands ended up being sold at a loss to Tata Motors of India, which is turning around the image of these brands.

- **Process:** Conventional wisdom holds that following process, routines would be the next way to create success. In contrast, the process in the luxury world is uncertain. For example, no one could predict that Chanel No. 5 would be so successful when thousands of perfume launches are failures. Thus its success is both creative and selective. The process may be known, but what will be successful is unknown. Night and day, the creator searches for a product that fits the brand. He travels, visits museums, talks to people in the street but also reads, refers to journals, analyses, asks questions, reflects, and may finally discover a detail that changes everything. A color may fuel his imagination, he may be struck by an idea, he may take the risk to go far beyond present-day routines and processes, never looking at other brands, break the rules and give birth to a product. This is the marketing process, this is the genesis of luxury.

- **Physical evidence:** It is necessary in the luxury world to understand art, food, architecture, and everything that is living. Creators who launch the products, all the "métiers of luxury," have to be as close as possible to the present-moment "mood." They visit New York and Tokyo, they are on the go all the time, in the midst of current happenings. They have to sense one or two years in advance what new colors and shapes will attract consumers. They have to marry two divergent concepts during their creation. They have to create the physical evidence, which is not only driven in some way by a mix of rational factors (price, price elasticity, brand positioning) but mainly by irrational factors (surprise, emotion, innovation). The logic is different. It is dominated by forces, which are in the field of "offers" and not in the ground of "demands." In the field of appliances, one knows the level of equipment a certain kind of household will buy, one knows that one cannot sell more than one or two TVs or refrigerators to a couple. In luxury, who can say how many pairs of shoes a brand can sell to a customer!

- **Productivity:** Marketing in luxury is not driven by market analysis of the potential customers. In luxury, traditional marketing studies are useless, as no one can assess the market reaction of a new product. A new dress, a new bag, or a new pair of glasses—it is almost impossible to predict if it will be a failure or success. Classic marketing tools may not be the answer. The luxury world in this case has no frontier and no limit. No explanation can be put forward to explain consumers' reactions. It is indeed a strange marketing paradox.

  The one distinctive feature of luxury marketing is that it is highly creative and discreet. When Moncler, the famous Italian brand, in the middle of Paris decides to show its ski jackets with snow and ski chair-lifts with men and women wearing ski boots, Moncler is going back to its roots and marketing its products—not as utilities for skiing but as a luxury brand.

  However, with more and more emphasis being put into marketing communication, it is challenging to draw a clear line between the marketing campaigns of big FMCG brands and those of luxury brands. In effect, they can draw inspiration from each other. For example, Coca-Cola's success with printing popular first names on its labels was picked up by Moët & Chandon. Moët & Chandon offered customers the opportunity to write a personalized message on their Impérial champagne bottles. This idea of customization is very successful, as it is a creative way of saying "Congratulations!," "Happy anniversary!," or simply "Thank you." To go one step further, customers can also ask for hand-customized bottles, which can be decorated in genuine gold or silver Swarovski crystals, according to their preferences and budgets.

  Productivity in marketing in the luxury industry essentially boils down to an *advance understanding of the future*. It is an understanding that emanates from the passion of people working in this industry. Can someone teach this? Can it be replicated productively? It is more like the job of an astrologer or a fortune-teller who is looking into the crystal ball. This marketing can be tough—no technique can help. What is the key? The answer is in finding the right talent. And talent is rare. Luxury brands are primarily dependent on talents that we can find only in the minds of creators and their abilities. Once the creators succeed, productivity soars.

- **People:** Brands need people who are expert in marketing. In the luxury world, designers are in fact the marketers. Consider the birth of the first Dior perfume, right after the creation of the couture house. It was the original idea of Christian Dior to complement a dress with a final touch. "I created a perfume to wrap every woman in glorious femininity, as though each of my dresses was emerging from the bottle, one by one" said Dior for Miss Dior. Before him no designer would imagine linking perfume and couture, but now almost every fashion brand has its own perfume, from the haute couture houses to fast-fashion brands like Zara. Another example is Karl Lagerfeld, who has rejuvenated Chanel No. 5 and made it the ultimate dream of almost all women, of all ages, all over the world. When he decided to turn the Grand Palais into a huge "Chanel Shopping Center" for its 2014 "Défilé"/catwalk show, in the middle of a busy food market, reinventing the packaging of Chanel, it was all that people were talking about during fashion week, like it or not. The creative director is by all means the chief marketing manager, and one of the best that one can find in the market. As the chief marketing manager, the designer must satisfy the nomad of today and of the future.

The Nomad

The world is becoming nomadic. The movements of travelers, tourists, and businesspeople is increasing, and it is no coincidence that the Airbus A380 was launched. As Jacques Attali wrote in his book Lignes d'horizon, *"There is no safe haven, the nomad individual will work without stopping because natural separations between night and day, and of time itself, have been abandoned. . . . For the first time in history, the nomad will have no fixed address. Our sense of ties will gradually fade to a memory. There will be nowhere left to hide."*

In the future, 2,000-seat airplanes will be slicing across the skyline. There will be huge airports and gigantic ships to deal with the movement of nomads. Nomads come from all over the place. Demanding customers travel the world, seeking riches and beauty and purchasing extraordinary clothes, flashy one-off pieces that make them feel and look good. They buy apartments or villas on beaches across the world. They feel at home in several places.

In 2014, more Chinese people visited France than Japanese. In 2020, there will be 200 million Chinese people traveling around the world, and 700 million tourists will visit Europe. Who and what will seduce then? How can we stimulate the appetites of nomads who think only of themselves, who want spas, body treatments, nature and seclusion, but are also attracted to design and receiving perfect service?

How do we communicate with these nomads?

How can we sell to the nomads of the future? What should we sell them?

Anything is possible. All sorts of stores can be envisaged for nomads, all sorts of products.

The nomads travel with electronic tablets, mobiles at their fingertips, browse, choose, purchase. They might enter a megastore, or a small boutique, they go everywhere, to places where a luxury goods store would never yet have dreamed of setting up business. Nomads are constantly on the move, pursued by information. They never stop working and stay connected.

What if we design flying stores? Mobile sales unit? Stores in trains dedicated to luxury, temporary stores, like kiosks set up where people don't expect them. It's up to us to discover new ways of becoming irresistible!

Everything revolves around the nomad's mobility. We don't know when or how the nomad develops an appetite, and luxury houses need to place their wares somewhere on their chain of desire.

Should we produce small sensual objects sold in unexpected places? Or should we invent transformable objects? For rich, demanding people who have no home and no fixed address, luxury goods should offer pleasure and serenity and be personalized, more egotistical than ever.

Nomads travel. They go to China, Japan, Hawaii, and the West Coast of the United States and then to the East Coast and to Europe. Where do they stopover? Where will they buy? How will they get back to base? Where is their base?

Nomads buy quickly, have things delivered, and want everything, right now. They often live in several places and feed on cult images and objects. There are no longer any settlers. The world is full of people who move and buy on the go.

Some goods are to be displayed or will complement goods that are worn. Luxury items help distinguish people and make them unique individuals in a homogenized, trivialized, sterilized world.

Luxury goods for nomads will be light, foldable, mobile, seductive, displayed, eternal. The quality must be perfect.

Innovation can be found everywhere, in fabrics, in the touch, scent, and aura of these goods. To persuade, creativity is a constant element, and competition is cut throat.

How can you seduce a nomad who sees everything, compares, hears everything that is going on, and gathers information at the speed of light?

It's a mad dash to catch the nomad's attention, but the key will always be in the same long-standing values.

The nomad is a human being, sensitive to beauty, elegance, and softness.

Nomads might like dark chocolate or praline—they know what they like and they have an appetite for it. They are in a way quite simple.

In this world where everything goes too fast, in which everything gets diluted, lost, where everything is public, everything is publicized, nomads are attracted to safe-haven products, natural products, signed products, tailor-made products just for them. The silence of the static luxury object will be a welcome contrast to the cruelty of unlimited speed.

Nomads need somewhere to hide and to feel protected.

The crowds of nomads imbue personalized goods with a certain extravagant quality. The fortunate paradox is that a nomadic lifestyle is compatible with all sorts of creativity that bring more comfort, more beauty.

The nomad will define luxury as the ultimate refinement to calm the anguish of traveling too fast. Fortunately, there is sure to be a contrast between the speed of travel, how random and fleeting it is, and the solidity of the purchase of a luxury good that the nomad will keep as a reminder of a flying visit. Eternity and the ephemeral will go hand-in-hand, and the object will offset the nomad's regret at having gone too fast, at not having taken the time to experience a sunset, or exchange a look of mutual understanding.

You can find refuge in the luxury of tomorrow.

Nomadism is an unprecedented path to luxury. It sets up in the middle of a large, unavoidable movement toward an emotional lifestyle, in the right place, at the right time, and in the best way.

Capitals for nomads are major cities: Beijing, Tokyo, Shanghai, Los Angeles, New York, Paris, London, and Berlin. From these places, the nomad will move on to other "peripheral" places that might be more suited to real, serene, reassuring luxury.

Nomads are attracted to monuments, museums, places of culture and relaxation, care and well-being, and luxury-goods houses should set up near attraction points such as these.

Emotion, desire, beauty, care, and culture are the natural companions of nomads—and of luxury.

The Eight P's of Luxury Brand Marketing for the Nomad of Tomorrow

Performance: When luxury goods were born due to creativity, attention to detail, and craftsmanship by the artisans, the goods sold themselves. The goods were bought by families, friends, and friends-of-friends. The owners, the creators did not chase their customers or push their goods to be sold using different tools of modern-day marketing. The creators drew customers by their constant pursuit of excellent product quality. For example, the Patek Philippe "generation" campaign harped on the fact that Patek Philippe watches were passed on to the third generation in a family. That is why Patek came out with the storyline "You never actually own a Patek Philippe. You merely take care of it for the next generation." Thus the concept of performance is associated with the timelessness of the product. Though a young woman may wear a Tiffany ring from her grandmother's wedding, she and her peers have their own tastes and preferences, they buy their own jewelry, and yet the products of earlier years are of such quality that they can be passed down from generation to generation. It is the excellent quality and their performance that makes luxury products desirable and timeless.

Provenance: Luxury brands have their own universe. The legend usually begins with an influential founder, a creative genius. For example, Chanel was much admired not only for the neat hand-sewn stitches on its famous tweed jacket, but also for the unique character of Coco Chanel. Coco Chanel, with her distinct signature style, gave the brand life, which still inspires women from all over the world today. Provenance doesn't always have to be a particular person: It can also be an iconic emblem, a history of a family, or everything that built the mystique of the brand. The combination makes up a story of a brand that with time becomes an integral part of the brand's story and personality. For example, those who buy Rolls-Royces are definitely not only paying for outstanding performance, but for its prestigious name, which has been associated with royalty for more than 100 years.

Paucity: Luxury is, by its nature, unnecessary, desirable, and exclusive. Luxury goods have to be earned. Luxury has to be inaccessible. The fact that it is accessible only to elites increases its desirability. Although luxury goods are no longer confined to only a small group of people, they are still relatively scarce compared to FMCG. This scarcity is certainly decided by the excellent performance of the products and the unique provenance of the brand, but also by marketing strategies, such as pricing, geographic differentiation of product offering, collaboration, and limited edition. For example, Hermès expresses the creativity of its brand through its very large collection; however, not all Hermès products are available in all of its stores. The stores have to order the products that they want to sell. At any point in time, no store of Hermès will have all of the collections. Paris stores will have about 35 percent of the collection. Each store will have a different assortment of products, which causes some products to be inaccessible and exclusive by design, not by planning. This also means that when one is a regular Hermès customer and one travels, one will always discover some products that are new.

Persona: The persona of a luxury brand is all the apparent elements that show the brand's identity. It is the personality, the character of a brand. It is conveyed by the visual advertising, by the consumer touchpoints, in stores and online as well, and by the events of brand communication. It is the ensemble of the brand's personality, the material and emotional values, the distinct and consistent brand image, and all the codes that make the brand identifiable. It is the fundamental key in the brand's visual advertising, to establish a clear, charming, distinctive persona, which the consumers can easily recognize even as it changes and evolves with time and can always relate to emotionally and actively. For example, companies use the persona of a brand, sometimes that of its creator, to encourage consumers to trade-up to more expensive lines when their disposable income increases. Armani is a good example: While Giorgio Armani Privé serves up haute couture fashion, it also offers lines such as Giorgio Armani, Armani CoUezioni, Emporio Armani, Armani Jeans, AIX Armani Exchange, Armani Junior, and Armani Casa, which portray the Armani persona while targeting different sets of consumers.

Personage: Brands use public figures or celebrities for promoting the brand. Brands use advertising to sell dreams. The advertisements are not for direct responses but to promote the dreams to many more people than the ones who can actually afford to buy them. Promoting the brand with endorsements from public figures and celebrities from movie stars to musicians, from political or royal figures to sportsmen, and from designers to bloggers is becoming more and more common. Endorsements from public figures continue to garner attention and credibility. However, given the fact that public figures can be associated with other nonluxury brands, and sometimes even competitor brands, it is a double-edged sword for companies to use celebrity endorsement as a means to increase the awareness of the brand. Using celebrity endorsement to increase the reach of a brand also in some way means that the brand needs some of the star's status to enhance its own status. It is in one way admitting that the brand cannot make an impact on its own. On the other hand, in emerging markets, with millions of potential new consumers, this is one of the ways to increase the brand awareness in countries where the history and the heritage of the brand are unknown. They have both to select the most influential figures without blurring the brand image with others, but also to find the most suitable endorser who is consistent with the brand ethos, brand aesthetics, and brand values. For example, the endorsement of Shah Rukh Khan, the number-one movie star of Bollywood, worked favorably for TAG Heuer to build its image in India.

Position: We will discuss further in the retail chapter how the choice of store location is vital in the luxury business. The competition for retail space is fierce, as availability of spaces for luxury brands is limited. Only the super brands in luxury business can negotiate shops in the most-sought-after places in the world: the Champs-Élysées in Paris, Madison Avenue in New York, the Hong

Kong International Airport, the first-class cabin on the Emirates Airlines—from thousand-square-meter flagship stores to ground-floor entrances in the world's biggest malls. In larger terms, position ranking is one of the most important parameters, not only in retail store location, but also in the choice of venue for events, in placement for media coverage, and in online inventory place when it comes to a digital strategy. Premium position means the highest exposure, maximum traffic, and prestigious image. On average, retail space amounts to about 35 percent of the costs in the luxury business, and the high rent may be coupled with questionable profitability. For example, retail space on the Champs-Élysées, a tree-lined avenue with broad sidewalks that extends two kilometers from the Arc de Triomphe to the Place de la Concorde in Paris, can boast 300,000 window shoppers per day and commands up to 18,000 euros per square meter. The Champs-Élysées was ranked as the third most expensive retail street in the world by Cushman & Wakefield, after Causeway Bay in Hong Kong and New York's Fifth Avenue. Sightseers can be observed photographing the Louis Vuitton flagship store, and there is often a line of people waiting outside to browse among the French fashion house's monogrammed bags and clothing.

Publicity: Publicity plays an indispensable role in branding as one of the most important ways to influence public opinion, right after visual advertising. Publicity is also a very sophisticated tool to increase the visibility of the brand, to forge a relationship with the customer, and to reinforce the feeling, the creative side of the brand. Publicity is a way to keep the aspiration high, such that the creator can communicate his or her vision in the long term. Thus publicity is not only limited to the launch of a new product, but it can also be a reward for VIP clients, or linked with other cultural or social events. It is one of the most powerful ways to generate buzz and draw attention to the brands, especially in fashion, where every year the fashion weeks are the most important festivals for buyers, bloggers, and reporters, and the film festivals are the most important events for celebrities. Again, the competition is intense, as influential brands can often get free buzz when celebrities wear their goods, while small brands need to compete to sponsor the outfits of a star. For example, in the summer of 2014, Van Cleef & Arpels showed its collection of high jewelry with the fairytale theme "Peau d'Ane," which means "Donkey Skin," at Château de Chambord in the Loire valley. The

French fairytale describes a princess who disguises herself with a donkey skin but in the end finds happiness with her Prince charming. The French jewelry house created artistic images with gemstones that gave a twenty-first-century interpretation of their own art, expressed with exceptional stones and their workmanship. It was like going back in history to discover the art, poetry, literature, and architecture of the early sixteenth century and of its place in nature. The event was complete with parakeets and owls clinging to the shoulders of masked courtiers parading on a terrace with fruit, flowers, and food; wine; and a wait staff dressed in Renaissance costumes like sweet princesses in silken dresses lit by jewels. There was a model of an enchanted forest, with a diamond barn hidden in emerald foliage; the chateau was recreated in diamonds circling a 39-carat Brazilian emerald. It was a rare event that had a combination of imagination and elegance far removed from the luxury world, which is more and more focused on celebrity, showmanship, and brand promotion. With no visible logos, the event transported guests to an enchanted world, while at the same time showcasing five centuries of the finest French traditions and, with a sweet simplicity, focusing on craftsmanship and skill.[1]

Pricing: Pricing is a delicate issue in the luxury business. Unlike FMCG, the demand for luxury goods is relatively inelastic. However, the information age and the growth story in emerging markets have brought democratization to the luxury industry. Consumers of today compared to those of yesteryear have far more knowledge of luxury brands. Consumers now are more price-sensitive and tend to pick the best buy. They have become more value-conscious. How to set the price is really an important paradox in the luxury business. The pricing strategy has to keep in mind that the price won't be so low that it dilutes the brand image but also not so high as to lose the desired number of potential customers. For example, in the luxury business it is almost universally understood that the price always reflects the cost, but in some cases it may not be so at all. It can be wholly dependent on the aspiration of the customers. An interesting question to ponder might be how to decide on the price of the first growth of Chateaux Margaux. If Dom Pérignon is a vibrant, living, perpetually renewed brand that evokes Dom Pierre Pérignon, the spiritual father of champagne, and is only produced when

---

[1]Menkes, 2014.

the grapes are exactly right, in that case what is the price of a vintage Don Perignon?

Figure 4.1 depicts the differences between the Ps of marketing in general brands versus luxury brands.

Cobranding: Does It Enhance Branding or Selling?

In the luxury world each brand is unique and has its own story to tell. One brand can hardly imitate and copy the success of another. However, as lifestyles of the rich and famous converge, collaborations between brands are more commonplace. It seems as though it is possible to create some synergy between brands, either in branding impact or in sales performance. The questions remains for cobranding: who, why, and how? Who does the brand choose to collaborate with? What objectives do brands have in mind for those collaboration? How has cobranding worked for both of the brands?

Some collaborations are not directly linked to sales; the choice is more about lifestyle. For example, Martini developed a brand with Dolce & Gabbana:

> The Bar Martini is the result of the collaboration between Martini and Dolce & Gabbana, two brands that blend Italian tradition and modernity.
>
> Crossing the threshold of the Bar Martini means entering another dimension. Guests at the Martini Bar are welcomed with a "total black" look: the only hint of colour is a red dragon rising from the floor of this place of relaxation, jealously guarded within Milan's flagship Dolce & Gabbana* Uomo boutique. The interior garden completes the experience.

Some collaborations are due to personal relationships or as an exception. For example, Hermès did a collaboration with Yamaha at the time that one of the family members was the boss of Yamaha at France. The idea grew from a special order made-to-measure upholstery that Hermès had been producing from the 1930s for planes, cars, and yachts. The collaboration with Smart was more of an exception, it seemed, as it was a limited series.

---

*http://www.dolcegabbana.com/martini/concept/

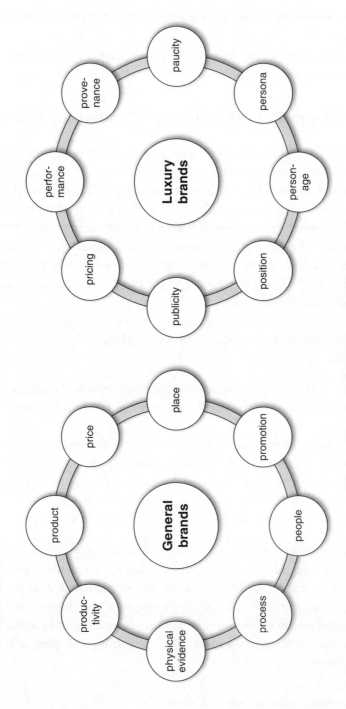

Figure 4.1 General Brands versus Luxury Brands

Some cobranding occurs at a more equal level to copromote the brands for the specific clientele of each brand. For example, BMW and Louis Vuitton collaborated on state-of-the-art luggage with green signature colors to complement the i8 sports car. This collaboration between premium automobile manufacturers and luxury brands is not something new. In the nineteenth century, when cars became the status symbol for the rich, Louis Vuitton, which was the largest travel goods store, created durable luggage pieces that fit in with the automobiles of the time and made a bold statement while perched on the roof. The collaboration between BMW and LV reinforces the shared values of creativity, technological innovation, and style. It synergizes perfectly with the pure expression of the art of travel.

Some collaborations have clear business goals: to boost sales as well as brand awareness and brand perception, for example, fast fashion and designers. These are the most common today. An example would be H&M's collaboration with McCartney, Viktor & Rolf, Roberto Cavalli, Comme des Garçons, Matthew Williamson, Jimmy Choo, Marni, Versace, and Lanvin. These collaborations have won H&M enormous attention and reestablished H&M as one of the leaders in the fast-fashion world. The collaborations won back many lost fashion fans and also regained the favor of fashion press and bloggers. Another would be Versace's collaboration with less-recognized brands like Maison Martin Margiela and Isabel Marant. From being sold out immediately on shelf, to remaining merchandising throughout the sales season, the focus of collaboration has switched slightly from being only sales driven to increasing brand awareness. For example, the result of the recent collaboration between H&M and Isabel Marant may have been more in the designer's favor.

It seems from the above discussion that collaborations are more about the marketing opportunities and less about the sales. Larger brands like H&M need to differentiate themselves from the intense competition by trading-up by working with respected designers. It may be that it the benefit of cobranding is the differentiation in a crowded market and the attention these collaborations draw.

Brand Extensions

Brand extension is the art of using a brand's image and proficiency in one area and stretching it to another area or an entirely new range of products.

This use of an existing brand in a new product or service category is a central growth driver for luxury brands. It is central to the business model of most luxury brands, since most of them offer a wide range of products, most often including fashion apparel, accessories, cosmetics, luggage, jewelry, watches, and sometimes cell phones, ski helmets, furniture, and bicycles. Had brands not been extending themselves, Hermès would still be making only saddles and Burberry would still be making only trench coats. On the other hand, there are two paradoxes within the framework of brand extensions of the luxury business. First, brand extensions imply that one has to move away in some sense from the original product that had a well-established history. Thus the new product has to be an innovation or a product extension or somewhat related to the history of the brand. In the luxury business, it is risky to move too far away from the history of the brand. Second, brand extension implies expansion and more products, which is contrary to scarcity. One can argue that scarcity will still be maintained within the product category by trading-up or trading-down.

Luxury brands have done extensions with relative ease due to their trading-down capacity. Brands such as Louis Vuitton, Gucci, and Chanel have expanded beyond their core business and offer a wide range of products, including fashion apparel, accessories, bags, watches, or jewelry. Some manufacturers of luxury products for brands such as Armani, Bulgari, Versace, and LVMH Group offer hotels and services under their brand. Although Armani began as a brand in the fashion industry, the offerings of Armani and its sub-brands range from books, flowers, furniture, and chocolates to restaurants, bars, and spas. With the use of cobranding, other brands, such as Prada, D&G, Armani, or Hugo Boss, have even offered mobile telephones. Dior's mobile phone venture was not successful. With these types of extensions, the luxury brands need to differentiate from their nonluxury counterparts. If not, the aspirational value will no longer be preserved. As discussed before, the trade-off between accessibility and exclusivity thus becomes a fundamental strategic challenge, which is particularly relevant in the context of brand extensions and growth strategies.

Other than growth strategies, brands agree to extensions in order to evolve from a luxury brand to a lifestyle brand. It is also a way to access more of a share of the wallet. However, not all such extensions are actually positively received by the consumers. For instance, in 1980, Pierre Cardin lent his name to pens, lighters, cigarettes, baseball caps, and so on. Clearly, this led to brand dilution, leading to a heavy loss for Pierre Cardin. Given that so many brand extension initiatives fail, it is imperative to ensure that some basic conditions are met. The brand must enjoy a heavy premium. The brand should be perceived to be one of the leaders in its area of business. The more revered the brand, the better it can extend. On the other hand, if the brand extension does not work out, the brand dilution is much higher in the case of a super-premium brand than of a premium brand. One has to think of brand building and not brand milking. Next, the core of the brand should be protected. In other words, brand extension is risky if the extension moves too far from the brand DNA. Brand adjacency and coherence is a condition for brand extension to be successful. This is the extent to which the brand extension is in line with the values personified by the basic brand. For instance, Cartier's expansion into high jewelry was in line with its basic portfolio of luxury watches and rings. Cartier's customers had to put in less mental effort to correlate watches and jewelry with each other. Hence, close adjacency assisted a profitable jewelry venture for Cartier. An example of a failed venture is when Hermès launched a lighter about 30 years ago. It was made by ST Dupont with some leather art created by Hermès. It did not work. The quality was not there, because the leather could easily be torn off. Maybe the creation was not strong enough, or maybe the coherence of style and quality was missing. It was basically a Dupont lighter with some leather.

Brand extensions could be envisaged in different ways. For example, Ansoff's grid, a two-by-two matrix, gives an idea of how extensions can be implemented.

	Current Product	New Product
Current Market	Market penetration	Product development
New Market	Market development	Diversification

When the product and the market remain the same, it is necessary to penetrate a market. For example, Berluti extended from leather shoes to menswear; to penetrate the market, it opened four stores in Paris.

Within the matrix, Berluti not only tries to sell more shoes, but it also wants to produce more new products for the menswear category. Berluti thus tried to increase sales by pushing the frequency of purchase higher. Similarly, all the luxury brands such as Dior and LV that have extended into high jewelry after 2005 have tried to tap the present market with new product development. Also, Gucci, Bottega Veneta, Ralph Lauren, and Prada have all have extended their lines from clothes to jewelry, handbags, shoes, sunglasses, and others. Hermès is the only brand that has still in 2014 not extended to sunglasses. The luxury brands who entered new markets in Asia with their current product are still in the market development phase in some countries, while creating awareness about their products in the minds of regional customers. For example, the geographic expansion of Armani in the Middle East and Asia led it to extend into nightclubs, cafés, and restaurants. Hermès' extension as Sang Xia in China is an example of diversification with a new product idea suited for the Chinese market.

In the luxury world, both vertical and horizontal brand extensions are common within the stronger brands. However, with the slowdown of the global market, many brands have turned back their attention to increasing the desirability and turnover of existing stores. Product extension has gone far beyond the original frontier: Hermès has added a stationery corner in its store on the Rive Gauche, Vuitton has stepped into high jewelry to enhance its luxury image, Armani has gone into house deco to express its lifestyle image, Guerlain has opened its own restaurant right under its flagship store on the Champs-Élysées and developed teas representing its perfumes. The frontier between each métier has blurred, with creating new products for highly demanding customers, most of whom are difficult to satisfy. Product diversification has become a key in brand extension.

Pricing

Economics suggests that with increasing price, the demand curve slopes downwards. The quantity demanded decreases. In contrast to traditional demand-based marketing, luxury is supply-based. The product comes first. Depending on the style and quality of the product, one sets the price based on the market perception, the amount of time and resources, and the related costs it takes to produce the product. The more it is perceived by the client to be a luxury, the higher the price it can fetch. Thus luxury economics is counterintuitive. Luxury goods are known to experience the Veblen effect, wherein the rising prices fuel demand for the product.

A recent study undertaken by a group of researchers revealed that the four main factors that influence the price of luxury goods are cost of goods sold, perceived customer value, predecessor prices, and competitor prices. It also revealed that more than half of the price-setting decisions among luxury brands are informed by the cost of manufacture and predecessor product prices. Twenty percent are set because of competitor price levels, and just a third are given a level according to their perceived consumer value. In this study, managers at luxury goods companies believe that in the consumer's eye, price ranks fourth in order of importance after brand/image, quality and design. The study in some way illustrates the rationale of pricing issues in the luxury world.

In a counterintuitive sense, the perceived customer value is the main reason why consumers tend to pay a relatively higher price for a luxury item compared to the functional utility that they derive from it. The symbolic or aesthetic utility to the price ratio is considerably higher for luxury goods than the utility value of the good. It means that consumers derive a status satisfaction or an ability to express their own styles from luxury consumption that is higher than the price they pay for it.

Apart from the above conditions, what makes pricing of luxury brands exceptional is the secrecy, the heritage, and the image associated with them. Very few luxury brands would openly proclaim the price of a luxury item that they are selling, though they closely follow their competitor's pricing as a benchmark. For example, when Bottega Veneta makes bags using the softest and most supple leather imaginable, the buyer doesn't care about the price the company quotes for this ultra-luxury product. The price, from the point of view of the customer, is not as relevant as the situational utility he or she derives from it.

Having said that, price should not be completely ignored. The Veblen effects can work, but only up to a certain price point, at which price elasticity may come into play. Price elasticity of demand is defined as the responsiveness of the quantity demanded to change in price. This could mean the quantity demanded could rise, fall, or remain

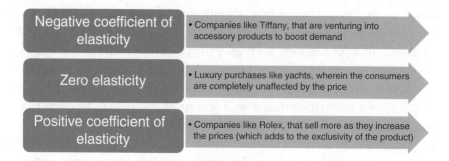

Figure 4.2   Brands and Price Elasticity

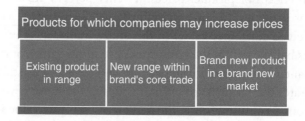

Figure 4.3   Types of Products That Have Price Increases

unaffected by a rise in price. The elasticity coefficient could be negative, positive, or zero (Figure 4.2). When the elasticity is negative, companies launch new products or extend their product lines to boost demand and thereby growth. At zero elasticity, price has no effect on demand. At positive elasticity, companies are better off to increase the price over time, which implies that with rise in price, demand also rises.

Traditional companies try to achieve economies of scale and cut down costs, and hence choose prices to propel demand. Traditional companies also want to increase the number of consumers within their ambit by competing on price. Luxury companies, on the other hand, try to push prices up over time. They want to increase the number of "wealthy" consumers within their ambit.

Increasing the price of an existing product without justifying why it has been done may not be acceptable to traditional customers. The Veblen effect does not apply in this case. Clarifying to the client the reason for the increase is always a good idea. For instance, Louis Vuitton always clarifies to its consumers in Japan if the exchange rates are eating into their profit margin, and only then will they increase the price of their goods.

When launching a new range, the aim of the company is to "trade-up" and not vulgarize the product. The motive is to increase the aspirational appeal associated with the brand. It is not to use in the wrong sense the status symbol associated with it. Thus it is a common phenomenon to launch a new range of products at a higher price point than the previous range. Also, the consumers believe that the new range is more evolved than the previous one, and thus must cost more for the company to produce. In this way the company is able to justify the higher prices, too. For instance, Tiffany & Co. hiked prices to clearly communicate its luxury position by using a larger proportion of gold and diamonds in their products. The story remained the same. This trading-up in prices was correctly accompanied by a trading-up in preciousness.

Storytelling: Culture, Event, and Communication

During the 1960s, the world of communication changed and marketing came into action. Luxury brands became the combinations of great offerings together with fantastic communication. The offerings from luxury brands were limited series, craftsmanship, and strong artistic vision. The offering was the product that didn't exactly fulfill a market or a need. And this is what created the market. It was visually recognizable and expressed a journey, an environment, a universe, that were coherent with the brand. The offer was an iconic product with fantastic quality.

With time, markets expanded and the luxury industry globalized their brand stories, which needed to be communicated to a diverse clientele residing across nations. From here on, the story of the brand was at the heart of a brand-building exercise that made a brand into a globally renowned luxury brand. It was about the unique history, the heritage, and the cultural roots of the brand, which could not be replicated by another brand.

The dilemma for brands was to decide which stories to communicate and which to not communicate. Should they express their uniqueness or their differences? Comparing products within a luxury brand category has very little meaning, as we have discussed before. The story that essentially can be communicated is based on cultural roots. For example, the codes are different, and this difference in codes has to be understood through semiotics. What needed to be communicated was what differentiated a Berluti pair of shoes from a Louis Vuitton or Christian Dior pair of shoes. Or the difference between Tom Ford's sunglasses and Moncler sunglasses. Here the consumer point of view was necessary, but the brand needed to educate and guide the consumer. For example, Chanel can be identified by its well-preserved code of using tweed or the symbol of the camellia flower. Thus the "offering" had its codes and the codes were not changeable. As another example, the Krug champagne brand portrays the dream of a man who wanted to give the best to his clients every year. He did not want to wait for a good year. This was the story that the brand needed to communicate, as it was the reason for Krug's existence. On the other hand, Chanel is involved in multiple foundations, especially involving children, but they don't communicate about it. In fact, very few even know about it.

The storytelling is also about cultural heritage. Chanel is a master storyteller in this regard. The interesting part of this discourse is to balance between reinvention of the thoughts of Gabrielle Chanel and the interpretation of Karl Lagerfeld. It's always about playing these two facets and knowing how to balance them, where to expose them, whom to expose to what, and not to communicate in a way that suggests any conflict between the two images. An interesting story concerned Chanel No. 5. The perfume placed Chanel in a situation where No. 5, while hugely successful, was perceived as being for only mature women. Chanel wanted to attract a younger audience. The management decided to shift the way women had always thought about the No. 5: Instead of talking about "My No. 5," they decided to focus on seduction, because women want to be seductive, and to actually have a man who would talk about Chanel No. 5. The idea in itself was very powerful, but the way it was executed with Brad Pitt as the celebrity spokesman boomeranged. This broke too many rules in one go and directly affected the sales of No. 5. They had to backtrack, and that's why they revived the myth of Marilyn Monroe, to go back to the roots of the perfume.

When Chanel launched the face cream *Le Weekend de Chanel*, they had a story to tell. Due to the complex world of beauty and the variety of cultural heritages of women from different countries, a simple story that could be understood universally by women was needed. Chanel created a differentiating and creative viewpoint on what beauty and skincare and in particular facial skincare are about. Thus they developed a range of facial skincare for the day called *Le Jour de Chanel* and for the night called *La Nuit de Chanel Le Jour* would make the skin more radiant for the day and ready for makeup. *La Nuit* is more for nourishing the skin and calming during the night. The creams feel different, they smell different, and they have different ingredient profiles. Chanel's innovation was to say, in effect, "Six days a week it's good to have a morning–night routine, but once a week, give your face a special treatment." The weekend (not in the literal sense) is one day of the week, whichever day one wants, for something that deeply cleanses and replenishes the skin. This product was called *Le Weekend de Chanel*. Chanel developed a completely new routine, which was basically the equivalent of what Clinique had done 25 years earlier when it launched its three-step series. The story needed to be told this way because this is what women could understand.

To promote the aforementioned stories of luxury brands events requires an important outlet. A shop is a very good place to talk about the story, as a one-to-one relationship occurs in a controlled environment. Fabulous single-brand stores are apparently one effective way to display the history, emotion, and the dream factor of the brand. However, it is costly and difficult to open stores all over the world. Luxury brands tend to leverage on art and culture elements to express the aesthetic and timeless value of their products. The short film *Odysée of Cartier* was a very well received on YouTube; the exposition Miss Dior has seen unprecedented success in each stop in the big cities throughout the world; and the biography of Coco Chanel has inspired countless women. Examples of events abound. Some of them are Louis Vuitton with VIP Maison openings, events at Johnny Walker house in Shanghai, events at the Martel pop-up cognac bar in Hong Kong International Airport, events at the Hennessy shop at Heathrow, and Burberry's events at Kean. The events were essentially taking away the very marketing aspect of the luxury house while injecting interaction or a creative angle to the business of reaching their elite customers. It was a way to rebalance the commercial aspect with a more cultural dimension. It explains also why so many houses have collaborations with artists, art galleries, and art events. Noted are Gucci Film Foundation, The Fondation Cartier for contemporary art, Le Cerc by Pernod Ricard in Asia, and others. In 2014, Fondation Louis Vuitton provided a permanent center for the charities, centered around the promotion of contemporary arts both in France and internationally. Designed by Canadian-American architect Frank Gehry to resemble a cloud of glass, the building resembles by twelve curving sails made up of 3,600 glass panels in the Jardin d'Acclimatation, Paris. These types of collaboration are very tax efficient.

An example of an event that is widely communicated is the Biennale des Antiquaires in Jewelry in Paris. The Biennale 2012 collection, presented in September at the Biennale des Antiquaires in Paris, was a resounding demonstration of Cartier's ability to celebrate its creative flair while mastering the highest and finest craftsmanship. With 155 unique high-jewelry pieces and precious objects, the Maison captured their imagination and fuelled the desire to own a piece of the Cartier history. The Biennale collection, complemented by a further 445 unique high-jewelry pieces, was unveiled to a private gathering of connoisseurs.

Similarly, with a theatrical multimedia event and an immersive new flagship, Burberry underscored the importance of storytelling in its China market.

"I think [storytelling] is important globally, but in China it stops things from being [mere] product and starts to give it life. Everything has a story—your clothes, buildings, videos, music. I think it is important people go along with this journey, otherwise it becomes a faceless product," Burberry's chief creative officer and incoming chief executive officer Christopher Bailey[2] told Business of Fashion, following a multimedia, Broadway-like show—billed as an "immersive, theatrical journey through the Burberry world of music, heritage, product, and innovation"—that the British megabrand was staged in Shanghai at one of the city's shipyards. He continued:

---

[2]"Christopher Bailey," *The Business of Fashion*. www.businessoffashion.com/christopher -bailey.

It's all about touching people emotionally. ... Tonight language doesn't matter—no matter where you are from, when you do something properly, people respond to that. It always surprises me how many people discover Burberry through our music projects for example. It's important to keep innovating with your product and keep telling different stories with it. History and heritage is important to have as a foundation, but you have to build on top of that to keep it moving forward. Technology helps us do that. . . . It's about fashion, music, dance, technology, and innovation . . . . It's about inspiring people and making them have an experience, tonight and everyday.

Digital Marketing

The digital channel has long been a question mark for the luxury industry. The digital channel can be accessed by one and all at leisure. The digital channel can be reached by the masses. The access gives wide scope for commoditization of the luxury goods industry. The information access from mass advertising in print media hoped to achieve recognition of a brand by the 1 percent of the population who could actually afford the products. There was an inherent pre-selection with glossy magazines and elite newspapers, journals where the luxury industry advertised. The remaining 99 percent of the campaign was to create awareness. But with the growth of digital-savvy consumers, the digital channel cannot be ignored anymore. The digital channel transcends barriers. The growing popularity and dispersion of digitalization, in particular social media, leaves a seemingly attractive opportunity to luxury brands. Only luxury brands have been slow to adopt and execute digital strategies.

The Digital Paradox

The slow process of adoption to execute digital strategies is inherent in the paradox between digitalization and luxury brands. First, luxury brands are built on tradition over time, whereas digital communication is a recent phenomenon. Second, luxury brand communication is usually constant and harps substantially on the brand identity and the DNA, whereas digital communication is dynamic and ever changing. Third, luxury brands are typically reserved for the elite, whereas the Internet is extremely democratic, especially in respect to social media. And finally, luxury brands exert firm control of all aspects of the brand communication, contrary to social media and the Internet, which are flexible and, especially for the case of social media, largely dependent on user engagement and contribution.

Though the paradox exists, the current geo-economic shift from the United States–Europe–Japan triad to the emerging economies of China, Brazil, Russia, India, South Africa, and other nations has witnessed the rise of the dominant luxury consumers from these regions. The consumption habits of this clientele are new and also expected to evolve over time. The arrival of new wealth centers that are redefining the profile of the luxury consumer offers opportunities. It also brings new challenges, chiefly catering to a dynamic nomadic class that carries its own value systems while traveling and shopping. The emerging middle class is increasingly Internet savvy. They are mobile and they use tablets and smartphones to search and research their interests before they actually buy. This behavior has led to potentially far-reaching implications for the distribution of luxury goods.

Given their age, location, and the era in which these consumers come from, it is perhaps not surprising that this generation of luxury clientele happens to be incredibly digitally savvy. According to a recent study, the average global penetration rate for smartphone usage is roughly 15 percent. However, in countries like South Korea, where smartphone saturation is highest (67 percent of the 50 million residents have smartphones), or in Brazil, where social media has been adopted by luxury consumers on an order of magnitude that dwarfs rates in first-world countries, it is of no surprise that brands would start leveraging this obvious opportunity. Among other emerging markets, clearly the Chinese rank as the world's largest Internet population and continue to adopt and adapt to new technology at a staggering rate, with over 720 million users online by the end of 2013. China's most popular micro-blogging site, Sina Weibo—long considered the biggest name in the Chinese Twitterverse, with a reported 500 million registered users—has some new competition, as the latest iteration in micro-blogging, WeChat (Weixin), is expected to overtake them in 2014. With such a reach in such a vast geographic spread, it is difficult to find the high-net-worth individuals. It is like searching for needles in a haystack!

After initial hesitation, even luxury companies from Italy and France—considered to be laggards in terms of web adoption—have come to embrace the opportunity to engage hundreds of millions of potential new customers via smartphones and tablets. Digital is not as easy to do as it seems. If done badly, without a concerted strategy, the democratizing effect can have adverse effects that can further erode the aura of exclusivity that has defined the brands for generations. Soul searching is needed to find the right communication strategy and social media platforms that will appeal to prospective consumers. The digital strategy needs to be real, authentic, experiential, and relevant for mobile consumers. Burberry, Gucci, and Ralph Lauren are the three frontrunners in digital strategy. Their campaigns illustrate different yet effective digital strategies. Burberry's digitalization is part of their brand culture and is communicated from the inside out. Gucci is ahead in e-commerce. Ralph Lauren is always the first to market with the most innovative ideas. Louis Vuitton is quickly catching up with a proactive and consistent digital strategy, focusing their communication on the art of travel.

The Mobility Paradox

Luxury revenues are about 5 percent of the world's sales of products. Whether luxury companies want to tap the remaining 95 percent is questionable. But it is imperative to create awareness among these new groups of multicultural, multimarket consumers. Studies have revealed that about 94 percent of the ultra-affluent consumers find out about products through digital technology and online information. Luxury merchants need to stay relevant and close to their customers, such as offering apps for mobile phones, a capacity that is slowly becoming an imperative rather than an option.

For example, Burberry's reopened its London flagship store. It brought to life the company's digital experience, allowing customers to connect to the boutique through numerous interactive devices. This connectivity helped to create an individual, customized experience.

During the opening of the store, the products were seen floating around the place, attached to golden helium-filled balloons. Full-length screens were turned into mirrors. Some items had chips attached that, when placed near a screen, initiated a presentation giving information about the product, including catwalk footage. There were no tills, just good-looking staff wandering about with iPads. This being London, and Burberry being famous for trench coats, from time to time there was even a "digital rain shower." The growth of mobile shopping through clicks meant that luxury brands are working harder to get people into their brick-and-mortar stores. In addition to opening new flagship stores across cities, Louis Vuitton, Hugo Boss, and Gucci also launched mobile sites.

The Brick-and-Click Paradox

Luxury goods retailers faced multiple challenges with e-commerce in 2012. On one hand, digital technology was a means to attracting a wider consumer base. On the other hand, there was the risk of cannibalizing brick-and-mortar sales, encouraging discount activity, and fueling online counterfeits. It was estimated that 80 percent of brands sold online using the Hermès label were fakes, for example.

Luxury branding may not be enough to capture new generations of consumers anymore. The new generation wants more than the product. They have to encounter the product and the experience both inside the store and outside, in the digital world. Thus most brands are uploading online pictures, movies, shows, and events almost immediately after they happen. Brands use modern art, screens, and anything that raises the aspirational level to get customers into the shop. Buying a product is about taking part even virtually in this glamour. But one has to balance the bricks (the physical stores) with the clicks (the online experience). As the Internet—and the mobile Internet in particular—is the fastest growing channel of retailing, there will be a tectonic shift from brick-and-mortar retail to online retail, which the luxury purveyors cannot totally escape. Sales of smartphones and computer tablets have surged globally, creating a different way to shop. The younger generation is more at ease with screens than with people. It is low-touch luxury, and its footprint is having a major impact on the way people shop.

On the other hand, for example, the opening of Vuitton's new Shanghai store—the largest shop in China—was a global event, with the brand taking out front-page ads in *China Daily*, *Shanghai Daily*, and the *New York Times*. Stores were springing up all over China. British fashion retailer Karen Millen opened its first Chinese store in Beijing in 2014, the first of 60 that it plans to open in the next five years, while American sportswear brand Michael Kors opened 15 stores in 2013–2014, taking its number to 20. Vuitton has 41, Hermès has 20, and Gucci has 39 stores in China. And they haven't even started looking at the so-called second-tier cities yet. Prada opened 65 stores in 2012, and plans to open 80 more a year for the next three years.

Similarly, some brands have realized earlier the importance of the digital space and have become leaders in the digital media across the world, notably Burberry, Ralph Lauren, Tory Burch, Estée Lauder, and Coach, as well as large brands such as Gucci, Louis Vuitton, Cartier, Dior, and Chanel.

The Reason for Social Media

Luxury is, by nature, product-oriented. A brand's value is based fundamentally on the excellence of its products. Though luxury brands never follow their customers' tastes or needs, it is certainly useful for them to better understand their consumers' desires. However, it is not always easy to get clients' feedback, because they may feel too intimidated or frustrated to make the aftersales contact. Social media has provided a free way for everyone to express their feelings, likes, and dislikes. It is risky, but also a great opportunity for luxury brands to get messages from their clients without any constraint or affectation, and to capture the preferences of their customers. Social media enables brands to draw detailed profiles of their consumers from their online activity and approach them more effectively through different media. For example, Burberry dedicates its Facebook page to its latest events, its Twitter account to celebrities' snaps, YouTube videos to its music project with artists, and furthermore it developed a Burberry acoustic playlist for its mobile application users, all of which together contributed to attracting a wider audience and conveying tailored messages to different customer profiles, which was either impossible or too costly for former avenues of mass media to address.

Social media has opened doors to give more consumers access to both information on products previously unavailable to them and discussions about the brands in a dynamic environment. The discussions can carry on with or without the direction of the brands themselves. The reality is that even a nonluxury consumer can provide his or her two cents online, where a third-world-country teenager is on equal footing with a bourgeoisie in Paris. Social media also allows brands to gauge consumer interest. They get feedback through discussion forums. These feedbacks transcend countries and cultures.

It can be assumed that social media is integrating itself into customer relationship management (CRM). Community managers for brands are the ones who manage the online community and feed the insights to the relationship manager. By creating group pages, retailers can create pages that have a viral marketing effect on consumers, luxury companies can use it to share news, promotions, and product launches.

Burberry, the iconic British luxury brand since 1856, started its digital investment in 2009 when the brand's retail performance dropped by 10 to 15 percent. Determined to find the solution in digital strategy, Burberry launched its first major digital campaign, the *Art of the Trench*, inviting the brand's loyal followers to post their own photos on their social networks, linking directly to the brand's website, which allowed the viewers to comment, vote, and repost their favorite images, and also to access the e-commerce site directly if anything caught their eyes. This campaign was successful and brought one million followers to Burberry by the end of 2009. Their concerted digital strategy has attracted 17.4 million fans and growing, who follow Burberry closely on Facebook, keep up with events, post, and share their personal stories. The brand declared a double-digital increase in revenue in 2013 and is ambitious to further develop its presence globally with a digital-integrated strategy.

Number one in jewelry and number two in prestigious watches, Cartier was always referred to as the king in jewelry and watchmaking for its knowhow and excellence since 1847. Cartier has created, for the first time in 2012, a three-and-a-half-minute film called *L'Odyssée de Cartier*. The three-and-a-half-minute film[3] follows the iconic symbol of

---

[3] White, 2012.

the brand—the panther—on a whirlwind trip around the globe where the panther brushes with key moments and locations from Cartier's rich history. The panther itself is steeped in Cartier's history: *La Panthère* is the nickname of Cartier's legendary designer Jeanne Toussaint, who created their first-ever piece of panther jewelery—a bracelet for the Duchess of Windsor. The panther travels to St. Petersburg in the snow, to China where he comes face-to-face with a golden dragon, to an Indian palace built upon an elephant's back and filled with glittering animal jewelry (many pieces of which reside in the Cartier archive), before leaping aboard the wings of an identical replica of the airplane built by Alberto Santos-Dumont to showcase the classic Cartier Santos watch (first commissioned by the hero of Brazilian aviation in 1904). The panther finally lands in Paris, the birthplace of Cartier, on Place Vendôme, where it meets supermodel Shalom Harlow at the Grand Palais. Cartier decided to launch the film online. Directed by Bruno Aveillan, the film was dedicated to displaying the values and inspirations of the brand in a universal scope, on a journey between dream and reality. The video has been viewed more than 17 million times on YouTube and brought sensational attention to the brand.

Tiffany & Co. has successfully translated their brand DNA into the social platform. While their company website has been primarily focused on e-commerce, Tiffany & Co. has used Facebook to speak of the brand's relevance in exclusive parts of society. Tiffany & Co.'s profile is filled with pictures of celebrities wearing Tiffany pieces, as well videos of Tiffany & Co. galas and parties, all of which trace back into the brand's importance to elite American culture. It also created the iPhone app that allows its users to browse their famed line of engagement rings. The app contains tools to help clients to purchase online, down to choosing the carat size and sizing the ring. The high-quality app carries the same simple elegance that Tiffany & Co. exudes in all of its brand's communications.

Guerlain created a six-minute film called *La Légende de Shalimar* (The Legend of Shalimar) in 2013. The film celebrates Shalimar, the perfume created by Jack Guerlain in the 1920s. The legendary perfumer was inspired by the story of the Indian emperor Shah Jahan, who built the Taj Mahal as a tomb for his wife. The name itself comes from the grounds surrounding the Taj Mahal, known as the gardens of Shalimar. The film was directed by Bruno Aveillan, who also directed the extraordinary Cartier *Odyssey*. Inspired by the legend of the Taj Mahal, the film takes us on the journey the Indian emperor went on in his attempt to join his beloved Mumtaz Mahal, played by Natalia Vodianova, who has been the face of Guerlain for some time now.

The above example suggests that social media has provided brands with new ways to communicate with customers, old and new. The digital-marketing challenge begins here. The challenge is to provide the customer with a digitally delivered experience that must be a subset of a recognizable customer experience created in any or all of the channels. To answer this challenge, fully functional brand websites are the first step. Websites are important, as studies have indicated that they fully trust companies with functional websites that are user-friendly. Utilizing Web 2.0 is another method of a customer touch-point, such as e-shopping. All of these methods enhance the customer experience. Customers trust the company website as a primary source of authentic information. A website is in fact the face of the brand in the digital space. It is directly communicating to the customer from near and far about new products, new markets, launches, events, and trends. The social trends are about information reaching the customer through their trusted peer group or directly through the companies. It is a push mechanism to reach out to both repeat and potential customers. That way social network is more popular than search engines.

For example, Prada and Lanvin both use YouTube with great effectiveness. Both show brand codes on the background of their sites, with varied content. Lanvin created a video showing models dressed in Lanvin designs dancing a silly dance with Albert Elbaz, the brand's designer, which went viral.

Bloggers are quickly gaining in popularity, especially with young, motivated luxury bloggers. Blogs have become a powerful tool that can influence the attitudes a consumer may have toward a particular product or brand. For example, Coach has harnessed the power of bloggers. The brand has monthly appearances by guest bloggers and will leverage style journalists during product launches. By associating the brand to influential bloggers and style journalists, Coach presents a culturally aware and supportive image of the fashion industry as a whole.

With the rise of smartphones, a branded application may offer luxury brands an effective portal to not only reach their target consumer, but (if done well) to increase the level of engagement between luxury brands and clients by opening a two-way communication channel. Gucci is the clear leader in this category. The brand launched their app way ahead of other luxury brands. The app has the *Gucci Little Black Book* city guide in case one wants to search trendy places to visit in top cities around the world, as well as look books and news from Gucci. One differentiating aspect of this app has been Gucci Beats, where the user can listen to playlists by Frida Gianni, the creative director, or mix their own music tracks and share them with friends. The app gives the user added value for downloading the app and a reason to return again. Others, like Chloé's app, are copies of their own website, or are too complicated to use, such as YSL's.

Instagram is the photo-sharing app that allows the user to take a picture and use several different artistic filters, then post not only to the Instagram feed (which other users can follow on Twitter) but also to Facebook, Twitter, Flickr, Tumblr, Foursquare, and Posterous. Instagram is well suited for the luxury industry, as it is visual, creative, convenient, and widely accessible. Instagram's popularity in the luxury industry is on the rise, with 25 percent of brands using this application. For example, in 2012, Michael Kors hosted a mobile contest on the Instagram application during which users could flaunt their favorite brand watch for the chance to win a limited-edition timepiece. TAG Heuer, Giorgio Armani, Hugo Boss, Rebecca Minkoff, Swarovski, and Porsche have used the Instagram mobile app in their communication efforts. For example, Italian brand Armani bolstered its social media presence through an Instagram effort in which consumers could upload images of themselves wearing their favorite sunglasses for the brand's "Frames of Your Holiday" campaign.

Contrary to Facebook, the Twitter population is more mature and educated; thus it is a perfect arena for luxury brands to communicate their image to intelligent and connected people. Though Twitter is not a top driver to a brand's website, it is a great medium to build loyalty in the consumer. In an effort to attract a younger and trendier clientele, Erika Bearman, Oscar de la Renta's director of communications, started tweeting under the handle @OscarPRGirl. She attracted more than 1,000 new followers a week and currently has more than 100,000 followers. Bearman has attracted such a following by simply sharing her experiences and life with her followers and joining in on the conversation.

Weibo is China's equivalent to Twitter. Vuitton was the first luxury brand to adopt a Weibo account. Weibo and Twitter have striking similarities, despite being culturally different. As with Twitter, the most popular pages are personalities, not brands. Culturally and artistically relevant content is also very popular. Chanel launched a Weibo account to promote Culture Chanel, an exhibition at Shanghai's Museum of Contemporary Art featuring carefully selected pieces from the brand's archives.

Foursquare offers geo-location and check-ins to connect travelers with nearby shops and services, and enables them to save money and unlock deals. Whether one is setting off on a trip around the world, coordinating a night out with friends, or trying to pick out the best dish at a local restaurant, one can use this application. Brands with the most check-ins include Louis Vuitton, Ralph Lauren, and Marc Jacobs. LV and Marc Jacobs have experimented with some of the industry's first geo-local programs.

Recent cross-sector studies[4] of e-commerce operations suggested that social media is not a significant driver of site traffic. Still, 90 percent of brands maintain an active presence across each of three major social platforms—Facebook, Twitter, and YouTube—and 61 percent have extended their efforts to Instagram, Pinterest, and Google+, keeping active programming across all six different platforms. Christian Louboutin, Michael Kors, Burberry, and Louis Vuitton have crossed 1 million followers on Instagram, while none has crossed 200,000 on Pinterest. Reports suggest that 60 percent of people say that they are put off by sales staff in luxury shops, and the number is even higher in emerging markets. Thus increasingly brands use Instagram, Tumblr, Pinterest, or Facebook to build communities of people who care about the brand.

E-Commerce

Providing information and doing business on the Internet are two different and divergent propositions. During the beginning of the digital era, most luxury brands distrusted all things digital. Digital is democratizing;

---

[4]Scott Galloway, *L2 Think Tank*, December 2013.

it's about accessibility. Luxury brand is about inaccessibility. To nurture the dream, luxury brands preferred to communicate to their consumers through tightly controlled traditional media channels (print, television, events, launches, direct marketing, point of sale, and others) to influence their purchases. There is nothing secret and inaccessible anymore, once information is on social media.

After years of ignoring e-commerce, luxury brands have woken up to this new profit opportunity and have started embracing it. Some brands that have been open to e-commerce include Burberry, Gucci, Bottega Veneta, Oscar de la Renta, Judith Leiber, Christian Dior, Hermès, Burberry, Tiffany, and Ralph Lauren. Recent entrants include Prada, Louis Vuitton, Yves Saint Laurent, Stella McCartney, Boucheron, Bulgari, Calvin Klein, Pucci, and De Beers. The latest brand to enter this club is Versace.

Discussion

Digital communication is a necessity. It provides more exposure and relatively low-priced advertising space on websites. It provides more engagement by first creating an open space for people to express and exchange their personal information and then pushing the story toward the consumer. In the luxury universe, the desire to know and to talk about luxury brands and products is even stronger. With social media, consumers have now unprecedented access to information about the brands and products, and have almost full freedom to express their feelings and comments on them. It caters to a larger audience instantaneously. No one has to be in a queue for hours to see the latest collection of Louis Vuitton or Chanel. Consumers can check their favorite brands on their computers, their tablets, or their mobile phones, anywhere and anytime that they want to. They can go back to check and recheck before they make any decision. A girl from the most remote country can have access to the Fashion Week catwalk through online video, just like any front-row celebrity. Targeting can be reasonably accurate to increase the number of potential customers with the demographic data that is available on the different social media platforms and with the interest of searches and visits. Like-minded consumers can be identified and reached with the same needs and interests through billions of small network circles. It is time-independent, unlike other channels such as print media.

Conclusion

The world of luxury branding is one of multiple paradoxes. It is a place where tradition and creativity collude, where ancient founders, recent artistic directors, savvy managers and youthful models meet and make magic together.

Where the key is building the dream, what makes you dream is the connection between the brand and the consumer. Consumers are ready to pay the premium because they love the brand and the experience. And when people love the brand, this is the magic. If you try to do it quickly, you destroy the dream because there is no fast track to luxury. Thus the paradox:

> "Building a brand takes time, resources and patience. Stakeholders are impatient; they want results every quarter—focusing both on growth and profitability."

This is how impoverished artisans by their sheer innovation and attention to quality rise to become emperors of incredible fortunes, which leads to the paradox:

> "Adam Smith spoke about the four necessities of production as land, labor, capital, and entrepreneurship. Karl Marx spoke about Labor as the most important factor. Capitalism spoke about squeezing Labor for maximizing output. Luxury respects craftsmanship and thus can justify the price of the product."

When understanding history is the quest to understand oneself, then one's reason for existence and one's values, which are timeless, have to be in line with the vision of the founder. There is always a tension between the past and the future. This is the tension, the contrast, that allows luxury products to continue to innovate, but with respect for their

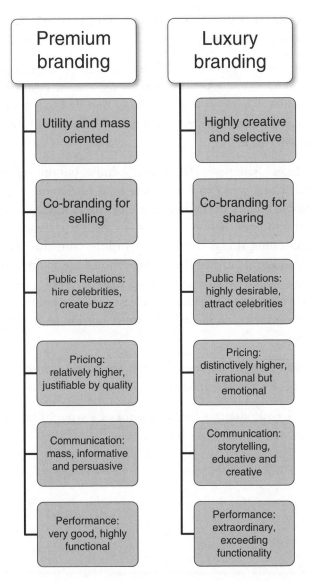

Figure 4.4 Differences in Branding Principles of Luxury Brands

roots. This tension is absolutely necessary. The day you break the tension because the roots are not there, you break the brand. Thus,

> *"Luxury needs to feed on people's experiences, their stories, made elsewhere, so it can understand the world better, expand a brand's vision, and innovate. Luxury is not an exclusive 'members only' club with a bouncer at the door; there is no need to have been born into this world to have access to it."*

Some brands will never sell in great volume, but this serves as a characteristic that one wants to have. As soon as one wants to include one product in the totality of the brand, it takes time, money, work, people, image, and resources. If one does not succeed, it is better to stop than to continue doing things that are not in line with the brand and can therefore damage its image. To manage the image is the most difficult thing in the world because everything that hurts the image hurts the business. If you control everything, at least you have control, and if there is a problem it is easy to identify the source of the fault. It leads to our final paradox:

> *"The more desirable the brand becomes, the more it sells, but the more it sells, the less desirable it becomes!"*

Figure 4.4 summarizes the discussion of some of the differences in branding principles of luxury brands.

Chapter 5

Brand Identity, Clients, and Ethos

*T*he young child walks with halting, hesitant steps as the grandfather walks slowly beside him, watching and encouraging.

Both are out for a stroll in a park adjacent to the Avenue des Champs-Élysées, just a few steps away from the luxury meccas of Avenue Montaigne and Rue du Faubourg Saint-Honoré.

On Sundays in this park, there is a puppet show, the last Guignol, and the grandfather and grandson find seats on a front-row bench.

Guignol hits the thief on the head and the child bursts out laughing as the grandfather smiles. What is he thinking? He certainly is not thinking about luxury, which means nothing to him in this precious moment when he is simply enjoying life, this warm intimacy between two beings who are enjoying each other's company without the encumbrance of wondering why. Guignol has finished. The grandfather and grandchild wander toward the merry-go-round.

Then the child speaks. He has seen and understood. His view is pure, simple, and direct.

He doesn't like the person in front of him, a "poorly dressed" woman.

He dislikes the color of the horse, an old faded gray, an ugly color!

This, too, is luxury, the observation of a child who reacts spontaneously without forethought, without constraints, the look of a child who guides the creator as closely as possible to simplicity, reality, a truth often in disguise.

The grandfather knows this perfectly well: The child's view is the key to luxury.

Brand Identity

Brand identity represents the *raison d'être* of the product, how it is perceived in the market, what the product stands for, how it is unique, what promise it provides and what value it offers to its customers. A brand's identity implies the history, savoir-faire, and mystique that make the brand special. For luxury brands, the core identity is depicted by the timeless essence or value of the brand that the customer perceives. This core identity does not change from day-to-day or cannot be altered easily. It is those intrinsic values that make a brand unique, valuable, rare and difficult to imitate. These intrinsic values are the ones that have cultural representations not only because of their roots but also because of their historical customers, their likes and dislikes, the archetype of aspirations, and how they perceived the brand when they used it for a certain amount of time. For example, in the words of Jean Paul Gaultier, "The nirvana of Hermès is Hermès! I like to twist their centuries-old codes a little and put in some Gaultier. For my first collection, I designed a leather corset with clasps reminiscent of the Kelly bag."

Brands through ages have been built with strong cultural connotations. This is so because culture integrates the accumulation of shared meanings, rituals, norms, and traditions among the members of society. In this way, luxury brands determine the overall desire a consumer feels toward different activities, narratives, products, and archetypes or aspirations. The luxury brand identity is closely linked to the narratives that are linked to a context and a subject. The narratives of context can be linked to time, place, lifestyle, founder, or group, whereas the narratives of subject can be linked to character archetypes, know-how or material used as craft or component. For example, Burberry has been related to the trench coat used in England, Rolex has been associated with sports, perseverance, and time, Hermès has been related to saddles and leather interiors, whereas Louis Vuitton has been associated with luggage and travel.

> *I love playing with classic things to make them new. The Vuitton monogram is an icon, over a hundred years old, but it's still something you can play with and make new.*
> **—Marc Jacobs, former chief designer of Louis Vuitton**

In this case, Louis Vuitton is a symbol of wealth, freedom, and travel. Travel implies a journey taken by a traveler to discover herself, others, and the world, learning about the meaning of life. Louis Vuitton represents rich French heritage, wealth, success, craftsmanship, quality, travel, timelessness, precision, and innovation. In all these descriptions, what stands out is the "art of travel."

Brands have been defined in many ways. Pirate ships raised flags on their masts with a threatening and terrifying symbol of death. Their victims fled or surrendered. Today brands are built collectively with messages that are sent through advertisements, public relations events, news articles, product designs, and customer experiences. So how is a luxury brand different from other iconic brands?

Most luxury brands have been built through time with a person, product, symbol, organization, or a mix of one or more of these as a frame of reference. It is so because the elements and patterns help to differentiate the identity through clarity and enrichment of the image. For example, a person might be Coco Chanel, Ralph Lauren, or Yves Saint Laurent. A product could suggest associations such as product scope, product-related attributes, quality, value, and a link to a country or region, such as Swiss watches or perfume from France, or a place like the Avenue Montaigne or Rive Gauche in Paris. A symbol could be the double-C logo of Chanel, the travel-trunk of LV, or the Kelly bag of Hermès. As an organization, it focuses on the culture and style of top management within the organization rather than on the specific attributes of the product, as is evident from the cosmetic industry, for example, L'Oréal and Estée Lauder.

Building and growing a luxury brand depend on managing some key paradoxes. The first paradox is to manage the *timelessness* and *modernity* of a brand. The second paradox is the trade-off between *exclusivity* and *accessibility*. The third paradox is to increase *brand awareness, brand mystery,* and *brand likeness* and manage them all together. The fourth paradox is to balance between *aesthetics* and *economic value.* The fifth paradox is to maintain the *brand identity from its historic roots while identifying the social, cultural, political, and economic trends of new and emerging markets.* The following quote depicts some key aspects of the paradoxes:

> *I'm not a fashion person. I'm antifashion. I don't like to be part of the world. It's too transient. I have never been influenced by it. I'm interested in longevity, timelessness, style—not fashion.*
>
> **—Ralph Lauren, founder of Ralph Lauren**

Many authors have tried to classify and present brand identity with different frameworks in order to explain the meaning that the brand depicts and how they manage the paradoxes. For example, Jean-Noel Kapferer developed a six-faced prism to demonstrate six sides of brand identity, such as *physique* (physical appearance), *personality* (inner source), *culture* (roots of the brand including communication), *relationship* (between the brand and the consumer), *reflection* (of consumer), and *self-image* (of consumer). These six sides are grouped with pictures of sender, receiver, externalization, and internalization.[1] Here the term *competitors* takes a back seat, as the luxury brand focuses on telling its story, be it from real life, as for Coco Chanel and René Lacoste, or invented from scratch, as for Ralph Lauren. These stories create identity and consumer relationships. Figure 5.1 depicts Chanel's brand-identity prism.

As depicted from the brand identity, Chanel embodies a strong woman who has climbed up the social ladder. This was Gabrielle Chanel's personality and background. Her modest origins and the fact that she had climbed up the social ladder at a time when most women did not have a prestigious career is part of the brand identity. To express this core identity, Chanel's retail locations worldwide have majestic staircases, symbolizing their founder's upward social mobility. Chanel also freed women from their corsets. Her idea was to dress

---

[1] Kapferer and Bastien, 2012

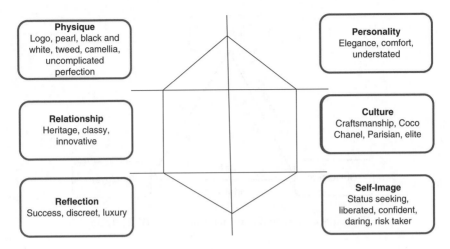

Figure 5.1 Chanel's Brand-Identity Prism

women who would favor convenience, comfort, and style. Doing so, she started a revolution by completely changing the code of women's dressing. The historical context of World War I may have favored this revolution, as well as Gabrielle Chanel's personality. In this post–World War context, women were working and needed to feel comfortable in what they wore. To this day, Chanel's style remains chic but convenient. The eternal classic of the Chanel suit is an example of elegance and comfort. Another important symbol of Chanel's Pantheon is the use of black and white. In terms of symbols, the black color is a symbol of masculinity whereas white represents femininity. Gabrielle Chanel was actually a pioneer by mixing masculine and feminine qualities, since the entire twentieth century was about mixing up and playing with feminine and masculine characteristics and stereotypes in fashion and in social behavior in general. Again returning to her roots, Gabrielle Chanel illustrated a mix of traits traditionally attributed to men and women—her strength and will to attain higher rank in the society and her general attitude portrayed an independent and self-confident woman. Many pictures portrayed her sitting on a staircase. Chanel clients are usually women who identify with these symbols of strength and success. They are in charge. They are successful and powerful or that is what they aspire to. This is in line with the image of Chanel

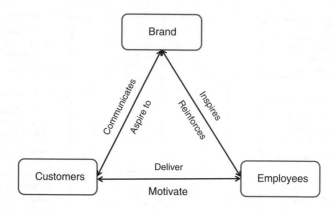

Figure 5.2 Brand–Customer–Employee (BCE) Triangle

women as seen in advertisement campaigns. The Chanel woman always look like she knows who she is and she gets what she wants. The symbol behind this representation is the queen. She is a powerful woman who seems confident, unafraid, free, respected, a risk taker and adventurous, successful, innovative intellectual, and elitist. Her posture shows strength and confidence. That is who Coco Chanel was or wanted to be seen as, and this is the identity picture of its clients. The key challenge for luxury brands like Chanel is to maintain this identity, which was created decades before. Together with maintaining the identity they have to be relevant, desirable, and inspirational today. It also has to be exclusive while being accessible, in order to achieve sales growth. Achieving growth in traditional markets while expanding in new markets entails exporting the brand DNA across cultures, recruiting new clients while maintaining the traditional aesthetics and thereby creating economic value. Figure 5.2 portrays the brand-customer-employee (BCE) triangle.

While managing the above paradoxes, another key word that represents core identity is often referred to as brand *nirvana*. For example referring to the American brands, Ralph Lauren's values include longevity, style, East Coast culture, Bostonian dream, American heritage, American dream, and timelessness. Amid them, the brand nirvana or core proposition of Ralph Lauren is "Bostonian dream." In the same spirit, brand characteristics of Coach include young, fun-loving, stylish, independent, cute and colorful, interactive, open, public, responsive, and trendy. The brand nirvana for Coach is "Let me be free" and "New York dream," which is based on the value of "fun." Brand identity for Coach is strongly transmitting the concept that they are different because the brand originates from Madison Avenue in Manhattan, New York. It doesn't matter whether they have a heritage or not. What matters to them is the fact that they are distinguished by their uniqueness. In the same spirit, for Stanley Marcus, founder of Neiman Marcus, there is a right customer for every piece of merchandise, and it is the retailer's prerogative to bring the two together and to prevent a mismatch. Brand values that Neiman Marcus aspires to are distinguished service, right service, professionalism, expertise, chic, high taste, customer satisfaction, insatiable curiosity, and passion. The brand nirvana of Neiman Marcus is "the right service." Thus the real offer of Neiman Marcus is to prevent the customer from making the wrong choice.

Luxury brands also play with paradox, altering images such as masculinity-femininity. Within this framework of multiple brand identity, the luxury product prides itself on being unique, the expression of a creative identity, of the intrinsic passion of a creator.

> *The image is born of itself, not of surveys showing where there might be a niche or a business opportunity, but in the very spontaneous identity of the creator, their background and their idiosyncrasies.*[2]
>
> **—Kapferer and Bastien**

For example, both Chanel and Armani seek to be masculine and feminine at the same time. Coco Chanel freed women from corsets, which were a symbol of confinement and restriction, by offering new designs with high spirit. She was innovative and intellectual, but simultaneously she argued that a girl should be both classy and fabulous. Armani, on the other hand, has the personality of a professional who is sophisticated, rich, free, classy, athletic, and successful. Moreover, the brand Armani, like Armani, embodies a person who is successful in his or her life, and pursues personal desires, such as dreams, adventures, and love.

---

[2]Kapferer and Bastien, 2009.

Armani projects the image of a smart professional who knows what he or she wants in life.

Marketing professionals calculate brand value by isolating the net additional cash flows created by the brand. These additional cash flows are the result of customers' willingness to buy from one brand more than from its competitors, even when another brand is cheaper. The hallmark of competitive theory is based on the premise that the beliefs and bonds created over time in the minds of customer through the marketing of the brand are the key differentiators. Thus customer equity is in fact the financial equity. Brands have financial value because they have created intangible assets in the minds and hearts of employees, customers, distributors, subscribers, and opinion leaders. These assets are brand awareness, beliefs of exclusivity and superiority of some valued benefit, and emotional bonding. This links back to the brand identity, referred to as the brand DNA circle, as depicted in Figure 5.3.

Ethos

Having dwelled on brand identity in the previous section, the main purpose of this section is to build the case regarding the difference between luxury goods and other categories of products. Luxury goods do not cater to primary needs. These are the products that no one really needs. Hence, organizations and brands that produce and distribute them need to make people dream in order to create the need. To succeed in creating the "dream machine," these organizations and brands must create an offer, an identity, a DNA that is capable of perpetuating the dream factor. When the market was local, in France or Italy, it was easy, but with markets becoming global the dream has to cross not only borders but also cultures. And different cultures dream differently; their aspirations are different. Thus storytelling has been a key enabler for the dream factor. A brand's story is built on its ethos, which is in fact the myth, the history of the brand. An apt example would be the intimate history of Marilyn Monroe and Chanel No. 5. Chanel enticed consumers with a two-and-a-half minute video featuring photographs of Marilyn Monroe as she appeared in *Life* magazine and *Modern Screen* magazine in the early 1950s, and included her famous quote about wearing only Chanel No. 5

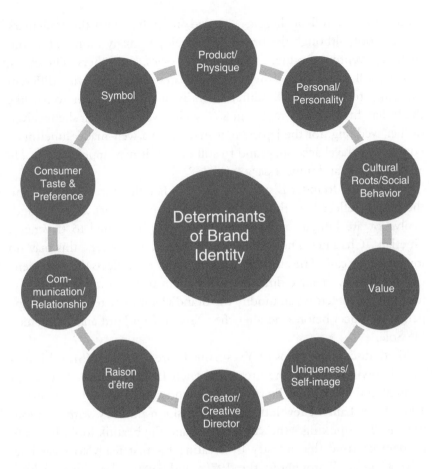

Figure 5.3 Brand DNA Circle

to bed. J'Adore, the perfume from Dior, tells the story of its creation in the short film *Le Parfum*. It emphasizes the story that the perfume was created from flowers around the world, combining the scents of Damask rose, Arabian jasmine, and Indian tuberose, while the glass bottles were blown in Murano, Italy.

A brand's ethos can also be communicated by the story of its origins, its founder, and the identity of the brand over time. When the founder creates a brand with his or her name, their character, the founder's understanding, beliefs, aesthetics, interests, and attitudes form the ethos of the brand. For example, Louis Vuitton still insists that its ethos be represented by roll-on luggage, crafted in leather with the trademark of LV motif, although the brand had developed many more extensions such as adventure products, fashion, accessories, and others. The ethos, though still true to the core, communicates differently with different meanings to its potentially different individual owners. For some, like the Indian bride, it may represent a very high-value gift that she received on her wedding; for the Japanese, it may mean a well-made, functional, convenient travel accessory; and to still others, it may appear to be only an overpriced and unnecessary suitcase.[3]

When the founder is still alive, such as Ralph Lauren and Armani, the brands reflect the ethos of the founders and owners. But as brands evolve or are bought by conglomerates, as it happened to Givenchy, Guerlain, Chaumet, Dior, Van Cleef & Arpel, and others, this may no longer be the case. The ethos remains the same as it reflects the core identity, while new creative directors at the helm may introduce some new ideals. New directors can modify the brand's legitimate territory, as happened to Gucci before and after the years of Tom Ford and Domenico De Sole.

Let's discuss the ethos of Yves Saint Laurent (YSL). YSL is historically known as one of the greatest French fashion houses. Yves Saint Laurent and his partner, Pierre Bergé, founded his eponymous brand in 1962. Saint Laurent revolutionized the fashion industry with creations such as "Le Smoking," the safari jacket, and the beatnik look. In 1966, he democratized the industry by creating his first ready-to-wear line, Rive Gauche. Throughout the 1970s and 1980s, the famed fashion house enjoyed success. Historically, YSL was known as an haute couture and ready-to-wear brand. Yves Saint Laurent enjoyed the company of women and was surrounded by female artists. He was inspired by muses such as Loulou de la Falaise, an aristocrat model and designer; Betty Catroux, a socialite and daughter of a diplomat; and Catherine Deneuve, the iconic French actress. This was not a coincidence. The Saint Laurent woman was seductive and possessed an artistic sense. She was unconventional and challenged the rules. This is what the Saint Laurent/Rive Gauche spirit was about. On the seduction side, the

---

[3] Berthon et al., 2009.

woman was sophisticated and fascinating. She played games, pretending to be innocent. Saint Laurent had created a tuxedo for women and some other feminine interpretations of masculine pieces like the blazer or the safari jacket. The archetype of this woman was the mistress, Parisian chic and unconventional.

However, by the 1990s, the brand was sold to the pharmaceutical company, Sanofi, and later to Gucci Group. While Saint Laurent continued to design for the haute couture house, Tom Ford took over design responsibilities for Rive Gauche where he infused the brand with his own personal "porno chic" aesthetic, ultimately making the brand unrecognizable to YSL loyalists. By 2002, Saint Laurent's personal problems overshadowed his ability to design and his haute couture house was eventually closed, leaving only Rive Gauche in the hands of Gucci Group. In 2004, Tom Ford left Gucci Group, and his protégé at YSL, Stefano Pilati, took over as designer of the Rive Gauche collection. Since Tom Ford's departure, Pilati and Gucci Group have been working toward rehabilitating the brand. It started by announcing in 2010 the opening of a new three-story flagship store on Avenue Montaigne, located in the Golden Triangle of Paris, next door to the world-famous Christian Dior flagship store. Since Ford's departure, the brand had been focused on returning to the roots of the brand and for many years did not engage in retail expansion.

The brand has also extended further into higher margin products, including leather goods and accessories and cosmetics. Although YSL has strayed from its roots in ready-to-wear, the brand has made investments into product categories that drive profits while maintaining the brand's identity. Under Stefano Pilati the brand returned to its original roots, its ethos as a trendsetter and tastemaker, and has produced some popular items such the Muse handbag and the Tribute shoe, which could be compared to historical YSL icons such as "Le Smoking" and the safari jacket.

In 2011, Yves Saint Laurent Couture decided to change its brand's name from the iconic Yves Saint Laurent that everyone in the industry called YSL to Saint Laurent Paris. This decision was made by Hedi Slimane when he was appointed as the creative director. This new name was supposed to restore "the house to its truth, purity, and essence—and taking it into a new era." It is true that Yves Saint Laurent has not been profitable for years, since Pierre Bergé and Yves Saint Laurent sold the brand. Some may wonder if the brand ethos needed rejuvenation. Instantaneously, criticism and anger was generated by that decision and it seemed that the designer has touched a sore spot, something considered sacred by fashion house lovers. It became clear that the name Yves Saint Laurent is part of the brand ethos. This actually was no surprise for anyone familiar with the brand, who knows how much the brand is the expression of its founder's personality. The reaction of some loyal clients was so violent that they created a logo expressing their hatred of the new brand name. This is not visible anymore. It has probably been erased by the brand. This vignette explains how valuable a brand name (and its ethos) is to its loyal clients.

The example of YSL shows that the ethos is powerful as the tool that allows potential customers to project themselves into the brand universe that has been the legacy of the brands. The brand universe is nothing other than all the ingredients that make up the brand identity. The intricate weaving of the ingredients of the identity strands, such as the founders, the creator, the era when the brand was born, its place of origin, the *savoir faire* and expertise, its original customers—is what they sell. It is not the product but the ethos. In summary, ethos is not visible to the consumer. It is not the color, the texture, the shape, or the size. Nor can it be described through the five senses. Thus for clients, especially new clients from new markets, the luxury brands today need to redefine and communicate the aesthetic of the brand to bring in the visible concepts for the clients to recognize and feel the ethos.

Clients

The previous section discussed the importance of brand identity and the ethos of the luxury brand. This section tries to understand how they relate to its client. When the brand has established its existence, potential clients can identify themselves with the brand and ultimately become loyal consumers.

Luxury consumption is not a rational decision. Here emotion takes precedence over reason: a brand's personality and essence create allure and entice consumers to abandon rationality and succumb to their desires. Yet, in a time when brands must manage the contradiction between maintaining exclusivity and growing their businesses through accessibility, the question of how a brand can lure its clientele takes precedence.

The published literature has come up with several typologies of consumers of the luxury industry depending on the categorization. The categorization dwells with "haves/rich" and "have nots/poor" in one continuum and "status seekers/public" and "nonstatus seekers/private" in the other continuum. Figure 5.4 provides a snapshot of the different types of consumers.

Nature of consumer: Keeping in mind the involvement of consumers in luxury purchases and their motives for purchase, researchers have tried to categorize different segments according to the classification between the haves and have-less and status-seeking. For example, *luxury hedonists* are not status seekers; they are usually young people who are successful and thus optimistic about life (Americans are a good example). They are pleasure seekers who like to live king-size with traveling and active social lives. They like to be up-to-date on the latest trends and love to spend on themselves in a guilt-free way. They use luxury brands as a way to express themselves to the world, as they have varied interests. They are fond of brands such as Marc Jacobs, D&G, Michael Kors, and others. The next group can be classified as *the traditional ones*—the loyalists, the fashionists, and the worthy members—who are mature, mostly male, and are of an older age group (for example, Japanese consumers). These are the *aspirational consumers* who like spending on themselves. Their purchases are driven by the need for quality and timelessness in their lives. They don't constantly monitor media for information on luxury items. They find out about luxury brands and trends more though word of mouth. The *luxury experts, the connoisseurs,* are the richest and the most educated (for example, French and Italian consumers). Highly creative and discerning, this segment is characterized by their openness. They are open to new people, new cultures, and new ideas. For them, luxury has to be of a discreet nature and not flamboyant. Paying close attention to products, they value superior quality and exquisite craftsmanship. They are not driven to purchase luxury products as a status symbol. They prefer natural products, such as organic products. They tend to purchase brands such as Hermès, Chanel, and Bentley. The

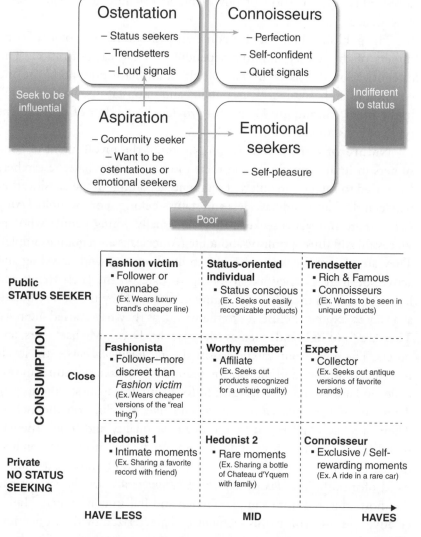

Figure 5.4 Different Types of Consumers

next segments are the *ostentatious, status-oriented individuals*, who are also the trendsetters. They are relatively financially constrained, thus finding it hard to meet all their luxury cravings, and wish to travel abroad. Highly fashionable, women and men in this segment are very sensitive about the brands and the logos that they display. Consumers in this segment are health conscious and spend a lot of time grooming themselves. They prefer brands such as Armani, Gucci, Prada, BMW, and so on.

Generalizing, the luxury consumer may be classified on the basis of characteristics such as (1) tastes and preferences and (2) nature of wealth.

1. **Tastes and preferences**: Consumers may be divided into categories. The first comprises the traditional luxury consumer—the elitists, the connoisseurs, who believe in established brands such as Hermès or Rolex. The other category comprises the democrats or the "new luxury consumers," who would have no qualms in accepting new brands if they were more satisfactory. These consumers know exactly what they want and are unwilling to settle for anything less in the name of tradition. They feel luxury should be available to all, and thus they spearhead the democratization of luxury.

2. **Nature of wealth**: Consumers can be rich, but that is not all. There is no color of money, but the time that one has been with money can have a bearing on consumption patterns. For example, those who are wealthy from the twentieth century, such as professional actors, sports personalities, and entrepreneurs, would have different consumption pattern from those who have newly acquired wealth through hardships. In the same light, those who have inherited wealth would have different consumption patterns from salaried executives and working professionals.

    Different types of customers have evolved over the past few years. For example, one consumer may no longer be a brand loyalist, wearing products from the same brand from head to toe. She has become more discerning while picking out the products she wears. There has also been a convergence in terms of dressing. Women of different ages can all dress similarly. The old have ways of looking younger and, irrespective of their age, everyone has started looking very similar. The following are the characteristics of today's luxury consumer:

- **Sharp**: He is well-traveled, familiar with different cultures, and intellectually sound. He is more aware of the minute differences between products. He is well informed about product characteristics. He understands the difference between genuine branding exercises and marketing gimmicks and questions the price premium that brands charge, refusing to pay a price that products don't merit. For instance, LVMH has been trying hard to sell its Dior and TAG Heuer watches in India, as most customers bought watches abroad as they felt models were not launched in time and were more expensive in India. Thus LVMH, despite not breaking even in India, is pushing hard to cater to the potentially huge Indian market, which is sharp about comparing prices worldwide.
- **Influential**: In the early days of luxury, consumers were many, but luxury brands were few. This led to the brand dominating the consumer. Given that competition among the luxury brands has intensified, the power has shifted to the consumer. Switching costs reduced as each brand underwent brand extensions. Consumers have greater options between products, brands, payment methods, and channels of purchase. Thus the locus of control has shifted to the consumer.
- **Unique**: Today's consumer knows herself and knows what she wants. Each woman is her own fashion designer. She uses her own mind and doesn't blindly follow what brands throw at her. She is bold enough to mix Chanel with Gucci and streetwear with luxury. She understands that people who don't know her gauge her from her clothes, so she ensures that her purchases suit her personality.
- **Demanding**: This consumer wants perfect quality, impeccable service, and superior craftsmanship. She is not willing to settle for anything less than the best. She craves customization and expects foresight from fashion brands, that they will understand her fashion needs before she spells them out. She wants creativity and authenticity from a brand. Her demanding nature can be illustrated by the rising market for custom-made luxury products, wherein each item is hand-picked by the consumer. Companies like Tiffany & Co. and Rolex are catering to this clientele with custom-made watches.

- **Attention span**: The need to be trendy propels this consumer to replace her clothes, shoes, and accessories frequently. Also, brands launch new products frequently, which encourages women to replace their wardrobes very often.
- **Ethical:** He wants brands that are socially conscious. He is not willing to wear shoes that are made by children in a developing country. He does not want to wear clothing that has been made in an environmentally unfriendly fashion. He likes to associate himself with brands that invest in social causes. He also likes it when brands share their values with him. For instance, a female consumer of this segment would purchase Viva Glam lipsticks to support the fight against AIDS in addition to enjoying a fashionable lipstick.

Discussion

Having segmented luxury consumers on the basis of their involvement and preferences, luxury spending has a cultural connotation. Culture has an effect both in terms of the kind of consumers (the demand side) and the kind of brands produced by the country (the supply side). Each country stands for a certain ethos: French tradition, German practicality, Japanese passion—all are well-established traits. On the basis of the nature of the people in a nation, luxury products evolve in the same way. When people buy a certain luxury brand, they also buy the culture that the brand belongs to. Consumers buying Hermès buy a little bit of France, and those buying Burberry buy a little bit of Britain, while those buying Ralph Lauren buy the American dream. For example, in the automobile industry, cars such as Ferrari, Lamborghini, and Maserati, have cutting-edge design and the most modern technology. It is no coincidence that all these cars are Italian. Cars such as Porsche, BMW, and Mercedes epitomize quality, efficiency, and comfort. These are all German brands. Jaguar (now owned by Tata Motors, a part of the Indian conglomerate of TATA Group), Bentley, and Rolls Royce all speak of British traditions and lifestyles.

It is a fact that consumers from different cultures have their own specific modes of behavior. Though the brands might sell the same product, the buying behavior differs from culture to culture, be it the brands they purchase or the way they use luxury items. For instance, one can try to recognize the nationality of a person from the way they wear their jewelry. French women have an understated style, as they are always worried about looking vulgar or out of place. Italians look for motion, and like decorative pieces that flow. German women buy their jewelry from their own salaries. Thus when they wear jewels, there is an aura of pride. They sport solid pieces of bold jewelry with ease. Indians are famous for consuming gold as jewelry not only during weddings but in their daily lives. In the perfume segment, the way perfumes sell in France is entirely different from the way they sell in Japan. This is probably due to the fact that the Japanese have a greater focus on natural scents. Perfume is considered unhealthy for babies in Japan, propelling mothers to give up perfumes. Only very understated perfumes do well in Japan. Strong perfumes sell heavily in other parts of the world, especially the Middle East and North America. In conclusion, though the product might be the same, the way it sells in different parts of the world might be different.

Pricing of Luxury Brands

The demand curve usually slopes downward, implying that as the price of a commodity increases, its demand decreases. It is another paradox in luxury business. Luxury goods are known to experience the Veblen effect, wherein the rising prices fuel demand of the product.

Consumers tend to pay relatively higher prices for luxury items compared to the functional utility that they derive from them. The functional utility to price ratio is lower for luxury goods. On the other hand, the symbolic utility to the price ratio is higher for luxury goods than normal goods, which means that the aspirational value for the luxury consumption is higher than the price they pay for it.

Secrecy is a part of the luxury business. This is due to the fact that pricing is not a major part of a luxury brand's strategy. For example, when Bottega Veneta makes bags using the most soft and supple leather imaginable, the buyer doesn't care about the price the company quotes for this luxurious product. The price, from the point of view of the customer, is not as relevant as the situational utility that he or she derives from the product.

Having said that, price should not be completely ignored. The Veblen effect can last, but only up to a certain point, when price elasticity may come into play. Let's analyze the various impacts that elasticity may have on luxury pricing.

Elasticity   Price elasticity of demand is defined as the responsiveness of the quantity demanded to change in price. This means the quantity demanded could rise, fall, or remain unaffected by a rise in price. Let's delve deeper into each possibility, working our way through examples.

Traditional businesses would try to achieve cost leadership while focusing on economies of scale to propel demand. Luxury companies, on the other hand, try to push prices up over time. They want to increase the number of "wealthy" consumers within their sphere of influence. Usually businesses would try to increase the prices through promoting (1) an existing product range, (2) a new range of products, or (3) a brand-new product in a brand-new market.

Increasing the price of an existing product without justifying why it is costlier may immediately attract unwarranted attention. The Veblen effect will not apply here. Clarifying to the client the reason for the increase is always a good idea. For instance, Louis Vuitton always clarifies to its consumers in Japan if the exchange rates are eating into their profit margin, and only then do they increase the prices. In the past couple of years, each year, luxury brands have elevated their prices by about 10 percent at least once, and usually twice. This is becoming the trend, and with this trend the luxury brands no longer are justifying the price increase to the extent that they did before.

When launching a new range, the aim of the company is to "trade-up" and not vulgarize the product. The motive is to increase the aspirational appeal associated with the brand, and not to pull down the name and status symbol associated with it. Thus it is a common phenomenon to launch a new range at a higher price point than the previous range. Also, the consumers believe that the new range is more evolved than the previous one, and more costly for the company to make. Thus, they are able to justify the higher prices too. For instance, Tiffany & Co. hiked prices to clearly communicate its luxury position by using a larger proportion of gold and diamonds in their products. This trading up in prices was correctly accompanied by a trading up in preciousness.

When launching a new product in an absolutely unexplored market, it makes sense for the luxury brand to fix the price at the lower end and slowly increase it. This is done in order to increase the trial rate of the product, given that it is a completely unexplored market.

Having discussed elasticity and related aspects of pricing, we now move on to how companies manage pricing. There are two distinct ways in which companies price their products: supply-driven pricing and demand-driven pricing.

Supply-Driven Pricing   In this case, the company sets the price of a commodity as it deems fit. Consumers indicate only whether they want to pay this price or not. As fixing the price now demarcates the brand's price territory, the company's responsibility is to ensure that the price evolves correctly with the offer. Also, the company must ensure that it is able to set the global price of the product carefully, to minimize arbitrage and have a healthy profit margin.

The company may set the global prices in two ways.

The first is a "cost-plus" strategy. Here, the differential between the prices of two countries is linked to the transport cost, customs, exchange-rate fluctuations, and local distribution costs. Thus each country has a different price, but the profit margin of the company is stabilized.

The second way to tackle this is by setting a very high common global price. In this case, the travel and distribution costs are considered to be too small to majorly affect the margin of the company. The common price closes all possibilities of price arbitrage.

Demand-Driven Pricing   In the earlier days of luxury, there used to be client-driven pricing. Giving one-time discounts and offers to win customers may be justified in this kind of pricing. Here the concept of yield management comes into play, wherein one time lowering of prices may be considered rational in order to spur a series of future purchases. A few things must be kept in mind by the customer: lower prices should not be at the cost of lower service quality. This will scar the brand name. Also, former customers should not feel cheated for having bought the product at a higher price and now witnessing others getting the same product at a lower price. Demand-driven pricing means that

Figure 5.5   Logic of Price Premium

the company should try to capture the entire consumer surplus (through differential pricing, capture the entire amount that the consumer is willing to pay). However, this should not be done at throw-away prices as a rule, as that will diminish brand goodwill. Figure 5.5 describes the logic of price premium.

Conclusion

To conclude in the words of Ravi Thakran, M.D., L. Capita Asia, "In branding a product, there are a few important aspects to remember. Firstly, it must have great quality. People tend to forget the price, but not the quality. Secondly, there must be creativity. Always stay ahead of the game and innovate further. Every new improvement to the product should always remain true to the DNA of the brand. You can't please everyone. To be a successful brand, you almost always have to not please someone."

Building a brand identity is painfully slow. Nothing happens quickly in luxury. The time in building the identity, clarifying the ethos, and being true to the clients is what is missed by many. It is something that is not factored in when one makes the calculation of sales with different pricing models. To make the brand well known is an art in itself. It is no longer a science. The meaning of the brand and what it stands for need to be clarified both internally and externally; the codes need to be defined; the brand needs to know who it is, what it represents and why it exists. One can buy an accessory and it is accessible. One can buy a little something, and one belongs to a certain group. When a luxury product is extremely exclusive, people forget it. It needs to be present, in the right way with the right dimension, but to be present is not the function of price. People need to think that they potentially have access to the product and dream about it. This is why the world is changing, and not everyone can be satisfied with the same dream. People dream differently. It takes a lot of time and courage to make people dream and yet do the right thing. Once people start dreaming, there is nothing to hide. This is when the codes become timeless and yet modern with a clear style. It takes ages before people really feel it. People associated with a brand feel it because it is seen all the time, but for the audience to feel it, it takes much more time.

That is why the use of story is perhaps the best way to convey the brand identity, its ethos to the clients. This is perhaps what people most want, the stories of today, the anecdotes, stories of people who are connected and who share experiences. People don't forget. If one speaks about a brand and associates it with an important experience in one's life, people will remember much better than if one merely explains the product to them. What is most important is that people enjoy it.

Chapter 6

Family Houses, Corporatization, and New Entrants

Twenty years ago, luxury was completely family-based in France. Families knew each other and their habits were well established. They would spend summers together in Monte-Carlo and winters in Zermatt. They worked at Place Vendôme, Rue du Faubourg-Saint-Honoré, or Avenue Montaigne.

It was the natural order of things. French luxury families were known and well established. Their customers were confident.

The House of Chaumet jewelers and watchmakers was the first family to rock the boat. Luxury was turned on its head. How was it possible? Shady dealings? And yet it was true: In the 1980s, the Chaumet brothers started down a path without knowing its course or where their journey would end. Confidence collapsed. Customers preferred to say nothing, abandoning their treasures to fraud and bankruptcy, so as not to risk a scandal and to be able to return to anonymity. But it weighed heavily upon them. The family jewels had slipped into an unpredictable torrent. Grandmother's diamond had been sold twice, with the emerald going along for the ride. In short, there was no public scandal, but the discreet and felt-lined world of luxury took a major hit.

The luxury planet was shaken, but the field had already been more broadly undermined.

The nephews, cousins, brothers, and sisters of luxury had had enough of seeing their parents or their uncles living high on the hog while they, as second in line, were left behind, since the rule was very simple: no dividends!

When income was limited all around, they made do, but as their hunger grew with the profits, the "bosses" had acquired a taste for privilege and benefits. Luxury was for them—and no one else—in the family.

True, some room was made for a cousin here or a brother there who was growing a little too impatient, but they were paid with "triflings."

And then came the avalanche. Businesses revived and strengthened and families that previously were merely comfortable became truly wealthy. The families then began to fall apart....

Some sold off quickly under pressure from shrewd gluttons who could see the luxury wave coming, while a few others resisted, and still others died in despair.

In 20 years, nearly every family in the luxury business disappeared from the scene: Boucheron, Guerlain, Chaumet, Lanvin, Fred, Kenzo, Givenchy, Gucci, Cartier, Arpels, Krug, Hennessy, Puiforcat, Canovas, Souleaïdo, Patou, and Vuitton—all sold.

The Taittingers sold Baccarat, le Crillon, le Martinez, Annick Goutal perfumes, Concorde hotels...the Bouilhets sold Christofle off very quickly to their cousin Borletti, who quickly resold it to the Chalhoubs...even Alexandre de Lur Saluces lost Château d'Yquem. The family that owned Cheval Blanc sold it to the Arnault Group.

Fortunately, we still have Pierre Frey, Hermès, Rothschild, Laurent-Perrier (the Nonancourts), Taillevent (the Gardiniers), Chanel (the Wertheimers), Rémy Cointreau (the Hériard Dubreuils), Michel Guérard, Delisle, Roederer (the Rouzauds), Piper-Heidseick, Weston, Bonpoint (the Descours), and many others, of course, who are still luxury families.

In this highly disrupted landscape, a few major entities were formed: LVMH, Kering, Richemont, L'Oréal . . . and they picked up the pieces.

Many died. Who remembers the wonderful Roger Faré, the most famous glovemaker of his time? Who remembers the incredible Draeger, the unrivaled printer? What remains of the images of Gelot, Jansen, Rouard, Paul Portes, Bianchini-Férier, Barroux, Leleu, Richard de Bas, Bagués, Jean Dessès, Jean Prud'homme . . . all famous in their day, and today unknown!

The families remaining today are tightening their ranks, but there are so few of them in France, Italy, and the United States, that they are regarded as survivors of the earthquake of planet luxury.

Will they hold up?

Over the past quarter-century, luxury sectors in Italy and France have faced transformations due to the evolution of the external environment and evolution of the family business in Europe. Family played an important role in the luxury goods industry, as the industry historically began as small-scale family-owned companies, especially prior to World War II when bonds of kinship were often more important in contract enforcement than in legal and regulatory institution.

Before the 1990s, the luxury business, particularly high fashion, consisted mostly of small privately owned companies, often run by the founder or his or her descendants. Many were poorly managed by conventional standards and suffered from the aftereffects of cultural and social chaos of the 1960s, which had left the luxury business in a delicate situation. The 1980s brought new opportunities for the luxury market, including favorable demographics, socioeconomics, and new cultural trends. Through developments such as the constant growth in affluence, the collapse of traditional family structures, and lifestyle diversification, luxury became an extremely heterogeneous and individual phenomenon in the second half of the twentieth century.

With the advent of the twenty-first century and considerable changes, first in the development of the luxury goods industry and then in the economic world, many of these luxury companies have transformed themselves from closely held, small-scale family companies into larger-scale, family-controlled companies with various product categories, and/or into publicly listed companies run by a professional manager, or acquired into a brand portfolio under an international conglomerate group.

At this phase, the role of family in the luxury goods industry transformed from the founders and/or designers of the brand to the brand's identity and personality. In the evolution of the luxury goods industry, from a small-scale individual family company to an international, multibillion-dollar industry, the family names of the men and women responsible for this transformation have become more familiar as brands than as individuals. Yet, as the modern industry struggles to reconcile its artisanal heritage with today's public offering, it is the personal, family connection that bridges the gap.

The industry as a whole has clear trends and it is helpful to understand them in order to predict which model can better integrate them and effectively deliver results based on them.

What Is a Family Business?

Family businesses are the oldest and the most common type of organizations across the world. Family businesses represent more than 70 percent of all companies in certain countries.

A family business is a business where more than half of the total shares are under control of the family members from one family. A business that has been passed from one generation to another, which includes family members from different related family units and may be across multiple generations, is also considered a family business.

In the luxury industry, family businesses at one time came in all sizes—from SMEs to big conglomerates that operated in various subsectors and countries.

But the majority of family businesses have had a very short life span; 95 percent of these businesses didn't survive after the third generation of owners. This was often due to the facts that successions were not well prepared to integrate into the management and that there was a lack of the good governance structures needed to survive long-term.

Development Cycle of a Family Business

It has been observed that generally, the corporate governance structure of a family business will vary depending on its stage of development

Figure 6.1   Brands of Different Sizes

and the family's percentage of ownership. The initial structure of an organization, in cases when the founder of the company was running the business, will be different than the structure when the next generation takes over, which will be different again from that of a business wholly owned by the family. The evolution is in three phases. In the "initial phase," all dimensions are concentrated in one family, groups of families, or the individual founder. As time goes by, the company grows and transitions ownership to the next generation, a stage called the "growth phase." As time passes, the company transitions to future generations, reaching "maturity-stage." When the firm reaches maturity, according to the model, the challenge is to renew and recycle in order for the company to continue. Figure 6.1 shows the evolution of family businesses.

Characteristics of Family Businesses

As seen earlier, family businesses evolve over time. They face particular situations and unique challenges during different phases. Family houses are supposed to uphold their *long-term focus and commitment*. In the luxury sector, strong commitment to the brand and delivering quality and service are a must. This is because the family name and family legacy are borne by the product. The family name in fact is the reason for the pride. The name of the brand is in fact the family name. It seems that the families have a different long-term business focus from shareholders, as they don't get caught up on quarterly targets. Instead they make what they consider to be the decisions for the brand, the benefit of which might be realized only far into the future. Family businesses also entail a type of *loyalty and commitment* from their employees, especially in the luxury sector. It has been observed that family businesses may face lower turnover. They are considered to be more humane in the workplace and employees are most often treated as part of the extended family. There is a level of care and concern. The turnover, however, might be higher at the upper-level positions, as there might be a "glass ceiling" for non family members. The professional managers may only ever be able to reach a certain level of the top positions. There always remains a chance that the topmost spot will be occupied by a family member. For this reason, it may be difficult to attract highly professional talent. But it can also be argued that, though professional managers may feel intimidated, they will work closely with the owner of the company. Another perception might be that the final control rests with the family, and the family members may strangle creativity and discourage diversity of opinions. But it has been observed that if objectives are clarified, the luxury industry has witnessed great leadership from family members and also from professional managers. Chapter 7 has further discussion about people working for the luxury industry. Figure 6.2 gives a snapshot that suggests why luxury family houses were able to outshine the conglomerates until the 1980s.

The luxury industry is abundant with examples that explain why luxury family firms failed to successfully maintain the business from generation to generation. Some of the reasons may be as follows: With globalization and the rise of emerging markets the owner lacked the *viability of the business* and could not *finance the growth options*. The owner either wanted to *exit* or died of old age. Succession planning does not always work, perhaps due to *infighting* between siblings, cashing in by family members, or the sheer *reluctance* of offspring to join the firm. Another occasional cause was the appointment of incapable members of the family who destroyed the company's value. *Succession planning* has always been a key concern: Family members who are not at the helm want out or are not comfortable discussing topics such as aging, death, and their financial affairs. Perhaps this is why at a global aggregate level more than 70 percent of family-owned businesses do not survive the transition from founder to second generation. Figure 6.3 provides a snapshot that suggests why luxury family houses were taken over by the conglomerates after the 1980s.

Figure 6.2   Reasons Luxury Family Houses Lasted until the 1980s

Figure 6.3   Reasons Luxury Family Houses Were Taken Over by Conglomerates after the 1980s

The luxury brands have historically been suppliers to royal families and other special clients.

A well-known artisan ("supplier to His Majesty") or a famous company (Saint-Gobain, makers of mirrors) were linked in a unique fashion to a trade, sometimes even to a single product (the Gobelin tapestries). This structure lasted until the Belle Époque, when Hermès was a saddler, Vuitton was a luggage- and trunkmaker, Christofle a goldsmith, but began to experience profound change after the First World War. The big luxury houses began to manufacture or to put their name to things that they had not originally known how to make.[1]

Overall, luxury family-owned businesses had a strong historical background that was deeply related to the culture in the region. The business ran over a half-century or more and they became integrated with the heritage of the country. People were proud of their names.

The Evolution of the French Fashion Houses

In the field of fashion, particularly that of high fashion, the evolution of the luxury industry is difficult to grasp. The departments of haute couture have always been true artisan workshops. They have usually been completely separate from the rest of the business, both economically and geographically. Yet without the haute couture, there would have only been, for the most part, a division of perfume and a division of ready-to-wear, at least until the 1990s. Haute couture has been both the origin as well as the facilitator for major developments in the luxury goods sectors. The financial investors who had bought the major luxury brands were less and less willing to finance the designers. The financial investors were not ready to accept the risk of failure linked to each collection. Since the late nineteenth century, a few key players such as Guerlain (perfumes) and Worth (haute couture) caused a revolution in the French luxury goods sector and helped to change the interests of the traditional clientele. In this period, a new definition of luxury emerged.

---

[1] Kapferer and Bastien, 2012.

The bloom of the "arts of fashion" started. From then on, people started to display their wealth with new status symbols, for example, the automobile, or via new identification factors such as perfumes or clothes ("la mode"). After World War I, new names emerged: Chanel, Poiret, and Schiaparelli become symbols of the *art de vivre à la francaise* because they gave an industrial dimension to their creations.

The situation become bleak with the recession of 1929. However, a few companies like Chanel managed to expand despite the economic downturn. Post–World War II, designers themselves became financiers, and that's when the luxury industry began to boom. By 1947, some designers—among them the couturier Lucien Lelong and perfumer Jacques Guerlain—founded the Comité Colbert. The foundation of the committee illustrated the changes triggered by the industrialization of the sector: In the coming 50 years, more and more brands emerged, but the number of companies owning the brands decreased, since several *"groupes de luxe"* emerged. Until the early 1970s, entrepreneurs in the sector changed from being creative designers and artists to establishing themselves as "industrials of luxury." This concept was new. It was toward a characteristic of the industry, namely the challenge of finding a balance between maintaining everything that luxury stands for (tradition, know-how, precious materials, scarcity, craftsmanship, and others) and economic requirements ("industrial scale" production, focus on costs, economies of scale, and others).

Fashion was the main beneficiary of economic growth during the glorious 1930s, which marked the beginning of a new era: various young designers followed the example of successful companies like Chanel and founded their own fashion houses, often with the support of some large entrepreneurs. The most famous examples are Christian Dior in 1947, Pierre Balmain in 1945, Hubert de Givenchy in 1953, Guy Laroche in 1957, and Andre Courreges in 1964. The large number of fashion houses (France had 106 haute couture houses in the late 1940s), the quality of the work, and the unwavering support of the international media were factors that contributed to the outstanding reputation of Parisian fashion. Moreover, after the economic crisis of the 1930s and the scarcity of resources in the 1940s, demand for beautiful objects picked up significantly, which allowed for the success of prêt-à-porter and perfumes. The perfume sector was the first one in the luxury industry to adopt mass production and to widen its distribution network to perfumeries and later also to airport shops. This led also to a certain trivialization and a greater accessibility of luxury products. The economic crisis of the early 1970s was a difficult period for luxury goods manufacturers: some houses that were already in difficulties didn't manage to overcome these, especially in the light of the evolution of society, the emergence of new ways of life, and an increasing internationalization until the end of the 1960s.

The economic situation of the luxury goods sector was very unstable throughout the 1970s and 1980s: Many believed that luxury was synonymous with continuous growth and record dividends proved increasingly difficult. Several businessmen (Bernard Tapie, Alain Chevalier, and Henry Racamier) started to invest in the sector to create new groups. Their attempts failed however, often due to the high costs of development. In 1989, the merger of Louis Vuitton and Moët Hennessy, the first luxury conglomerate, created the birth of an industry. This event changed the luxury world and ushered in a movement of corporatization, acquisition, and expansion of family businesses within the fold of a conglomerate. At the end of the 1990s, Francois Pinault founded a similar group that became the main competitor to LVMH. During the same period, Hermès started to diversify its operations. The Groupe Vendôme (owned by the Richemont family), with its prestigious brands (Van Cleef & Arpels, Cartier, Piaget, Chloé, Lancel, Montblanc, and others) emerged as another major foreign competitor of the French luxury houses. By the end of 2002, 12 out of 77 members of the Comité Colbert belonged to LVMH. Over half of the members of this Comité belonged to luxury conglomerates. Witnessing the changes, in 1989, Christian Blanckaert, then president of the Comité Colbert, defined the luxury goods industry as being "characterized by six points: international perspective of the management, high-quality products, a strong and coherent image (often with a connotation of the *art de vivre*), accessibility for the grand public in terms of the prices, creativity and innovativeness and a perfectly chosen, controlled, and managed distribution."

The Evolution of the Italian Brands

Italy is a country with a long history of successful entrepreneurship across many sectors. In addition to fashion, art, literature, and music,

Italians became known over the centuries for a wide range of excellent products—olive oil from Tuscany, cheese from Reggio Emilia, and vinegar from Modena, to name a few. Entrepreneurs and their family enterprises have stood at the center of the Italian economy, which has greatly influenced Italians' view of business. Italian middle-sized companies have some similar characteristics across different sectors and industries. These common features show clearly how history has shaped this dynamic section of the Italian economy. Family-run businesses tend to focus on long-term goals and viability rather than short-term gains, because owners wish to pass their companies down to future generations. Yet a number of factors can hamper their economic growth and prevent them from focusing on innovation, anticipating market trends and producing high-quality goods. Many suffer from a lack of strategic vision among the founders, family members' inability to communicate effectively, excessive control by the entrepreneur, and conflicting opinions among family members on which direction the business should take.

The origins of a large part of the Italian Mittelstand can be found in many industrial districts scattered all over the country. They were entrepreneurs and they started with small and medium-sized enterprises that concentrated mainly on textiles, clothing, furniture, and footwear businesses. These small entrepreneurs, who successfully coordinated the resources that were present around them and, if necessary, expanded by creating extensive distribution networks, are at the origin of many of today's medium-size companies. A relevant example is the case of Della Valle group (internationally known through brands like Tod's), which emerged from the Marches shoemaking district. More or less the same conditions of entrepreneurial family-based organizations have fostered, during the 1960s and 1970s, the consolidation of the Benetton group, and later the creation of Diesel. These examples highlight the importance of the relationship between these middle-size corporations and their surroundings, especially that of local production systems as industrial districts.

Since the opening of the formerly highly regulated markets (Cold War era) and the proliferation of Asian-made products as well as the introduction of the euro, Italian companies have been forced to change their strategies to catch up with their international competitors. Organizational changes were needed to adapt to the changing environment. The family organizations voted almost unanimously to integrate vertically so that they could control the complete value chain. The emerging organizational form favored a family controlling a large number of internationally scattered, independent productive units (frequently run through joint ventures with local entrepreneurs). The birth of these "pocket multinationals" was a consequence of a rational strategy aimed at the minimization of administrative and coordination costs. With this change of small to medium-size corporations came also a transformation of the entrepreneurial role. The transition from the small workshop to a structured enterprise generally was carried on by the second and sometimes the third generation of the founder's family. Usually, the "younger generations" had a higher educational level than their ancestors, who had often received little formal schooling. Formal education was compensated by a high commitment and attachment to their own companies. The enlargement of the firm's boundaries and the adoption of a relatively complex organizational structure brought about a transformation of the decision process. The decision-making process seemed to be much more participative than in the past, when it involved coopted managers or professionals. The family remained, as in the past, the main decision-making structure, influencing the succession strategies. Familism[2] was, however, still a dominating feature, especially when succession strategies are considered.

After the terrorist attacks of September 9, 2011, Italian family businesses went through a difficult phase. Luxury family goods companies depended on tourists, particularly Asians, visiting Europe. However, the fallout from the dot-com boom, the events of 9/11, SARS in Asia, and the beginning of the war in Iraq dented consumer confidence and decreased international travel.

By contrast, the financial and economic crisis in 2008 affected Italian luxury goods companies only slightly, and especially those few companies that were present on different international markets recovered quickly from the downturn. Post-2008, Italian companies struggled with their competitors in France. French firms dominated the luxury-goods industry with 36 percent of the global market share.

---

[2]Defined as the identification between the family and the enterprise and the consequent adaptation of the company's goals and strategies to the family's benefit.

During 2009–2014, the luxury industry witnessed the acquisition spree of Italy's family-run businesses. Many of the Italian family businesses such as Bulgari, Brioni, Loro Piana, and others had been acquired by the French conglomerates. But there still remained some robust, independent family houses such as Ermenegildo Zegna, Ferragamo, Luxottica, Moncler, Prada, Armani, Dolce & Gabbana, Tod's, and others. The main challenge for these family firms was to keep growing profitably to compete effectively. The growth needed to happen in terms of turnover and geographical expansion, especially in the Asia Pacific region, an area where the new generation of luxury customers were fast rising. They had to think of succession planning and the next strategy. They were all managed differently within complex organizational structures that had their own strengths and weaknesses and were perhaps impossible to generalize. Their key strength was in fact in the diversity of these management structures. Figure 6.4 depicts the key engines of growth for luxury houses.

The larger challenge in Italy was for the smaller family-owned companies with sales of US$20 million to US$40 million, trying to break into the US$200 million range. This type of expansion was traditionally

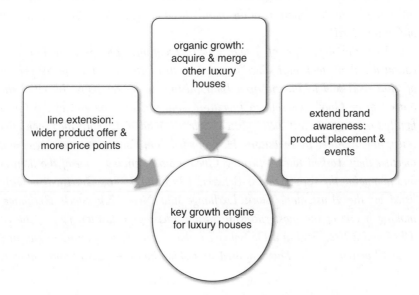

Figure 6.4   Key Engines of Growth for Luxury Houses

done by relying on markets in the United States, Europe, and Japan through forging close links with department stores, distributors, and high-net-worth buyers. Entering markets in countries in the growing regions, such as the frontier markets of Asia-Pacific, Russia, and Latin America, was more complicated because they often lacked consumer retail infrastructure. Additionally, the demand for Italian goods started to move away from ready-to-wear to leather goods to accessories. Some examples of family businesses are illustrated in the next section.

Gucci (Kering)   *Gucci was founded in 1921 by Guccio Gucci in Florence, Italy as a small leather-goods shop and saddlery. The brand grew from strength to strength and by the mid-1950s had shops in London and New York. Guccio Gucci passed away in 1954 and was succeeded by his son Aldo. Aldo then transformed the family business into a global brand. He invented the "GG" interlocking logo.*

At the height of its success, Gucci could count Grace Kelly and Queen Elizabeth II as loyal customers. However, by the 1970s, family feuds had taken over the company, over licensing, over the direction of the company, and over who was the real head of the company. By the early 1980s, Gucci was overlicensed, with its logo on every product imaginable from headscarves to key rings to lighters. The infighting led to the departure of the brand's head designer Paolo Gucci (grandson of Guccio Gucci).

After the departure of Paolo Gucci, Dominico De Sole, a Harvard-educated Italian, took over Gucci's operations in North America and 50 percent of Gucci was sold to Investcorp, a Bahraini investment company. In 1993 the other half of Gucci was sold to Investcorp, and this was the end of the Gucci family's involvement in Gucci. Mr. De Sole was made CEO of Gucci soon after it was fully acquired by Investcorp. He promoted Tom Ford to creative director and together they worked toward turning Gucci around, ending a lot of the licenses and managing the supply chain. Between 1995 and 1996, Gucci was publicly listed on the Amsterdam Stock Exchange and New York Stock Exchange, making it one of the most successful initial offerings in fashion ever. Between 1994 and 2002, Ford and De Sole were able to turn Gucci around—revenues grew 32 percent a year. They acquired six fashion houses—Yves Saint Laurent,

Balenciaga, Aiexander McQueen, Stella McCartney, Bottega Veneta, and Sergio Rossi—as well as Boucheron, a jeweler, and Bedat, a watchmaker. When Kering bought the group in 2001, almost all of them were leaking cash.

Bernard Arnault noticed Gucci's evolution and slowly started buying shares in the company. All this came to a head when Arnault launched a takeover bid for Gucci. Ford and De Sole fought him off and decided to team up with Francois-Henri Pinault of Kering. This was the birth of the PPR group (now known as Kering).

After Pinault acquired Gucci, he bought Yves Saint Laurent (YSL), a company that was overlicensed and performed poorly. De Sole and Ford went to work transforming the new group. Ford was designing for both Gucci and YSL and De Sole focused on vertically integrating YSL and bringing to an end the numerous licenses, as he had done during the turnaround of Gucci. Balenciaga, Bottega Veneta, and Boucheron were also bought by De Sole, bringing together multiple brands under the Gucci group umbrella. However the relationship with Pinault (of Kering group) was soon over for De Sole and Ford, who both left Gucci group in 2004. It had also financed two new labels: Stella McCartney (former designer of Chloé) and Alexander McQueen (former designer at Givenchy), and most recently Brioni was purchased by Kering. It was a journey for Gucci, from a small family shop to one of luxury's most dramatically run family businesses. It evolved to be a luxury powerhouse. Key in its success was the shift from family managers to professional managers and designers. What almost killed the company was family infighting. It is doubtful the company would have survived had it not been bought by Investcorp, its shares floated, and professionals brought in to manage the company.

Prada   Prada was started in 1913 by Mario Prada. It began as a luxury store based in Galleria Vittorio Emmanuelle II in Milan, Italy. It started selling leather goods: handbags, trunks, and small leather accessories as well as beauty cases and other articles of value. By 1919, the company had grown by name and was known for its fine craftsmanship and exclusive design. It was named the official supplier to the Italian royal family.

After World War II, Mario Prada lost interest in his business, and the company continued without much happening. In 1958, Luisa Bianchi,

Mario Prada's daughter, took over running the business. The company continued for another 20 years with little to no real success to talk about. Things started to turn around for the company when Luisa's daughter, Miuccia Bianchi Prada, took over the business in 1978.

In 1979, Muiccia partnered with Patrizio Bertelli, a leather–goods manufacturer from Tuscany. Their business relationship evolved into a romantic one and they married in 1987. Together they built up Prada into a leather goods and accessories company. In 1993, they opened Miu Miu, a new brand that was an extension of Prada, which focused on women's fashion and accessories. Miuccia was the creative brain behind Prada, and Patrizio headed the business side of the company. Patrizio built the company from a value of $25 million in 1991 to $750 million in 1997. Patrizio took advantage of the war for Gucci that was taking place in the late 1990s and sold Prada's 10 percent share in Gucci to LVMH for $140 million in 1999. Within six months of having sold the Gucci shares, Patrizio went about building the Prada group. He bought a stake in three different companies: Helmut Lang, Jil Sander, and Church and Co., thus creating a fully privately owned luxury group. Patrizio's overspending meant that by the 2000s the company had a growing debt estimated to have been about $1.7 billion by November 2001, about the same as that year's revenues. To make matters worse, the CEO and the designer of Jil Sander both quit.

After this event, Prada started to prepare for its initial IPO. However, because of the terrorist attacks of September 11, 2001, it had to put off the IPO. The group had to shed Jil Sander and Helmut Lang. Both companies were sold off and the group soldiered forward. The company continued to grow and later even acquired Car Shoe. Today, the group is made up of Prada, Miu Miu, Car Shoe, and Churches and Co. It was finally listed on the Hong Kong Stock Exchange after an IPO in June 2011 raising $2.14 billion. It was a much–needed financial injection that by this time had acquired large debts. With the IPO, Prada was still managed as a family business, as a majority of its shares were still family held. Its growth was slow, and it wasn't until Patrizio partnered with Miuccia that the company started to grow from a small family business that was draining family funds to one of the big players of the luxury industry of today. It was strong enough not to fall into the category of small family business in the luxury industry that either dwindled into nonexistence or that were bought out by one of the large conglomerates. It continued to grow by focusing on acquisitions and strengthening the Prada brand; thus, Patrizio and Miuccia managed to build a leader in the luxury industry. What was key in the whole equation was the aggressive acquisition but also the focus on the cornerstone brand. The IPO in Hong Kong brought a much-needed capital injection into the group to help it continue to expand.

Salvatore Ferragamo   In the world of designer shoes, the brand Salvatore Ferragamo is a star. Mr. Salvatore Ferragamo became famous when he moved to Hollywood in the 1920s and made bespoke shoes for film stars. In 1923, he took over the Hollywood Boot Shop in California and was known as the "Shoemaker to the Stars." In 1927, he returned to Florence, the center of the Renaissance, where later in 1936, he bought the historical Palazzo Spini-Feroni and opened the first Ferragamo store. The company flourished after World War II, expanding the workforce to 700 craftsmen producing 350 pairs of handmade shoes a day. Salvatore Ferragamo died in 1960 at the age of 62. After his death, his wife Wanda and later their six children (Fiamma, Giovanna, Fulvia, Ferruccio, Massimo, and Leonardo) ran the Ferragamo company, and made his name live on as an international company.

The Ferragamo family was among the first to go to the Asian market. In 1989, it opened its first store at Hong Kong, early expansion to the Asian market. In 1998, Ferragamo licensed its eyewear line to Luxottica. In 2001, Ferragamo created and launched in house its first perfume. In 2007, Ferragamo licensed its watch line to Timex. And the year 2011, saw the launch of its first jewelry collection, in collaboration with Mr. Gianni Bulgari, grandson of the founder of Bulgari and a renowned jewelry designer himself. The same year, the company was quoted for the first time on the Stock Exchange market in Italy, after the failed attempt in 2006. Now, the Ferragamo family has built a luxury fashion empire, released books, opened a museum, and branched out into hotels and restaurants. The opening of the Salvatore Ferragamo Museum in 1995 in the Spini Ferroni Palace, the historic headquarters of the brand, is dedicated to the founder's history and his celebrated shoes, and is nowadays referred to alongside mentions of famous museums such as the Louvre of Paris and the Victoria and Albert of London.

The brand had always been run by the family members until 2006, when Michele Norsa was appointed CEO. Michele Norsa was the first CEO named outside of the Ferragamo family. He had more than 35 years of experience as a CEO of Italian-family firms in diverse sectors such as fashion (Benetton), publishing (Rizzoli), and luxury (Valentino). Norsa orchestrated the successful IPO for Ferragamo. He had done the same for Valentino before. Norsa used the 22 percent of the company to open 25 stores, of which 10 were in China, thereby doubling its number of stores to 66. He also refurbished the flagship stores in world capitals, such as London and New York. In 2014, Ferragamo expanded its operations from luxury shoes, to bags, eyewear, silk accessories, watches, and jewelry, perfumes, and a ready-to-wear clothing line.

The appointment of a professional CEO heralded the family business going global. With the appointment of a CEO, Massimiliano Giornetti, from the family, was named the chief creative director (CDO). He was working within the business for the previous 12 years. The young CDO was placed in the spotlight in the latest brand events, giving talks to editors about his inspiration, in contrast to previous Ferragamo occasions, where the emphasis has been on the family history of the company. Ferragamo was in fact boosting the visibility of its creative director, as Dior did for Yves Saint Laurant.

Since the appointment of the new creative director and chief executive, the brand has made a significant effort in expanding its business globally, especially in Asia and particularly in China and for Chinese customers, achieving a €282 million turnover in 2013. Best known for their luxury footwear, the brand's portfolio has grown over the years to include ready-to-wear clothing, silk scarves, accessories, and jewelry.

Drawing inspiration from other cultures and art has always been in the brand's DNA. Today the critical point is how to create synergy in branding and retailing to gain maximum business growth from the product category expansions, in order to strengthen and rejuvenate the long-history luxury brand, Salvatore Ferragamo.

Armani   Giorgio Armani is another tangible example of a brand that has a strong founder as its asset who plays an important role for the development of the firm and the strong existence of the brand. In 2010, Giorgio Armani produced €1.2 billion. Giorgio Armani is a designer and businessman who created the empire of Armani. Nowadays, it is one of the conspicuous icons of the Italian luxury brands. He is a very detailed person who has a solid desire to create the world of Armani, offering Italian timeless lifestyle for consumers. The stretch of the product line of the business started from fashion and moved on to cosmetics and home products. Armani's vitality and ideas for his business built the company as one of the most influential players in the industry

Armani launched extensions of its product lines. It has about 15 lines, including outlet. It started with the couture and expanded to a sports line, accessories, cosmetics, and home products, and then extended to hotel resort range at the end. Armani started with men's suits and from that point, it has always been keen to keep a balance between menswear and womenswear each time it has launched a new line. Also, Armani was a pioneer of making luxury affordable before the concept of masstige in the luxury marketing arena existed. Clearly, this was a major success of Armani, which expands its customer profiles in terms of gender, ages, and social classes. The licensing business is a huge success factor for those firms run by entrepreneur to stretch their product lines worldwide. Though there was no choice besides licensing in the beginning due to the lack of financial support, it was a wise choice to implement its strategy since Armani has been successful with licensing business through its history. Armani managed well to find the right partner and distributors while strictly controlling its brand, partly by guaranteeing it's "Made in Italy" promise by hiring Italian manufacturers. The licensing business started from apparel to hotel resorts. For instance, L'Oréal is the partner for the perfume business and Armani had an agreement with Fossil for watch manufacturing and Luxottica for eyewear.

Dolce & Gabbana   Founded in 1985, Dolce & Gabbana is one of the leading international firms in the fashion world. The founders, Domenico Dolce and Stefano Gabbana, had always been the creative and stylistic inspiration of the brand. Together they were the originators of growth strategies based on balanced development and focus on the core business. Over the years, the creation of collections was integrated with many of the brand's activities, such as publications, cultural, and social events. They were done at the Metropol space in Milan, the blogazine Swide.com, the Martini Bar, the Gold restaurant, and others.

In 1989, Dolce & Gabbana opened their first store in Japan under partnership with Kashiyama Co. They started to export to the United States, where they founded their own showroom in 1990. In 1992, the brand launched its first in-house perfume, the same year that they presented their first men's collection. The perfumes were a huge success and won an award for men's perfume for the brand. In 2001, they launched their children's wear collection. In 2006, the company started a new journey in accessories and leather goods for men and women. The company also stepped into cosmetics, with Scarlett Johansson as the face of the advertising campaign. The first fine jewelry line came in late 2011 with 80 pieces, including bracelets, necklaces, and, later on, watches.

In 2012, due to the underperformance and blurring of the brand image, the company decided to erase the sub-brand D&G and integrate into its main brand Dolce & Gabbana. In the same year, Mr. Dolce and Mr. Gabbana made their debut in couture with the collection Alta Moda after 26 years of designing ready-to-wear. The first-ever haute couture line made history at the San Domenica Palace Hotel in Taormina, Sicily. With 73 looks full of Dolce & Gabbana signature style, the Alta Moda collection was, according to Mr. Gabbana, the cofounder and the designer of the brand, "not because of us, but the customers. They really do not want to see their dresses in a magazine."[*] His partner, the other founder and designer of the brand, Mr. Dolce, commented that, "This is our style. It is not a trend . . . Here, we are completely free. So for me this is not work but pleasure."[*]

Currently, the company is present in 36 countries. The group designs, produces, and distributes high-end clothing, leather goods, footwear, and accessories. It also manages the production and distribution of beauty and eyewear, timepieces and jewels through licensee partnerships.

Zegna

A great family makes a great company, a great company makes a great family.

—Gildo Zegna

[*]http://fashion.telegraph.co.uk/article/TMG9390006/Dolce-and-Gabbana-couture-First-look-at-the-autumnwinter-2012-collection.html

Zegna has been the leader in menswear. They hold this position by maintaining utmost quality in their fabrics in each step of the value chain, from selection of the finest raw materials to development of innovative customer relations. Gildo's grandfather built a series of business-related infrastructures for his fellow citizens: He built roads to schools and always took a sincere interest in the welfare of the work force in the wool mills. And his sense of social responsibility—his commitment to people—endures as a basic principle for the family of Zegna. The company has assimilated and enlarged upon Ermenegildo Zegna's environmental awareness. The group is presently involved in a number of major conservation projects, expression of the good corporate citizenship that has distinguished the company throughout its history. Inspired by the grandfather's legacy, the new generation of Zegnas are carrying on his work—weaving the future on the loom of the past.

Tod's   Tod's S.p.A. engages in the production and sale of shoes and leather goods under the Tod's, Hogan, and Roger Vivier brand names. It offers shoe collections for women, men, and children under the Hogan brand. The company also offers a range of casual wear, including seasonal men's, women's, and junior's collections under the FAY brand. It sells its products globally. The company is based in Sant'Elpidio a Mare, Italy. It is presided over by businessman Diego Della Valle. Dorino Della Valle started the shoemaking business out of a basement in the late 1920s. Diego Della Valle, Dorino's elder son, expanded the workshop and turned it into a factory that started manufacturing shoes for American department stores in the 1970s. Diego brought in innovative marketing strategies in the early 1980s, kept the handmade manufacturing process, and went on to create brands of lifestyle named Tod's, Hogan, and Fay. Roger Vivier, maker of high luxury shoes was acquired in the mid-1990s and developed during the beginning of this millennium. In 2003, Italian designer Bruno Frisoni was hired as Roger Vivier's Creative Director. The Della Valle family, which owns a majority of the luxury maker, also has stakes in RCS Media Group, the football team Fiorentina, and other companies. All members of the family were born in the middle Italian region of Marche, and many of them continue to reside there.

Versace   Gianni Versace S.p.A, is an Italian fashion label founded by
Gianni Versace in 1978. The first Versace boutique was opened in Milan's
Via della Spiga in 1978, (though the Versace family are from Reggio
Calabria) and its popularity was immediate. Today, Versace is one of
the world's leading international fashion houses. Versace designs, mar-
kets and distributes luxury clothing, accessories, fragrances, makeup, and
home furnishings under the various brands of the Versace Group. Gianni
Versace was killed by Andrew Cunanan on July 15, 1997. His sister
Donatella Versace, formerly vice president, then stepped in as creative
director of Versace, and his elder brother Santo Versace became CEO.
Donatella's daughter Allegra Versace has owned 50 percent of the com-
pany since 2004, a wish expressed by Gianni in his last will. Versace's Style
Department employs a group of designers and stylists who work in teams.
Each team is specifically dedicated to each fashion line or label. These
teams operate under the close supervision and guidance of Donatella
Versace. There are several lines that make up Versace. They are Versace
Couture, Versace Jeans Couture, Versace Home Collection, Versus, and
Versace Collection. In addition to clothing and accessories, Versace also
operates a hotel, the Palazzo Versace.

The Versace label named Versace Couture includes high-end, often
handmade apparel, jewelry, watches, fragrances, cosmetics, handbags,
shoes, and home furnishings. Traditionally, the couture is presented on
the runway during Milan's fashion week, but this has not been strictly
the case in recent years. Couture dresses in this line may cost about
$10,000 and suits cost approximately $5,000. Donatella Versace directly
heads this line and designs a vast number of the items. The Versace label
named Versace Collection is the second high-end line of the group and
is designed for younger, more fashionable people; the logo is discreet
and consists of the outline of a V surrounded by the classic Greek frieze
or is signed with the word "collection" written smaller in black at the
bottom line of the name Versace in outlined letters or in white. The
Versace Sport line ended in 2008 due to extensive counterfeiting of
this line, damaging the Versace group image. Versace Jeans Couture, a
casual clothing line, focuses on informal clothing and high-end denim
and classic Versace print shirts. It is readily available and comparably
affordable, but has been discontinued in the United States for the most
part. This line is distributed through 56 boutiques and flagship stores,
and 1,800 multibrand points of sale, including Internet-based shops.

Versace Sport encompassed active wear and accessories. The name was often printed on T-shirts.

Versace planned an IPO in 2006, but it was not realized. In 2011, the group returned to profit. In 2014, it sold a 20 percent stake to Blackstone for €210 million to fund expansion before taking another chance at an IPO.

Family Business during Crisis

Even with the dominance of French luxury conglomerates such as LVMH and Kering, some family businesses have managed to not only survive but to also retain their place as strong competitors. Although family firms grow and flourish for many different reasons, analysis of family businesses globally reveals that the most critical factor to their success is the families' coordinated and sustained long-term strategy for growing and controlling their businesses. This strategy can take many forms, but usually involves the exercise of patience in investing capital, the retention of companies through tough times, long-term development of talent, a focus on core businesses, the maintenance of strong and enduring values, and an emphasis on long-term performance over quarterly gains.

It is seen that luxury family businesses survived the crises relatively better than their bigger competitors. Experts argue that this is mainly due to the fact that in periods of economic difficulties the long-term vision of family entrepreneurs is a true competitive advantage.

Moreover, businesses run by a team or family members tend to be more resilient and more likely to succeed than any other kind of company since they have one indisputable defining quality: the family. Since family businesses have their name and reputation associated with their products and/or services, they strive to increase the quality of their products and services and to maintain a good relationship with their partners. Several studies have shown that family-owned companies do indeed outperform their nonfamily counterparts in terms of sales, profits, and other growth measures.

During the crisis and much before, there was debate that the formation of the LVMH Group in 1989 would lead to the extinction of family-run businesses in the luxury goods sector. The arguments put forward were based on lines of diversification rather than focused on business. It was touted that the nature of retail of luxury industry requires a consolidated sales force and would look for stronger vendors to support them. The competition became international and more and more volatile, and thus a portfolio of several brands would hold a better position to face these challenges since it allowed for diversification of risk, economies of scale, and exploitation of synergies along the entire supply chain.

Family Businesses of the Future: Corporatization

Family businesses will continue to play a greater and greater role in world economies into the next century. Data suggests that more than 50 percent of the leaders of family businesses in the United States think their businesses will be owned and managed by two or more of their children. Two brands that require discussion in this regard are Jimmy Choo and Brunello Cucinelli.

Jimmy Choo

Jimmy Choo, one of the new entrants in the luxury goods industry, was founded in 1996 by Tamara Mellon and the London-based couture shoe-maker, Jimmy Choo. Jimmy Choo was already known around London for his made-to-measure shoes; he was well known within certain social circles in London for his craftsmanship and had a solid customer base of celebrities and royalty. Tamara Mellon brought the finances and Choo brought his name to the partnership. However, in-fighting broke out between Ms. Mellon and Mr. Choo. Mr. Choo struggled to make the transition from a couture shoemaker to a ready-to-wear shoe designer and was upset when his niece Sandra Choi took over as the company's creative director. By 2001, Ms. Mellon and Mr. Choo were ready to split.

In 2001, Choo's 51 percent of the company was bought by Equinox Luxury Holding, the fashion arm of Phoenix Equity Partners, a private equity fund, for approximately $10.6 million. Mr. Robert Bensoussan, one of the shareholders of Equinox, became CEO of Jimmy Choo.

Tamara Mellon held on to her 49 percent stake in the company, and Ms. Sandra Choi became the creative director of the brand.

In 2004, Equinox sold its stake in Jimmy Choo to Hicks Muse Tate & Furst for £101 million. Mr. Bensoussan remained as CEO and the Mellon family's stake in the company remained the same. The company continued to grow at an extraordinary rate between 2004 and 2007; the number of stores went from 23 to 60. Hicks Muse Tate & Furst became Lion Capital LLP. Partnering with the private equity firms was paying off for Jimmy Choo. Financing was not an issue and it had a strong enough financial base at all times to aide in its expansion.

In 2007, Lion Capital LLP was ready to sell its share of Jimmy Choo. TowerBrook Capital Partners, an international private equity fund, bought the 51 percent stake in Jimmy Choo for £185mn from Lion Capital LLP. In three years Lion Capital LLP had made £85 million by buying and selling Jimmy Choo. The company continued to grow and began to diversify its product offering; they introduced handbags and small leather accessories into the collection. Shortly after the sale to TowerBrook Capital Partners L.P., Mr. Bensoussan, CEO of Jimmy Choo, left and was replaced by Mr. Josh Schulman. Tamar Mellon still owned 41 percent of the company and remained as the company's president even after Mr. Bensoussan left.

In 2010, TowerBrook Capital Partners announced they were looking to sell their stake in the shoe and accessories company. The company's revenues had more than doubled since in May 2011, both Tower Brook Capital Partners LP and Tamara Mellon sold their stake in Jimmy Choo for a value of £500 million ($811 million) to Labelux GmBH, a luxury goods company from Germany. Labelux was Jimmy Choo's first non-private equity owner since Mr. Choo sold his stake in the company in 2001. Although Ms. Mellon had sold her stake in the company, she remained as Chief Creative Officer, while Mr. Schulman also remained as CEO and Ms. Sandra Choi as the creative director of the company. The management of the company looked as if it would not change. However in November 2011, Ms. Mellon announced that she would be leaving the company and Mr. Schulman would be leaving as well in the reorganization of the company.

As a new entrant in the luxury business, Jimmy Choo managed to survive outside of a luxury group, thanks to financing from its multiple private equity stakeholders. It was co-founded by Ms. Mellon and its eponymous designer Jimmy Choo, but quickly evolved into a listed company. The company was never structured as a family business. Apart from Ms. Mellon, co-founder and the biggest stake owner of the company, it always relied on a business manager. The aim of the company had always been to make solid returns on the investments of its private equity owners. The company was able to grow and develop as quickly as it did because of the fresh capital investment that came each time the ownership of the company changed hands. The constant change in ownership did not affect the company's performance because one thing always remained the same: Tamara Mellon, the face of the company. The constant injection of capital meant that the company could invest in retail and expand without worrying about how it was going to raise the capital to further develop. To date, Jimmy Choo has had four leveraged buyouts.

In 2014 the portfolio of iconic luxury brands such as Jimmy Choo, Bally, Belstaff and Zagliani within the Labelux holding structure were fully integrated into parent group JAB Holdings, the management of the investment arm of the billionaire Reimann family. In 2014, JAB Group executed a £1 billion ($1.7 billion) float in London for Jimmy Choo.

Brunello Cucinelli

Brunello Cucinelli is an Italian company in the fashion industry that produces high-end cashmere clothing and accessories. The company controls the whole value chain from design to manufacturing to distribution. Combining its Italian heritage, outstanding quality, and artisan craftsmanship with great creativity, Brunello Cucinelli has built up a strong brand identity and positioned itself in the absolute luxury segment of the market. The company was founded in 1978 while cashmere was only produced in a natural color, but Brunello Cucinell, the founder of this company, thought that colorful cashmere could be a breakthrough; therefore he established the first cashmere knitwear company in Ellera di Corciano in the province of Perugia. The product range was expanded through the multibrand wholesale distribution strategy. First of all, the company purchased stakes of Rivamonti, a producer specializing in design and producing wool knitwear in the mid-1980s. Following this, the company acquired Gunex and expanded its product line to women's skirts and trousers. At the same time, the company established its U.S. branch, which is responsible for the import and sales of cashmere knits in the U.S. market. In 1994, Brunello Cucinelli started its men's collection and opened the first boutique in Porto Cervo. Starting in 2005, Brunello Cucinelli opened directly operated stores (DOS) in Milan, Paris, New York, and Miami, and franchising shops, such as ones in London, Tokyo, Moscow, Saint Petersburg, Sylt, Cortina, and Saint Tropez. Those stores are opened on the main streets of major cities in Italy and abroad and in some exclusive resort locations

Cashmere, a very rare fiber, is the main raw material of Brunello Cucinelli's product. To secure the highest quality cashmere, the company cooperates with the most prestigious cashmere spinners in Italy and has signed long-term contracts to provide the highest quality yarn. A clause in the contract suggests that the contract would be renewed every three years in order to ensure the unhindered supply of stable quality and softness of cashmere.

All Brunello Cucinelli's products are made in Italy, relying on the internalization of intellectual and manual skills. The strong commitment to the high quality and focus on every detail at each stage of manufacturing led the company to manage the whole process of production, from raw material to the finished products. As a result, Brunello Cucinelli employs the top craftsmen in the field, those who maintain high quality and produce creative products. They could ensure this control over the value chain due to their new prototype research and long-term commitment to their production process.

The Brunello Cucinelli Group markets its products through several different channels, which include DOS (directly operated stores), outlets, and the online boutique (retail distribution channel) or through franchising (wholesale single-brand distribution channel) located in prestigious areas, as well as through a presence in the wholesale multibrand distribution channel. Until the end of 2011, the group had stores in 53 countries, with a network of 20 DOS, 39 single-brand franchise stores, and an online boutique, plus a network of over 300 dedicated corners in the multibrand retailers.

Brunello Cucinelli adopts a strictly selective strategy in distribution. The company chooses knowledgeable distributors who not only appreciate the true value of this brand but also reinforce the brand image in the local markets. By doing this, the company preserves the exclusiveness of

Brunello Cucinelli. The 59 stores of Brunello Cucinelli over the world in the prestige luxury locations could ensure the transfer of the brand identity, and ideas of culture and lifestyle. In the multibrand sales channels and particularly in luxury department stores, Brunello Cucinelli products are often presented in dedicated places: "soft-corner" (discreet) corners and shops within shops.

In order to not only have financial stability but to also raise its visibility and attract talent for international expansion, Brunello Cucinelli listed itself on the Milan stock exchange in 2012. Unlike other luxury brands such as Prada, which went to the Hong Kong Stock Exchange, Brunello Cucinelli listed in Milan because its founder, Mr. Cucinelli, had confidence in his home country and was proud of being Italian. After the IPO, the majority of shareholders are still members of the Cucinelli family. Although Brunello Cucinelli could not take advantage of the Asia market, Mr. Cucinelli has an optimistic vision of future global development, since brand visibility and financial support have increased due to this listing.

Changes during Transition from Family Business to Corporation

The sustainability of the conglomerate business model has been questioned since it was born. The formation, growth, and success of LVMH opened up opportunities for ailing family businesses to be acquired and run within a conglomerate. It revolutionized the luxury industry's traditional ways. As a series of acquisitions were orchestrated and the acquisitions integrated, family businesses and designer brands such as Givenchy, Cristallerie de Saint Louis, Céline, and Kenzo were saved from going bankrupt. The turnaround story was fascinating as brand after brand was turned around and its heritage protected. The turnaround occurred by rejuvenating the brands, launching new products, undergoing expansion, and leveraging existent synergies within the group. With the success of the growth-through-acquisition model, the formation of similar conglomerates such as Richemont and Kering was triggered, and another wave of new acquisitions of some of the most renowned brands in fashion, jewelry, cosmetics, and other sectors began. It started to become clear that the size of these groups contributed in relevant manner to the growth, diversification, synergies, opportunities, and better vertical integration that were all necessary for the success of the brands involved. The transition of the smaller brands to be come part of the larger group. Though freedom was maintained for each brand to operate independently, strict financial rigor made them responsive to the market. The products that they created needed to have a market, and the market needed to have consumers aspiring to those products.

Not all the brands were acquired. Some smaller business houses and designer labels remained faithful to their original market position as family-owned brands and focused on serving niche segments, specializing in their core business while highlighting the importance of craftsmanship and creativity. They were small in number. They were strong enough to resist the offers of acquisition from the luxury conglomerates. Some of them prospered while remaining independent. Among them were names such as Hermès, Chanel, Tiffany, and the Italian brands. They had extremely robust balance sheets and enjoyed unprecedented brand recognition. Hermès, for example, was consistently ranked very high in value within all luxury companies, proving to be a vivid competitor regardless of its apparently old but most efficient business model. Figure 6.4 shows the different engines that drove the growth of luxury houses.

It remained a challenge during this transition to compete with the conglomerates. Funding for sustainable growth and to compete with brands such as Louis Vuitton and Gucci remained a challenge. Most of these family businesses had to go public in order to provide the appropriate amount of financing required for the global expansion. The 1990s were famous for the number of IPOs of fashion houses, including those of Ralph Lauren, Tod's, and Hermès. The advantage was still in favor of the IPOs, as the family still kept the controlling interest. It meant that the pressure from shareholders was much less demanding than that from the conglomerates. The competitive advantages during the transition were more or less similar for both the conglomerate and the family house, as Table 6.1 shows.

Table 6.1 Competitive Advantages of a Conglomerate and a Family House

Competitive Advantage of a Conglomerate	Competitive Advantage of a Family House
Strategic imperative: • Global positioning of different brands • Access to strategic resources • Economies of scale and scope • Synergy • International expansion Organization imperative: • Management quality • Organizational design • Shared research and development • Integration into selective retailing Operational imperative: • Merchandizing know-how • Product line extension • Inventory management • Sourcing and supply-chain integration Financial imperative: • Financial discipline • Synergy in marketing budget • High bargaining power—advertisement and retail space	Strategic imperative: • Common shared values defined by family (not shareholders) • Strong commitment • Loyalty • Stability • Expansion as a consequence of business strategy • Emphasis on long-term creation of value rather than quarterly gains Organization imperative: • Flexible and prudent decision making • Homogeneity in internal culture • Long-term development of talent Operational imperative: • Partnership with suppliers Financial imperative: • Not answerable to shareholders for every quarter • Decision can be consensus based • Not in a hurry

Succession Planning

With the transition from family houses to conglomerates, another key issue was succession planning. The stars of yester years were talented, creative, and charismatic, and they created an empire with their own names. What happens when they retire? Be it a family house or a conglomerate, the luxury businesses are still run by individuals who are immensely passionate about the business.

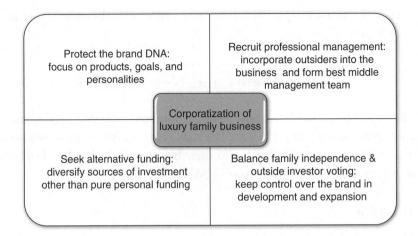

Figure 6.5   Corporatization of a Family Business

According to the literature on family businesses, seven of ten family-owned businesses fail to make the transition to management by the second generation, and only one in ten makes it to the third generation. Simply put, the statistics are against the successful continuation of family businesses over multiple generations. Based on the previous discussion, most of luxury brands were founded in the nineteenth century as small-scale family businesses, or later, a large number of these establishments were being managed by members of the second or third generation. Figure 6.5 depicts the corporatization of the luxury family business.

Armani is a case in point—a very specific one, though. But the luxury industry is in fact full of these personalities who were and are larger than life. The brand of Giorgio Armani was very well grounded, and it is tied to the founders but may not be able to stand alone for long once Mr. Armani retires. What will happen to the Armani brand after Mr. Armani? Will it continue to be as strong, or will the empire slowly deteriorate? And what if the founder himself is better known than the company brand? Giorgio Armani has clearly built a worldwide business, but it is very much dependent on his own involvement. What happens when he moves on? The question then becomes: How will the next-generation entrepreneurs be able to preserve the brand identity and keep it profitable?

Entrepreneurs and New Entrants

The rising trend has been billion-dollar businesses created by designers with their own names. They are the new entrants. We discuss two such new entrants who have developed their brands—Tom Ford by himself, and Marc Jacobs with help from LVMH Group.

Tom Ford

Thomas Carlyle "Tom" Ford is an American fashion designer and film director. He joined Gucci in 1990 as the brand's chief designer for its women's ready-to-wear line. At that time, Gucci had a very blurry brand image—"No one would dream of wearing Gucci," said Dawn Mello, the company's creative director at the time. The brand was struggling to re-establish its status in women's fashion. In 1992, Ford took over Richard Lambertson's position as the design director, leading the brand's ready-to-wear, fragrances, image, advertising, and visual merchandizing. In 1994, Ford was promoted to creative director. In 1995, he worked with French stylist Carine Roitfeld and photographer Mario Testino to create a series of new, modern advertisement campaigns. Between 1995 and 1996, sales of Gucci increased by 90 percent. In early 1999, luxury product conglomerate LVMH initiated a takeover bid on Gucci. Tom Ford and Domenico de Sole, CEO at that time, were not comfortable with the management style of Bernard Arnault. Ford and De Sole approached PPR (later Kering) group. François Pinault, the group's founder, agreed to purchase 37 million shares of Gucci, equivalent to a 40 percent stake. Arnault's share was diluted to 20 percent. At the same time, Tom Ford was the largest individual shareholder in Gucci. During Ford's 10 years as creative director at Gucci and Gucci Group, sales increased from US$230 million in 1994 to almost US$3 billion in 2003, making Gucci one of the largest and most profitable luxury brands in the world. When Ford left in 2004, Gucci Group was valued at US$10 billion. He was also behind the decision of Gucci Group buying Yves Saint Laurent and was named in 2000 the creative director of that brand as well.

In April 2005, Ford founded his own Tom Ford brand. Having already built his fame as a designer at Gucci, his new fashion lines for men became a big success. Domenico De Sole joined in the start-up and became chairman of the company. In that same year, Ford partnered with Marcolin Group to produce and distribute optical frames and sunglasses. At the same time, he cooperated with Estée Lauder to create and produce the Tom Ford Beauty brand, and he posed for his own named fragrance advertisement campaign. With the fame of Tom Ford as a celebrity-like public figure, the eyewear and beauty products with his name became huge successes, which funded the launch of his first luxury menswear collection. The strategy was to focus on superior fashion design and luxury products, attention to detail, and made-in-Italy roots, while the production and distribution under the Tom Ford label were licensed to Ermenegildo Zegna in February 2006. In April 2007, Tom Ford opened its first flagship store in New York at 845 Madison Avenue for luxury men's ready-to-wear and made-to-measure clothing, footwear, and accessories. Later, in autumn 2010, he presented his much-anticipated womenswear collection. The first unisex store opened after the womenswear launch in Beverly Hills, California. In 2014, there are 98 freestanding Tom Ford stores and shop-in-shops in locations, such as Milan, Tokyo, Las Vegas, Dubai, Zurich, New Delhi, Shanghai, and Russia. The Tom Ford brand in 2014 is valued close to $1 billion, and is continuing to expand worldwide.

Marc Jacobs

The talented fashion designer Marc Jacobs was born in New York City on April 9, 1963. After graduating from the High School of Art and Design in 1981 he entered Parsons School of Design. As a design student at Parsons, Jacobs met Robert Duffy, an executive with Ruben Thomas, Inc. when he showed his senior collection. After seeing Jacob's collection, Robert inquired about having Jacobs develop a ready-to-wear collection for Ruben Thomas, Inc., under the sketchbook label.

This conversation started a partnership, called Jacobs Duffy Designs, Inc. The main concepts of this partnership were love for fashion and commitment to quality. The partnership and concepts remain the cornerstones of the company today. In 1986, Jacobs designed his first

collection bearing the Marc Jacobs label with the support of Kashiyama
USA, Inc. The following year, Jacobs was awarded the Council of
Fashion Designers of America Perry Ellis Award for New Fashion
Talent. In 1989 Jacobs and Duffy joined Perry Ellis and were named
vice president of women's design and president respectively. While at
Perry Ellis, Jacobs created a designer collection and was in charge of
the various women's licensees as well. In 1992, the CFDA once again
gave Jacobs a distinct honor: Women's Wear Designer of the Year.
In the fall of 1993, Jacobs Duffy Designs, Inc. launched its licensing
and design company: Marc Jacobs International Company, LP, and in
1994, the company licensed to Look, Inc., and Mitsubishi Corporation
for distribution of the Marc Jacobs designer collection in Japan. Soon
after, Marc Jacobs International Company, LP, entrusted Iris S.R.L.,
the Italy shoe producer, with the production of all Marc Jacobs shoe
collections. Then in 1995, Jacobs launched the first collection of men's
ready-to-wear.

In 1997, Jacobs was struggling to keep his namesake brand business. Bernard Arnault approached him with an irresistible offer that
Jacobs relaunch the famous but stodgy Louis Vuitton label in return
for LVMH underwriting Jacobs's design company. Therefore, Jacobs and
his partner, Duffy joined Louis Vuitton as artistic director and studio
director, respectively. During his tenure, Jacobs worked on many of the
French luxury house's lines, including handbags, men's and women's
ready-to-wear, shoes, and small leather goods. Jacobs's designs helped
boost sales to the tune of €3.8 billion for the Louis Vuitton brand,
which accounted for 60 percent of LVMH's operating profit. At the
same time, the sales of Marc Jacobs brand increased to about $75 million
by a 50 percent investment from LVMH. The company launched its first
handbag collection in the fall of 2000 and a second Marc Jacobs store
was opened on San Francisco's historic Maiden Lane in August 2000.
The first freestanding men's collection store opened on Bleecker Street
in New York City in September 2000, marking the beginning of what
would become a street of shops. In the same year, a licensed agreement
was signed with L.S.A S.P.A., an Italian company based outside Milan, to
produce men's and women's ties and scarves. The secondary line, Marc
by Marc Jacobs, was launched in the Spring/Summer 2001 Runway
show. The Marc by Marc Jacobs collection included shoes, handbags,

and other signature accessories. A licensed agreement with Calza Turifi-cio Rossimoda S.P.A. was signed in 2001 to produce all women and men's Marc by Marc Jacobs' shoes. In September 2001, the company launched its first fragrance. The scent, called Marc Jacobs Perfume, was inspired by gardenias in water. The launch took place on the Pier 54 on the Hudson River and was staged as a benefit to a dozen downtown New York City charities. However, in 2003, the USA fragrance divi-sion of Marc Jacobs brand was sold to Coty, Inc., under the decision of LVMH without informing or consulting Jacobs. In the following year, perfumes under this brand still continued to be launched. In 2005, the company launched its third women's fragrance, called Blush, which was inspired by the scent of blooming jasmines. All fragrances till 2014 were developed and produced by the company's fragrance partner, Lancaster Group US, LLC. The company's eyewear collection is produced by Ital-ian luxury eyewear partner, Safilo SpA. The company also launched the company's first watch line with its partner, Fossil, and a collection store in Paris.

In 2004, the company had a distribution agreement with Imaginex Holdings, Ltd. (a division of the groups whose companies include Lane Crawford and The Joyce Boutiques) for distribution in the territory of Hong Kong and Mainland China. It was also the beginning of a part-nership that included the opening of its first flagship store in Shanghai in August 2004, as well as stores in Beijing and Chengdu. The first U.S. multibrand store opened in July 2004 on Boston's Newbury Street. March 2005 marked the opening of two stores in Los Angeles: a col-lection store at 8400 Melrose Place and a Marc by Marc Jacobs store located at 8410 Melrose Avenue. In the same year, Marc Jacobs launched its first watch line and a collection store in Paris, in partnership with Fossil. Later that month the company opened a collection store at the Bal Harbour Shops in Bal Harbour, Florida. In January 2008, a Marc by Marc Jacobs boutique opened in Chicago's Bucktown, and several limited edition fragrances were launched. The fall brought openings in Paris, London, Madrid, Istanbul, and Athens—all with their first Marc by Marc Jacobs locations. 2009 saw the start of a new venture formed with Sumitomo Corp. that meant the start of a new beginning for the Marc Jacobs business in Japan.

In 2014, Marc Jacobs Collection and Marc by Marc Jacobs's stores were in 35 countries around the world. In Asia Pacific, there are 29 stores located in Korea, 13 located in Hong Kong, 20 located in Taiwan, and stores in 23 main cities in Japan.

Trends and Discussion

With the downturn in the economy and with a not-so-upbeat forecast in Europe in 2014, such as the threatened accession of Crimea by Russia, globalization may pose a challenge to family-owned SMEs, which account for up to 90 percent of Italian companies and around 60 percent of French companies. The threat arises from the lack of financial power that the family-owned luxury goods firms require for international expansion to compete against international conglomerates and to attract buyers to their products. On the other hand, many economists are optimistic that Italian and French firms can capitalize on their sense of beauty and style through effective branding of their trademark craftsmanship.

With the discussion on growth and profitable growth across geographies, it seems reasonable to conclude that globalization has placed new demands on even the best established brands and that could cause old strategies of attracting high-net-worth customers to fail. It may not be only the pull phenomenon of attracting the customer to one's stores in their home country but also the effect of the push phenomenon of reaching out to those high-net-worth customers in distant mature and emerging markets who do not have a passport or do not travel as much as their Western counterparts. Following on those lines of discussion, Asians, especially the Chinese, are now the biggest consumers of luxury goods. So the key question would be to ask how the family businesses can travel across borders, and if so, to which destinations?

Historically, there have been three strategies to leverage brands globally. These three strategies were the key growth engines for the luxury houses. First, the growth engine was by inorganic growth, thereby acquiring family-owned luxury brands, a strategy that was followed by LVMH, Kering, and Richemont. Second were line extensions, which involved offering consumers different designs at tiered price points. Examples would be Armani's wide range of clothing lines and luxury goods, Hugo Boss's red-and-black line, and others focusing on different customer segments. Third was extending brand awareness through product placements, gala events, advertisements, and other methods. The general trend for family houses was thus a choice that was dependent on the amount of resources one could deploy.

Despite growing popularity of the conglomerate model, there is no optimal route to growing a family-run luxury goods business, managing its succession, or growing a particular brand within it. The optimal strategy will always depend on the company and its products, goals, and personalities. Yet there are some general guidelines in this context. Investors like to see that families can incorporate outsiders into the existing business model and believe that family firms need good middle management. They also advise businesses to protect the brand DNA and find the best professional management possible. Ownership remains one of the key issues of internationalization and expansion of family businesses. For example, the case of Etro, a growing family-owned fashion and textiles house from Milan, showed that family businesses in the luxury sector can internationalize without giving up their independence. Over the past years, Etro has been growing slowly but in a structured way while also managing the transition from the vision of its original founder to that of the next generation. Its ample internal capital and collaborative family members have allowed Etro to retain its independence.

Nevertheless, it may not always be the case: The majority of family companies that historically financed their businesses through personal resources now realize that they need to seek alternative funding to compete globally and penetrate new markets and that this might entail giving up ownership (or part) of the family business.

From analysis of the luxury business houses, its road toward corporatization, to the birth of conglomerates, it is clear that its evolution has led to vertical integration. The challenge faced by most luxury brands, especially the family houses is how to finance their expansion, control their production, protect the value chain, and promote core values while minimizing counterfeiting. The story of Louis Vuitton focused on their ability to vertically integrate and scale-up. It was imperative in developing the company and growing it further. For its successful growth story, diversification of the product offering, vertical integration, and control of the supply chain have been key success factors. The conglomerates owned a large part of their manufacturing and retail outlets. They could synergize, share existing resources, take advantage of cumulative sourcing and advertising, create supply-chain efficiencies, and foster economies of scale. With their portfolio of brands, they also had high bargaining power in retail outlets, luxury malls, and luxury streets. The new entrants, on the other hand, had to adapt faster, especially when they did not have the backing of large groups or exterior financiers. For example, Jimmy Choo, due to its solid financing base, was able to grow at a double-digit rate. We have also seen that a weakness that haunts the family business is the issue of succession planning, as seen in the case of Hermès and the important role professional managers play in the growth story of the brand.

With time, the number of smaller players, with a turnover in the range of €20–50 million, has shrunk. Raising financial resources for expansion has been the most important challenge for the smaller houses. For example, in the case of Prada, Hermès, and a number of other companies, going public did not mean that the family lost control. It meant that though they remain majority shareholders, they need to answer to shareholders who care about quarterly returns. Those who have succeeded on their own have involved and had the help of professional managers.

There have been a number of new entrants over the years in the industry, but very few are alone and unassociated with any group or conglomerate. Conglomerates owned and nurtured a large number of the new entrants, as we see in the case of Gucci group with Alexander McQueen and Stella McCartney. Having the financial backing of a group meant that professionals had been at the helm from the onset and that they have had strong financial bases to enable them to compete in an extremely competitive industry. The added advantage was that they were able to lean on the larger brands from the group to negotiate retail space and advertising space and share part of the supply chain. This gave them an advantage in controlling their costs while leveraging their competencies of the group. For any new entrant, the opportunities availed to them would be few and far between. The question that still remains unanswered, which will only become clear in time, is whether there is room in the luxury industry today for small independent players, and if

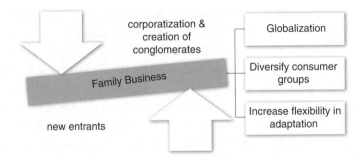

Figure 6.6   Paradoxical Challenges Faced by the Luxury Family Houses

there is, how they can survive in a competitive market that is completely privately owned.

On the other hand, the paradox of maintaining heritage and increasing the bottom line is a common struggle in this industry. The activities of the conglomerates show that size alone cannot overcome this paradox. While conglomerates have been creative in exploiting synergies across brands, they have not always been successful. Some brands garner the profit—the so-called star brands—while other brands in the portfolio continue to be loss-making. Today's loss-making brands in the portfolio may be the star brands of the future. While portfolio theory will accept ebbs and flows in profit generation, it is more often the case that for most conglomerates one or two brands represent the majority of the profit. Further, the less-successful brands often erode the profits of the other portfolio brands. Figure 6.6 summarizes the paradoxical challenges of the luxury family houses.

To summarize, three key organizational trends in the luxury industry that affected family businesses, leading to corporatization and creation of conglomerates and spurring new entrants, were globalization, increasing diversity of consumers, and flexibility in adaptation. They embraced new cultures while remaining true to their values and heritage, which in fact gives them their competitive advantage.

Conclusion

It is evident that if there weren't successfully built family-owned luxury businesses, luxury conglomerates would have never been able to shape themselves into what we see today. They rely on the heritage and tradition brought in by these family-owned companies, which give them the legitimacy to play in the luxury field. Conglomerates do make sense in the luxury-goods sector, which requires large marketing budgets to drive sales and increase product visibility, but the heritage of each brand is what fundamentally allows them to exist. From this perspective, it can be said that the family businesses are in fact stronger than the conglomerates, given that they build the base for further development. Even if conglomerates seem to be a route with no return, there always has to be room for the family-owned businesses to shine, as this is really the part of the luxury industry that best creates the myth and the mystery of true craftsmanship behind unique products.

With increased competition in the luxury market, a critical issue for family houses as well as entrepreneurs is how to leverage the substantial growth and preserve the brand autonomy. The biggest luxury conglomerate could be a panacea for the family-owned business. However, to some extent, being one part of a luxury conglomerate portfolio could have the dependent brand facing a disaster or being a neglected orphan under the umbrella of a multibrand conglomerate. Therefore, to be or not to be a part of the multibrand companies is a question that needs a rethink. Sometimes it may be the only way to survive. Financing through the capital market could be the white knight for them. The critical issue would be how to balance long-term development and short-term sales growth under the pressure of stockholders. And the question remains: Is the growth of a luxury brand sustainable in the long term?

Chapter 7

Management Styles in the Luxury Industry

People in the luxury industry are often referred to as homoluxus. The homoluxus should always know that the life span of luxury brands is varied and totally surprising. The homoluxus is wrong to believe that the luxury brand will be successful forever! He is convinced that he is eternal and nothing can happen, protected by his brand, sure that he is and will remain successful. He is applauded in his social circles. He can see his own name or the name of the company he leads, in the best streets of all the cities. He is thrilled to speak about his brand, is in all the magazines—his image is seen everywhere, usually with charming ladies and stars, dressed in black tie. How can he be afraid of anything?

Nothing really scares him. The homoluxus loves journalists, even if he denies this—he says that he hates to talk about himself, but he keeps telling everybody what he thinks. He knows what is good for his brand, and what is not appropriate. He says that he loves working as a team but very often we observe a "one-man show," or at the least, he imposes his view with authority—the homoluxus does not like contradiction or opposition, he is so sure of himself! He will never die, this is certain. He does not care, in fact, even if he keeps saying that he is obsessed with the question—the homoluxus is living in a paradox, a small figure, a huge name, an immense ego, a modest attitude internally, a sense of esthetic—who knows what the priorities of the homoluxus are?

He is everywhere but actually no where; he travels constantly; he has a drug, the mobile phone, but pretends to be on the ground all the time, especially when he is in the air. He is the best, he loves his brand. He will love the next one same as the last one, with the same type of love. He is confident he will reach the sky even if reality shows a different picture—he cannot admit his mistakes, why should he? The luxury world hates mistakes, failures, death—these are alway the responsibility of others—the crisis, the creators, the shareholders, but never the homoluxus himself.

There are some homoluxi who are better than others. The truly best one is asking himself what to do, whether to go further, and with whom. He is like Mao Tse-tung on the long path, walking, running with a group of "complice," afraid to fall, to fail to win the target, to choose the wrong place or the wrong price for the stars, to recruit the wrong creator. He is scared—he knows how fragile a luxury brand can be, how it is important to be aware of the "ephemeral." He is aware of the risk of collapse, which comes so quickly in luxury. He is not obsessed with money but with the product and its quality. He is not in a hurry, has time, and he is not under pressure; he is zenlike in his focus, and has nothing to demonstrate. Does he still exist in the luxury forest or is he a dinosaur?

As discussed in Chapter 3, most of the industry's iconic brands were established more than 100 years ago and were originally owned and run by families. In France, these companies were called "maisons," or houses. From the 1980s onward, Bernard Arnault (LVMH), Francois Pinault (Kering), and Johann Rupert (Richemont) began to apply the strategies of large, multinational corporations to the luxury industry. By acquiring many of the traditional family-owned and -run brands, the three major luxury groups—LVMH, Kering, and Richemont—were founded, thereby recreating an industry that had been not only fragmented but run by the heads of each maison.

Formerly accessible to only a small, elite group of consumers, luxury was democratized during the late twentieth century. Brands became more accessible. For example, many companies began introducing brand extensions, such as eyewear and perfumes, into the luxury landscape, thus attracting larger (and younger) audiences. Another development during 2000–2014 was the expansion of most luxury brands into emerging markets. The main focus was on Asia and the high-growth BRIC nations, with the greatest growth area being that of Asia. China in 2014 represented a significant share of the revenues of most luxury companies.

Luxury has been built on the foundation of certain principles that can be neither ignored nor compromised. It is a culture and a philosophy that requires understanding before the adoption of business practices because its intricacies and output are essentially different from other types of goods.[1] Its path dependency points to the culture, heritage, and style that need to be understood in order to practice it with flair and spontaneity.

Path Dependency: Management Styles

The creator: *One concocts extraordinary olive oil that the creator presents in beautiful, elegant bottles. The creator intends to sell them in luxury delis, and he will no doubt succeed. The creator has the energy, the taste, the talent, and the patience that it takes.*

Another loves jewelry, makes one-off pieces with stones that she finds from who knows where. Another mixes colors, matches fabrics, and makes necklaces of unusual shapes.

One creator was a designer, but his former luxury house laid him off after closing its doors. He opened a little boutique, but it didn't work; he wasn't a good manager. He is a creator, not an accountant.

Then there's the one who makes sandals and the other one who makes dresses. They are all in luxury's waiting room. They struggle.

Creators often have plenty of illusions. Mistakenly, they think that luxury designers can do anything they like! A creator's freedom has to be based on rules and knowledge; otherwise, nothing good can come of it.

---

[1]Okonkwo, 2010.

That said, the golden rule in real luxury is to make sure creators have no managerial responsibilities, and are given a free rein. The truth is that luxury can only work if the products are unexpected and unplanned.

If design becomes standardized, there is no chance of surprising the customers and making a sale. Producing articles that resemble others, that have a feel of "déjà vu," would doom the luxury market to failure.

Creation goes beyond a system or habits. The organization of a luxury house has to allow for this.

Of course, creators can be unbearable megalomaniacs, demanding and obnoxious. But it's in their nature, and the rest of us just have to accept that.

Luxury needs entertainers. Luxury could not exist without artists.

Creators drive luxury and so sometimes reason must give way to imagination, reality gives way to the irrational, and truth succumbs to dreams! That's what luxury is all about. At least, that's how it should be.

What is the common thread running between Gabrielle Chanel, Hubert de Givenchy, Yves Saint Laurent, and Christian Dior? Are all the names of designers or brands? This is one of those rare questions where one can never be wrong. These are names of designers who gave their names to their brands. In the earlier days of luxury, the designer stood for the brand. Each brand displayed the eccentricities, the enigma, and the individuality of the designer it stood for. What remains important to date is that the designer gave identity to the brand, making the designer and the brand inseparable. Thus we were in a regime, where the "Creator was the Controller." But can the creators actually run a global business or manage the value chain of the business? What will happen after they leave the brand? And when they leave, most important, who is going to sell their brand?

The store manager: *Martha must be about 50, but that's not important. The important thing is the energy that she has.*

She is striking. She's elegant, tall with long flowing hair. Her energetic walk conveys her vivacity and immediately gives a good impression that seduces the visitor.

Martha is a great saleswoman. She knows it and she is proud of it.

Her lightly tanned skin and the scattering of freckles on her face give her a mysterious, animal-like quality that conveys her taste for freedom. It is obvious that Martha is an independent woman.

This morning she is wearing a full-skirted blue dress designed by Jean Paul Gaultier for Hermès. Her beauty is impeccable—not aggressive, but serene. It is the way she looks at you that makes her beautiful—as well as her clothes, her height, and the color of her skin.

Martha is dignified. That is obvious.

She is not one to be scorned or humiliated. She is prepared for everything, from tough negotiations to difficult questions and unexpected arguments.

Martha is good at selling because she loves it.

She likes the challenge of the job and the products. She takes her share of responsibility for the brand. She sells only what she knows.

Martha was a sales assistant, promoted to be a supervisor, now a manager of the whole store. She now manages a large team of very different people, who are difficult to lead. They are so different that it is surprising she can actually manage to impose her point of view.

Yet she sees everything. When the customer enters the store and speaks to a sales assistant, Martha, from a distance, observes the gestures—the salesperson who suggests, the customer who touches, weighs, examines, and replaces the precious object delicately, or clumsily.

Martha is vigilant as she has a full overview of the store. Her attention is like radar. Nothing escapes her. She always chooses the right vantage point from which to observe all goings-on in the store. Quickly, she makes her way toward the men's department where she can hear that an irritated customer, impatient to obtain an answer to his question, is on the verge of leaving. Martha sees that the person serving him is too slow, that another pair of sales assistants is whispering in the corner (not about work, she imagines). They are giggling like two schoolgirls and this is neither the time nor the place. The shoes are brought to the customer, but in the wrong size. Martha anticipated this and hurries over to smooth matters over with the gentleman and makes sure another lady who has been waiting patiently is served a coffee.

Martha is a fairy. Her magic wand gives her store a tone, a rhythm, and a style that would not be there without her.

She chooses the flowers, tidies up, refolds a shirt, moves a tie that has been put in the wrong place, murmurs instructions, gives advice, picks up a stray piece of paper, sees a customer to the door, says "good morning" and "thank you," and generally plays hostess and boss, nurse and psychologist. A sales assistant is in tears because a customer told her she was "too poor to buy a bag like this for yourself!"

The cruelty of the remark caught the girl off-guard and she crumbled. Martha explains, reassures, and the saleswoman goes back "on stage" once the injury has been bandaged over.

Martha directs a "company of actors," as she calls them. The sales floor is their stage and their role is to "bring happiness." Martha leaves her worries at home—her mother's paralysis, her father's Alzheimer's, the stress of her son's "A" levels, and her daughter's exams.

Martha had decided that when on duty she has to put her anguish to one side and be a dream-maker. She pilots her store from the top deck and keeps it shipshape with the regal air of a mighty admiral directing a battle.

Martha takes her role as leader very seriously. She enjoys motivating her team, seducing her clients, and practicing her art.

For Martha is, in essence, an actress. She is a woman of few words, and what she does say, she always says calmly. For the rest, her stature and the way she holds herself are all the eloquence she needs. She is a store manager.

As depicted in Chapter 2, two decades ago, the luxury industry model was almost completely dominated by the family business. However, the rivalry between Bernard Arnault (LVMH) and Henry Racamier created a historic structural shift within the industry as each aimed for market control through growth and acquisition. As a consequence, the industry started consolidating, and family houses that could not survive were absorbed within the multibrand conglomerate, except for a select group of French and Italian companies such as Hermès, Chanel (Wertheimer Family), Armani, Prada and Tod's to name a few. These tectonic shifts from the family business model to corporatization pushed the luxury industry away from its historic style of management as the key factors of success become finance instead of family, and the focus shifted to the colossal conglomerate instead of the small, artisan business, which became "inadequate" for a global business strategy.

To understand the management styles of the managers in the luxury industry, we need to dwell briefly on the role of the managers—and the usual typology of the management styles.

By definition, the role of a manager is to plan, organize, lead, and control. Since managers perform multiple roles in an organization during the strategy-making process, their method of acting will depend on their style of management. Figure 7.1 depicts strategy making as a design and as a process.

Under the same circumstances the roles of leaders are different. They are there to define the future and vision of the company, inspire, and change the employees, and energize and innovate the organization. More often than not in the luxury sector the role of the evolutionary process as a decision-making style has been more prevalent.

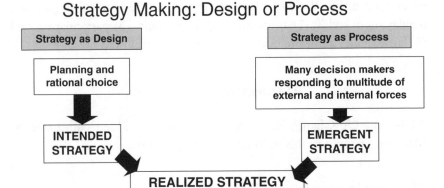

Figure 7.1   Strategy Making—Design or Process

Literature over the past 70 years depicts management styles that incorporate both the contents of decision making and the process of decision making and are aligned to goal setting, strategy formulations, and strategy implementation. Management style is also profoundly influenced by the distinctive environment, social culture, and climate in which an organization operates. The distinctive way in which managers perform the various functions in an organization decides their management styles. There is a core management style that reflects the values and norms of a culture, and this is practiced in the given organizational climate and culture. Three axes are usually analyzed: (1) degree of control in decision making,[2] on a scale from autocratic to democratic; (2) degree of production- or task-oriented and people- or relationship-focused;[3] and (3) social orientation—human capital linked with knowledge and customer orientation. Such a core management style may have variations that include *conservative style, entrepreneurial style, professional style, bureaucratic style, organic style, authoritarian style, participative style, intuitive style, familiar style, altruistic style, innovative style,* and so forth. Given the choices, an unlimited number of management styles can

---

[2]Robert Tannenbaum and Warren Schmidt developed the Leadership Continuum Theory in 1958.
[3]Blake and Mouton, 1972.

be visualized. For the sake of simplicity we will focus on four primary management styles: (1) autocratic, (2) democratic, (3) participative, and (4) laissez faire, all in the context of the luxury industry.

Managing Paradoxes

As discussed in Chapter 4, the luxury industry is ridden with paradox. Managing people in this industry is also a paradox.

The Ambidextrous Luxury Manager

Combining the right and the left brain: The left brain uses logic, facts, and science. It is pragmatic and forms strategies. The right brain is creative, imaginative, perceptive, risk taking, and oriented toward the big picture. Managers in the luxury industry are required to understand the unique properties of the luxury experience, manage highly creative people, apply tough management disciplines, and be sensitive to the cultural nuances involved in running a global business.

Speed versus time: The manager has to grapple with timelessness and profitability. For example, Hermès and Chanel might be of the opinion that they are not looking at short-term profits, yet during every quarter they have to keep an eye on the revenues, which in turn will determine their growth and investment plan. The focus on profitability is now extending across the portfolio to highly prestigious, loss-making brands, and the introduction of International Financial Reporting Structures is forcing greater transparency in financial reporting by large groups. The speed of growth and the time required have a direct bearing on the talent management of the companies. On one hand they have to nurture talent that understands and communicates the story of the brand, the product characteristics, timelessness, quality, and service of the luxury business, while on the other hand they have to cater to the speed of marketing, sales, and after-sales in international markets.

Everywhere or not: The luxury manager has to understand French and Italian *savoir faire* while selling products in Shenzhen, Sao Paulo, Singapore, or San Francisco. Dispatching expatriates to manage stores is one realistic option, although the expatriates more often than not do not speak the local language. The expatriate manager on his or her "colonizing" mission of emerging markets is probably well equipped but finds himself or herself short of understanding the local nuances and can be a failure. Research from Martens & Heads shows that not more than 15 percent of the actual operating CEOs are from the local emerging market. Also Maxine Martens, CEO of Martens & Heads, rightly questions, "How many French or Italian luxury firms that do 30 percent of their business in Asia have 30 percent of their top management from Asia?"[4] Some propose that with globalization and corporatization, the luxury industry should also follow the path of the global corporation. They should also hire more locals in the emerging markets and bring more emerging markets professionals to the HQ.

Internal versus external: Should the ambidextrous manager be found internally or should she be headhunted externally? Research shows that there is a trend to hire executive people outside the luxury industry because they have more experience dealing with crises and global expansion in emerging markets. There are highly capable leaders in other sectors whose experience managing brands and whose international mindset could be invaluable to luxury businesses needing to operate more effectively in a globalized marketplace. The big question is how to identify those leaders who can bring new skills and a fresh outlook, adapt to the idiosyncrasies of the sector, empathize with the product and the consumer, manage the creative process and get the best out of existing talent, handle operational complexity, shorten the production cycle, and yet remain flexible and agile enough to respond to and run with innovative ideas.

Leaving it up to employees to take the initiative and gain education and experience on their own, however, is a gradual process that has prompted many eager companies to look for an alternative quick fix by pursuing talent outside the luxury industry. Gucci's Robert Polet was president of the ice cream and frozen foods division of Unilever before joining Gucci in 2004. LVMH has recruited several non-industry leaders, including Laurent Boillot, formerly of Unilever. Liberty plc hired Geoffroy de La Bourdonnaye, who was with Disney for many years before joining LMVH, while Dr. Bruno E. Sälzer worked at Beiersdorf and

---

[4]Luxury Society, 2010.

Schwarzkopf before becoming CEO of Hugo Boss. Stanislas de Quercize, president of Cartier and ex-president of Van Cleef & Arpels, started his career at Procter & Gamble.

But the big three, LVMH, Richemont, and Kering, although open to external high-potential recruits, are undoubtedly more comfortable trying to nurture employees who are already within the organization or at least within the industry, and are now investing in their talent resources to nurture leaders for tomorrow.

Big or small: The big three, with time, have transformed themselves into multicultural, multibrand conglomerates. While it is difficult to generalize, managers coming into the industry from outside tend to be more effective when joining larger businesses than smaller ones. Culturally and in other ways, it is easier for larger companies to assimilate outsiders, but that is not to say that smaller companies could not benefit greatly from an infusion of leadership talent with experience of different sectors and global markets. The challenge is to find leaders who possess a high level of sensitivity and who recognize the importance of preserving the inherent value of a brand.

International versus local: The industry is in a state of flux and is undecided. There is little consensus, even from an academic point of view, on how to modernize the luxury industry. Those who defend exclusivity and brand coherence are equally passionate about adapting to, and meeting the needs of, emerging markets. Some state that local distribution will be the key to success, and that new ways of doing business (such as going digital and e-commerce) are critical, while still arguing against employing mass-market tactics for fear of diluting that sense of exclusivity and even opulence that is the very hallmark of luxury. Thus, where can one find this manager, the leader who is best equipped to handle the seemingly contradictory elements of developing new markets, opening up new distribution channels, adapting to diverse cultural expectations, and preserving exclusivity and brand coherence, while operating within a far tougher, more competitive commercial environment?

Manage talent in the digital era or stick to the traditional: The competencies required for the digital and the traditional luxury world are not the same. To be ambidextrous is a key challenge. Burberry and Polo Raph Lauren have embraced the digital world with ease, while many are still struggling. For example, Burberry is often recognized as a digital luxury leader. With two enthusiastic advocates steering the company, CEO Angela Ahrendts and chief creative officer Christopher Bailey (now promoted to CEO, since Angela Ahrendts left for Apple in 2014), the firm has intertwined creativity, technology, and management in a way that has helped generate consumer interest in Burberry's products via its digital projects. Through their Art of the Trench crowd-sourcing site, a three-dimensional Livestream show, and, most recently, an interactive digital ad campaign, Ahrendts and Bailey have facilitated collaboration across several functional departments, making everyone work together in the name of digital innovation.

Thus the ambidextrous luxury manager needs to have a portfolio of skill-sets that will make him or her comfortable in this industry. Figure 7.2 explains the ambidextrous nature of style in the decision-making process.

As in all industries, one size does not fit all. The luxury industry has witnessed a sea of change in the internal and the external environment during the past 20 years, and the styles of top management have evolved over that time. The specificities pertaining to these changes had profound implications on the styles of management and governance of these companies.

Familial Autonomy

"Family ownership is very specific to French luxury," once commented Elisabeth Ponsolle, General Secretary of the Comité Colbert. The Comité Colbert, founded in 1954 by Jean-Jacques Guerlain, consists today of 75 houses of French luxury, each with different histories, cultures, sizes, and management. However, they share common governance rules and are willing to co-promote their values and know-how. The term "houses," as opposed to the luxury company members of the Comité Colbert, illustrates their respective stories and the transmission of their know-how from one generation to another, which retains the secrets of their creations. Indeed, most of the members of familial business, and the family CEOs of the Comité Colbert, call each other "*chef de maison*" and not chairman or CEO. Thus, the span of control and decision making by definition is with the *chef de maison*, who renders complete autonomy to the brand. For example, the House of

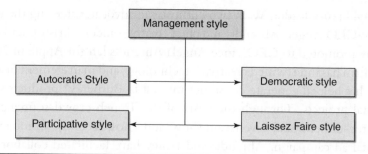

	Management Style	Pros	Cons		
	Autocratic	Instruction is forceful Facilitates fast decision No unexpected side track due to lack of communication among staff New policies/changes can be implemented swiftly	Staff feel de-motivated as they are not consulted Do not favor innovative ideas from staff as they will not be considered anyway Lack of discussion has a negative impact on team work Wait for instruction thus causing delays No initiative from team members		
	Democratic	Encourages group decision Everyone can voice their opinion Opinion from staff considered important and value adding Reduce implementation conflicts	Decision made may not be the best for the company Time consuming Conflict among support and non-support group Staff may not have enough knowledge about the decision		
	Participative	Boosts staff morale Idea generation Networking among team Friendly Reduce implementation conflicts	Time consuming Staff feel offended if their ideas are not implemented Sometimes consultation may look artificial and not genuine if idea is not implemented		
	Laissez Faire	Maximum delegation Manger can devote more time to strategy formulation Learning and knowledge-creating atmosphere Seen as empowering staff May create synergies between different subsidiaries	Less control Trust might be hampered Overall goal might not be achieved Time consuming in some emergent situations		

Figure 7.2 Differences in Management Styles

Lanvin was founded by Jeanne Lanvin in 1889. Bernard Lanvin, the grandnephew of the founder of the couture house, is today head of the fragrance division and always refused to give up control of the couture, ready-to-wear, and fragrance businesses. Similarly, Pierre Frey founded the manufacturing house in 1935, and 75 years later the company is still 100 percent family-owned with Patrick Frey as head of the house since 1978, and has managed to keep control and expand internationally.

It is observed that there are three types of luxury companies that exist today. The first ones are the luxury houses that were built by several successive family generations. These are still run by the descendants of the founders like Estée Lauder and Hermès. The second type is those houses acquired by rich families from their founders at the very beginning that still remain with those acquiring families, such as Chanel (with the Wertheimer family) and Guerlain (owned by LVMH Group). The third category is those conglomerates that have built a portfolio of luxury brands within their own structures focusing on specific luxury sectors. In general, it was observed that family companies were more often profitable than listed financial groups, and survive well, at least while the family has the ability and will to manage the house. One reason might be the style and principle of management, as they care more about people, the relationship with their employees and their customers, and the value and the image of the name (which as previously discussed is often their own name), rather than profits. Moreover since they are not listed companies, they are not bound to reveal their financial figures or development strategies. This freedom results in minimal distraction in implementing their consistent strategy while maintaining control over the brand. This in turn allows them to emphasize and focus on long-term positioning rather than short-term quarter-wise profit motivation.

Resisting the Financial and Stakeholder Pressure

Some families have managed to maintain their independence, such as the Hermès family, the Wertheimer family (Chanel), the Frey family (Pierre Frey) and the Tribouillard family (Leonard Fashion) and many others in France and in Italy. Each of these families has created profitable business models that encircle powerful and independent brands, with minor debt and fixed expenses. For instance, Hermès has been very successful. They attained a double-digit operating profitability of around 32 percent in 2013 that was the group's best performance ever recorded since its partial introduction in the stock market in 1993. Then-president Patrick Thomas declared that "These results reflect the quality of our company business model and the efficiency of the employees who are implementing it."

Hermès owned around 20 stores in China, with an annual expansion rate of two to four stores. Hermès never borrowed from the bank, but disposed of a large treasury of cash, allowing them to manage to finance shops and projects. Having increased its financing power by 42.5 percent in conjunction with the rationalization of the working capital requirements, the net treasury of the group had increased. In 2013, Hermès pursued its investments in the development of its distribution network. It opened in 2014 a Maisons Hermès in Shanghai and stores in Thailand, Malaysia, and Korea.

Hermès, along with Prada, is the most profitable company in the world of luxury. This is why there is no potential synergy with any other player in the industry. It is also why Hermès does not need anyone to support its capital structure. Due to unprecedented success of Hermès, both at home and in international markets, it has long being the target of the LVMH Group. The Group for years was purchasing bonds and stocks on the financial market. This aggressive entry of LVMH into the capital structure of Hermès brought nothing positive to Hermès. Still LVMH, increased its stake in Hermès to more than 20 percent. This is the reason the family members fought back by creating a controlling family holding for more than 50 percent of the share capital within the group. Their reaction sent a clear signal that they would do anything in their power to block a possible takeover by the conglomerate. "Hermès is not managed on financial principles," said Patrick Thomas, the first nonfamily CEO, "it is managed on the principle of the artefact in the best possible finish with the finest raw materials, with creativity as strong as possible that make people come into our stores and the strong assertion of the Hermès style." He continued to state that "All these features have nothing to do with a group that is much younger, and which is essentially a financial strategy group. And if you give economic control to financiers, they will kill the economy because they want short-term results. Finance should be a means to develop the economy but not the objective of the economy." The message was well understood. Axel Dumas and Bernard Arnault agreed to a peace agreement in September 2014. According to the agreement, LVMH will keep only 8.5 percent of Hermès shares, and the Hermès family will now control directly about 70 percent of the shares. This is a victory for Hermès and also a fantastic deal for LVMH, which in the process made a profit of over €3 billion.

Similarly other families have succeeded and managed to stand up for their independence. Each of these families has created profitable business models that encircle powerful and independent brands, with negligible debt and fixed expenses, which has allowed them to be independent and in full control.

Leonard, a French house created in 1958 by Daniel Tribouillard, had a geographical expansion strategy, and thus in 2013 it was more famous in Japan than in France. The simplistic design of an "orchid on silk," which has been the signature symbol of his brand since the 1970s (when the first shop was opened in Paris) is famous there. It all began in 1958 when Daniel Tribouillard developed his idea into reality and made the brand name famous for its fully fashioned printed pullovers. Rapidly, he was known as "the man behind the flowers." He remains the proprietor of the company and refuses to sell to a big group. In Asia, printed patterns are still highly fashionable, and the public is in awe of Leonard's creations. From design to canvas to garment, the Leonard creation process stands out as unique in the world of Parisian couture. Despite past achievements, the future lies in the preservation of identity. It remains one of the last French family businesses in the ready-to-wear sector. Strong bonds between the French house and Japan have grown during the hundreds of trips made by Daniel Tribouillard and Nathalie, his daughter, to Asia. Today, 80 percent of the sales of Leonard are generated abroad, of which 60 percent are in Asia. In addition, many licenses have been granted in Japan. It is evident that the brand is turning its strategy toward Asia; however, it remains rooted in France, which has pros and cons. Nathalie Tribouillard, managing director of the company commented that: "France remains the reference in terms of creation and quality, but if the government doesn't make efforts to reduce the charges that bear upon enterprises, we risk to be no longer competitive." This was true in 2013 when companies found themselves in a difficult situation with a permanent change in government fiscal policy.

Conglomerate: Strategic Mix of Independence

However, in the process of globalization, family-owned luxury houses find it more and more difficult to fund the necessary expansion and communication for their brands. This is where the big conglomerates have entered the picture.

Three conglomerates—LVMH, Paris-based Kering, and Switzerland's Richemont—have doubled their combined share of the global luxury market over the past decade. In 2013, they posted a total of $45 billion in sales out of the $234 billion that Bain & Co. estimates was spent on luxury goods worldwide.[5]

As discussed earlier, these groups are considered to be multibrand or multiproduct players. They operate on a large-scale with turnover figures usually over €3 billion. These groups, such as LVMH, Kering, Richemont, and Swatch Group, have reached a high level of diversification compared to their smaller competitors.

Examples of Styles

Houses from different countries can generally be said to have their own approach in management styles.

The French

France is luxury.

Louis Vuitton, Chanel, Hermès, Saint Laurent, Cartier, Christian Dior, Baccarat…these, together with others, are recognized brand names, all of which are French.

The French are on a parade. High fashion is like a flag waving in the wind, announcing perfumes, clothing, wines and spirits, hotels, accessories, shoes, bags, and so forth. Televisions relay the message, images enchant, and French luxury is present.

---

[5]Matlack, 2011, 79–83.

A number of brand names come to mind as representing top luxury—Chloé, Sonia Rykiel, Lanvin, Longchamp, Agnès B., Leonard, Bernardaud, Bonpoint, Givenchy—constituting a French armada. The Americans counterattack with Tiffany & Co., Ralph Lauren, Donna Karan, and Calvin Klein, while the English do their part with Dunhill, Burberry, and Paul Smith. Even the Germans won't be left out of the luxury market, taking up the rear with Escada, Hugo Boss, Jil Sander, and others.

The Belgians innovate with Martin Margiela, Dries Van Noten, and Ann Demeulemeester in the lead.

With so much at stake, the entire world wants a piece of the luxury pie.

But France still leads with 50 percent of the world market.

The jewelry market has been the subject of a bitter fight. Entering into the fray are Cartier, Tiffany & Co., Harry Winston, Van Cleef & Arpels, Bulgari, Boucheron, Fred, Chopard, H. Stern, and others. Here again, the French have a top-rank position.

In watches, France, thanks to LVMH, is regaining strength against the Swiss, who dominate with Rolex, Omega, Jaeger-LeCoultre, Baume et Mercier, Breitling, Patek Philippe, Audemars Piguet, Breguet, Vacheron Constantin, Girard-Perregaux, and Blancpain, among others.

France is in the lead in the luxury market thanks to Louis Vuitton, Hermès, Hennessy, Cartier, Moët et Chandon, Chanel, Christian Dior, Rémy Martin, and Lacoste, who together dominate the luxury business world in terms of sales. Their ranks are joined by the major French hotels and conquistadors of cuisine, such as Alain Ducasse and others.

It's wise to benefit from, invest in, act, and take shelter behind the red, white, and blue umbrella that naturally promotes the international development of French luxury companies.

LVMH: Bernard Arnault   Bernard Arnault says he is deeply involved in the creative process, far more than his peers. He believes that in the creative and highly seasonal fashion business, the ability to match effective CEOs with temperamental designers can make the difference between a star and a failure. He believes that "to have the right DNA in a team is very rare. It's almost like a miracle." Deemed the "Billionaire Matchmaker," in the past 20 years, he has formed close creative bonds with designers and managers. He was always at the helm of the decision making during final key appointments. His vision of the luxury and fashion industry as he states it is: "This link to creativity, it's not far from art, and I like it very much. You must like to be with designers and creators. You have to like an image. That's also a key to success. And at the same time, you must be able to organize a business worldwide."

The key to success can also be the ability to build a "dream team" with a strong collaboration between the CEO and the creative director. In this case, the manager has to create a nonconventional style of management. He needs to give autonomy to the creative director and be able to deal with paradox, contradictions, and uncertainty.

> *Artists must be completely unfettered by financial and commercial concerns to do their best work. You don't "manage" John Galliano, just as no one could have "managed" Leonardo da Vinci or Frank Lloyd Wright.*
>
> **—Bernard Arnault**

In almost all its acquisitions, LVMH maintained the creative talent as an independent pool without attempting to generate synergies across product lines or brands. Lately, though, the sourcing has slowly been centralized to gain synergies and cost savings with a centralized purchasing mechanism.

Arnault's secret was to "remain deeply involved in the creative process, far more than his peers ... convinced that the ability to match effective executives with temperamental designers can make the difference between a star and a failure in the luxury goods business." The article quotes Arnault as saying that "If you think and act like a typical manager around creative people—with rules, policies, data on customer preferences and so forth—you will quickly kill their talents."

For example, Bernard Arnault does not believe in managerial limit setting. In 2000, Galliano sent models down the haute couture runways wearing dresses made of newspaper. To block the plan would have crushed the designer's spirit. When Dior manufactured the dresses in news-type printed fabric, they sold out immediately. It was a huge success for Dior.

Therefore, one can deduce that the management style of a luxury CEO is significantly different from any other market. They must work within both the business environment and the artistic world, where the typical personalities encountered are polar opposites of each other.

Arnault believes that innovation is the primary factor of importance for growth and profitability. "Our whole business is based on giving our artists and designers complete freedom to invent without limits." This suggests that human resources and management are critical as the company tries to build a work environment that promotes creativity as well as adherence to strict business discipline. However, it is the vast range of disparate and diverse brands that causes the problem for coherence.

Another concern is the ruthless pursuit toward the bottom line. LVMH believes in running businesses profitably. Managers are supported as long as they make money over the stipulated minimum. "You have the freedom as long as you exceed your targets. Once you do not ... there is no freedom anymore." For example, LVMH acquired the old French brand Céline in 1988. But for years it did not do much with it. In 2008, Arnault found Phoebe Philo, who was the former creative director of Chloé. He instantly believed Philo to be the perfect match for Céline. He gave his full support and freedom, as always, to the new Chief Creative Officer. In the following two years he erased all the old collections, closed the unperforming stores, refurbished the main stores and moved the headquarters to London. With substantial investments and losses for two years, Phoebe Philo proved her talents and rejuvenated the house, which has now become one of the most profitable and desirable brands in the luxury world.

However, industry insiders cite that all is not well with a financial man like Bernard Arnault at the helm. His management style has been described as providing "constrained freedom" The emphasis is on profit, and if any division or company did not deliver, it would promptly be sold off. This approach contrasts with the traditional and creative view of haute couture, which although it loses money on different sets of collections, waits for the market to accept its designs over a period of time.

The group's leadership has been sustained by new product launches, store openings, and increased investment in communications, but the key to its success rests with Bernard Arnault himself and his personal view of what makes an appropriate management style in this industry. In 2010–2011 and in 2011–2012, LVMH grew with remarkable speed, breaking previous records, which Arnault attributes in part to the long-term strategy "pursued, unchanged, throughout the economic crisis."[6] In his 2011 letter to the shareholders, he speaks of the wide range of brands that are strengthened and respected by the LVMH group and states that each "builds its own future on its own culture and its historic know-how ... we give them all the nurturing and support they need for long term development."

Hermès: Jean-Louis Dumas

> *Be natural, say what you want to.*
>
> **—Jean Louis Dumas**
>
> *He helped a lot of people to bloom.*
>
> **—Pascale Mussard (niece of Jean Louis Dumas)**

Jean-Louis Dumas within Hermès was an icon in his own right in the luxury world. Some consider him a legend. He assumed the leadership of Hermès in 1978, at a low point in the company's fortunes. In his nearly 30 years as the company's chief executive, he transformed it into one of the world's most successful luxury brands. Jean Louis Dumas was both a business-oriented CEO and an artistic director. He was a very atypical leader who cultivated his garden with creative talents and exceptional know-how. He was a visionary, guided by the love of people, of beauty, of travel and culture. He made Hermès much more than a "luxury" brand. In fact, Jean-Louis never used the word luxury. He created a "maison" of talents, excellence, craftsmanship, and creativity, and he achieved a goal that he didn't even have: he made Hermès the most luxurious brand in the world—some people say that it may be the "only one left."

> *We've got to remain true to ourselves, but we've got to change constantly. And it's that tension which is at the heart of Hermès. You have to make a reaction. You have to surprise. You have to astonish yourself. Be always on a wire, a thread.*
>
> **—Jean Louis Dumas**

---

[6]LVMH Letter to Shareholders, 2011.

With a free, sometimes audacious hand, he shook things up by hiring exciting new designers, extending the company's lines, and creating iconic products such as the Birkin bag, inspired by the actress and singer Jane Birkin, and expanding internationally and taking the business into new markets such as China. He also invested in companies like the glassware maker Saint-Louis, the tableware company Puiforcat and the fashion house of Jean Paul Gaultier. In 2003, Dumas again surprised the industry, this time[7] by hiring Jean Paul Gaultier as creative director.

I would love to work on it. It's a house that allows for great creative freedom with no limits.

—Jean Paul Gaultier

Jean-Louis Dumas's style was different from the rest. Frederic Mitterrand, the French Minister of Culture described him as follows: "Jean-Louis Dumas was an extraordinary man whose charisma was entirely devoted to creation and excellence. His name, his person, and his humor, remain inseparable from the famous maison—Hermès. Man of taste and culture, passionate for drawing, he knew how to treat the designers with the kindness and respect they deserved. He did not hesitate to make bold decisions, as when he invited Jean Paul Gaultier to reinvent ready-to-wear at Hermès. He devoted his whole life to serving this great house and French creation, which he has succeeded in renewing the codes and traditions with an endless imagination and vision."

At Hermès, the management style was clear. No member of the family got a position unless he or she deserved it. If an outsider was better qualified, he or she would get the job. When Jean Louis Dumas promoted his niece Pascale Mussard into advertising and public relations, she was at first surprised, as she was shy and wasn't sure she would fit the job. He told her, "be natural, say what you want to." He believed in her. "He helped a lot of people to bloom," she said.

During Jean-Louis Dumas's time, Hermès's core business strategy was to produce products that were of unrivalled quality using traditional craftsmanship and the finest quality natural materials such as leather and

---

[7] After he had hired Martin Margiela.

silk. The house had built its success over time with an excellence and authenticity of expertise in craftsmanship and prided itself on core values of elegance, timelessness, and quality creations. The Hermès strategy was to continually expand and innovate its product range while at the same time staying true to its roots and continuing to produce timeless creations. Some legendary models have never gone out of style and are still produced today, such as the iconic Kelly Bag and silk scarves.

A key management style was to maintain extremely high levels of in-house production and treat people extremely well. Hermès produced more than two-thirds of its products in house with manufacturing operations that encompass more than 30 production units spread across France and one each in Great Britain, Italy, Switzerland, and the United States. To keep up with demand, the group further expanded production capacity over the years. In 2015, it plans to open several more plants in France.

Another key management style was to retain tight control over outsourced production, carrying out targeted audits to ascertain that its suppliers operations meet the group's expectations. In some cases, the company buys into carefully selected companies to ensure the stability of these relationships. Hermès maintained its long-term strategy of maintaining control over its know-how and distribution network. The group continued to invest in projects to expand production capacity in its different sectors. As an "outside" successor of Jean-Louis Dumas, Patrick Thomas followed Jean-Louis Dumas' style and succeeded extremely well in pushing sales and profitability to a level that was never achieved before. Pierre-Alexis Dumas, the son of Jean-Louis Dumas; Guillaume de Seynes, another nephew of Jean-Louis; and Henri-Louis Bauer, a cousin, took over as the new management team in 2014, under the leadership of Axel Dumas as the CEO of Hermès.

Hermès' business style has a dual focus of accentuating the house's unique position as the ultimate in quality and craftsmanship while at the same time focusing on business growth. Hermès' core business strategy was to have "full control of the value chain, own stores, no licenses, no delocalization of production, worship of the product, products partly handmade, importance of creation, capitalization on heritage and history."[8]

---

[8]Kapferer and Tabatoni, 2010, 17.

The family "dream team" was fully dedicated to pursue this strategy in the future.

The Swiss

The Swiss are known for their watches. The Baselworld is the place to be. In 2014, the watch trade show in Basel in Switzerland attracted more than 150,000 visitors and 1,400 exhibitors from 40 countries, and generated about $2.8 billion in revenue. It all started in 1917 when a handful of Swiss watchmakers collaborated to organize an exhibition to show the world the delicate craft of watchmaking and promote the value of "Made in Switzerland." The heavyweight independents were Rolex, Patek Philippe, and Audemars Piguet. The rest were part of multibrand conglomerates, such as TAG Heuer of LVMH Group, the watch brands such as IWC, Jaeger-LeCoultre, Officine Panerai, and Vacheron Constantin of the Richemont Group and Breguet, Harry Winston, Blancpain, and Omega, among others of the Swatch Group.

The Swatch Group Ltd., hailing from Switzerland, is the number one manufacturer of finished watches in the world. The Group not only manufactures finished watches but also is in the business of producing jewelry, watch movements, and watch components. The journey of Swatch Group started in 1983, when the first Swatch watches were released. The following years have seen the recovery of the Swiss watchmaking industry as a whole, and the establishment of The Swatch Group as a strong, diversified industrial holding, a leader in the watch business that is based out of Switzerland. The watch industry is Switzerland's third largest exporter after the machine and the chemical industry. Switzerland harbors the retail operations of most of the world's most sought-after brands, often found concentrated on Zurich's Bahnhofstrasse and Geneva's "luxury mile," the rue du Rhône.

Richemont: Johann Rupert

Richemont has weathered the economic crisis to date and is in a strong financial position. There will still be plenty of challenges ahead but we are confident that Richemont's Maisons will surmount them.

—Johann Rupert, CEO

Rupert described his management style as "hands off" and depicts how he often adopted a disguise to check up on some of the group's boutiques. He is quoted as saying "I don't need to worry about operational issues. I know I can trust my colleagues to do that. I'm no longer involved in supply-chain management, the IT infrastructure or even, come to that, the financial disciplines. We have the people to do all that. Don't postpone until tomorrow what you can delegate today."[9]

Admittedly, it was more of a holding of a group of individual companies. "Years ago, I determined that we would vertically integrate to the fullest extent. Although that was not the most popular, or financially lucrative, choice, I made sure every brand had its own manufacturing and structure. Each could be autonomous." It is interesting that this approach worked so well in this case, while LVMH has been known to experience problems trying to follow this model. Perhaps the answer lay in the fact that the Richemont brand range was much smaller and much more interrelated. In addition, despite the autonomy, synergies still existed behind the scenes. Rupert introduced structural changes early on, so that each of his brands, known as "maisons," could enjoy independence over their products, strategies, and communications. The model has been copied by rivals, notably LVMH, but remains conspicuously distant from more autocratic styles of competitors such as Swatch Group and other groups that focus on a founding father, such as Georgio Armani.

Brand control in Richemont rested in the hands of the strategic product and communications committee, which is "the ultimate brand guardian. We have a very collegiate style, and people with immense experience, going back years. We are Richemont's institutional memory."

Rupert is a man of frankness, which seems typical of his affable style. He has earned respect around the world as a great business figure, who hints at a certain personal distance from luxury goods and the social circles that surround the industry. "In an industry characterized by high-profile leaders, Johann Rupert stands out as an exception. Unlike Bernard Arnault, chairman and chief executive of LVMH, or the father-and-son teams at Kering and Swatch Group, the Richemont boss is content—even determined—to remain out of sight. Richemont holds no news conferences and Mr. Rupert gives few interviews."

---

[9]Simonian, 2007.

The group keeps to the background in favor of its brands. "I even discourage my colleagues from getting into the papers too often. I'm against this trend of turning businessmen into cult figures," he says. Rupert's vision is clear: "All we're trying to do is keep the products and the message consistent. If we do that right, the numbers will come out right, too."[10]

Rolex: Hans Wilsdorf   Rolex is a private foundation. It has benefited from a remarkable stability since its beginning and an unparalleled consistency of purpose of its founder. It has five CEOs in its century-year old history. The private nature of the foundation has enabled the company to control and innovate. Each of its leaders in turn has made bold moves, embraced progress, and broken with tradition when necessary to ensure the success of the company. Rolex never lost its focus. It has only three values linked to its DNA: timelessness, sports and adventure, and reliability. Its strategy revolves around these three words. It has no brand extensions. It has only watches and only five models—Daytona, Submariner, Sea Dweller, Yacht-Master, Milgauss (with date-just, day-date, or date).

Hans Wilsdorf, the founder, started the company in 1905 and envisioned the wristwatch in an era of pocket watches. He was fascinated with watches and obsessed with creating movements small enough to be worn on the wrist, at a time when men's fashion favored large-face pocket watches. With a visionary spirit, he detected that a reliable and accurate wristwatch could change the overall market.

After Hans Wilsdorf, Rolex engaged in almost half a century of leadership under the Heiniger family. André Heiniger became managing director in 1962, two years after Wilsdorf died. He was a true commercial strategist, moved by inspiration and enthusiasm, always keeping his profile low. Like Hans Wildorf, he had a strong sense of anticipation and was continuously pursuing perfection. André Heiniger was one of the greatest visionaries of contemporary watchmaking. One important decision, for instance, was to remain faithful to the mechanical watch. He also gave rise to partnerships with sports events and personalities of world

---

[10]Simonian, 2007.

renown. Upon André Heiniger's leadership, philanthropy efforts were developed and the Rolex Award for Enterprise was created to honor and support pioneering individuals whose projects have brought major benefits to their communities and beyond. Under André Heiniger's leadership, Rolex experienced years of expansion. He brought the company to the next level, defined its marketing vision, and contributed to increasing the brand's recognition, paving the way for the next chapter in the history of the company.

In 1992, Patrick Heiniger, his son, succeeded him. He was focused on strengthening the defense of the brand worldwide and, most important, he was responsible for the fundamental strategic choice of vertical integration of Rolex's means of production, guaranteeing control over the manufacture of the essential components of the brand's watches and thus ensuring its autonomy. He was responsible for increasing quality and productivity within the company.

Patrick Heiniger left the company in 2008, but remained as an advisor. He was succeeded by Bruno Meier. This was the first time the company was not run by either Wilsdorf or a member of the Heiniger family. Well aware of the challenges arising from globalization, he steered a careful course between the legacy of the past and the demands of a constantly changing world to allow Rolex to build on its success. Under his leadership, Rolex continues to optimize its industrial and commercial structure to heighten its passion for innovation and perfection.

The Italians

Despite arriving in the world of ready-to-wear after the French, the Italians have the strongest worldwide sales in this segment. The advantages they have over the French are those of novelty, diversity, and reach. A point to be noted about the Italian brands is that they mostly started out with accessories: the beginning of great designers was in Gucci handbags, Fendi fur, and Prada shoes. However, they slowly increased their reach to include ready-to-wear collections, which became an instant hit with the ladies. Despite never having promoted *haute couture* (which is a very French concept), these Italian brands were never afraid to hit Paris fashion week with their latest collections.

The Milan fashion show. You have to be there.

Along with the French, the Italians are the kings of world luxury. They are everywhere in fashion—clothing, wines, and hotels—everywhere you go! Italy has numerous luxury brand names: Armani, Prada, Furla, Gucci, Bulgari, Versace, Moncler, Ferragamo ... but the country that comes to mind throughout the world when luxury is mentioned is France.

Armani has built a luxury empire encompassing everything from sunglasses to haute couture and luxury hotels. Armani even makes television sets, fountain pens, jewelery and all sorts of accessories that look like a disorganized ensemble "à la Cardin," in true Italian style, packed with charm, and as always, rather successful, too. On planet luxury, Armani pops up at every street corner, in one disguise or another, under his own trade name or that of one spinoff or another: Emporio, Armani Casa, Marni, Armani Collezioni, Armani hotels ... So what will be the next Armani venture? And what does the future hold for the Armani group?

Now that Gianfranco Ferré is dead, Valentino is standing aloof. Versace has been through tragic rough patches, but the family still knows the ropes ...

Tod's is the one that has beaten them all to the post, its founding president Diego Della Valle being a darling of the media. Tod's is a planetary success story, an Italian symbol of luxury and creativity positioned in the best places, a conquering and innovative spirit.

Luxottica, the discreet maker of Rayban sunglasses, also makes eyewear for Chanel, Versace, Prada, Bulgari, Tiffany, Dolce & Gabbana, Paul Smith, Ferragamo, and others. With more than 60,000 employees, it produces more than 40 million pairs of eyeglasses on three continents. And the world's No. 1 eyewear maker is the Del Vecchio, another Italian luxury family business, with sales of over €7 billion.

The list of the Italian luxury players goes on forever, featuring Armani, Moncler, Prada, Gucci, Dolce & Gabbana, Pucci, Versace, Zanotti, Valentino, Furla, Fendi, Bulgari, Ferragamo, Cavalli, and Rossi, not to mention Ferrari and all the others ...

Italy is the kingdom of design, and Torino is the capital. The Italians often group their export operations with those of the rest of the family, but will they find a way to join up like the French, creating large groups in order to brace themselves against the competition of tomorrow, or will they wither away when their founding fathers die?

The French believe that the Italians view LVMH or Kering with envy and are forced to admit that they have never been able to create one almighty, all-encompassing luxury conglomerate. The timing would be perfect now that so many questions arise about the future of family-run businesses left to their own devices through lack of planning for their succession. Will Armani, Ferragamo, Versace, Prada, among others, find a solution for the future, or will they crumble under the pressure of family quarrels and poor succession planning?

Where succession is concerned, Italian luxury is still in the ice age compared with its French counterpart, having failed to plan ahead. As a result, some superb talents have already passed over to the French side, led by LVMH or Kering such as Gucci or Pucci, and other may follow suit! Will the Italians know how to preserve their luxury houses, or will French luxury become Franco-Italian? This may turn out to be the best option, because the great Italian brand names will no doubt prefer to fly the French colors if they survive. We can all live with that. In the end, Europe is here to stay at the helm of world luxury for many years to come, and within Europe, the Franco-Italian pair is way ahead of its time.

Armani: Giorgio Armani

When people stop to ask me for an autograph, what I hear most often is, Mr. Armani, you make beautiful things, but I like you so much as a person. You are so nice, so real. That's my reward. Being famous very often means sacrificing your privacy and that of others. I have never compromised. I learned to get where I am by work, I learned slowly. I wasn't certain of succeeding. I am trying to optimize my ability, which still seems very acute to me, to manage this empire as if I were immortal—for now, I should add.

—Giorgio Armani

Giorgio Armani sees himself as a talented designer, an idol, someone famous, a celebrity. He is the type of leader who likes to have control of every detail. He created his company from scratch, building it up into a successful empire with a lot of hard work and a hands-on attitude. It is all about him, and he manages his empire as if he were immortal. He oversees every aspect of the business and makes all the decisions. Giorgio Armani was a pioneer in terms of making luxury affordable a long time before the concept of "masstige" came up in the marketing arena. As early as 1979, he launched Armani Collezioni, first in the United States, then a year later in the rest of the world as a diffusion line. But even more innovative was his vision in 1981 to create the world of Emporio Armani, a brand that he decided to create as valuable and strong as Giorgio Armani but more affordable and also more creative and fashionable, with one concept in mind: to make fashion affordable for the masses. This was still quite revolutionary at the time for a brand that remained luxury positioned, as Emporio Armani distribution was and still is restricted to free-standing stores and shops in prestigious department stores. One of the key ingredients to success was the passion, professionalism, and consistency brought by Giorgio Armani and his team of designers in the development of all the collections from Giorgio Armani to Emporio Amani, from Armani Collezioni to Armani Jeans. Mr. Armani has always controlled every detail of every collection. For him, whether the product was Giorgio Armani or Armani Jeans, a suit or a pair of jeans, did not make a difference: He wanted to check and control every product with the same attention before giving his final approval. This level of control has been essential in maintaining the consistency of the brand identity with so many brands created, so many product extensions, and so many partners involved.

> *There is no doubt that there are difficult years for the fashion and luxury market. Nevertheless, the good results achieved by the Armani Group consistently bear witness once again to the strength of our brand and confirm the solidity of our successful business model. We continue to believe in our vision, our goals, and our strategic choices, and this belief encourages us to maintain a long-term view in any initiative we undertake.*

—Giorgio Armani

Gucci: Domenico de Sole and Tom Ford   Domenico de Sole and Tom Ford formed a very famous dream team—the "Dom-Tom" power duo. They conceived the turnaround of Gucci from a suffering leather goods company into one of the world's hottest luxury goods company.

One important aspect of this dream team was that they had mutual respect and total trust in each other. Domenico de Sole recognized that Tom was a creative genius and gave him freedom to work in his field, while Tom recognized Dom's management skills and abilities as the company's CEO. "Our [Tom Ford and Domenico de Sole's] mutual respect for each other and total trust in each other's abilities has been key to our success," stated Tom Ford.

After Domenico de Sole and Tom Ford's teamwork, Gucci was in the hands of another good team—Patrizio Di Marco and Frida Giannini. "I don't have to tell Frida to do anything other than to be herself. She's made beautiful products from the beginning." said Patrizio Di Marco. Di Marco was also very successful in turning around Bottega Veneta, giving full creative freedom to Thomas Meier, a former employee of Hermès. The team, creative director Frida Giannini and her partner at home and at work, Patrizio di Marco left Gucci left in early 2015 as Gucci's designs of floral bags and its double-G logo became too popular to retain the exclusive cachet their price tags demand.

Prada: Patrizio Bertelli and Miuccia Prada   Prada, the Italian family-owned brand, has long been known for its intense management by its owners, Patrizio Bertelli and Miuccia Prada. The Bertelli–Prada partnership is the heart of a firm that has thrived for the past quarter century as a distinctly family-run enterprise. Bertelli, Prada, and her siblings own close to 95 percent of the company. Bertelli and Prada serve as chief executive officer and chairman, respectively. Bartelli brings the same intensity to the business side of the brand as she does to the creative. Past and present executives describe him as an indefatigable and charismatic boss with an intimate knowledge of the company, from the stitching of shoe seams to the color of the walls in Prada boutiques. He has the last word on everything from hiring to how many precious skins to order for a line of handbags. When a top manager leaves—and several have after clashing with the boss—Bertelli often takes over the position in an interim capacity. Executives are loath to make decisions without his approval, and few dare to contradict him. "It's the law of the jungle," says Gian Giacomo Ferraris, chief executive of Versace, who worked at the Prada group earlier this decade. "He expects a lot from himself, and therefore from others. Either you play at his level, or he writes you off." One example could prove Bertelli's autocracy and bad temper. When he was overseeing the decor of a new Miu Miu store in Manhattan in 1997, he did not like a mirror and smashed it simply because he thought the mirror made people look fat. Bartelli loves his autocratic style and his total control over the creative designers. He believes in the crucial points that the creative and commercial needs of the brand have to be on equal footing for the company to be a true success. Thus, designers have to make consensus between their creative thinking and the demands imposed on them by the managers. Clashes between the creative and business sides have led to legendary bust-ups, and resulted in the German designer Jil Sander's acrimonious exit from her eponymous firm when Prada bought it in 1999.

As the decision maker of the company, the Bertelli-Prada duo is so important to the business that when the company was preparing a stock-market listing, banking advisers laid out as a "risk factor" for investors any eventuality that the two might decide not to work together anymore. According to the brand's COO Sebastian Suhl, "They are not managers, they are owners and entrepreneurs, and they are the brand!"

Coach: Lew Frankfort and Reed Krakoff

> Before [Lew Frankfort] acted, he began to formulate a plan. He likes to have a vision and a sense of where he's going. That way he can communicate his expectations to his staff and others.
>
> **—Marilyn Much, journalist at Investor**

Lew Frankfort has been with Coach since 1979. He stepped down in 2014. He brought Coach from a $19 million company to a $3.6 billion international group. What vision did he have for the brand?

> I realized that we were plateauing. I recognized that I needed first to transform myself from believing that Coach could continue to be successful as a house of American leather goods, to believing that it [. . .could] evolve into a modern American lifestyle accessories brand. At the same time I knew I had to persuade consumers to embrace the changes at Coach.
>
> **—Lew Frankfort**

He decided to recruit Reed Krakoff as president and creative director of Coach, who introduced accessories and new products to the stores monthly instead of semiannually, and he increased the profitability of the company by supplying in Asia.

They're [Lew Frankfort and Reed Krakoff] an excellent balance for each other, which is critical. One is strong operationally; one is a strong creative force. It's rare to find that combination.

—David Lamer, analyst with Ferris Baker Watts

They balance each other and acknowledge their individual strengths, with Lew Frankfort focusing more on the operational aspects and Reed Krakoff on the creative side of the business. They see each other as partners and have a very open and frank relationship, saying exactly what is on their minds, and thus setting a good example for the rest of the company. The trust factor also plays an important role.

We are partners in running the company .... We tell each other exactly what's on our minds, and that sets a good example for the rest of the company. Usually we don't even have to debate, but if we were to have a debate about an issue, we trust each other. Not only do you need to know your business and your customers, you need to understand the pulse points of your business, you also need to be nimble to adapt. I strongly believe in situational leadership—modifying my leadership style to fit the skill set and experience level of the person I'm working with—to appropriately "tell, sell, collaborate, or delegate" the project at hand. I am driven in part by a blend of striving for excellence and a fear of failure.

—Lew Frankfort

The leadership of Lew Frankfort has become legendary in the luxury world. His vision, planning, sense of the future, communication, and methods of managing the expectations of his staff and others led Krakoff to comment "the key to Lew's success as a dynamic and inspirational leader is in his ability to orchestrate a decision-making process that is both inclusive and incisive."

Lew Frankfort is a humble leader who is not afraid to admit when he has made mistakes. And he is proud of that fact. To him, the best managers are those who have experienced both success and failure. He considers every mistake he has made as a true learning experience, and he is always striving for excellence. He also adapts his leadership style to fit the person with whom he is working.

> *I'm flexible. I don't fall in love with my designs . . . . I'd rather not have an "It" bag; I'm very humble about our business. If no one says anything about [the prospective bags I am walking around the office with], I know they're probably not great. But if I walk by the catalogue people and [they] say "Oh my god, when is that coming out?", then you know you have something. It's a handbag; it's not your taxes. It has to be emotional.*
>
> **—Reed Krakoff**

Coach is a consumer-centric brand. CRM has played a major role in Coach's success. It's not that easy for a designer to set his ego aside and rely as much on consumer research as on his own creativity. In order to constantly innovate, Reed Krakoff had to be humble, focus on the business, and be creative at the same time.

Analysis

What is perhaps even more indicative of a good management style, however diverse, is that the companies discussed—LVMH, Hermès, Richemont, Rolex, Armani, Gucci, Prada, Coach—increased their revenue from 2010–2014, indicating a strong ability to recover from the global financial crisis.

The company that stands out the most in regards to this is Hermès, followed by Prada and the rest of the brands. Hermès was the only company to increase revenues consistently for the whole Group from 2008 to 2014. After completing the finest years in Hermès history in terms of development and profitability, it is worth reflecting on the key attributes that drove such a result.

Another identified criterion to the successful management of a luxury brand is brand identity, as it is vital to both the immediate and sustained success of a luxury brand today. Each company analyzed has a strong brand identity. They all understand the importance of heritage and authenticity, and place paramount emphasis on product and service quality, as well as on creativity and innovation. Each recognizes the importance of having a strong brand positioning and an excellent brand image and presence worldwide. However, it is worth evaluating to what extent each individual company is able to achieve this.

The family-owned companies have been able to develop over time at their own pace. After 170 years, it is rare to see a company still guided by the very essence of its beginnings, and to see the founding family still retaining the largest shareholding block and responsible for shaping the philosophy and performance of the business. Hermès' focus is on value rather than volume. They have a commitment to their craftsmen, allowing them large amounts of freedom so as to encourage as much innovation and creativity of their métiers as possible. The link to their heritage and equestrian theme has always and will always be there. Yet it is constantly being evolved and mixed with an element of surprise. Hermès creates innovative new products while maintaining existing favorites and bestsellers. Their motto "Everything changes. Nothing changes." perfectly embodies the essence of the brand. Hermès took things slowly and gave time for its dream to flourish and spread, a path it was only able to take due to being a family-owned company. It was this elongated process of brand-building, production, marketing, and selling that has resulted in the timeless aura that characterizes the brand.

Prada also was able to take the time it needed to evolve as a brand at its own speed. Mario and his brother ran the company at their pace until Mario's daughter, Luisa Prada, took the helm. Muccia Prada joined the company and eventually took over from her mother in 1978, with Bertelli alongside her as business manager. Even then, Muccia was allowed time to implement her creativity and transfer it into design. It is no doubt this freedom and encouragement of innovation and creativity that have contributed to its success. "Prada's originality made it one of the most influential fashion houses."[11] At Prada the technical acumen and commitment of employees is also extremely highly respected, and Prada offers rewards and growth opportunities in order to retain

---

[11]Carrie Grosvenor, "Prada: From Suitcases to Oscar Gowns, from Milan to the World." www.lifeinitaly.com/fashion/prada.asp.

talent. They have stayed true to their heritage as a producer of travel articles and accessories made with sophisticated techniques and the finest materials and extending their product range without losing sight of where they began.

In contrast, the brands that are owned by companies that have been successful are seeking growth and profitability. They want star brands that will be their "cash-cows." LVMH, Louis Vuitton, Christian Dior, Hennessy, and more recently Sephora are treated in this way. With the slowing of growth in China it remains to be seen how the traditional star brands can be cash-cows. The brands were strong and resources were deployed preferentially to make them stronger, such that the brands could perform wonders with their consumers. In contrast, the brands within these companies that were not as strong might not be given the time and attention they need or they be overshadowed by these star brands.[12] One need only look at what happened with Michael Kors. "Was I mistreated?," Kors said in an interview. "No. Was I neglected? Yes. I never felt as though there were a strategy at LVMH as far as pitting the designers' against each other or the brands against each other," Kors said. "It's just that I never felt anyone was watching the smaller companies at all, but everybody was spending their time on the two first-born children—Louis Vuitton and Christian Dior. In a way, if you're a nice kid, no one pays attention to you. If you're a bad kid, you get spoiled."[13]

At Kering, Gucci was their "star brand," and during the era of Tom Ford, it completely lost sight of its heritage and its link to horses. The brand was promoted as having sex appeal and high-octane glamour. It was perceived to have lost its magic, and the real story of Gucci was forgotten. When Tom Ford left the company the brand struggled, and his successor, Freida Giannini, had to go back to the archives to gain inspiration and draw again on the heritage of the brand. This illustrates the fact that luxury brands need time to develop both their image and their identity, and sometimes, with the way company-owned groups are

---

[12]Star brands are defined as those brands that are timeless, modern, fast-growing, and highly profitable.
[13] *Women's Wear Daily* (April 2004).

managed, this is not possible. And the management style is a key to develop and understand the brands. Another lesson is to say that brands are far more important than creators and managers, and when Tom Ford and De Sole left Gucci, the brand did not suffer and growth continued.

The common thread that was revealed during the description of the leaders and managers that run the houses, brands, or the conglomerates was their dedication and the consistency in their vision, their passion for the industry and their brand, their relentless capacity to create, innovate, and at the same time to run their businesses globally. All understood the need to have a high level of in-house production and a high level of control over suppliers that resulted in high quality. All understood the importance of a powerful distribution network, the need for a strong global presence (particularly in the emerging markets of Asia, especially China), and to work toward optimizing all of these aspects as much as possible.

The dominant style as seen from the above description would be in the continuum from an autocratic to a laissez-faire style of management, but what is certain is that all those who are at the helm of the luxury business have their own very special style of management. The autocratic yet hands-off style might be actually a variant laissez-faire style, because managers were not passively leaving decisions to their employees, but leading with a clear know-how of the industry. The conglomerates have pressures on their bottom line coming from their stakeholders every quarter. The family-owned brands had no such pressure and could take it slowly and focus on the long term. This made them less efficient and slow to respond to the changes in the environment. But in the end the industry seeks profits to sustain itself. The craftsmen and métiers also need to be protected. This could only ensure that the skills of the craftsmen and their specialization were protected, nurtured, and encouraged to foster. This would ensure that innovation and creativity be sustained to serve the ever-increasing number of wealthy people of the world.

Conclusion

The luxury market is complicated and diverse. At each spectrum lies a different managerial approach, from the large global multibrand conglomerate to the small, exclusive family-run "maison." As has been discussed, neither method leads to Eldorado. Certain brands are today successfully managed by these large corporations, but issues of neglect still, and will always, exist. At the same time, the security and stability of joining forces has led many irreplaceable and unique labels to abandon traditional luxury ideas in favor of more commercial, global business practices through acquisitions and mergers. Despite this trend, some maisons, notably Hermès and Chanel, have managed to survive and prosper. It is the job of the leader to lead. The role to create a pathway into the future remains central.

Luxury is a world of details. Everywhere, the detail makes the difference, and also for a manager. It is a world where to succeed, the top guys must have a hand-on-management style and not to be global and strategic; to have a vision, one needs to speak the language of the brand, it is not easy.

Managers from outside will succeed and have succeeded as the past has witnessed.[14] If they get the rules right there is no reason to succeed, if not they are rejected by the others. Competence, human capacity to drive others, hard workers, physically capable to jump from Europe to Asia and America, and being able to withstand all climates are necessary. To be a manager in the luxury industry, physical endurance, good mood,

---

[14] Managers have replaced "chefs de maisons" on the luxury planet. They come from all horizons: Yves Carcelle from textile Descamps, for LV; Sydney Toledano from Lancel, where he worked for many years with the Zorbibe brothers. Patrick Thomas was with Pernod-Ricard, the famous French group, and was hired by Dumas to manage Hermès. During the 1990s, Dumas had chosen managers from outside the luxury world to manage Hermès, Mireille Maury, Gilles Duval, Christian Blanckaert, and Patrick Thomas. All of them had no experience in luxury. Mireille Maury came from Saint Gobain and Gilles Duval had been in the distribution of mass-market products. Christian Blanckaert came from Thomson. In the Pinault-Kering group, the artisan of the Gucci Group buy was Serge Weinberg, who had been a civil servant before his appointment as CEO of CFAO, a distribution company famous in Africa. François Pinault hired many managers from outside the luxury world and his son as well. Robert Pollet for Gucci came from a large food company. These managers succeeded very well, all of them. Some never stayed, like Fabrice Boe-Dreyfus who was the general manager of Hermès for a few months only, coming from L'Oréal, or Veronique Morali, a very capable manager who never found a position that suited her capacities within the Chanel Group.

good health, and good listening skills not only in the home market but in international markets is a necessity.

One must remember that the key to succeed is to understand first that in famous houses, no one is waiting for you to succeed. When LV or Chanel or Hermès have been successful for more than 100 years, it is useless to come as a fighter or a Zorro to explain how to perform. The manager must first listen a lot to capture the subtlety of the luxury game, leave the creators aside, understand the product, spend a lot of time in the stores, and contribute to better business methods. They must change their orientation, put themselves in the mood of the brand, meet employees inside and clients outside, watch the reactions of everyone in various countries, and reflect. It is a long process of understanding, and it takes time and requires qualities of modesty, humor, and rapidity to grasp all details.

Different houses, brands, and conglomerates have different management styles according to the personalities of the leaders, the internal and external environment in which they are operating, the situation the brand is facing, and other specificities such as size, expansion, retail network, and others. Indeed, there are some successful practices that could be taken as references. But there is no recipe for the best single style of management for the industry. A mix of the styles might be needed in implementing certain strategies, solving some problems, or managing a complicated situation.

However, the human factor creates challenges for brands. The people behind these brands have worked for decades, and the brands have survived through two world wars and multiple global fiscal meltdowns while building up their images and sustaining them. An economic crisis cannot fracture the values, principles, and standards that fuse the founding family or creator of the logo.

Each brand recognizes the importance of both profitability and protecting the brand identity and image at the same time. Thus, as has been seen, with very strong and unique leaders, managers, and owners dominating this industry, the overarching theme is undoubtedly in managing the creativity and bottom line, which seem to be at loggerheads, thus creating the homoluxus.

In 1930, Gabrielle Chanel signed a contract with Samuel Goldwyn to be costume designer for United Artists. Gloria Swanson was one of the actresses who wore Chanel dresses.

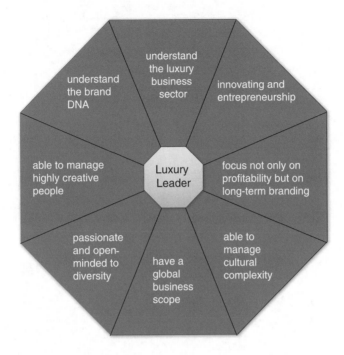

Figure 7.3 Characteristics of a Leader in the Luxury Sector

Mademoiselle Chanel was always full of audacity. She dared to use an inexpensive fabric—cotton jersey—and even back then, she had no qualms about designing a suit for working women. Her tweeds were made especially for her in Scotland. Around the same time she also started making costume jewelry. To Chanel, fashion was on the streets. So she dared to be different.

Chanel, Saint Laurent, Cardin, Courrèges—they were all daring and paid no heed to what the others were doing. The luxury world abounds with people who dare, people who are totally free and independent. They are simply themselves, and they design as they see fit. Figure 7.3 depicts the characteristics of a leader in the luxury sector.

These people are everywhere in the luxury sector, because the freedom to design is not the privilege of a particular field. On the contrary, it is to be found in all luxury markets, from champagne to fashion, from cognac to hotels or watches.

Luxury products in all sectors simply need to be unique and extraordinary, like a Stradivarius violin. This is inescapable.

Chapter 8

Skills

Craftsmen are the unknowns of the luxury world. They come from extremely varied backgrounds, they are passionate about doing a good job, and they perform their crafts with well-deserved pride. Luxury is not a word that means anything to them. They are driven by beauty, perfection, a polished finish, and excellent handiwork.

They know they are the "Last of the Mohicans," but they are happy about this. Some were trained on the job, some in schools, some were sons of craftsmen, and they all pull together as one. In the word "craftsman" there is "craft," and in "worker" there is "work"—as in a work of art. Craftsmen and workers are artists, and they put their stamp on their work. A luxury craftsman is committed to his product: He marks it and may see it again.

A craftsman gleans his knowledge by watching, certainly not by reading. He teaches by demonstrating. He learns by observing and he passes on his know-how.

A great craftsman also knows how to behave with clients or in society in general. He knows how to explain, listen, and demonstrate. He is passionate and demanding.

If he knows how to *do* as well as how to *be*, then his future is mapped out with a major luxury house, but if he is on his own, then he is fragile. The luxury craftsman is part of a team, he never ceases to learn new things, he has to adapt to new models, new workshops, and new supervisors. He travels, learns from talking to others. His life is one long discovery. He is the true representative of luxury and holds the key to the treasure trove: know-how!

It takes time to be a successful craftsman: time for learning, time for training, time to listen and to watch, time to try and try again. A work of art takes time and a luxury goods craftsman is part of a long-term investment. It is indeed the most valuable element of the production process for luxury goods. Adam Smith spoke about labor as one of the necessities of production along side land, capital and entrepreneurship. As these skill-sets are rare, valuable and not easy to learn and imitate, they justify the price of the product.

With the rise of the luxury conglomerates and the growing numbers of wealthy people around the world, especially in new emerging markets, the luxury industry experienced a phase of phenomenal growth during the last decade. Due to growth in foreign markets and scaling-up of operations, the scarce resource has been the skill required to produce exquisite goods in terms of both economies of scale and economies of scope. Scale and scope begs the question of how we find the special skill-sets required for (1) craftsmen who have the tacit knowledge of the brand DNA, (2) designers who understand and create innovations around the brand DNA, (3) salespeople who translate the story of the brand to the diverse and increasing numbers of consumers across different cultures, nations, and continents, and (4) managers who can run the business not as a small- and medium-size enterprise but as a global corporation.

The four different types of talent have the ability to use their left brains and right brains effectively. While the left brain uses logic, attention to detail, facts, figures, present and past, and complexity; acknowledges reality; and is strategic, practical, and safe, the right brain uses feeling, creativity, imagination, attention to the big picture, symbols and images, present and future, philosophy and arts; appreciates spatial perception; comprehends knowledge; and is open to possibilities and risk taking. In this industry craftsmen have to be skilled in balancing the right- and left-brain functions to a certain extent, whereas the designer has to be more skilled in right-brain functions. Sales staffs, on the other hand, need to be more skilled in left-brain functions with skills development of the right brain. Managers need to be more skilled in using the left brain while acknowledging the right. It is a difficult balance, and it becomes more challenging with the expansion and growth of this industry.

The phenomenal growth has caused some luxury conglomerates to outsource some of their activities to skilled labors in different countries, mostly countries with low-wage workers, to increase profitability. In this way the industry saw a period of transformation and renewal. But customers crave "Made in France," "Made in Italy," or "Swiss" watches. A key question then is how to manage phenomenal growth, scale-up the production of the goods while keeping the DNA intact, and produce in the home country, where skilled workers are fewer and farther between?

Bottega Veneta offers a good example of this. Tomas Maier, design director for the brand, is committed to conserving Bottega Veneta's know-how, preserving jobs in the area where the company originated, and ensuring the survival of certain vital skills which might otherwise disappear. To do so, he has taken the initiative of creating leather-braiding schools in the Veneto region around Venice. Fighting hard to pursue what, for him, is a highly personal issue, he has succeeded in making his expectations of sustainability an integral part of Bottega Veneta's outlook. In other words, Bottega Veneta now seeks to make permanent a particular business and human resources quite beyond its current agenda and its own immediate interest.

In the same vein, the business of luxury is not any longer a local business. Neither can it be run on a local business model. The industry has become global, and the luxury companies need to be run by skilled professionals who not only understand the intricacies of the business but also can operate on a global scale. Gone are the days of one, two, or four shops in different regions of France or Italy. Emerging customers are educated, digitally savvy, and abreast of the changing ways in which the products and services are designed, marketed, distributed, and consumed. One of the undoubted strengths of the luxury industry has been the power of brands' heritage and core values to attract passionate and patient individuals who appreciate the creativity, craftsmanship, and cachet of working in this industry. But this is no longer enough. To thrive in this current transformative period, the industry is seeking breakthrough talents with specific skill-sets that are entirely new to luxury while enabling the existing talent pool to adapt and change with the times, keeping them excited and motivated.

In fact, the future growth in luxury industry would mean understanding the sociocultural context that is combined with knowledge of the well-informed consumers who, with their original interpretation of the context, can be catered to with innovative and creative products. Fresh talents with versatile skill-sets will be needed to ensure the sustainable development of the luxury industry.

Historical Craftsmanship

Craftsmanship is the key to luxury, because I think the time has come back to restore the value of the expertise of craftsman and to look to the solid foundation of the past to create the new.

—Fulvia Visconti Ferragamo

Luxury goods have existed for centuries, as the royal and aristocratic classes around the world have spent their fortunes on extravagant handmade clothing and accessories. The luxury brands that are well known today are approximately 100–200 years old. However, the industrialization of the luxury goods market took place in past couple of decades. Most fashion and accessories, jewelry and watch brands, such as Rolex, Hermès, Louis Vuitton, Boucheron, Cartier, Prada, and Versace, started out as small French or Italian family businesses, centered around a person or a creative designer and an authentic material. At that time, the requirement for skill-sets in luxury businesses was simple and limited, because the business were operated as family businesses that served and satisfied local customers to a great extent, and in some case regional customers and special-order customers. The skill sets mainly focused on their passion for excellent craftsmanship and creative design that had their signature differentiation. For example, the story of Boucheron and the Swiss watch industry demonstrates how history had a part to play in the creation of this brand and the sector.

A Boucheron sapphire necklace—a jewel of this kind requires infinite patience to seek out the finest stones; it then requires some 500 hours of labor to assemble; all on top of the 14 years of study to master the skills required to make one. Because a luxury product is the result of such painstaking efforts to meet the highest expectations of quality, it is not subject to the whims of style or season. A Boucheron necklace becomes a family heirloom, a tuxedo by Yves Saint Laurent will be a classic for generations. Timelessness is not just about the product, but also about the brand value and all the nonmaterial things which it represents.

The Case of the Swiss Watch Industry

The first mechanical clock was invented in Italy and England around the mid-fourteenth century. The oldest clock tower dates back to 1352. Over the course of 700 years, the mechanical clock epicenter moved from Italy to Germany to France to England to Geneva, and finally to the Swiss canton of Jura, where it remains today. The first wrist-watch was a piece commissioned in 1810 by the Queen of Naples from Abraham-Louis Breguet (1747–1823). Breguet is often thought to be the greatest watchmaker of all time. During this time, the rapid innovation of watches from a clock-tower to a wristwatch worn by the Queen of England paved the way for how the watch was manufactured. Watches went through the manufacturing cycle of ad hoc local production to a division of labor between artisans who produced one-of-a-kind timepieces to uniform assemblies of interchangeable parts. Switzerland, located in the alpine region with high mountains and narrow valleys, had few natural resources. Conditions such as the terrain and cold winter climate made agriculture difficult, and in-house handicraft industries such as textile, cheese, chocolates, and watches were developed to supplement agriculture.

Watchmaking was introduced in the middle of the sixteenth century by the Huguenots—the French refugees who were persecuted because of their Protestant faith. These refugees settled in the French-speaking

Geneva and expanded from there to the Jura Hills near Neuchatel. Geneva was a city of merchants who understood trade and were skilled in the craftsmanship of watchmaking. Around 1785, some 20,000 persons worked in the watchmaking industry of Geneva and produced 85,000 watches per year and another 50,000 watches in the region of Neuchatel. The long winters provided lots of idle time in this region and the relatively soft hands of cow herders were well suited for watch manufacturing. The herders were also willing to work for low wages, as watchmaking was relatively well compensated compared to working on farms. Watchmaking became synonymous with jewelry making due to the intricate complicated parts and the use of precious and semiprecious stones, enabling watches to withstand wear. The settlement of Protestant refugees from France brought not only experienced workers but the related and supporting skillsets of commercial networks for export trade. During the same time, Germany, Britain, and France became involved in two world wars. Switzerland's location in the center of Europe, its multilingual population, 500 years of democracy, neutrality, and peace with trading and exporting competencies became a capability to trade across the world even in wartime. At the turn of the twentieth century Switzerland overtook Britain, France, and Italy and became leaders of accurate and precise manufacturing of watches.

Entrepreneurial Designers

Family houses were entrepreneurs and started their businesses with passion and belief in what they did. For example, Hans Wilsdorf was passionate about watches and started a watch trading company when he was 22 years old in London in 1903. So did Van Cleef, Arpels, Guerlain, Krug, Rothschild, the Chaumet brothers, Coco Chanel, Breguet, and others. They did not have any shareholders and their objective of business was not maximizing shareholder value; they did not feel the need of hiring functional talents such as finance, retail, marketing, branding, or for the positions of CEO, CFO, COO, or HR.

The Case of Hermès: Saddle Trunk

Thierry Hermès, who was born of a French father and a German mother in the German town of Krefeld, was the sixth child in his family.

He moved to Paris in 1828. Being trained and talented in leatherwork, he opened a workshop on Grands Boulevard of Paris in 1837 that specialized in the horse harnesses that were required by society traps, calèches, and carriages. The products created from leather by Hermès were inspired by the dynamics of animal power and grace, movement and travel, nature and outdoors. The business offered a model that was built on stitches that could be done only by hand. The famous saddle stitch, which required two needles working two waxed linen threads in tensile opposition, was a fine, graphic stitch that would never become loose when done properly. Thierry's customers were socialites, the Parisian beau monde, and European royalty, including Emperor Napoleon III and his empress, Eugenie. But Thierry's real customer was the horse. It was his passion to make the horse and its rider comfortable with a leather holster that was immaculate. Its richness lay in the fine leather and in the elegant saddle that revolved around the life of a horse. After Thierry retired in 1880, his son Charles-Émile inherited the business, moved to 24 Rue du Faubourg Saint-Honoré, and added a custom business that required measurements from both the rider and the horse.

The Case of Louis Vuitton: Travel Bag

Louis Vuitton was born in Anchay, Jura, France, in 1821. He moved to Paris at the age of sixteen in 1837 and apprenticed with luggage- and trunkmaker Monsieur Marechal. With the apprenticeship, he trained himself in the art of fine-luggage creation. During his apprenticeship he worked as a luggage packer for upscale Parisian families. This experience gave him insight into the world of luggage and the needs of wealthy travelers. In 1854, he opened his first store in Paris, creating Louis Vuitton Malletier, or Trunkmaker. He began by designing the first flat-topped trunks that were lightweight and airtight, clearly innovating and differentiating his products from other trunkmakers, which had rounded tops for water to run off. The rounded-top trunks could not be stacked in railway cars. To save trunks from water he designed the waterproof signature gray "Trianon" canvas. The "Trianon" trunk quickly became popular as a symbol of cosmopolitan living and elegant traveling. The same year, Vuitton created innovative trunks to accommodate the voluminous crinolines worn by France's Empress Eugenie, wife of Napoleon III. The "Empress" trunk could be considered the beginning of Vuitton's carefully crafted image as a brand of luxury and celebrity.

By 1860, Vuitton was already successful enough to open a larger factory in Asnières-sur-Seine to accommodate the increased demand for his goods. During the next decade, Vuitton created many innovative designs, including the first Vuitton wardrobe trunk, which contained a rail for hanging clothing and small drawers.

The Case of Zegna

Angelo Zegna, a watchmaker by trade, started weaving wool from four looms. Of his 10 children it was the youngest, Ermenegildo, born in 1892, who was the young entrepreneur; Ermenegildo, when age 18, founded the Lanificio Zegna (wool mill) in Trivero, in the Alpine foothills near Biella, thus creating the Ermenegildo Zegna Group in 1910. His passion was to make fabrics that had to be "the most beautiful in the world." Following his passion, he started producing and sourcing fabrics of outstanding quality and design that were avant-garde. Ermenegildo's skill in sourcing was way ahead of his time. He sourced quality natural fabrics directly from their country of origin and brought innovation in product in his homeland, Italy. This vision of integrated sourcing with highest quality weaving laid the foundations for a fully vertically integrated company and one of Italy's most acclaimed family-driven enterprises. Again, much ahead of his time he understood the meaning of sustainable production and the importance of forging a relationship with the local territory and the community. He understood that the beauty of the natural environment and people's well-being were indispensable. Angelo Zegna, son of Ermenegildo, described his father's achievements: "I see four forces acting throughout my father's life. First of all, he was born in the right environment to develop his business aptitudes. There were various small firms competing in a small area. Secondly, he was always determined to get the better of his British rivals by offering creative Italian fabrics with unbeatable quality. The third force was an exceptionally open mind, especially regarding the social welfare of the territory and redistribution of value to workers. Lastly, there was his fundamentally important relationship with nature, his awareness that natural resources are limited and that we must protect them. He was an ecologist long before the term even existed!"

The Sales Team

There are some unique features that separate a luxury employee from a regular employee.

One type of employee is trained for rigor and intelligence. They are trained to look into financial understanding of the situation. They are practical and understand the strategic underpinnings of a decision. They have a highly developed left brain, and these include the banker, the doctor, the lawyer. The other kinds of employee are creative and artistic. They think laterally and not literally. Through their artistic talent and imagination, they create things. Boasting a highly developed right brain, these include the architect, the musician, the dancer, and so forth. What is interesting about a luxury employee is that he or she must have a mix of the above two contrasting traits. He needs to be a practical artist, which sounds counterintuitive. However, this is the oxymoron that every luxury employee lives with. He has to be a strategic player with a dash of creativity. These two diverse skill-sets are not easy to find in a single employee, and even if found, it is difficult to manage these employees.

The challenge that luxury employees face is pertaining to how to make profits without compromising on the brand DNA, grow without diluting the brand offer, be less accessible and still sell as much. For instance, Louis Vuitton has expanded its reach to many remote parts of the world. Ninety-four percent of young Japanese women own a Louis Vuitton, making the brand less exclusive. The other extreme is Hermès, which is known to have much greater profit potential. Hermès on the one hand can innovate, customize, and woo the Chinese and the Japanese. However, they are noted to stick to their cultural roots, their heritage, and they are not immediately interested in market share. They embody French aristocracy, deeply Protestant in their ways. Thus, they are unwilling to compromise on their craftsmanship, their excellence in quality, and their manual production process. They think for the long term and not for short-term gain. It is part of the family ethics. With the above two examples, it is evident that the skill-set required for working for LV is different from the skillset required for working for Hermès. Another example to be noted in this regard is that of the Italian brand Bottega Veneta. They are known to offer the most exquisite craftsmanship. The striking feature about Bottega is that people are less aware of the brand than its competitors, like Armani. This indicates a heavy upside potential for Bottega Veneta, which it does not believe in capitalizing upon, as that would imply the brand losing its understated DNA. The brand prides itself in its delicate subtlety and not on quarterly sales revenues. However, the discrete and no-logo brand image works well among its customers and at the same time boosts the bottom line of the company.

The Professional Managers

The first generation of entrepreneurs and designers were retiring by the late 1970s. The family businesses were inherited by their children or were passed to the immediate relatives. With the expansion of their businesses, both new challenges and opportunities became prominent. The craftsmen, designers, and owners of the brands did not know how to embrace globalization effectively when more and more of their customers were from distant countries. They did not have the management depth to embrace growth, expansion, and profitability. That was probably the reason that in the 1970s, many of the French firms, especially fashion houses, suffered from a variety of management and ownership problems. These firms lacked capital and were not yet mass-marketing their wares. The 1980s saw a revitalization of luxury firms. One reason was the use of celebrities to promote brand awareness, such as using the Academy Awards to showcase designer clothing. Another reason was the influx of capital to these firms. Leading this trend was real estate manager Bernard Arnault, who took control of Agache-Williot-Boussac-Saint-Frères and kept only its affiliate, Christian Dior. Arnault soon thereafter took control of Louis Vuitton and Moët-Hennessy, and united them under LVMH. From 1985 to 2006, he took over 64 brands. With this came the consolidation and the business groups of Richemont in 1988 and PPR (now Kering) in 1999. This consolidation required distinctive skill-sets drastically different from what was needed historically. They gave rise to multibrand conglomerates whose business models incorporated globalization, professionalization, commercialization, centralization, and profit maximization for their shareholders.

In order to deal with this new business strategy the conglomerates needed to create new structures around the brands. They started employing line managers who were trained and skilled to manage fast-moving retail businesses and were able to manage a professional workforce. These called for various new talents with diversified skill-sets such as strong leadership, effective communication skills, efficient strategy-making skills, and financial skills. In fact, the luxury conglomerates forgot the position of Chef de Maison (Chief of the House) and began to hire CEOs or other important staff for their management from other industries. For example, they hired Conchetta Lanciaux, Yves Carcelle, Lew Frankfort, Sidney Toledano, Christian Blanckaert, Tamara Mellon, Stanislas de Quercize, Daniel Piette, Ravi Thakran, and others.

In the mid-1980s, this new group of professionals was ushered into the luxury industry. They had no luxury background before they entered this industry. For the past 25 years they have steered their brands successfully through cyclical environments. They have some skills-sets in common. They possess well-functioning accounting and financial skills and were invariably educated in a business school of high repute. They have proven records of well-rounded management and open communication skills. They possess exceptional leadership skills and have proven records of recruiting, motivating, and retaining talent. They have a keen insight for change and development within the market vis-à-vis market entry, expansion, extension, and acquisition. They have a knack and an intuition about strategy formulation and implementation of skill-sets across markets, while staying true to the brand's DNA. They understand the attributes of luxury brands they work for. They understand the brand's core value and position in the market.

Skills Required

In the last three sections we discussed the evolution of skills in the luxury industry. The three multibrand conglomerates specify somewhat different skill-sets that are required to be successful in the industry, yet are also specific to the conglomerates.

The professional environment of the LVMH group is shaped by excellence *and* exacting expectations, *reflecting our constant contact with
the magic of creativity and with unique expertise in a tremendous number of different skillsets around the world. Our working environment is
entirely focused on luxury, making it especially stimulating for people
who are* creative, passionate, *and have an* entrepreneurial mindset.
*LVMH is a veritable "ecosystem," counting over 100,000 people with
an incredible wealth of experience and opportunities.*

*When people join LVMH they choose an environment that is fas-
cinating and* passionate, *embarking on a professional journey that is*
stimulating *and profoundly* meaningful. *Joining LVMH means being
part of a Group that is the leader in its industry and enjoys a global
presence, a Group where* passion for aesthetic quality *and* creativity
goes hand in hand with a commitment to excellence *and to being the*
best. *It means playing a part in an ecosystem that is constantly evolving
and reinventing itself. It means contributing to the work of* teams *that
are rich in talent and* diversity. *When people embrace the LVMH experience, their own story becomes interlinked with that of the brands whose
rich heritage* we represent as we perpetuate the "Future of Tradition."

**—Chantal Gaemperle, Group Executive Vice
President, Human Resources and Synergies**

According to LVMH, it has a decentralized organization where each
brand manages recruitment independently to meet its specific needs.
The skill-sets required are varied. It recruits *exceptional* people capable of
combining *pragmatic* and *creative* thinking with an *entrepreneurial mindset*
and *international vision.* They seek people who feel a *strong affinity with
luxury products.* An unyielding commitment to *excellence* and an ability to
anticipate the future while *respecting the DNA* of our brands are essential to
a fulfilling and successful itinerary in the prestigious environment of the
LVMH group. The LVMH group considers *diversity* to be a great asset.

Compared to LVMH, Richemont Group requires the following
skill-sets:

*Richemont and its Maisons are committed to preserving the finer busi-
ness values of* entrepreneurship, integrity, *and* creativity. *They offer
talented and skilled people diversified and engaging development opportunities along their career path, both nationally and internationally.*

Moreover, they encourage them to build on their strengths, develop their skills and support the achievement of the Maisons' business success. They look for people who want to contribute *to the successful history of our Maisons, who aim for* excellence *in whatever they do and share our long-term vision. They ask the best of our people and steer individuals towards achieving their* personal excellence. *We are committed to providing an environment where* professional competencies *are continuously developed; where* trade skills *are the finest in the industry and where professional development is considered a priority.*

The Richemont Group manages by objectives, empowers people to take initiatives *and expects the employees to actively contribute to the Group's success and show* commitment *to the Maisons and* loyalty *to the Group. They are committed to preserving* high standards of performance *and* unsurpassed quality *in their everyday business activities. They see it as a privilege to work for, and represent, excellence, tradition and prestige. This is why their employees act as an* ambassador *of the Maison they represent and for the Group as a whole, just as Richemont is dedicated to providing excellence in shared services to our Maisons via our network of regional subsidiaries. They conduct their business in accordance with management principles that place value in our people's successes, namely:* trust *and* loyalty, mutual respect. *At Richemont they apply the word "Métier" (which in English means workmanship or "a highly skilled line of work") as an honorary term to credit those professions working at the heart of our luxury business, and which require a* unique savoir-faire, expert qualifications *and* accomplished dexterity.*

The Richemont values are: entrepreneurship, creativity/innovation, customer focused, learning culture, craftsmanship. Core competencies are entrepreneurial spirit, creativity/innovation, customer focus, learning culture, challenging partnership, team player, integrity and trust, self-management/leading by example, managing and developing teams.

---

*http://www.richemont-retailacademy.com/

The Kering Group has the following HR strategy.

The aim of the new Group HR mission, which is aligned with the Kering vision, is to empower our employees to fulfill their potential and creativity by fostering their skills and performance in the most imaginative and sustainable manner. Three main trends will support the Kering effect on HR: global, digital, and sustainability. The idea behind the HR strategy is to enable our brands to flourish through accessing and sharing, among other things, a talent pool, expertise, standards and best practices. It means that brands, while benefiting from the created synergies and following the guidance of the Group, will be able to exercise their autonomy: a concept that can be summed up with two words: "roots" and "wings." Taking care of our employees in the same way as we do our customers and making talent development a managerial principle will inspire and guide Kering leaders.

                         —Belén Essioux-Trujillo, Senior Vice President Group HR

The interviews and survey among luxury professionals show the following skill-sets are being sought after by the luxury sector. The skill-sets needed are diverse and have been clustered along three axes for the four levels in Table 8.1. The four axes are (1) fit with the changes in the environment, (2) fit with the luxury sector related to the right brain, (3) fit with the company culture, and (4) competency related to left brain.

Managing Talent

Some of the main challenges that leaders are faced with in the twenty-first century are globalization, increasing stress on the environment, increasing speed and dissemination of information technology, and scientific and social change. But these aren't the only challenges the executive faces while managing a global corporation. In 2010 and 2011, the luxury industry reported exceptional results, much more than expected. The years 2010 and 2011 were record years for some of the luxury brands, including Louis Vuitton and Hermès. Some of the factors that helped the luxury industry ride the economic crisis were

Table 8.1 Skill-Sets Sought after by the Luxury Sector

Figure	Changes in the Environment	Fit with the Luxury Sector (Right Brain)	Business Competency (Left Brain)
Craftsman	Training in the métiers Creativity Innovation Intellectual maturity Flexibility, humility, and willingness to learn Desire to build an effective succession plan Aesthetic quality	Understand the brand DNA Sensitive to the creative element of the business Creativity Autonomous Entrepreneurial Integrity Excellence Passionate Respect for the company culture	Commitment Trust Loyalty Learn-on-the-fly
Designer/ Creative Director	Design capability Ability to adapt Resilience Curious Adapt-on-the-fly Agile	Understand the essence of the brand DNA Understand the six senses with keen interest in art, sculpture, music, theatre, museums, and walking the streets. Appreciation of Indian royalty and grandeur, French couture, German precision, Japanese sophistication, Latino flamboyance A great ambassador of the brand Able to manage cultural complexity Autonomous Entrepreneurial Integrity Excellence Passionate Respect for the company culture	Global Digital Sustainable Commitment Trust Loyalty

(continued)

Table 8.2 (*Continued*)

Figure	Changes in the Environment	Fit with the Luxury Sector (Right Brain)	Business Competency (Left Brain)
Sales Force	Agile Ability to adapt Curious Flexibility, humility, and willingness to learn	Understand the brand DNA Sensitive to the creative element of the business Customer seduction at retail stores Ambassador of the brand Fluent language skills Able to manage cultural complexity The art of storytelling, building personalized relationships, social confidence, knowledge, conversational skills, flair. Employees in the luxury sector should feel like stars themselves Integrity Excellence Passionate Respect for the company culture	Drive sales around the world Manage boutiques Global Digital Sustainable Learn-on-the-fly Trade Commitment Trust Loyalty

Manager			
Agile	Understand the brand DNA	Strong commercial sense
Ability to adapt	Sensitive to the creative element of the business	Understanding complex distribution systems
Open to change	Good rapport with the creative director and manage the creative process	Multifunctional experience in different companies and in different markets
Flexibility, humility, and willingness to learn	A great ambassador of the brand	Knowledge of retail and merchandizing—manage boutiques.
Resilience	The art of storytelling, building personalized relationships, confidence, knowledge, conversational skills, flair, feel like stars themselves	Good team player, able to delegate
Curious	Able to manage cultural complexity	Global
Desire to build an effective succession plan	Entrepreneurial	Digital
	Integrity	Sustainable
	Excellence	Trading
	Passionate	Commitment
	Respect of the company culture	Managerial courage
	Leadership skills of self-knowledge, solution-oriented, decisive decision making skills	Capable of working in an autonomous, destructured, corporate environment, while establishing a coherent structure at the brand level
	Edgy and avant-garde	Open to mobility
	Manage celebrities	Learn-on-the-fly
		High employee engagement
		Trust
		Loyalty

an increase in global travel, a stronger U.S. economy, and continued expansion across the emerging BRIC markets (Brazil, Russia, India, China), where there was an insatiable thirst for luxury. But things have changed. In 2013 and early 2014, sales warnings were issued for the major brands, especially Louis Vuitton and Gucci, mainly due to the decrease in sales in mainland China.

As the luxury industry changed, so did the role of its CEOs. Executives tried to understand the specificities of working in the luxury industry, such as the need to manage creative staff and their egos, be strict about management disciplines, and have the soft skills necessary in running a multicultural global business. But these skills were not readily available inside the maisons that created the brands. A study by the Luxury Society mentioned that "there is a shortage of talent with the skills, experience, and vision necessary to navigate the crisis and steer luxury organizations through a period of transformation. The pool of talent within the industry is too limited not to consider outsiders of the industry *and* insiders in particular instances."

Talent Prospecting (Pool)

LVMH realized it back in 1991. With international expansion and scaling up, the major concern for LVMH was finding the right talent pool. The then–HR director Concetta Lanciaux confided that her primary concern was to "have the best managers who not only understood the business but also how to sell." Lanciaux's challenge was particularly difficult because there was no school where one could get trained executives to manage luxury brands. Most firms were small, family-owned companies, without trained personnel or a proper succession plan. LVMH had to recruit and develop talent from different fields. Regarding the mobilization of LVMH's resources, Bernard Arnault commented,

> In a global context, the progress of LVMH in 2003 was based above all on the excellence of the fundamentals and its capacity to mobilize its internal resources. We could rely on our traditional strengths, namely the talent of our managers and employees and their determination to make the difference, the appeal of our major brands, the certain values—more than ever in a difficult period, the creativity and excellence of our products and the power of our distribution networks. We are continuing

to deploy the organic growth strategy [...] while still carrying out the sale of nonstrategic assets, we will maintain strict management focus, enabling us to reinvest the cost savings achieved in the driving forces of our growth.

Talent Acquisition (Recruitment and Induction)

The three major conglomerates have developed in-house mechanisms to recruit talent that will be leaders for tomorrow. They consistently engage themselves to recruit from the best business schools in France (such as ESSEC, INSEAD, HEC, ESCP-Europe, and others) and abroad. For example, LVMH carried out various original initiatives for young people in France and abroad to develop talent for the luxury industry. It was through these initiatives that primary school children, high school students, art students, young artists, and designers, as well as those closer to the group's new work opportunities, such as college and higher education students, MBAs, could benefit. In 1991, for example, LVMH partnered with Paris-based business school ESSEC to launch the luxury brand marketing LVMH ESSEC chair, funded with FF10 million equivalent to €1.5 million. Further partnerships were launched in Asia as well.

LVMH also instituted a strong company-wide induction program as well as on-the-job training to introduce the world of luxury to its capable, bright novices. It also encouraged and passed on the know-how, skills, spirit of excellence, and the attitude that conveys, through its creations and products, an exceptional art of living, which has been appreciated worldwide. The awakening and education of young people with these values had has been considered an essential part of the Group's goal. External recruitment of fresh talents is a strategic pillar of LVMH human resources policy.

In the case of Kering, the key goal of their relations with educational institutions has been to attract new talent while adapting recruitments to the prevailing economic environment and the diversity of activities and professions of the Kering group. Kering has been conscious of its image as an employer and has wanted to position itself as a preferred employer. The group and its subsidiaries have therefore chosen targeted institutions (business schools, universities) with which specific actions and partnerships have been set up: participation in forums, conferences centered on the group and the leading associated professions among the brands, and resume-writing workshops to support students in their search for an apprentice position or a permanent job. For example, Kering has long been a partner of ESSEC within the program "Pourquoi pas moi? / Joining a business school—Why not me?" This setup is to help young people from modest origins and with high potential to access high-quality education by developing their social capital and their self-confidence. K's entities (headquarters or outlets) open their doors every year to junior college students enrolled in this program to allow them to become familiar with their environment and professions, thus helping these students prepare for a future career path.

Talent Identification (High Potential)

LVMH has invested in hiring people with experience in other industries, such as consumer goods, and select people "who could understand good taste." Lanciaux cited engineering and business schools as specific sources of talent. During 1995, Lanciaux explained, "With some 40 brands potentially competing against each other in the group, recruitment and everyday business becomes complex. In the case of our group, what builds value and profits is the ability to act in an autonomous way and create new products. The business is built on the number of innovative products that come out every year—20 percent to 30 percent of the turnover is based on new products. Therefore our companies' senior executives have to have a large dose of autonomy and creative capacity. People use these as aspirational products, so we need people who manage and dream—and make others dream."

In 2013, the Group had more than 60 brands in its portfolio. LVMH started its FuturA program to develop its high-potential recruits. FuturA has been constituted as an international program to search and develop external or internal experienced high-potential executives, enabling LVMH to deepen its lateral talent pool. The objective was to recruit and develop people who had the potential to take up Group key positions within a five-year horizon. The selection process identified people with 5 to 10 years of professional experience and a proven ability to learn and adapt in increasingly complex environments. As future leaders within the LVMH group, High Potentials were supported by special initiatives to spur their development.

Data showed that 66 percent of the senior management jobs at the Group level are filled through internal mobility. Fifty percent of high potential employees are non-French and are trained through LVMH House, the training program for executives, and LVMH Experience, the training for high potential managers who have recently joined the group, which is used as an integration tool and springboard for moving into leadership positions. LVMH Perspectives offers managers a way to speed up their career by learning from two different perspectives: the first is self-knowledge, and the second is being aware of and facing strategic challenges.

Kering-Gucci Group in 2010 developed a different approach with its "Heritage Program," mainly looking for passionate individuals with strong backgrounds and interests in the luxury goods sector. The management committee was interested in finding and training experienced people from fields other than luxury, from which they might be able to gain new ideas and alternative strategies to implement. The reason Gucci strongly believed in such profiles was based on its past experience with its previous CEO, Robert Polet, who came from the ice cream and frozen foods division of Unilever and was mostly known for his ability to think outside the box (e.g., he was the first one to leave design decision exclusively to the designers, much unlike previous executives). In fact, through his work between 2004 and 2011, Polet proved that integrating different experiences and knowledge from the fast-moving consumer goods industry was a major advantage.

Talent Development (Retraining)

The three Groups tried to create changes within by training and educating their talent resources. LVMH, Richemont, and Kering all have put in place programs—LVMH House, LVMH Experience, LVMH Perspective, Kering University, Richemont Creative Academy—where they train managers to help them improve their core competencies.

At LVMH, training is distributed between the Group, its business divisions, and the brands themselves, always focused on enriching the skill sets of employees and sharpening their performance. Training programs address needs that were identified and discussed during annual performance appraisal interviews. Technical skills are the responsibility of brands, which sometimes pool training across business groups. At the global level, the Group proposes a broad array of training in management, sales techniques, marketing, project management, and languages and cultural awareness, all centered on the distinctive LVMH ecosystem and its experience in luxury and serving specific clientele segments. Training is organized at the regional level—Asia, Japan, the United States, France, the United Kingdom, Switzerland, Spain, and Italy—as well as by the brands.

For example, from 2000 onward, Kering University has offered training development programs for its managers on various contemporary issues and perspectives in order to support and facilitate the deployment of Kering's strategic positioning. Kering University programs are in line with Kering's challenges, such as Digital Academy, internationalization, performance, innovation and entrepreneurship, leadership, change management, personal impact, innovation and creativity, risk management, strategies and negotiations, and new buying behaviors. The subjects developed by Kering University allow the group's current and future leaders to stay ahead of change.

In the case of the Richemont Group, it promoted training and retraining of its employees in several different ways. Its 16 brands ran different programs such as retail staff training at the Montblanc Academy, employment staff training at IWC, A. Lange & Söhne's in-house watchmaking school, Cartier's training center for watchmaking, and Piaget's "Les Ecoles de la rue du Louvre" in Paris that is managed by the French Jewelery Association.

Amongst many other training programs, Richemont supports the Campus Genevois de Haute Horlogerie in Geneva, the Creative Academy (Masters Program in Arts & Design that imparts specialized training in design for applied arts, in particular jewelry, watchmaking, and fashion accessories) in Milan, and the Richemont Retail Academy in Shanghai, China, which collaborates with WOSTEP (Watchmakers of Switzerland Training and Educational Program) around the world in cities such as New York, Hong Kong, Shanghai, Tokyo, and London. For example, the Richemont Retail Academy opened its doors on November 11, 2011, in Shanghai. It was a one-of-a-kind recruitment-selection and sales-development center, created to source, select, and train the next generation of sales personnel for its maisons' boutiques in China, including second- and third-tier cities. Student trainees follow an intensive eight-week program, following a curriculum created specifically for the Academy. Held entirely in Chinese, the course blends classroom training with "on the job" work in boutiques. The course covers etiquette and the importance of service as well as a technical knowledge of watches and jewelry. The program is run five times per year and prepares some 200 new boutique sales professionals.

Talent Performance (Performance Appraisal)

One of the executive vice presidents of the LVMH agreed that the group sought to foster creativity not only among its design teams but also with professionals throughout the business. He compared the process to mixing the perfect cocktail—LVMH tried to build a work environment that promoted creativity and at the same time adhered to a strict business discipline.

At LVMH, Chantal Gaemperle, the group executive vice president, human resources and synergies, explained that the annual organizational management review plays a pivotal role in identifying talent and succession planning. This dynamic process is central to recognizing the contributions and talents of the Group's people. It ensures advancement within the Group by identifying key positions, internal resources, and the human resources needed to drive continued growth at LVMH companies. The operational management review is linked to the regular performance appraisals that identify employees' strengths and opportunities for improvement, as well as their personal goals. These appraisals serve as the basis for concrete action to enable people to achieve fulfilling career objectives. The LVMH group has focused on internal mobility—both geographic and functional—as a cornerstone of their talent management policy. This cross-fertilization of experience within their ecosystem under the unifying umbrella provides a space for development.

At Richemont, along with continued investment in learning and development, the Human Resources departments across the Group work with managers to facilitate opportunities for employees to transfer between Maisons. This internal mobility has mutual benefits, providing greater career development opportunities for employees and helping to retain skills and talent within the Group. Regular performance management review and annual individual development plans have always been a critical element of the core strategy to retain, motivate, and develop its employees. The Group saw it as a way to develop, recognize, and reward talent. The Group has also developed a specific Performance Management learning and development program specifically for managers, aiming to support them in implementing the process within their teams. The program has been designed to be an ongoing and incremental learning path that leads to retention and integration of high potential managers.

Talent Retention and Integration (Compensation and Benefits)

LVMH's aggressive growth through acquisition created both challenges and opportunities. On one hand the brand needed to be preserved, and on the other the owners and managers needed to be absorbed, retained, and integrated until the time that the brand could be scaled. LVMH tried to treat such moves sensitively, with a vision of integration. Lanciaux commented: "First of all, it was about respecting, identifying, and then preserving all of the assets of the company—not changing everything at once. One of the mistakes that companies in this situation make was to change everything and bring in their own culture. When we buy these brands, we buy them to develop them. To develop the brand, the first thing one needed to know was what makes that brand. Very often it's a number of people who are behind it, often invisible. . . . One has to find them, make them visible. This means that we have been able to preserve the integrity of these brands. Our style is not to go in there and replace everybody—never." According to industry sources, LVMH's compensation policies for senior managers and high-potentials were much above the industry average.

While at Richemont, managers in maisons, regions, and functions were responsible for managing the performance of individual employees. They were guided by the Group's performance management process, which supports transparent compensation and rewards decision making using clear job responsibilities, annual strategic individual objectives, and the development of personal competencies. All managers and virtually all other employees at Richemont undergo formal performance management reviews leading to individual development plans.

To ensure equitable treatment across markets, Richemont's corporate Human Resources function performs a number of internal and external benchmark studies comparing reward and compensation practices. This information is used in an annual salary review to ensure equitable treatment of employees and that salaries and benefits remain competitive relative to their peers.

In summary, talent management in the luxury industry requires creativity. It is not only the managerial talent that needs to be managed but also the designers and creative talent. Figure 8.1 depicts the talent cycle.

Talent Exit (Right Sizing)

Talent exit has been a key issue in this industry. The industry is small, with a total of about 110 brands (excluding automobiles, hotels,

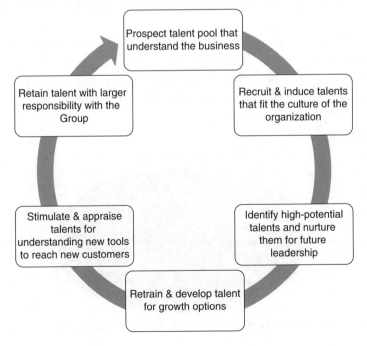

Figure 8.1   The Talent Cycle

yachts, and others). People usually move from one brand to the other. "Up-or-out" syndrome is prevalent, as people working in this industry have to continuously reinvent themselves, be creative, be agile, and perform. Thus, the three big groups needed to plan the succession and the exit policy with precision and professionalism. For example, finding 60 CEOs and 60 creative directors, managing them, and planning their succession, if not thought out properly, could indeed be a challenge.

At Richemont, employee turnover and retention data is closely monitored by the applicable country, maison, functional area, and type of employee contract. Naturally, the turnover rates vary by maison, by country, and by function. For example, in Switzerland, where one third of the Group's permanent employees are based, the turnover rate is below 10 percent. This is in line with market averages. The turnover rate is higher in countries where retail activities predominate, such as mainland China and Hong Kong. Richemont believes that through group-wide efforts with respect to new employee induction programs and ongoing performance management and retention strategies, employee turnover rates in those countries will stay below market averages.

In 2012, Richemont data revealed that 42 percent of employees have worked for the group longer than five years and the average length of service for employees is 6.4 years. These figures reflect the expansion in the underlying businesses spanning 2000–2010 in particular, in terms

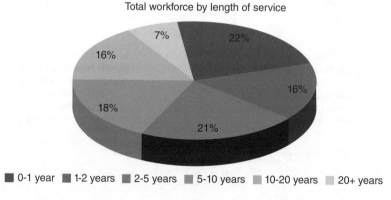

Total workforce by length of service

■ 0-1 year ■ 1-2 years ■ 2-5 years ■ 5-10 years ■ 10-20 years ■ 20+ years

Figure 8.2 Total Workforce by Length of Service

of geographic coverage and the growth in the group's distribution and retail activities. See Figure 8.2 for the details.

Conclusion

The changing needs for hybrid skill sets is a reflection of many new dynamics in luxury industry: the digital revolution, globalization, faster and improved customer feedback, structural changes in the industry, new business models, and more cross-relationship between governments. Hence, the willingness to learn and successfully use new skills is an increasingly attractive employee trait at all levels of the organization. Currently, the luxury industry is undergoing a very big transformation in the new environment of globalization and is facing some serious challenges such as social media, Asian over-reliance, the South American alternative, emerging luxury, and changing consumption trends. In order to be adaptable or survive in this complicated and competitive luxury business, various professionals in different domains are needed urgently. For example, one of the most important trends of the luxury sector now is to expand to emerging markets such as China and India, and there is a great need for cross-culture experts who can move seamlessly between the countries, cultures, and languages, ensuring that the essence of the brand is not lost in the transition as the industry continues to globalize. However, it does not mean that business talents with specific skill-sets outside the luxury business outweigh the creative geniuses who are the messengers of the brand. Future success can only be generated by balancing these two categories.

There has been an ongoing debate about the ideal leader for a luxury brand. Is the manager supposed to be from within the industry or without? Is she supposed to be formally schooled or is mere talent is enough? Is her nationality of any consequence, or is culture of any importance in this regard? Should she belong to the luxury family or can she be an outsider?

The question of industry: Is it necessary to be from a luxury background to be able to lead a luxury firm? The answer is no. It is a evident that belonging to a luxury background certainly helps leaders, as they understand the industry well. However, if a leader from another industry walks into luxury, it is the manager's ignorance in itself that can be used to the brand's advantage. This new manager brings with him/her a fresh perspective to think outside of the box. The manager does not have a fixed way of looking at things and can infuse the company with a new lease on life. The general conclusion is that employees grow mostly within the luxury industry and become leaders. However, mere talent is enough for someone to make his/her way into luxury at any stage in one's career.

The question of family: Luxury brands still continue to be family held. Brands such as Patek Philippe, Richemont, Chanel, Hermès, Tod's, Armani, and Missoni are still closely held and follow the tradition of the children taking over the family business. Even LVMH and Kering are controlled by families. If becoming a luxury leader implies that you have to belong to a family that owns a luxury empire, the answer to that question is no. One must remember that these luxury dynasties were started by men and women with no initial backing in luxury. They made these luxury empires from scratch. The Richemont dynasty was started in 1941 by Johann Rupert's father, Anton Rupert. He started out with a dry-cleaning business in South Africa, moving onward to tobacco. His son Johann was not too keen on the family business, and was an investment banker with Chase Manahattan earlier. It is evident from the story that the father did not have a luxury empire to start out with, but the son did. So one can be in either situation and still manage to lead a luxury company to further success.

The question of culture: In order to protect its brand's DNA, is it necessary for a leader rooted in the brand's culture to lead it? Do the French have to lead French companies? If an Indian leads the French major Hermès, would Hermès become any less French?

Creating a tempest in the French haute couture world, an Italian was appointed creative director at Christian Dior in 1989. Gianfranco Ferre's appointment was criticized because French haute couture was uncomfortable opening its tightly guarded doors to other nationalities. It was believed that this showed disrespect to the spirit of creativity that the French prided themselves on. However, a fact that the industry realized only later was that fashion is not conventional or contemporary, old or novel, French or Italian. In the globalized world of today, the Italians dress like the English and the English dress like the Italians.

Another brand that created history with its turnaround in this decade was Burberry. The British trench coat company had recruited an American, Angela Ahrendts, as CEO and an Italian designer, Christopher Bailey, as its chief creative director. Both transformed Burberry in a period of seven years (2006–2013) when Angela Ahrendts and Christopher Bailey tripled its revenues to $3 billion and a stock market return of 300 percent and successfully revitalized a 150-year-old brand that had lost its way. In 2014, Ahrendts moved on to join Apple as senior vice president of Apple's retail stores, while Bailey took over as CEO. These two anecdotes only stress the fact that luxury leadership transcends time, space, and nationality.

The required skill-sets to succeed in the luxury industry are changing fast. The skill-sets are needed from diverse industries, diverse markets, and varied business functions. Figure 8.3 summarizes the wish list of skill-sets that may be required for the person wishing to be a leader in the luxury industry. Together with this skill-set, one has to take into

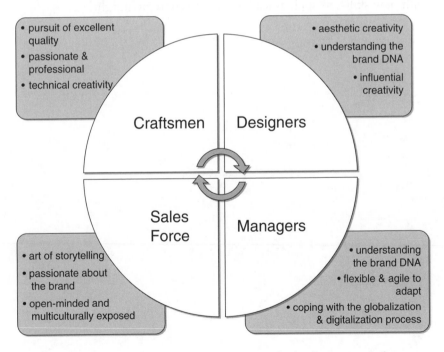

Figure 8.3   Skill-Sets Necessary To Be a Leader in the Luxury Industry

account that the new global challengers from emerging markets are playing prominent roles in global luxury markets. These challengers are rapidly globalizing their businesses and competing with luxury companies for market share, resources, and talent both at home and abroad. The family businesses are fast dwindling. They are either eaten by the multibrand conglomerates or bought out by private equity companies or by family houses from the East. For example, LVMH Group bought Bulgari and Loro Piana, whereas the Kering Group bought Brioni. The Mittal family bought Escada and Labelux acquired Jimmy Choo. Eurazeo bought a stake in Moncler, whereas the Qatar Investment Authority bought Harrods and Printemps. From the above-mentioned examples, it is evident that with globalization, democratization, and growth in emerging markets, gone are the old days of standing alone with a few boutiques and delivering excellent results or being large without delivering. In both cases, the brands will be acquired, as it is time consuming to create luxury brands. Will the future growth of luxury industry be driven by the creative genius with traditional skills, or by business talents with new skill-sets such as leadership and strategic insight?

Chapter 9

Services: The Point of Sale

The welcome: *Sales assistants are chatting to each other in a corner. Luxury shopping is not what it should be. Even worse, an assistant greets the customer with a stare or a rude comment.*

"*So, what do you want? I am busy for the moment.*"

"*Can you make sure that the children do not touch anything?*"

"*What is that dog doing in here?*"

Or a sales assistant is putting away some articles while a customer waits to be tended to. Well, the customer could wait all day, because she obviously is not wanted.

A sales assistant sneers, saying: "You've never heard of this bag? How did you miss the advertisement campaign?"

The client is totally inept, poor thing!

A client walks into the store. The girls at the checkout counter are talking. He starts looking around and a sales assistant enquires politely, "May I help you with anything in particular?"

*"No," responds the client. "I am not looking for anything in particular."
And he storms out!*

*A customer returns a dress. "This dress has already been worn!" cries the
sales assistant.*

"No it hasn't," replies the lady, "I simply tried it on again."

"Well, it is too late, it cannot be returned now, and where did you buy it?"

"Here."

"But who sold it to you?"

"I have no idea."

*Skills in greeting customers are sometimes horrendous, or even blatantly
nonexistent. On other occasions, the reception is simply magnificent.*

*At the entrance to the store, a hostess greets you with a smile and ushers you
in. Then she guides you around the shop. The customer has no obligation to buy,
children are welcome, they even have toys for them to play with, dogs are welcome
too. Browsing through the store becomes a wonderful enchantment.*

*Greeting the customer is never a question of money, it is the result of moti-
vation and pride.*

*Luxury becomes superb when it is dealt out generously, and welcoming a client
is an act of self-effacing generosity. It takes little more than a simple, attentive
look, escorting the customer to a counter or dressing room. There is absolutely
no need for insincere flattery, just a light touch, a gentle sense of humor, without
going too far.*

*The welcome epitomizes luxury; it flatters the mind and attracts the customer
to the product, while complementing it.*

*The welcome to a luxury shop can be the best in the world … or it can be
appalling. Just like luxury itself.*

Luxury used to be "ordinary goods for exceptional people," but more
and more it is believed to be "exceptional goods for ordinary people."
In times such as now, major luxury brands are converging in terms of
the 8Ps—*product performance, paucity, price, provenance, position, publicity,
persona, personage*—the notion of service excellence is one of the clear
differentiators between the different segments and categories of luxury
goods.

Service and luxury appear as intertwined and interdependent as
excellent quality and luxury. The notion of service includes the soft-side
of providing the service during prepurchase, as well as in-store services

during and at the point-of-sale (POS) and post-purchase. Employees working on the sales team and in boutiques, as well as managers and designers, are all intricately involved in the process of total product and service offerings. While providing service, the flow of customer management process is intricately linked to how each brand engages with the customer. The people and process are explicitly and directly in contact with the customer, whereas the physical evidence is implicit to the customer. The physical evidence encompasses the environment in which the service is delivered, in terms of communication, service performance and intangible experience relating to the potential customers and customer satisfaction. The concept of flagship stores and well-designed boutiques thus plays an important part in the services offered by the front-line personnel and reflects on the productivity of the people involved in the sales process at the POS.

Following the above notion, luxury goods consumers have evolved over the past decades. They are aware of more choices. They are more knowledgeable. They are also more traveled and more exposed than their predecessors. They can easily compare and contrast not only between brands but also across geographies when they look for luxury goods. At the same time, brands have extended their DNA and become more diversified, tending to be "generalists." For example, Louis Vuitton and Dior extended their offers into high jewelry and watches, while Cartier strengthened their leather-goods range. Similarly Berluti extended from leather shoes and briefcases to ready-to-wear and bespoke collection. Brands have become cross-gender, with Dior going for menswear while Hugo Boss has developed styles for women.

Due to the phenomenon of designers becoming "generalists," the luxury industry has also significantly evolved through the effects of four major trends, which include globalization with access to goods, democratization with access to different segments, diversification with access to different product ranges, and digitalization with access to comparable and competing information. Due to the four mentioned phenomena, the place where the relationship between the customer and the desired brand occurs, the point of sale, appears as the epicenter to have significant impact. Beyond the mere influence on customer perceptions, satisfaction, and loyalty, the role of service appears as multilayered, catering to the communication of the true DNA of the brand, to meet and cater to new international customer expectations, to be different in design and style, to be timeless and yet modern, and to remain relevant to different cultures across national boundaries.

Issues in Point-of-Sale

With globalization, democratization, and digitization, managers in the luxury industry are faced with a dilemma. From their home base they need to access foreign markets not only in terms of geography but also in welcoming foreign consumers from new and emerging markets. This in itself means that actually managers are managing much more than only a brand. What they are in fact managing is a dynamic consumer base with different mindsets, different cultural orientations, different idiosyncrasies, and different buying behaviors. For example, in emerging markets consumers often use the term "How costly it is?" In mature markets, the consumers ask "How expensive it is?" Though the connotation of both the questions is the same, the inner meaning is different. At the POS, the sales representative can interpret the question in a different perspective depending on her knowledge about price and cost and based on her life experience, as well. Thus in the luxury business, more and more sales representatives are hired from new markets while keeping the diversity of consumers in mind. This simple example of cultural connotation radically changes the foundation of luxury branding.

Due to the issues in luxury branding with people, process, and physical evidence, traditional luxury brands are now faced with opportunities on the one hand and challenges on the other. On one hand, emerging markets bring high-net-worth individuals, exponential growth and consumption, low-cost production, and high technological advances, whereas the challenges faced are how much to democratize, digitize, and globalize while keeping up with the development path without blurring their own identity.

At the point of sale and service (POSS), the challenge translates to what type of image the brand would like to portray to its new generation consumer. Is it the image of a parochial mindset, a diffused mindset, or a global mindset? A parochial mindset at the managerial level and at the POSS would mean a mindset that remains blind to diversity across markets and cultures. There are few incentives, if any, to adapt the processes to local conditions in a foreign market and in extension to foreign consumers in their home markets. On the other hand, a diffused mindset would mean that the managers and employees at the POSS would have a deep understanding of the local culture and local market. Furthermore, a global mindset of managers and employees at the POSS means not only that they understand and acknowledge the differences and diversity of cultures and markets but also that they have the ability to synthesize across this diversity.

Moreover, traditionally, brands have entered the global market via distribution models including but not limited to internal expansion, mergers or takeovers, licensing, franchising, joint venture, or noncontrolling interest points of sale. Complementing this, luxury brands also include flagship stores as the most prevalent and strategic method of market entry that provides controlled POS with ample brand-to-consumer benefits, no matter the market.

In light of this, along with various POSS, it seems there is a coherent strategy to differentiate the brand across markets. For example, they offer to differentiate their brand through new concepts like pop-up shops such as Hermès' pop-up scarf installation and user-generated digital media such as Burberry's "Art of the Trench" satellite web page in order to make an unforgettable imprint on the consumer's mind.

The paradox that emanates at both the managerial and POSS level is which strategic posture and communication method to adapt? Is it effective to be French or Italian, selling the finest French and Italian products in a parochial approach, or to have a diffused posture like that of fast-moving consumer goods such as Unilever or later on P&G, or to inculcate a global posture like that of Japanese firms, which are leveraged on the basis of standardized, highly efficient product–market structure?

The Customer Dimension

Customer relationship management (CRM) traditionally involved technology, people and processes. Technology managed the database of the customers, and processes were aligned to give the customer an integrated service, from creating awareness to sales and after-service. In the luxury industry, the relevance of people and the emotional connect has been much more of a focus. Selling a luxury product requires simple human attention. This is true across the entire value chain from production to sale. Similarly, products sold by salespeople taking an active interest in the consumer, trying to cater to his every need, are valued more by consumers. Just by way of contrast, the hypermarket or fast-food delivery is "self-service." Luxury restaurants with Michelin-rated five-star chefs such as Alain Ducasse, on the other hand, that offer experiential dining, believe in waiters flocking around the clients, live music being played, and a five-course meal presented at the pace that the client is comfortable with.

An effective consumer experience involves two aspects. First, it must create positive emotions and memories to target customers and second it should deliver the targeted brand values. From the moment the customer enters a store until the exit, there are five elements that need to be taken care of. These elements include store outlook and interior decoration, product, price, service, and the feeling of pride (Figure 9.1). Brands like Louis Vuitton do well on store outlook, decoration, and product. However, it has been widely reported that the attitude of the saleswomen may not work in Louis Vuitton's favor. Saleswomen are known to be scornful with customers who don't look as though they can afford a Louis Vuitton.

It must be one of those continuing paradoxes. Louis Vuitton by any standards is one of the best-selling luxury brands in the world, with the highest brand image in the brand rankings for consecutive years. Since 1999, Louis Vuitton maintained a global database to coordinate customer service actions. By closely monitoring customer information, LV could give personalized offers to each customer and catch fraudsters who come to buy LV products in France in order to sell them in their own country. Managing customers in groups of countries, Louis Vuitton could manage the same customer, whether she shops in Belgium, France, Germany, the

Figure 9.1 Elements of Customer Happiness

United States, or Japan. Apart from tracking its customers closely, Louis Vuitton also offers lifetime guarantees, a proof of the quality of their products.

There are many kinds of services that a luxury brand can provide to its clients to boost customer satisfaction. These include services that enhance the shopping experience for the consumer, provide timely after-sale service, give certain privileges to the consumer, and provide other value-added services. For example, the brand can educate the consumers on how to drape certain scarves or how to use makeup. Estée Lauder in 1991 wanted to capture the attention of its clients by providing a 25-minute free makeup video. This helped to educate their customers for achieving better results. Chanel launched its Makeup Artistry program to expand the reach of its national makeup artists. The aim was to offer the most up-to-date trends to consumers by training the in-store beauty artists. The aim was to have seven trained artists at the top, who teach the latest techniques to in-store artists, who can then teach these skills to the consumers. A pan-American contest was held to pick the top seven artists who would train everyone else. It worked on a simple trickle-down effect. Not only did this become a value-added service for the consumer, enhancing her happiness quotient, but it also boosted Chanel's sales as the artists taught clients how to use Chanel beauty products.

As an example, the brand can proactively engage with consumers to enhance their shopping experience. They can on one hand be exclusive in their engagement, using their CRM tools, and on the other hand interact in a one-to-one manner. Two perspectives need to be catered to at all points of the interaction: First, the customers' perspective about what they want, and second, how the company wishes to define its products and services. Managing perception of service is always a greater challenge than managing the actual quality of service offered. In this respect, more so in the luxury and super-premium segment, the client needs to be the central priority. Selection, training, and development of personnel is the minimum requirement for an effective customer service function, but it is not the sufficient parameter. This is so because all the dimensions of service quality can be influenced directly by a company's employees (Figure 9.2). For example, Sephora produced different formats of makeup as an in-store concept. One such concept was to make

Figure 9.2 Elements of Delighting Customers

a 600- to 750-square-foot store resemble a backstage environment, with makeup stations, lighting, and coordinated music. A separate entrance to enhance the experience was also provided. Each such store was touted to have over 1,200 Make Up For Ever SKUs. Another concept by Sephora was that of "Superfoods," where Sephora tried to use food items for beauty purposes. The whole theme of the store was centered on food, where store employees called "Quickies" wore lab coats with bright T-shirts underneath. With two machines, they would provide quick 20-minute treatments such as Coconut Kiss lip treatment, Breakout Star acne treatment, The Big O lifting facial, and others. Dior on the other hand started a concept of having a "residential" store. Dior introduced parquet floors, snow-white Louis XIV chairs, cocoon-shaped salons and certain other signature Dior elements like white lacquered walls, glass box cases, and leather upholstered banquettes. The front room was filled with handbags combined with classic moldings and furnishings. The aim was to remind the clients of their dressing room, where they could patiently sit and try on their clothes, bags, and shoes. The "home-like" feel that Dior wanted to provide to its customers was meant to encourage people to relax and take their time. This helped kick off the experience of "wardrobe shopping."

Together with enhancing the in-store experience, another focus for the brands has always been to enhance the shopping experience of consumers by reducing the time they spent standing in queues or looking for different colors or sizes for a particular item. Prada, for example, introduced a system in which every product and loyalty card carries an RFID chip, which is tracked on a Bluetooth connection. Through the chip, loyalty cards activated a database on the shop's computer to tell the salesperson information about the client. When the client takes a particular item to the trial room, the salesperson can see all the items on the screen outside, since each item has a chip attached to it. The screen enables the client to request different colors or sizes without leaving the trial room.

Once an expensive product is bought, it is expected that the consumer won't be in the mood to spend exorbitantly on getting it repaired in terms of both time and money. For example, many luxury brands such as Rolex, Hermès, and LV have universally recognized after-sales service. Rolex takes care of common problems faced by watch lovers concerning repairs and servicing. Rolex's service center in Singapore is known for its speed and rigor. One can take any Hermès product into any of its stores in the world either to return or to repair it.

Other companies offered value-added services as well. Estee Lauder provided its customers with a Skin Imaging System to analyze their skin type. The system comprised a camera shaped like a telephone receiver connected to a video monitor. The camera runs over the skin, providing a magnified image and showing what exists beneath the skin's surface. On providing this bit of information to the client, Lauder skin experts diagnose the problems that the clients face and offer a solution from Lauder's product range. In order to establish its reputation as the skin expert, Clarins opened up spa facilities in its skin-care product shops. This was done in order to pamper the consumer with a pleasurable experience, boosting loyalty and thus sales. It was believed that the spa service would help the brand express itself. These facilities gave the clients a moment to themselves, where they could experience the product. Ermenegildo Zegna created a loyalty card for customers who bought a tailor-made suit worth $1,500 or more. The loyalty card provided benefits such as repair during the two years after purchase. Zegna could also refit the suit for the client if he so wished. The suit could be made at the client's home or office. The card also gave the client access to Oasi Zegna in the Piedmont region of Italy where he could have a walk or go horseback riding. In the same vein, the Privilege Club of Porsche gave special privileges such as hotel reservations, customer care in emergencies, business service center services, and special dinners for Porsche clients. The hospitality industry is a classic example of providing additional services that leave a smile on the face of a consumer. This ranges from a welcome drink, room upgrades on arrival, complementary laundry, complementary airport pick-up, complementary newspapers and magazines, and complementary fruits and wine in one's room. Credit card companies like MasterCard, Visa, and American Express offer luxury credit cards to their wealthiest clients. This entitles them to services such as a personal wealth manager, home delivery of most items, and others. For example, Carrie Marcus once alluded that "It's never a good sale for Neiman Marcus unless it's a good buy for the customer."

After-sales service has always been an important part of the whole service process, sometimes even considered the key to grade a brand's quality of service. Especially for jewelry and timepieces, customers are highly concerned about the turn-round time, the price and the guarantee of after-sales service. A good after-sales service experience may win over the loyalty of a customer who will be likely to repurchase and to spread positive word of mouth. The satisfactory level of the after-sales service is not decided by the size or the position of the brand: unlike in-store service, which can be influenced by many factors such as size of the store and luxury facility, after-sales service is decided more by the strategy of the brand and by the formation of its sales staff. There are some successful practices in both big brands and small brands that can be learned from. For example, the after-sales service of Cartier is worth mentioning. Cartier, the leader in high jewelry worldwide and the star brand of the Richemont Group, has been established as the king in jewelry. However, this strength has brought difficulties for the brand in watches, as it is always suspected to be more a "fashion" or "jewelry" brand than a real watch brand, if not considered as "off-piste" in the horology world. The fact that their watch store is more often located in the jewelry section than in the watch section also led to such an impression.

However, Cartier has long understood the concept of "service" better than its competitors. The excellent quality of their after-sales service for their watches has won them allocades from which customers have experienced the same quality of finish from the finest jeweler. In the after-sales service for watches, Cartier offers several options for customers to choose from as their own needs, from a rapid service of battery replacement at £35 or a simple polishing service at £50, to a complete service that covers repairing parts such as the water-resistant gaskets, polishing, and movement disassembly, starting from £160. It also offers more specific service such as providing a wide range of straps for changes, varying in colors, materials, finishing techniques, and styles, from lizard in matte and gloss finish, to alligator and Kevlar, trying to ensure the customer's delight. The service is not limited to watches and jewelries, but also extends to its writing instruments and leather goods, which are given the guarantee that "a Cartier should last for a lifetime." While its rivals such as Rolex and Piaget are often criticized for offering expensive repair service, Cartier wins in the after-sales service, with extremely knowledgeable and helping staff, guaranteed turn-around times, and a variety of service offers at reasonable price points.

In summary, there are a number of ways that brands have focused on the customer satisfaction dimension. Some have defined a multilayered service offering based on customer loyalty, which categorizes customers based on their loyalty and/or spending in order to put more focus on the VIP customers. The idea was to give greater attention to those customers as opposed to excursionists, and to provide them with privileged exclusive services. An example is to create an exclusive club such as platinum card holders for airlines, hotels and provide additional services for those elite members. Another way to extend services that are practiced by the luxury brands is giving invitations to special sales to special clients and friends of the brands. Luxury houses are not focused only on sales but also concentrate on the type of sales.

CRM provided the brands with a systematic and comprehensive approach to access customer information. This systematic approach paved the way to personalized service. Whenever possible, luxury companies were able to use market research data and consumer profiling to understand buying behavior patterns. This option was based on a customercentric view of the organization that has provided a flexible IT solution. Coach utilized this concept effectively across its stores as it conducted focus groups and surveys and gathered marketing intelligence to gain better insights into its customers' needs. Lew Frankfort said, "Today, we don't just sell products, we build relationships with our clients." Coach's growth had always been based on fulfilling the consumers' needs and expectations. It had positively anticipated and responded to, not only fashion trends, but also to consumer preferences. When the first Coach store opened in 1981, Lew Frankfort spent the first days talking to consumers about their habits. He was an ardent believer in finding out what the customers thought. He strongly believed that the better he understood them, the better job Coach could do. Coach started CRM at a very early stage. In 1987, Sara

Lee paid for the market research. Coach was able to identify precisely the profile of its core consumers. They were 35-year-old affluent and professional women who got their first Coach bag as a graduation gift and now owned three or four. It was the description of a preppy high-profile American woman from those early days. Coach spent more than $3 million per year on research. Lew Frankfort explained it as the "logic behind the magic." The company had contacts with more than 75,000 actual or potential clients each year to keep track of the perception of the brand, gauge brand awareness, and assess shifting consumer tastes. Surveys could be in a form of telephone surveys of 500 people at a time, in-store polls, or in-depth interviews. Among the recurrent questions, consumers were asked what the company could do better, and what customers like and don't like about Coach. With these surveys, Coach's R&D team undertook in-depth analytics. As an example, they were able to analyze the behaviors of their clients, how frequently they go to the store, the conversion rate of the store, and so forth. This understanding of the business has helped Coach maintain its profitability even in recession periods. The brand also believed in testing before launching a new product, to limit the risk of uncertainty. A year before the launch of its signature collection, Coach showed samples of the collection to a few hundred consumers in 12 stores in Japan and the United States. This enabled them to forecast demand. Six months prior to the launch, they did a test in 12 stores to see how fast the bags would sell.

The salesperson needed to be qualified, trained, and empowered at the POSS. Their soft skills needed to be enhanced as they were interacting with high-net-worth clients who were looking for an experience in the luxury environment. With empowerment, training, and a flexible organizational structure, sales associates could spontaneously contribute to problem solving and potentially anticipate customer needs. For example, the sales staff of luxury retailer Ralph Lauren were empowered to make split-second decisions without having to check with a manager. The experience of a delighted customer is not an easy task to sustain, which in a sense reinforces the aspirational link between the brand and the consumer. As an example, a luxury beauty institute in the United States created "Innovation Stations" that highlighted the technology of innovative skincare products and other items, as well as "Play Stations," allowing for extensive product testing. According to the industry and the company culture, this option can be extrapolated into various forms. For example, the chef Pierre Hermé created one-to-one sessions where customers can create a pastry for a special event.

The Service Dimension

Historically, luxury goods companies have neglected the service dimension in the true sense of the word. They did it due to some inherent quality of luxury goods that has been explained in Chapter 2. Luxury goods by definition are of exquisite quality and craftsmanship, invariably aesthetic, rare, extraordinary and symbolic. The brand equity is enough to sell such an article. Moreover, the nature of the product, the power of the brand, low competition between specialized brands, and the rarity went against the common notion of service as a differentiator. With the growth of the sector and competition from new consumers from Asia, Latin America, and East Europe, the different aspirations regarding luxury goods have changed with time.

With the expansion in mature and emerging markets, the service dimension has become a key differentiator. Why this is so? With diversification in their product category more and more brands feel the need to touch the heart to increase their presence in the share-of-wallet of the customer. For example, Hermès was known for their saddles, while Montblanc was famous for its writing instruments. But today, they both offer accessories such as belts and watches. To be relevant to the customer in all their segments, luxury brands started to understand the necessity of focusing on their customers in terms of their satisfaction, their relationships, and ultimately to their delight. As this dimension is an act, an experience, a performance that is intangible, perishable, inseparable, and variable and it does not result in the ownership of a tangible object, it needs to be practiced and institutionalized.

The institutionalization may be in the form of adoption of practices moving forward from customer satisfaction to service quality. Essentially, to understand the process, first there is the notion of customer service. Luxury consumption in no way ends with the product. Luxury does not end with the product. It is the entire experience of hearing about a product, going to the showroom, sifting through all the products, clarifying your doubts, and then making a purchase. Also, this process does not end here. It is critical for a brand to offer exceptional after-sale services. It is difficult to imagine authentic luxury without stellar service. If the service is poor, luxury escapes. For example, Berluti opened its flagship store in 2013 at 14 Rue de Sèvres. In an interview, Antoine Arnault, Berluti's CEO, commented that:

> People come not only to shop, but to share a moment with us. They spend on average 45 minutes per visit in the 4,300-square-foot unit. They shall spend time for the bespoke tailoring, following the acquisition of Arnys. The dozen tailors that came with the acquisition of Arnys will provide individualized service to their old and new clientele. The store blends elements of Berluti's roots as an haute cobbler that includes streaky brown leather walls and parquet ceilings with original furnishings from Arnys, such as the leather-topped Louis XV desk. One of the store's unusual features is a patina bar, where clients can bring their Berluti shoes for repairs or a serious polish. To provide the same level of service and environment, Berluti plans opening stores in important locations in Tokyo, Hong Kong, Shanghai, and London. The firm should have … 45 directly owned stores [by 2014] that will cater to the high-end men's wear across the globe."

Second, with the economic crisis and austerity measures across nations, luxury companies strengthened their ties with their customers as a means to differentiate themselves. The companies went back to their loyal customers, were attentive to their needs, and connected with them at an emotional level. Nothing is more valued by consumers than human attention. They want to be pampered while they are at the store. Third, customer service needs to adapt to the changing behavior of the consumers. It is evident that with increasing knowledge and availability of more information, consumers are becoming more discerning and demanding. The new consumers tend to ask more questions when they step into a store. One would expect luxury to be solely driven by pleasure and away from critical questions of customers. That was before. Now, they want to know what they are spending on. They are moved by press reports, tweets, and blog entries. A bad incident can reflect poorly on a company's service. When Oprah Winfrey was turned away by a Hermès showroom, as it had been shut down for a private event, it reflected poorly on Hermès' service quality.

Service quality by definition is the perception of the consumer prior to the encounter with the brand due to reputation and word-of-mouth. This is an interpersonal process that is culturally bound and relates to professional manners that speak about the brand image. The concept of service quality rests on the different understandings between their stakeholders. Five main gaps have been usually identified. The first is the *management perception gap*. This is the knowledge gap that arises due to the differences between consumer expectations and management perceptions of consumer expectations. Management may think that they know what consumers want and proceed to deliver, when in fact consumers may expect something quite different. The second notion is the *quality specification gap*. This is the difference between management perceptions of consumer expectations and service quality specification. Management may not set quality specifications or may not stipulate them clearly. Alternatively, management may set clear quality specifications but these may not be achievable. The third is the *service delivery gap*. It is the difference between service quality specifications and the service actually delivered. Unforeseen problems or poor management incentives can lead to a service employee failing to meet service quality specifications. This may be due to human error as well as to mechanical breakdown of facilitating or supporting goods. The fourth gap is the *communications gap*. It is the difference between service delivery intention and what is communicated about the service to customers. Examples include promises given by promotional activities that are not consistent with the service delivered. It usually arises from a propensity to overpromise. A typical example would be first-class travel, which may have been promoted with glowing images and messages in glossy high-end travel magazines, but in the end falls below the level of service expected by customers. The fifth gap is the *service quality gap*. This arises due to the difference between what customers expect and what they receive. The service experienced is not consistent with the service expected.

Summarizing, the gaps can be bridged by assurance, empathy and employee engagement. The assurance is dependent on the employees' ability to convey credibility and inspire trust and confidence. Showing empathy means to be attentive to the customers. The service quality ultimately depends on the frontline employees who deliver the firm's promises, create an image and promote those services. The frontline employees in that sense are the real face of the brand. Studies have shown that new customer services are about the customer experience that can be provided before, during, and after the consumption and interaction with the brand. For example, the experience before could be of website, hotline, catalogues, design, colors, social media, PR events, launches, press, advertisements, and others. Both Burberry and Ralph Lauren were further advanced in the digital space than other competing brands. The sales experience could be appealing to the six senses in the store, through design of the store, in-store welcome, product knowledge, and contact with the salesperson. It could be the words used, eye contact, body language, special attention, and others. After the consumption, the interaction could be either at the place of sales, VIP club, virtual community, maintenance advice, after-sales exchange, the exchange process itself, special attention during the discussion of exchange and others. Some of the recent examples of engagement with customer experience would be an interactive show window display at Porsche design stores, branded lifestyle extensions at Chanel and Beige in Tokyo, Bulgari Hotels and Resorts, Cheval Blanc, and customer-learning centers of Apple. Other total service experience has been provided by Nespresso relaxing lounges, in-car check-in service at the Hôtel Plaza Athénée in Paris, personal concierge services for the Visa Black Cards, American Express Platinum Card, and the Pink Ladies in London, to name a few. Figure 9.3 summarizes the discussion.

Conclusion

It has become imperative that brands develop dedicated, knowledgeable sales forces. Salespeople are the face of the brand, and it is the human interaction that helps in converting a purchase. Revolving technology to aid the buying behavior is crucial. Consumers of today and tomorrow would like to have the options of interacting with the brand before,

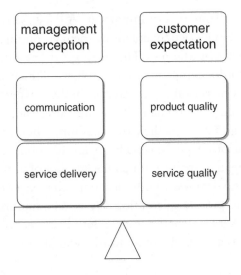

Figure 9.3   Management Perception versus Customer Expectation

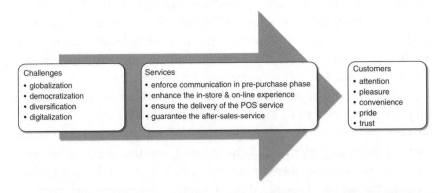

Figure 9.4   Challenges, Service Dimension, and Customer Engagement

during, and after the purchase. It is again imperative that such channels be made available to the consumer to engage with them. It is easier said than done. Figure 9.4 depicts the challenges, the service dimension, and the customers' expectation in term of experience.

Customer experience and engagement is more than customer relationship management. As luxury industry flies across borders, following at least the elite clients is very important. A database of their likes and dislikes can go a long way in maintaining the relationship. LV understood that much earlier than the rest. The retail spirit has always been one of the key values in the company's roots. Luxury salesmanship is not about the price but about assisting the customer in their experience of fun and enjoyment during the purchase. They are purchasing something they want, something that serves their own passion. They are looking for an indulgent, luxurious experience. They want to connect and feel at ease when they come in to spend a substantial amount of money, so the transaction needs to go seamlessly without too much anxiety over pricing and negotiating. The process of seamless sale is very important, as without good customer service, there are no referrals or repeat business. Since the luxury goods are purely aspirational, switching to another brand is also seamless.

The heart of the sales is the sales staff. The sales staff need to show their passion and be informative when selling to clients. The process needs to be involved and ideally should be fun and exciting for everyone involved. This will let the sales staff and hence the brands stay in touch with their customers, or potential customers, and build a relationship by following up and staying current. Perhaps the best way to stay in touch is not by bothering people, but by informing them about something they've already expressed interest in. Customers looking for an experience need to feel welcome in a comfortable setting. It's an art to take customers through the numbers of any particular transaction and get them to understand without being assertive. Then it becomes more about sharing the experience, building the relationship, and helping the sale to happen. What a luxury customer wants from the sales person is not a sales pitch, but assistance in making a decision that demonstrates that the customer and the salesperson are on the same team. It is important to let the customer know that it is okay to spend money and enjoy their life with the product. The product is special. It is neither about the money nor about the product characteristics. It is about the feeling, the experience, and the feel-good factor about owning the product. There's nothing bad about it—that's what luxury is all about.

Case Study: A Man in a Wheelchair—the Extra Mile

As he glanced casually through the window from the inside of the boutique, a Hermès sales assistant noticed a man in a wheelchair across the street, in front of a shop that belonged to a competitor of Hermès.

The sales assistant observed the situation. He opened the large door of the boutique, that gave access to the side street, Rue Boissy-d'Anglas.

He could see that the wheelchair was somewhat jammed, and that its owner was stuck there on the other side of the Rue du Faubourg Saint-Honoré.

He crossed the street and asked the man, who appeared to be an elderly British visitor, whether he needed any assistance.

The man in the wheelchair nodded and replied, in faltering French, "Oh, yes, please, I think my wheel is broken."

The sales assistant immediately called his colleagues to come and help. He and two others carefully lifted the gentleman from his wheelchair and settled him in a plush chair inside the Hermès store. Then they offered to mend the wheelchair on site.

The gentleman looked as if he could not quite believe his eyes.

Twenty minutes later, the wheel was repaired and the man safely seated in his chair again.

He bid them good-bye and left, thanking them profusely.

One month later, they received a letter. The gentleman, who turned out to be an Irishman, claimed that he had "never seen anything like this." . . He wrote: "I had never imagined that Hermès could be a place where they do not deliver some kind of sales spiel or try in one way or another to push their products because it is their job to sell. I was amazed that they would go the extra mile and help someone on the other side of the street, taking the trouble to carry me back to the store, with no concern

(continued)

(Continued)

for names or details, and that they would be prepared to mend a wheelchair, no questions asked. Among the staff present, no one knew that I am a loyal customer and have been for as long as I can remember. To me, your approach reflects the quintessence of a luxury brand: showing patience and respect, offering help, and not going all out to sell."

That day the Hermès store displayed long-held values, showing a different aspect of luxury in which selling is not the issue. Acting in such a manner was purely and simply an expression of family business ethics. That day, the staff at Faubourg Saint-Honoré made their team, indeed the whole company, very proud.

They had done the right thing, at the right time, and with the right attitude. That day, the word luxury regained its true depth of meaning.

Chapter 10

Systems and Operations in the Luxury Business

D ue to the growth and expansion of the luxury industry, the way of managing the back-end of the business has changed. During most of the twentieth century, one, two, or three shops had to be managed for each luxury merchant. The craftsmen used to work in their workshops either above the shops or in the basement. The raw materials were processed and stored nearby, and the finished products were brought from the shop floor directly to the stores. The owner could supervise the full value chain from sourcing and procurement to sales. He, himself, was also the designer, and he supervised the operations and manufacturing. When a friend or a friend's friend visited his store as a customer, he would come down, market the product, and sell it himself. He alone guaranteed the service for the specially crafted goods that he made on his shop floor. The customer could in fact visit the shop floor, could see how intricately the products were made, and could even chat with the workers as they sometimes made special made-to-order materials. Gone are those days.

Luxury companies today manage hundreds of stores across nations. The sourcing has to be done from multiple locations across the world. The crocodile skin has to come from a crocodile farm in Singapore or Australia, while the wool has to come from an alpaca farm in Peru or the cashmere from Inner Mongolia. And all the raw materials have to reach the shop floors on time. The processed products have to reach the Bejing store or the Delhi store on time, and that should coincide with the launch of the product in Paris, Milan, New York City, or London, because the buyers are waiting. The customers know all about the products, as they browse on the Internet. They have compared the products and are highly knowledgeable about the competition, as well. They are not the earlier small group of family, friends, and extended friends of the owner. They come for those exquisite products from faraway lands—from Japan, from China, from Nigeria, or from India.

But how does a company deliver the products that are made in France, Italy, or Switzerland to customers all over the world within such a short time span? How does a company educate those customers twice every year about new offerings? How does a company track the products? It is not a shampoo that is the same product sold everywhere, instead, it is an exquisite pink python-skin bag. There are only two of them made this year. One has been taken to be shown to an oligarch in Moscow, whereas the other one is being stored in Shanghai. It has to be brought back to London to be shown to a member of the royal family of Kuwait. From the two shops and one workshop, the luxury business has changed over time. It needs to be managed with state-of-the-art logistics, a global supply-chain, and customer management systems.

The Challenge

The luxury industry has evolved into a global industry with the requirement of global systems and processes to manage the business. One could argue that is why it is difficult to manage such a global operation. Procter & Gamble and Unilever are managing their products internationally and with success. The difference is in the perception of the brand value. The aspiration needs to be created, the story needs to be communicated, and the service has to be delivered with utmost care for such high-involvement products. The traditional strategies for maintaining the international network of high-net-work customers are changing every day. The expansion has created complexity, and the speed with which it needs to be managed across nations has become uncertain. These luxury firms have to look beyond single global system strategy and structure to create new sources of value. The challenge is perhaps to focus on multiple strategic systems objectives in the search for efficiency, flexibility, responsiveness, and finding innovative solutions at the same time. Some of the key parameters that need attention for luxury goods are the 10 Cs, as follows.

1. **Content:** Luxury goods are by definition creative. Luxury goods companies, again by definition, design and deliver products that are unique and handcrafted. The way the operational excellence and customer intimacy need to be delivered could only be through storytelling and the creation of content around the brand.

2. **Customization:** Customization or making special-order products has always been a strength for luxury brands right from the days of the maharajas of India to today's custom-made products, limited-edition products, special-event products, country-inspired products, year-of-the-Chinese-calendar products, and others. They have always been a priority to make the customer feel special and cared for.

3. **Convenience:** The luxury customer can go to great lengths to acquire what inspires him or her. Maybe the product that she is looking for is rare and not available. Creating convenience for the preferred customer and thereby extending added service is thus important. With the Internet, though, specifications can be understood but still the product may not be available when one reaches the store.

4. **Cost or time value of price:** The real cost a consumer bears for purchasing a product exceeds the price tag. The real cost includes the cost of transport, the opportunity cost of the time the consumer spent to reach the physical store, parking time, and so forth. Due to differences in tax structures and the constant fluctuation in exchange rates, the home location of a luxury firm such as Paris,

Milan, or London most often offers the best price for the products. The famous queue of Japanese tourists and now Chinese tourists outside the stores of the Champs-Élysées reinforces the power of the cost. Thus, to be sensitive to the time value of price, the systems need to evolve to understand the trends and respect these customers who come from faraway lands to have a piece of their aspiration, their dream.

5. **Computing:** The back-end systems also need to process and generate data about billing, taxation, and tax refunds; identify repeat customers; coordinate functions, and track the processes up to the sale, so that the customer experience is seamless inside the store. An intelligent system sometimes allows sales personnel across the world to identify customers and thus find information about the tastes and preferences of an individual.

6. **Customer franchise:** Customer franchises are the summation of all the positive feelings that a customer experiences toward the experience—be it his ability to trust the brand or the confidence she has in the brand. Customer franchise is a direct consequence of the branding efforts of a company—its positioning and the place that it enjoys in the mind of the customer. It is imperative that this information be documented and available across the organization to better serve the luxury customer.

7. **Customer delight:** Customer service does not mean well-behaved employees standing behind the service desk alone. A customer is definitely at ease if the sales speaks his or her language. Figure 10.1 shows the six basic ways customer delight may be achieved.

8. **Community:** Building a community by inviting people during special occasions, regular mailings, keeping in touch with new product launches, and inviting people for brand promotion events go a long way to build and nurture the network of loyal customers. The network of people interested in the product discusses their experiences and also discovers what others from similar social strata are up to. This experience can make or break the sales of a product. Once again, to use this type of information, strong back-end systems are necessary to enhance the total experience for the customer.

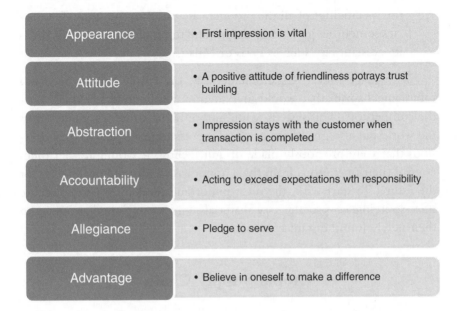

Figure 10.1   Six Ways to Achieve Customer Delight

9. **Communication:** The systems at the back-end should be able to code the brand offer and the feedback. Since the customers hail from multiple nations their expectations are varied, diverse, and different. Communication channels between the company and the consumer and between consumers becomes an important marketing input. The exchanges help consumers make up their mind about a product. The company database shows the buying pattern of return customers.

10. **Customer value:** Though luxury consumers are ready to spend a fortune on their purchases to address their emotional and psychological needs above and beyond their functional needs, they need to be assured of the value's worth. The satisfaction that a consumer obtains from a product, or in economic terms, the "utility" that she derives from the product, determines the customer's values. One of the best ways to transmit customer value is by ensuring a powerful brand experience (in addition to the product) in the country where the purchase is being made. Thus the salesperson needs to be aware not only of the total brand experience but also

the specificities of all the product categories in the store. The stories sometimes go back to the life and times of famous personalities in a distant city such as Paris or Milan.

To manage the 10 Cs simultaneously, the family houses needed a robust mechanism that would give them a competitive advantage over the competitors. This system would not only track their products across the world but also give them data and reports to make professional decisions that were previously made on gut feeling. It would also let them control their operations from their home base and strategically plan for the future. To start with, the most important necessities were to secure their sourcing, to procure raw materials, and to ship their products to their newly found distant customers.

Global Supply Chain

The role of efficiency in supply chain management (SCM) is something that businesses can't ignore. It has become increasingly important for firms in highly competitive (mature) markets. A well-coordinated and implemented supply chain process gives the firm a competitive advantage as it is difficult to imitate for competitors in the short term. Sustained competitive advantage in a supply chain involves vertical integration across the value chain. The shift was predominant as luxury companies integrated their suppliers and started using more technology-oriented processes to reduce time to market their products globally. Collaboration and trust became important among the stakeholders in the value chain.

As luxury companies became global they were forced to integrate SCM systems aimed to reduce manufacturing cycles, reduce inventory levels (raw materials, semi-finished and finished goods) to streamline the flow of information, to remove bottlenecks, internal and external, and to ensure reliable delivery, fast, at the right time and right place, to customers. But it also aimed to increase profitability by making SCM more responsive and effective.

Over the years, high-end fashion houses paid far more attention to product design, craftsmanship, and image than to the mechanics of keeping their stores stocked. When new designs caught on, they often sold out quickly, and the companies were often ill-prepared to speed up production and distribution. Experience suggests that with increasing costs of advertising, promotion, and retail space, synergies are not enough for profitability. Return-on-net-assets (RONA)—used to measure company's financial performance—also means that sales per square foot have to be monitored closely. In addition, it means that the shops need to stocked with products all the time and replenished.

Many brands have long regarded limited-edition products as a way to bolster their cachet. As a result, customers often found themselves on waiting lists for popular merchandise. As an anecdote, the popular story about the Birkin bag needs to be told. As a journalist writes,

> *To fend off customers, Hermès has found an innovative policy. Since the demand far outstrips the supply of Birkin bags, they ask customers looking for Birkin bags to come to the store and try their luck. Most of the time the Birkin bag is unavailable. Usually if the customer is a repeat customer the sales staff after asking the name will go and check the database. Once the sales staff is satisfied that the person is indeed a return customer, (s)he is instructed to tell that the customer needs to visit the store again and again until she is lucky. The sales staff is very kind to give his or her visiting card. But once the customer calls them with the number from the visiting card, they are instructed not to give the information about the product over the phone. It is somewhat an innovative marketing ploy whereby the customer has to visit the store to try her luck to buy a 7,000 euro handbag!*

But the market is changing, and the objective remains that products be always available in stores. It is also true that Hermès increased its production of Birkins, but the demand far outpaced the supply. Fast fashion labels such as Zara and H&M have thrived by spotting trends quickly and filling shelves with new products every fortnight by implementing a very efficient and sophisticated global supply chain. Their success has forced luxury and higher-end rivals to rethink how they do business, and now most of the luxury brands place importance on speed to market. After decades of relying solely on their designers' instincts, for example, some luxury fashion houses, including Italy's Gucci Group, are now using focus groups to find out what consumers actually want in advance.

More and more luxury brands operate more like a successful modern retail store to serve customers better by keeping their boutiques fully stocked with popular merchandise. They educate their sales staff to be more aware of the systems in their supply chain, including modification of the distribution system and the way salespeople serve customers in the stores.

However, tampering with the production can pose a risk to the brand's image. Indeed, customers pay a fortune for luxury products partly because they have bought into the notion that skilled craftsmen make them the old-fashioned way. But the reality is somewhat different. There are limitations to doing things the same way they were done in the olden days due to the sheer scale and scope of the luxury business of today. Without a well-entrenched assembly-line production system with skilled craftsmen, together with efficient SCM, it's not possible to reach out to customers in hundreds of stores globally, keep the stores filled with both the classic and the new designs, and replenish them continuously.

For years, luxury-goods makers have thought about supply and demand differently from other consumer-goods companies. In most sectors, running out of a product when demand is strong is considered disastrous. But production is limited for some luxury fashion items. The industry has begun to rethink that approach. For example, Hermès International has hired another 300 factory workers to reduce waiting lists for best sellers like its €5,000 Kelly bag. Hermès craftsmen still stitch most of the bags by hand, signing them when they finish. Louis Vuitton, which has annual sales of nearly €7.4 billion, had announced that the supply chain changes will help it meet a goal of at least a 10 percent annual sales growth for the next several years. Versace SpA recently hired a division of Computer Sciences Corp. and Giorgio Armani SpA hired Oracle Corp. to help make their supply chains more efficient. Burberry PLC, Cartier, and Prada SpA have retained German software firm SAP AG for the same purpose. As an example of the experiences of Louis Vuitton, the following case study illustrates how it implemented global SCM by introducing process reengineering, creating a logistic hub and training programs to accompany the new way of working.

Case Study: Louis Vuitton

Louis Vuitton, a unit of LVMH implemented its global supply chain. With help from McKinsey, Vuitton made its manufacturing process more flexible, borrowing techniques mastered by carmakers and consumer-electronics companies. The new factory format was called Pegase, after the mythological winged horse and a Vuitton rolling suitcase. Under the new system, it takes less time to assemble bags, in part because they no longer sit around on carts waiting to be moved from one workstation to another. That enables the company to ship fresh collections to its boutiques every six weeks, from twelve weeks before.

On the manufacturing side, it used to take 20 to 30 craftsmen to put together each Louis Vuitton "Reade" tote bag. Over the course of about eight days, separate workers would sew together leather panels, glue in linings and attach handles. With the implementation of Pegase, clusters of six to twelve workers, each of them performing several tasks, can assemble the $680 shiny, LV-logo bags in a single day. Vuitton was releasing a new handbag each season. But the factories, which were working on long-term schedules, remained out of step. If a seasonal bag became a hit, the company wasn't capable of ramping up production.

Vuitton executives imported lean production processes developed by Japanese carmakers, which enabled their factories to react quickly to changes in vehicle orders. The Japanese approach seemed to offer a way for Vuitton to shift production to the handbags that were selling best. But Vuitton's manufacturing procedures weren't conducive to such flexibility. Each factory had about 250 employees, and each worker specialized in one skill, such as cutting leather and canvas; preparing, gluing, and sewing it; making pockets and stitching the lining; and assembling the bag. Specialists worked on one batch of bags at a time. Half-completed purses would sit on carts until

(continued)

(Continued)

someone wheeled them to the next section of the assembly line. Because craftsmen were specialized, it was nearly impossible for Vuitton to quickly switch workers from one task to another.

The realignment of the process to fit the SCM plan was carried out as follows:

- The first step was to train workers to handle multiple parts of the assembly process. Gluing, stitching and finishing the edges of a pocket flap, for example, became the job of one worker, not three. To minimize waste of time, the production process for each product was divided so that each worker would need the same amount of time to complete his or her allotted tasks.
- The factory floor was reorganized accordingly. Mimicking the small-team format used by Japanese electronics makers, Vuitton organized workers into groups of 6 to 12, depending on the complexity of the bags or wallets they made. For maximum efficiency, Vuitton arranged the groups in clusters of U-shaped workstations that contain sewing machines on one side and assembly tables on the other. Workers simply pass their work around the cluster. As workers were less specialized now, they could produce more types of bags, which gave Vuitton more production flexibility.
- The reorganization extended beyond the factory floor. A distribution center in France used to send products directly to Vuitton's stores around the world. The company implemented a global distribution hub outside of Paris that shipped the products to six regional distribution centers: two in Japan, two in Asia, one in the United States and one near Paris for European orders. It enabled a process whereby within a week of a product launch, stores around the world would feed sales information to France and production was adjusted accordingly. Factories worked on a daily schedule, compared to a weekly schedule before the reorganization.

- The reorganization's final stage—named Keepall—was implemented in the stores. In the past, salespeople advising customers would disappear into stockrooms when products weren't available on the shop floor.

  Now, Vuitton assigns a few employees at each store to the stockroom. In the flagship Champs-Élysées store in Paris, items are sent via service elevator from a basement stockroom to the cash register. They arrive wrapped in tissue paper. Early indications that the reorganization is working have prompted LVMH officials to consider extending the new factory format to other divisions.

Customer Relationship Management

With globalization and the expansion of markets, maintaining a customer database across nations, engaging them, and keeping track of their spending habits offer key challenges for the luxury business. Slowly but surely, luxury brands have recognized the true importance of customer relationship management (CRM) as it relates to short- and long-term brand success. Nine out of ten luxury CRM executives believe that having a customer centric culture and values are linked to long-term growth and financial success of the brand. It is imperative that a system is maintained whereby managers can track the customer retention rate. Traditionally RFM (recency, frequency, monetary value) was the type of data most commonly found in luxury CRM systems and used in marketing campaigns for luxury brands. The luxury brands are slowly adopting more formal customer experience research. Before the most commonly used source of knowledge about the customer experience was from the sales executives. As demand was always greater than supply, customers were pulled toward the brand; the brand was not pushed toward the customer. But with the expansion of luxury brands across global borders, a definite need has been felt to educate the new consumers, who get wealthier as time goes by. Thus along with market access, the process of educating the employee about different markets and the story of the brand is a long one. Once it is achieved, a true customercentric culture will emerge. Also key performance indicators (KPIs) are sometimes not aligned.

In order to evaluate why a customercentric culture needs to be adopted by luxury brands, it is necessary to understand that the luxury environment has changed over time. Before companies had goods that were sought after. Each brand had its specialization, such as *ébénistes* (cabinet makers), *tapisseurs* (upholsterers), *menuisiers* (carpenters), and other artisans who made beautiful products for the court of Versailles. Competition did not exist like it does today. Each one had their own space, be it the jewelers or the perfume makers. Initially luxury companies controlled what they made available to consumers, directing price and quality controls. But today's environment has changed. There is intense competition. The bargaining power of consumers has increased with time. Technology and access to information has made consumers much more knowledgeable and products more comparable.

With competition, luxury companies would like to know more about their customers—perhaps not necessarily their buying behaviors, but definitely their aspirations and their lifestyle. Also they would like to protect these customers from their competitors by measuring *recency, frequency,* and *monetary value* of purchase patterns. It is the type of data that luxury companies currently utilize in their existing systems. For example, customers who made a recent purchase are more likely to purchase again, compared with those who have not or those who have purchased only one or two times. Customers who pay the most are more likely to buy again. The most valuable customers tend to become even more valuable the more they spend. The lifetime value of a customer is critical to developing an effective CRM system. Customers of high potential value may be those who are young professionals or up-and-coming professionals, who spend now but will potentially spend more in the future as they mature and become loyal to the brand. The CRM efficiency can help in creating and maintaining the "dream factor" for these luxury consumers. In mature markets, new technologies to track spending patterns within the brand or the conglomerate universe are finding large potential for innovation and productivity gains within the loyalty landscape. For the emerging markets, it is easier to measure due to two reasons. First, the

CRM system is already in place and time tested in mature markets. The traveling customers usually have to provide the details of their nationality for value-added tax refunds. Creating the CRM profile becomes possible once the system is globally integrated. Second, CRM knowledge is already integrated in the retail process.

The CRM is intrinsically related to the retail strategy of the brand. Luxury retailing demands a "hands-on" approach in terms of high service interactions, personalized communication, and providing superior service. For example:

> ... a member of Kuwati royal family aspires to the Chanel brand. She usually shops in Kuwait and Bahrain. In Kuwait and Bahrain, she has the status not only of a repeat customer but also that of the royal family, who spend a considerable amount of resources on the particular brand. She comes to Paris for work. She and a friend visit the Chanel stores at Rue Cambon and then at Avenue Montaigne. Though she is clad from head-to-toe in Chanel products, even the latest white Chanel sneakers from the Fall 2013 collection, the sales staff does not recognize their royal customer. She is just another customer who visits the store from the Middle East who is wealthy. In the salesperson's mind, there is no dearth of wealthy people from the Middle East who often shop in Paris. The customer is perplexed. She has not been treated the way she is used to. She tells her friend to inform the sales staff that she is a regular customer and is looking for some specific products. The sales person is very helpful, but she cannot do much. Her name does not appear in the database, or her passport details. The customer's friend then has to reveal that she is from the royal family. The sales staff goes inside and calls the Chanel boutique in Kuwait. Once her identity is confirmed, the whole shop wakes up.

In the luxury environment there exists a low profile of shoppers' behavior, but shoppers have high expectations for customer service. The challenge is in keeping customer expectations consistent throughout all stores. Measuring salesperson interaction is a management issue as well. Microsegmentation is the key challenge. If the focus shifts to macrosegmentation, the notion of personalized customer service might get lost in translation.

The state-of-the-art situation in luxury CRM and supply-chain management is to have a diverse multichannel approach to customer loyalty. Data can be obtained from different sources such as feedback from sales associates in the store during purchase, at the point of sales (POS), from online browsing patterns, and via cross-channel loyalty tools that align the customer with cross-channel customer demand. The two most effective strategies that are usually implemented are customer affinity and preference, and personalized promotions across channels. This can measure, to a certain extent, the lifetime customer value and the competitive advantage of the brand vis-à-vis their closest customer in the category.

More and more, real-time customer data is being used to understand the aspirations and the trends of the repeat customers and also of the new customers. This data is slowly becoming a priority, as it affects inventories and the resultant supply chain. It seems that 30 percent of retailers are using real-time data and plan to fully implement POS tracking as well as online web trafficking in real time.

In the luxury environment, control of the distribution and supply chain to get products to different markets is not shared. So sharing data from supply chain database is proprietary information. The CRM system the company uses is reflective of how the brand is managing its exclusivity. The decision-making process drives value. This is because because of the strong emphasis on controlling the supply chain and retail distribution. It is a top-down approach.

From the operations and system perspective, the key challenges will be to improve the customer experience, integrate demand-driven methods into product designs, and execute and develop industry-leading innovative methods to maintain loyalty.

To achieve all of this, most luxury firms have already adopted an integrated enterprise resource planning system like SAP that manages all the business operations and customer relations. The concept of CRM has been around as long as people have been buying and selling. The data were kept on diaries, notebooks, and ledgers, all of which were handwritten. With advanced technology, the key to a good CRM remained the same. It was to effectively store information about customers. It is in fact a strategy that a company uses to manage customer interactions, tracking the customer profile and what they buy in the store. Using this data, the store can offer its customers incentives or information about offerings so they buy more from the store. The CRM software also helps companies manage the customer relationship process. The key is in uncovering and storing information about customers. The more they know, the better they can manage their product lines and product offerings. It involves acquiring the customer contact information and keeping notes throughout the sales cycle. By tracking this type of detailed data, companies can compile reports and data regarding the products that are purchased. They can do as little as send out "thank you" notes, birthday cards, and anniversary cards for a purchase, or more.

Linked to CRM in the integrated value chain is the process of just-in-time (JIT). Stores need to be provided the products in a manner such that there is neither a dearth of a particular product nor excess inventory, thereby controlling cost. Integrated enterprise resource planning software, such as SAP, enables real-time processing that allows companies to react to situations in their supply-chain process. The integrated core functionality of the software tracks finance, production, planning, sales and distribution, and materials management. Product costing, human resource needs, and quality control are integrated in the system.

Together with CRM, the next step for luxury companies is to focus on speed to market. Whether a luxury product is destined for a company-owned store or offered in a higher-end department store, design leadership and speed to market continue to distinguish these brands. Making runway fashions ready-to-wear and getting them in the hands of eager shoppers requires a well-integrated, coordinated, and thoughtful approach of planning and execution. Luxury retailers have had significant success managing narrower collections of garments and accessories, producing smaller lots (albeit with much more detailed fabric, trim and construction requirements), and simplifying operations. They also mitigate risk by removing most replenishment and limiting the product's on-shelf lifecycle. Luxury retailers have also been continuing to closely emulate supply chain giant Zara, which continues to break the conventional speed barrier with tightly controlled and integrated design, manufacturing, and demand-driven product management. Zara's latest innovations involve implementing store-level technology that provides managers more control over ordering products and choosing among distribution options that speed the shipment of in-demand products. The result has been further reduced lead times that put an even greater challenge in front of retailers hoping to compete. Zara's fast fashion and use of information technology at the store level and at the corporate level have been studied extensively. The main challenge always remains to balance accessibility and exclusivity.

Moving further, the use of appropriate technology that speeds innovation and customer insight is the next frontier in managing customer aspirations. In-store technology for luxury goods is more focused on simplicity and reducing the focal point during the transaction. Few engage high-tech support such as handheld devices (like tablets) or kiosks. The checkouts are deemphasized, with registers hidden to the point of invisibility, as is the case with Ferragamo and Bottega Veneta stores. These retailers deemphasize the commercial transaction to an extreme, such that it adds to the comfortable, exclusive nature of the experience. On the flip side, the ubiquity and familiarity of handheld devices means that even luxury-goods shoppers would likely be comfortable with an employee using a smartphone personal digital assistant to access their customer record and then tailor the in-process shopping experience, taking into account personal shopping history and known preferences.

Slowly, with so many stores to manage, luxury is moving toward the integrated retail experience. Retail is in the detail. Luxury goods retailers' focus on quality of design, speed to market, and comfortable, even simple, shopping environments with thoughtful, well-trained, and neatly dressed multilingual employees is a powerful model. It is a good baseline for aspiring midrange and upper-scale specialty retailers and vertically integrated manufacturers. This also reflects the luxury brands' requirement to maintain its exclusivity. Such is the case with Chanel, with well-dressed employees wearing Chanel apparel in all stores. Ferragamo also practices this strategy, with its employees wearing black uniforms and Ferragamo shoes. Retailers that are truly demand-driven will set themselves apart from the competition by choosing particular points of service at which to excel. The use of IT and sophisticated information-driven tools such as QR codes, electronic specification, VIP identification techniques, mobile apps, and handheld devices like smart phones and tablets all engage the clients and make their interaction inside the store a pleasant experience.

Information Technology

As distances between production facilities increase and pressure for fast delivery increases, the coordination of these dispersed manufacturing resources becomes a critical activity. If the logistics system is well positioned, it becomes a bridging strategy and structure in the new competitive environment. It is imperative to recognize that logistics play an integral role in creating the "fit" necessary to achieve competitive success, especially when the products have to be "Made in France" or "Italy" or "Switzerland." Most of the upwardly mobile high-net-worth individuals are using mobile applications on their handheld devices to access information before they shop. It is thus imperative that the luxury companies align themselves with this trend and provide their clients with the information they need to make their decision while inside the store. Brands such as BMW, Mercedes-Benz, Burberry, Louis Vuitton, Ralph Lauren, Chanel, and others have their own apps to provide their clients instant and updated information. For example, Chanel is organized in terms of a business unit. To protect its exclusivity, like most luxury brands it does not allow its consumers to purchase online. It also protects against counterfeiting and accessibility of many of its product lines. In that respect, Ralph Lauren is a leader in its superior web and mobile applications. In some markets, Ralph Lauren is a mass brand with its Polo label. To differentiate itself, the brand has Black and Purple labels. It has managed to balance its technology-based marketing campaign and its CRM to become one of the undisputed leaders in the lifestyle brand category. With Ralph Lauren, consumers may also purchase online. But Ralph Lauren had faced shortcomings in implementing its worldwide SAP structure to capture all sales in all areas globally and locally. Since it has also taken control of licenses in China, Mauritius, and other locations recently, its mass marketing capability in controlling CRM has been effective.

Another example has been Ermenegildo Zegna, which has an excellent record in its e-mail and web campaigns. They understand the details that are of value to their customers. The company builds affinity and keeps the relationship with the customer close to their value, with hand-woven fabric, silk and materials that are sourced from the finest wool in far-off countries such as Australia, Mongolia, South Africa, and Peru.

For example, Zegna targeted consumers with an e-mail offering free shipping on its Autumn/Winter 2011 collection as a Thanksgiving gift and was one of the few retailers to offer a turkey-day-themed promotion. Free shipping may be seen as one of the most valuable incentives to offer to luxury buyers, especially since they are paying high price points for goods. It is a gesture, as they believe they deserve a break, even if it is only a few dollars. The Zegna e-mail provides links to its social media pages and the Zegna mobile application. Burberry, in their digital communication, expressed that they had not focused on a CRM system but rather on a digital presence online. The company realizes the impact of its online and social media effect on the brand's bottom line. Their operational excellence is focused on its supply chain, IT, planning, and replenishment. They agreed that this focus enabled them to respond more effectively to strong consumer demand, something that they could not have handled a couple of years ago. Their focus on digital marketing helped them extend their region awareness where social media plays a key role. They had more than one million unique visitors to their Art of the Trench site and more than two million views on YouTube. They currently have more than four million Facebook fans, and that number grows every minute. They bought back the licenses in China and their SAP is being rolled out in that country. They are yet to have a full CRM database and rely anecdotally on certain markets. For example, foreign customers dominate the luxury consumption in London. It is the Chinese, the Russians, the Middle Eastern customers, and a lot of Europeans. Though a lot of improvement has been done to improve the supply chain over the past four to five years, they are still focused on speed to market and replenishment of seasonal collections and identifying the best sellers. Like most luxury companies, capital expenditures and infrastructure are not a focus. Instead, they have focused on digital.

Brands like Ferragamo and Van Cleef & Arpels are secretive about their systems, logistics, and supply-chain methods, but resources show there is a CRM system in place or that one is being developed that results in a focus on the U.S. and French markets.

Conclusion

To put it holistically, researchers have argued that each cog in the wheel within the broad framework of operational process—the supply chain followed by customer relationship management—should lead to a total customer experience[1] (Figure 10.2). Managers have become increasingly aware of the need to create value for their customers in the form of experiences. To carry out such a strategy, luxury companies must gain an understanding of the customer's journey—from the expectations they have to the assessments they are likely to make when it's over. This is the way that they tell the story of the brand and create aspirations within the customers. Research shows that by using that knowledge, companies can orchestrate an integrated series of "clues" that collectively meet or exceed people's emotional needs and expectations. The internalized meaning and value the clues take on can create a deep-seated preference for a particular experience, and thus for one company's product or service over another's. A clue is anything that can be perceived or sensed, or recognized by its absence. Thus, the product or service for sale gives off one set of clues, the physical setting offers more clues, and the employees—through their gestures, comments, dress, and tones of voice—give still more clues. Each clue carries a message, suggesting something to the customer. The composite of all the clues makes up the customer's total experience. For example, measuring concretely the actual functioning of the product (the intricate story of the scales of the crocodile skin or the delicate python skin) is a clue. The service offered while showing the product and explaining the number of movements of a tourbillion is a clue. The emotions and the senses, which include the smells, sounds, sights, tastes, and textures, as well as the environment in which it is offered, are all clues.

The experiences the same customer has when visiting the LV flagship store on the Champs-Élysées, the Hermès Faubourg Saint-Honoré store, and the Chanel store in Rue Cambon are entirely different. The feel of leather upholstery, the tone of voice of the person answering the customer, the décor are all clues that envelope the functionality of a product and the service. This category of clues includes two types: "mechanics" (clues emitted by things) and "humanics" (clues emitted by people). Such clues tend to address emotion rather than reason, as people consider whether to buy or move on.

To build this competency so that it becomes a capability within the organization, luxury companies might want to analyze their shops,

---

[1] Berry, Carbone, and Haeckel, 2002.

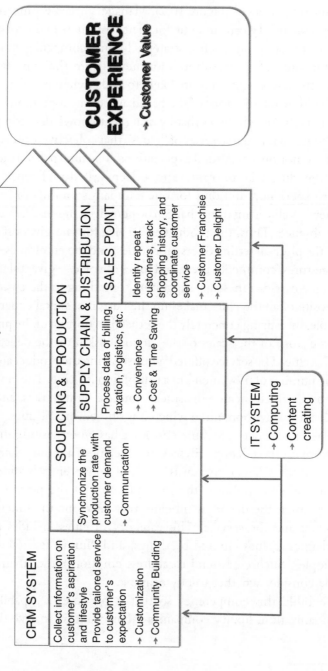

Figure 10.2 How to Create Value in Operations and Systems for the Customer Experience

using hours of video footage and examining frame by frame, watching facial expressions, gestures, and body language in order to understand customers' emotional states in various situations. To complement this information, it might be helpful to conduct in-depth interviews with customers and employees to find out how people on both sides of a transaction feel about different aspects of an experience and the emotional associations that go along with it. For example, it is easy to monitor the growing anxiety of a potential customer about whether she will find what she has came for after traveling all the way from China or the Middle East. People in this situation behave almost like children, wanting to buy a product at that moment. The customer does not need it, but the experience and the product will make her happy, her self-esteem will soar, and she will achieve a state of self-actualization. This experience can then be translated to the basic motif that reflects the organization's core values and branding strategy. The motif acts as the unifying element for every clue in the newly designed customer experience.

Customers always have an experience. It may be excellent, good, bad, or indifferent. The key is how effectively the company manages the experience. Managing both the functional and emotional experience of the customer increases the chance of emotional bonding between brands, customers, and luxury companies. This bond is a sustainable competitive advantage that is difficult to replicate. It is rare, expensive, and cannot be imitated or substituted. This may be the next frontier where luxury companies can strengthen customer loyalty for the next generation.

Chapter 11

Retail, Distribution, and E-Commerce

*T**he duty-free market is worth more than €30 billion, €10 billion of which is in luxury products. LVMH holds the biggest share of duty-free shopping, with a majority interest in DFS (duty-free shoppers) and sales of more than €2 billion.*

Most duty-free stores are in airports, except in Hawaii, Korea, or on the island of Okinawa, Japan, where huge shopping malls are allowed to sell duty free.

The shopping center at Okinawa is an incredible example. Tourists, mainly Japanese, but also Chinese, Korean, and Taiwanese arrive at the airport. The Duty Free Shopping service meets them at the airport and takes them to the shopping center in cars that they will keep for their entire stay on the island. Before they return the cars, they fill up the trunk with duty-free purchases.

It is a military-style organization that takes care of tourists and does not let go of them. The DFS center in Okinawa is huge. There is everything there: restaurants, hundreds of shops with a special area for luxury products, where all the major brands are present. It has to be admitted that it is rather like a cattle market, and a far cry from what luxury is usually considered to be.

Quite surprisingly, major luxury brands set up in these inland, town-center shopping centers!

In Waikiki, Hawaii, or Okinawa, the most beautiful brands are displayed next to umbrellas and cheap lingerie. This can sometimes be strange and humorous to see.

In Hawaii and in Seoul, for example, all the customers are Japanese; they arrive at these temples of duty-free shopping in coachloads. Hordes of people shop and leave.

The sales figures for the airports are amazing, with London and Seoul being the winners. They sell more than a billion dollars' worth of duty-free retail goods, followed by Dubai, Singapore, Amsterdam, Paris, Hong Kong, Bangkok, Frankfurt, and Tokyo.

Luxury at the airport—why not?

In Europe, airport stores are no longer duty free. Prices are the same as in local markets, except if brands sell at discounted prices, which is permitted, but costly.

When duty free was stopped in Europe, companies threw up their hands in despair, predicting the apocalypse, job losses, and diminished sales. They turned out to be mistaken; duty-free business at the airport is flourishing and is there to stay.

In airports, travelers buy anything from clothes to cars and shoes. Duty-free shops can sell any type of goods and services, because customers have time to kill and do not feel guilty about shopping. They wander around, looking, observing, as they have nowhere to wander off to.

Airport sales are an excellent way for luxury brands to enter the market. It could even be a good idea to specialize in goods for sale in airports. Millions of potential customers remain to be won over, and in an enclosed space with potential customers who are relatively available and who have purchasing power, it's just a question of capturing their attention and inciting a desire.

At the same time, innovation in the airport market is faltering.

A luxury house may set up business in terminal A, where Japanese airlines arrive and depart. Then all of a sudden, JAL, ANA, and all the Asian companies move to terminal B and the luxury house is back to square one with no Asian clients, but Latin American ones instead. The hard-won customer is now in the other terminal, and the competitor brand there suddenly has masses of Taiwanese and Chinese to sell to.

One brand weeps, and the other jumps for joy.

Luxury poker is a game you play at the airport.

Do these uncertain prospects account for the fact that Louis Vuitton has never set up in an airport?

Channels of Distribution

With globalization and the rise of wealthy consumers across the world, distribution is one of the key elements in the value chain of the luxury goods industry. In earlier days, it was different. Most producers of luxury brands harped on their aspirational value. It was all about the brand and thus related to branding of their goods and brand management. With the spread of luxury aspiration across consumers and across geography, the focus for most has shifted to efficiency in the distribution of the products. Distribution is also about execution. The brands have to make their goods available to the consumers in distant lands at the right place, the right time, within the right environment, and at the right cost. How to reach them and at what cost are the key questions with which luxury companies are grappling today.

Luxury houses decided to focus their attention on their distribution channels and redefine ways to efficiently reach the new customers through diverse ways. The distribution channels can be categorized into five main areas. They are directly operated stores, franchises, wholesale distribution, travel retail, and licensing. Simply described, it is a function of control and capital required. Of course if the control

Figure 11.1   Distribution Channels in Luxury

and capital required are high, the profitability is also high. Figure 11.1 describes the various distribution channels that are available for luxury goods companies.

These channels differ in the degree of control, capital requirements, and profitability:

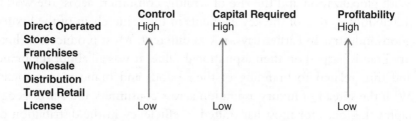

From the 1990s, the luxury retail sector began reaching its consumers through the aforementioned ways. They intensified their distribution methods through direct retail formats with an increased number of stores, innovating as they went with different store formats such as flagship stores, large format stores, and multistoried stores inside prestigious malls and department stores, shop-in-shops, and others. To disseminate information across different geographic locations they developed online business models with selective and still limited revenue generation. They also pre-established shops in duty-free areas for travelers. To supply products to these diverse clienteles, they had to evolve their production methods from manufacturing a few pieces to hundreds or thousands of pieces, depending on the number of stores they had. To keep in line with this model, they had to innovate their structure of inventory turnover that depended financially on extending their product line to accessories such as handbags, perfumes, cosmetics, and others. This product and distribution strategy enabled them to target not only a wider customer base but also to democratize the luxury goods industry, keeping in mind the future consumers.

Many argued that this global distribution strategy on crafts and art would reduce the perception of exclusivity, aesthetic and technical superiority, distinction, and singularity, and in the long run will threaten the legitimacy of the brand. The challenge was to redefine, rethink and reevaluate how to balance broader distribution while reasserting the singularity of the offerings.

To address the issue of brand legitimacy with a global distribution strategy, luxury brands such as Vuitton, Dior, and Chanel have linked traditional legitimacy based on craft skills and know-how to charismatic legitimacy. The charismatic legitimacy is based on an exceptional charismatic persona together with the creative director who designs the products as they reinterpret the codes of traditional legitimacy within the context of the changing environment of today. Charismatic legitimacy, for example, has been based on creating devotion to (adoration of) the exceptional character of a leader, dramatized in his or her persona and the compliance of followers with the leader's mission out of affectionate devotion to this persona, such as Louis Vuitton, Miss Dior, and Coco Chanel. Charismatic legitimacy was combined with the creativity and artistic interpretation of Marc Jacobs for Louis Vuitton (until 2013), John Galliano for Dior (until 2012), and Karl Lagerfeld for Chanel. The interpretation of the charismatic legitimacy by the artistic director was communicated to create its strategic value in marketing of the brand within the different channels of distribution.

Retail

With global expansion, an integrated global retail distribution strategy that creates a satisfying and unique shopping experience in the stores has become a necessity. It is not only to differentiate each brand from its competitors but also to communicate the unique features of the brand to its respective customers. In retailing, one of the most important characteristics is execution. This can be best done through directly operated stores. It is about bringing the best-designed product to the right kind of

shop at the right time. It is said that "retail is in the detail." It is important that during retailing, the perceived value of the product with better
quality and higher prices seamlessly transmits the cultural and historical
heritage of the brand the same way that it transmits in its country of
origin. When compared to fashion that is subjected to short-term cycles
and perpetual change, luxury is for the longer-term traditions. In a way,
there is no intrinsic luxury good to sell. It is for the retailer to organize
and govern the access to luxury goods for consumers. This organization and access has to be in the same way in which luxury evolved and
expressed in a particular cultural context. The access to the retail outlets thus in a sense needs to be hedonic and multisensorial to connect
with customers on an emotional level. The retail outlets thus should
provide for the high "ratio" of intangible value to price. The successful
luxury retail strategy relies on the logic of adoration, which has a charismatic basis. Thus we witness in mature markets a growing presence of
luxurious shopping districts that remains highly sought after. High-end
department stores continue to expand internationally through physical
stores and online. Premium department stores are opening stores in new
markets. Several department stores started offering international delivery.

Flagship Stores   In the past 10 years, as part of the integrated global
retail strategy, there has been a rise of numerous impressive flagship stores,
not only in their established markets such as Europe and the United
States, but also in emerging markets. Luxury brands used to choose New
York, London, or Paris for their biggest flagship stores, as these cities
provide more credibility and visibility. Now many of them have moved
to metropolises in mainland China such as Shanghai and Beijing for their
new flagship stores, after Tokyo, Hong Kong, and Seoul. For example,
in 2014, Louis Vuitton opened its largest flagship store in Shanghai, the
Louis Vuitton Mansion, after they opened one in Marina Bay Sands
in Singapore. Hermès opened its flagship store in Shanghai in 2014.
These new Louis Vuitton stores, all designed by famous retail architect
Peter Marino, feature the entire range of Louis Vuitton products, from
ready-to-wear for men and women to leather goods and accessories,
as well as limited special merchandise. With the existing 42 boutiques,
including eight flagship stores already in China, the idea was to capture
customers by providing them the *ultimate luxury experience* and a holistic
image of the brand.

In that sense the retail space is also about *communication*. It is a crucial communication vector for luxury brands. The space has to provide the elements of fantasy, charisma, and privilege while maintaining the cultural heritage of the brand. Robert Polet, the previous CEO of Gucci, once said that "Nobody needs another handbag. The need to have it factor has to be created, and the customer says 'I need to have that $2,000 bag, and my only worry is that it be in stock. I want it now.' This is the emotional desire of the brand, the power of the dream."[1]

The retail space plays an important role in evoking this *feeling and associated emotions*. The shopper needs to be seduced by the lavish surroundings, a Disneyland of desire. To build this desire and the context has driven Prada and Louis Vuitton to work with famous architects to design flagship stores in emerging markets at an incredible pace.

Yet the stores need to portray a *consistent image* both geographically and spatially. The retail space must correctly evoke the codes of the brand, with no disconnect from what is going on in the advertising or on the runway; otherwise there is a risk the consumer will become disenchanted. For example, Aldo Gucci defined the appeal of authentic luxury goods in 1938 when he hung a sign in the brand's first store in via Condotti, Rome. It read: "Quality is remembered long after price is forgotten." Ironically, few people can remember what the store's original interior looked like, because it has been redesigned to reflect each incoming designer's interpretation of the Gucci brand. Lately the transformation was overseen by Frida Giannini, who took over from Tom Ford as Gucci's chief designer in 2005. Working her way through the chain of stores, she has changed Ford's black-and-chrome aesthetic and replaced it with her own lighter, more gently nostalgic vision. As each successive designer tweaks the codes of the brand, its original values disappear under layers of artifice. But is the image depends not only on the store—the location is also significant.

Upscale stores are invariably located in elegant districts that create an elegant, sophisticated microworld of their own. Examples abound. Paris has Champs-Élysées, Avenue Montaigne, Rue du Faubourg Saint-Honoré, Rue Cambon, Place Vendôme, and others. London has its Regent Street, Tokyo has its Ginza. As luxury shoppers want to reinforce their perceptions about quality, emotional reward, and then price,

---

[1] Passariello and Meichtry, 2007.

the exclusivity or status of the *location of the stores* becomes a key differentiator. For example, after Louis Vuitton opened its first mainland
China "Maison" at Shanghai's Plaza 66—its fourth location in the city
and 39th nationwide—was in Anhui province in its capital city in Hefei,
at Intime Center, in 2013. Hefei is little known outside of China, and
certainly not widely known *within* China as a very luxurious city. But
over the past several years brands like Gucci, Burberry, and Bally have
transitioned from small sales counters at malls like Wanqian, Shangzhidu,
and Drum Tower Business Plaza to full-fledged locations at Intime, making it the city's premier high-end mall over the course of one year*. An
interesting fact is that in the city of Hefei, 90 percent of VIP shoppers
are under the age of 35.

However, the big-store retail strategy can be a challenge even for
big brands due to the high level of investment, the difficult choice of
location, and the high rent in those locations. The flagship stores demand
more input at both the financial and the managerial level, especially in
the emerging markets of Asia, Latin America, and Africa, which are
more complex to manage because of the different cultures and business
environments. Another fact is that, due to the high taxation on luxury
goods in these markets, customers from these regions today tend to shop
overseas for luxury goods. For example, Europe has been profiting a
lot from travel shoppers, especially those from China, while the local
market in mainland China has been down, where the average luxury
goods price is 9 percent lower than that in Hong Kong and 28 percent
below mainland China. With over 1 million Chinese travelers in France
spending an average of $1,000 per capita, Paris may soon see Chinese
police protecting their travelers in Paris!

As a big-store retail strategy has its pros and cons, some brands have
downplayed this strategy and concentrated more on a mixed strategy.
For example, one of them is Ralph Lauren. It started making neckties
for men and gradually became the leader of lifestyle for menswear and
womenswear, developing a wardrobe fit for the denizens of *The Great
Gatsby*. Ralph Lauren has not invested as much as its competitors in the
expansion of its retail presence. Ralph Lauren has been relying heavily
on franchising and licensing in most markets, where they may not have

---

*http://jingdaily.com/louis-vuittons-inland-china-empire-set-to-grow-even-larger/20296/

a directly operated store. Their low retail presence in important markets such as Europe and China may be why the brand was witnessing a dilution of its value in these markets. In China, many consumers associated the Ralph Lauren brand with only the Polo and Denim lines. That was reflected also in the brand's travel retail performance, which explains why Chinese tourists account for less than 2 percent of Ralph Lauren's Paris flagship store sales, while its rivals, such as Burberry, have been earning up to 50 percent of their sales from Chinese tourists.

To cater to this deficiency, since 2010 Ralph Lauren has been expanding its flagship store network together with its new merchandise categories, particularly accessories. By opening its biggest flagship store in Kuwait, following the opening of its first flagship store in Moscow, the brand is eyeing expansion in the Middle East, Russia, and Brazil. It also has plans to restructure and develop its retail network, particularly in Europe, and to grow its store base through concession shops in China, in order to boost the presence of the brand. This ambition was shown in the company's decision to expand retail spaces dedicated to womenswear and accessories, including the Blue and Black labels. Since 2010, this expansion strategy has been implemented, starting from a flagship store in Milan to the recent plan to redesign and expand the layout of the Paris store to better showcase its growing accessories merchandise. Besides reorganization of existing stores, the company has been opening new mono-brand shops, with one store in New York dedicated entirely to women, and one men's-only flagship store in Hong Kong (the first men's-only store in Asia). Ralph Lauren realized that its focus on a digital presence became in one way its weakness in communicating its brand image consistently across consumer categories. It is trying to re-establish its luxury lifestyle status and respond to growing demand in new markets. The appointment of Valérie Hermann, former CEO of Yves Saint Laurent and previous director of Women's Ready-to-Wear at Dior, as the new president of luxury collections for Ralph Lauren clearly showed the ambition of the brand. The new big-store strategy aligns with other big luxury brands and emphasizes the retail tradition of the brand.

Wholesale

The concept of wholesale sales is rare in the luxury industry. Wholesale is mainly prevalent in the watches and the wine and champagne sectors.

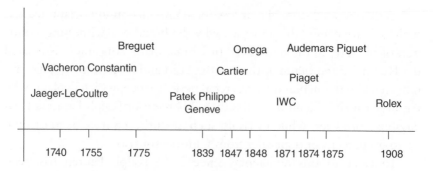

Figure 11.2   The Birth Years of Brands

The nature of the wholesale business can be examined from the watches sector.

Luxury watches were created as early as 1740. Figure 11.2 depicts the time frame when the 10 well-known luxury brands were founded. Their birth was not entirely sporadic. Three brands—Breguet, Vacheron Constantin, and Jaeger-LeCoultre—date from the 1700s. The brands Omega, Cartier, Patek Philippe, Audemars Piguet, Piaget, and IWC began in the 1800s. Rolex was founded in the 1900s.

The fact that these three clusters existed in the watch industry suggests that gaps were identified in the industry by owners of companies. This gave rise to multiple brands that came up to target the various emerging segments. It gives an idea of how the market segmentation evolved based on watch complications, the advent of newer technologies, and changing consumer preferences. It indicates how important heritage and legitimacy were for the watch industry.

All the watch brands follow a wholesale strategy as part of their distribution plans. They book orders at watch fairs like the Basel Watch Fair and provide multibrand retailers with their brands, which are pre-booked during the fair. In this way, with a concerted strategy of directly owned stores (DOS) and multibrand retail chains, luxury brands can reach their customers with ease. The watch brands using this strategy can be present in Italy, the United States, Germany, Japan, China, and France, and with multibrand stores in New York, Singapore, Hong Kong, and some other Asian cities. Some brands such as Rolex, Cartier, IWC, and Jaeger-LeCoultre have made a strong presence with both DOS and through multibrand stores in mainland China. Patek Philippe is the only brand that has been following a consistent United States-centric retail strategy, and its expansion plans in China indicate that it does not plan to expand like its competitors in Asia.

Brands such as Vacheron Constantin, Patek Philippe, IWC, and Jaeger-LeCoultre have expanded in the United States, Europe, and Japan. Omega is one of the most aggressive in this sector in terms of expansion through the wholesale market.

Comparing the various retail presences of the 10 brands, it was discussed that watch brands were following different strategies in their expansion plans. For example, Cartier was expanding its retail presence in mainland China along with Omega. Rolex, Audemars Piguet, and Patek Philippe were the major players of the industry in terms of sales and were independent players. All the other seven brands were part of the luxury conglomerates. On average, Rolex is the largest vis-à-vis sales (€4.1 billion), followed by the whole Haute Horlogerie (HH) group (the other seven brands had a total sales of about €2 billion). Cartier with €2 billion sales was a key player by itself in both the regular and jewelry watch segment.

Luxury Pop-Up Stores   Another format that has gained momentum is the pop-up store. They have proved quite successful in the United States and Western Europe. Pop-up retail stores are stores opened for a short duration. It denotes that for a determined or undetermined period of time, customers can expect to enjoy the brand experience. It allows for feedback on a flexible retail model that could lend itself to being permanent within the space or within that general area. The spending on the interior design and rents are negligibly small. The concept of pop-up stores revolves more around creating a "buzz" rather than generating sales. It primarily serves as a channel through which the fashion brands engage directly with consumers and test the market for a more long-term retail commitment. For example, BMW embarked on a pop-up store in central Moscow with their 7-series model. The pop-up store was complete with a library, reading space, snacks and bar, and a display space with one model. It may be a trend in the future for luxury brands to use pop-up stores to display their creativity. This is because brands are working on different ideas with an ever-increasing number of designer and artistic collaborators who are housed in the world's most luxurious retail stores. Also, for example, Gucci opened a pop-up store in London's Covent Garden to celebrate the launch of its trainer range with Mark Ronson. Louis Vuitton opened seven pop-up stores around the world to celebrate the launch of its collaboration with the Japanese artist Yayoi Kusama. British shoe label Nicholas Kirkwood was using a series of pop-up stores to grow its global presence. He opened seven pop-up stores in 2014, starting with the first pop-up store in Printemps, on Boulevard Hausmann in Paris, in March, and from there the brand will host pop-ups in six other cities.

Licensing

The luxury goods industry has been taking the licensing route since the beginning of retail expansion. Licensing is a favored option, as it lets a brand enter a new market with relative ease and minimum investment. Licensing contributes a significant portion of total revenues for many luxury goods companies. Thus, the luxury-goods companies selectively disclose and investors carefully review data on the mix of owned and franchised or licensed operations. For example, groups such as LVMH have no strategic licenses, while Gucci had a limited number of strategic licensing partners. Specialty apparel brands such as Polo Ralph Lauren and Armani rely on a greater mix of licensed sales. Compared to that, Hermès has no licenses at all, and Chanel has licenses only for eyewear.

Though a licensing distribution strategy has proved to be a quick and efficient way to increase the scale and scope of luxury businesses, in many cases it has resulted in a tarnished brand, particularly for those who overextend their licensing activities. This is because the risk of diluting the brand with time exists if the license agreement cannot be controlled and the partner cannot be trusted with the licensing agreement. The experiences of each luxury brand are different, but the trust issue has consistently emerged to be one of the most painful experiences. It is clear from these experiences that an appropriate mix and structure of licensing activities is crucial for a company to be successful within the luxury goods industry. As companies mature, they seek full ownership of the licensed business to increase control and provide a platform for greater value extraction. Writing-instrument companies such as

S. T. Dupont and Montblanc and eyeware businesses rely heavily on the licensing business model. The well-known licensing companies are Safilo and Luxottica for eyewear, Fossil and Swatch for watches, and L'Oréal for beauty and cosmetics. The infamous cases in which brands diminished their value through licensing were those of Gucci, Polo Ralph Lauren, Calvin Klein, and Crocodile, among others.

Tom Ford and Dominico De Sole saved the Gucci brand by buying out hundreds of licensing agreements when they rejuvenated the brand. Polo Ralph Lauren had to be rebranded as Ralph Lauren, as the Polo brand was licensed and copied throughout markets. Calvin Klein and Crocodile have lost their luster due to licensing. More recently, Tom Ford used the licensing retail strategy to grow his brand.

Case Study: Tom Ford

Thomas Carlyle "Tom" Ford is an American fashion designer and film director. He joined Gucci in 1990 as the brand's chief designer for its women's ready-to-wear line. At that time, Gucci had a very blurry brand image. Dawn Mello, the company's creative director at the time commented that "No one would dream of wearing Gucci." The brand was struggling to reestablish its status in women's fashion. In 1992, Ford took over as the design director, leading the brand's ready-to-wear, fragrances, image, advertising, and visual merchandizing. In 1994, Ford was promoted to creative director. In 1995, he worked with French stylist Carine Roitfeld and photographer Mario Testino to create a series of new, modern advertisement campaigns. Between 1995 and 1996, sales of Gucci increased by 90 percent. In early 1999, luxury product conglomerate LVMH initiated a takeover bid of Gucci. Tom Ford and Domenico de Sole, the CEO at that time, were not comfortable with the management style of Bernard Arnault. Ford and De Sole approached PPR (later Kering) group. François Pinault, the group's founder, agreed to purchase 37 million shares of Gucci,

(continued)

(*Continued*)

equivalent to a 40-percent stake. Arnault's share was diluted to 20 percent. At the same time, Tom Ford was the largest individual shareholder in Gucci. During Ford's 10 years as creative director at Gucci and Gucci Group, sales increased from US$230 million in 1994 to almost US$3 billion in 2003, making Gucci one of the largest and most profitable luxury brands in the world. When Ford left in 2004, Gucci Group was valued at US$10 billion. He was also behind the decision of Gucci Group to buy Yves Saint Laurent and was named the creative director of the brand as well.

In April 2005, Ford founded his own "Tom Ford" brand. Having already built his fame as a designer at Gucci, his new fashion lines for men became a big success. Domenico De Sole joined in the start-up and became chairman of the company. In that same year, Ford partnered with Marcolin Group to produce and distribute optical frames and sunglasses. At the same time, he cooperated with Estée Lauder to create and produce the "Tom Ford Beauty" brand, and he posed for the advertisement campaign for the fragrance with his own name. With the fame of Tom Ford as a celebrity-like public figure, the eyewear and beauty products with his name became a success, which funded the launch of his first luxury menswear collection. The strategy was to focus on superior fashion design and luxury products, attention to detail and made-in-Italy roots, while the production and distribution under the Tom Ford label were licensed to Ermenegildo Zegna in February 2006. In April 2007, Tom Ford opened its first flagship store in New York at 845 Madison Avenue, for luxury men's ready-to-wear and made-to-measure clothing, footwear, and accessories, where later, in autumn 2010, he presented his much-anticipated womenswear collection. In 2014, there were more than 100 freestanding Tom Ford stores and shop-in-shops in locations such as Milan, Tokyo, Las Vegas, Dubai, Zurich, New Delhi, Shanghai, and Russia. The Tom Ford brand is presently valued at close to $1 billion, and is continuing to expand worldwide.

Case Study: Prada

The Prada Group is a global powerhouse in luxury goods, a business icon in combining industrialized processes with sophisticated workmanship. The Italian luxury group has now under its roof notably four brands—the star brand Prada, which contributes to more than 80 percent of the group's sales, the younger sister brand Miu Miu, "the other soul of Prada," representing over 15 percent of the sales, the historic British brand Church's for luxury men's footwear, and the Italian brand Car Shoe specifically for driving moccasins. The Group operates mainly in luxury handbags, leather goods, footwear, clothing apparel, and accessories, registering €3.59 billion net sales in 2013. The products are sold in more than 70 countries worldwide, mainly through retail and wholesale models. The group has a retail network of more than 491 directly operated stores, generating more than 80 percent of the total net sales. The wholesale network is highly selective, including luxury department stores, independent retailers, and franchises in the big cities worldwide, from which, however, the sales have been slightly shrinking from 2009 onwards. The decrease is detected mostly in Europe, due to the economic crisis, though compensated by the four duty-free franchisees opened in Asia. The group also operates under licensing agreements in eyewear, fragrances, and mobile phones; however these are minor activities from which the royalties account for only around 1 percent of the group's net revenue.

The main brand Prada was founded in 1913 in Milan by Mario Prada, grandfather of the current CEO Miuccia Prada. The historic store is located in the prestigious Galleria Vittorio Emanuele II in Milan, and has been a favorite of local customers with its Italian aristocracy and avant-garde fashion style, attracting millions of tourists every year. The leather goods segment registers both the biggest part of sales and the fastest growth,

(continued)

(*Continued*)

while the impressive success is mainly sustained by the brand's iconic handbags and modern styles. The brand has kept delivering a double-digit growing performance everywhere through its 301 directly operated stores (DOS), except in Italy due to the overall downslope of the economy. The major sales in 2013 came from the Asia Pacific area, accounting for around one-third of the sales, excluding the travel retail revenue generated by Asian tourists. The revenue from the Middle East area has been on the rise since the opening of the first Prada store, while the market still remains to be developed.

Innovation in retail is at the core of Prada's success. Since Patrizio Bertelli joined Prada in the late 1970s, he has broken new ground in the luxury world by introducing a new business model in which he kept direct internal control over all production process while aggressively eyeing international expansion. The products are made in 11 company-owned sites, 10 of which are located in Italy and one in Great Britain, and by a network of external contractors who are strictly supervised to follow the standard of craftsmanship, quality, and reliability, from the sourcing of raw materials to the fabrication of prototypes, including in-house and outsourced production. The innovation also lies in the distribution model, where Prada was the first brand to launch a new type of store known as "Prada Epicenter," designed by internationally known architects, integrating the brand's cutting-edge products with the modern merchandising store setting. The brand enjoys state-of-the-art visibility on an international scale, and ranks 72nd in Interbrand's top 100 most valuable global brands in 2013.

Outlet Stores

Discounted luxury channels are another distribution outlet that is expanding, especially in the United States and Europe. In the midst of the economic downturn, some retailers preferred outlet stores, which were usually away from the city center, in comparison to expensive locations. They were likely to remain more price sensitive and offered discounted prices. Outlet villages have been performing well and are expanding in Eastern Europe. High-end department stores are expanding their discount formats in the United States. Flash sale sites are gaining prominence in the luxury goods market. Luxury retailers should perceive discount channels as an opportunity to encourage shoppers to trade-up. Luxury houses are now focusing more on menswear, children's wear, and the introduction of beauty ranges. Luxury retailers are introducing dedicated menswear stores. Luxury houses are keen to further develop their children's wear offerings, and are experimenting with beauty products. Pop-up stores are used to generate greater excitement and brand awareness within the outlet stores. An example of an outlet store that has gained prominence is the Val d'Europe.

With around 200 shops covering an area of 20 hectares, an architectural mix of separate houses and glass and steel constructions inspired by late nineteenth century Parisian architecture, Val d'Europe belongs to the new generation of commercial centers, providing a combination of unique shopping and comfort for the visitor. Its grand walkways and sumptuous halls take the visitor on a journey through a town center and a rural village offering exclusive specialty boutiques in a village-like atmosphere in the Ile de France.

The store merchandising consists of not only last season's merchandise but also "limited-edition" merchandise, which has never been sold in main stores for various reasons. This is more appealing to customers, and it's also easier for brands to position the price (contrary to conventional wisdom, outlet pricing is not necessarily discounted pricing). It also comforts the loyal clients that what they bought in the store will never be sold at a discounted price in outlets, which helps to keep the brand's prestigious image and enhances the client's loyalty by separating target customer groups. For example, Céline strictly applies a no-discount policy; it does not participate in any kind of sales promotions in its department stores, rarely organizes private sales, and selects different merchandise for its outlet store.

Luxury brands always provide value-added after-sales-service; however, purchases done in outlet stores do not benefit from the same service, and customers need to pay for services such as altering or repair. Also different exchange and return policies apply in outlet stores. Normally no exchange or refund is possible for outlet merchandise. By doing this, luxury brands create a distinction between their directly operated stores and outlet stores. By this way, they can protect their loyal clients and also recruit new customers.

Travel Retail and Duty-Free Stores

Travel retail is a steady growth sector in the luxury industry. Travel retail refers to the sales made in outlets at airports and duty-free shops, plus shopping on airlines during the flight and on cruise ships. With a Compound Annual Growth Rate of 7 percent, the duty-free retail market has delivered consistent strong growth since 2000. This success has been despite major terror incidents, regulatory changes in the European Union, and the worst recession since 1929. The growth of the travel and tourism industry in 2013 contrasted with overall global economic growth that was flat or even negative. The strongest growth was in international demand for travel across national borders for leisure and business purposes. With further investment planned by the major players and traveler numbers expected to rise, duty-free retail is forecast to grow strongly. On average, sales of goods in airports, on cruise ships, and in duty-free shops grew 9.4 percent to €55.8 billion in 2013 and are set to reach more than €100 billion by 2023.

Retail success in the duty-free sector is dependent on contributions from the three major actors, known often as "trinity" stakeholders. The trinity stakeholders are the landlord, the retailer, and the supplier. Figure 11.3 shows the relationship between the trinity stakeholders and the consumer.

- **The landlord:** The landlords are the airports. They are like the shopping centers: They provide access to the passengers and the retail space for duty-free retailing. Their expertise lies in promoting the airport as a destination for shopping. The exclusive and highly sought-after nature of the retail space that the landlords own or manage means that risks to the landlord are low. They are responsible

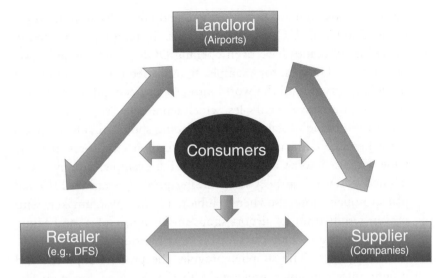

Figure 11.3   Trinity Stakeholders

and play the important role of boosting passenger flow and therefore retail footfall. Thus, any duty-free business models will link the landlord's rental income to passenger numbers in one form or another. With limited duty-free retail space available, most privately owned/ managed airports will invite bids from retailers in an attempt to secure the highest possible rental income. The airports at Dubai, Singapore, Hong Kong, Macao, Hawaii, Frankfurt, and New York City are some of the most sought-after landlords in the travel retail world.

- **The retailer:** Retailers provide the store expertise and knowledge that are required to operate duty-free stores profitably. Sales revenue is the most common performance indicator for retailers. The trinity is a very specific model, as so many airports adopt minimum annual guarantee (MAG)–based rental structures. For example, duty-free-shops have long established a dominant position in travel retail. DFS, the giant duty-free shopping chain, which was acquired by LVMH, witnessed a growth in sales of 19 percent in 2013. The growth was contributed mainly by its new concessions in Hong Kong. LVMH's beauty brands such as Dior, Guerlain, and Givenchy were in direct competition with L'Oréal luxury brands. To respond to this trend, many luxury brands have been opening DOS in airports and travel destinations. Hermès, for example, transformed the 50 boutiques it has in airports around the world into proper freestanding shops as a way to capture travel retail sales, which represent a "significant" portion of the brand's total sales. Freestanding shops provide shoppers with the same familiar environment as in their city stores. It is the same with the jewelry and watch sector. For example, Tiffany & Co. opened its seventh airport store in Singapore's Changi in 2013 and plans to open more elsewhere. Hublot, a luxury watchmaker, with proven results from its airport shops in Changi, Dubai, and Hong Kong, may choose Frankfurt for the next location.

- **The suppliers:** The supplier provides the product expertise and insight into consumer preferences that is required for duty-free shops. As a result of the global and high-income nature of traveling passengers, suppliers benefit from brand exposure, resulting in relatively low risk. Currency fluctuations in various international travel retail channels may reflect retail price points and pose difficulties to margin and wholesale price management. Furthermore, because of a high loyalty rate for popular traveling areas where airports hold more power in price negotiation, sometimes brands do not have direct control on the travel retail price and promotions that could be inconsistent with the brand's strategy and brand image. The suppliers need to keep an eye on the overall offer in the travel retail.

- **The consumers:** The ever-changing mix of travelers, the consumers, flowing through airport terminals provides unique challenges and opportunities. Some of the key challenges that can be overcome are as follows. First, the rising middle class, affluent travelers from across the emerging and emerged world, are forming an important segment for duty-free retailers. To harness and attract these customers, the luxury brands need to have a consistent offering across markets. The sophisticated customers often compare prices across geographic locations. Second, an increase in a brand's presence in high-profile travel-oriented locations with the brand's signature decoration and highly recognizable merchandising setting has to be coordinated and responsive across and within markets. Third, specific product offerings and extended product categories have to be tailored to travelers' profiles and travel destinations. To boost the offerings there will be a need to introduce occasion-specific campaigns. This could be targeted regionally and locally to target the travelers and to increase the effectiveness and efficiency of marketing. Training of sales associates and travel retail teams is a necessity. The sales force and the travel retail teams, especially in promising travel retail destinations, need thorough knowledge of the brand, the luxury positioning, and travel culture. The three together would be needed to provide high-level service to the travel retail customers and to engage with the travelers within a limited time and space.

Of the travel retail consumers, the phenomenal rise of the Chinese traveler, in particular, is of great interest given the growing importance of luxury in the duty-free retail world. Tourism spending accounted for up to 12 percent of total spending worldwide in 2013, while spending by Chinese tourists in Europe was closer to 20 percent, according to Bain & Company. In 2012 and 2013, the world's biggest spender in luxury was China, while Chinese tourists alone could be spending as much as €140 billion a year, representing nearly 70 percent of the global luxury market, within which €74 billion were spent overseas. According to the United Nations World Tourism Organization, the Chinese made 83 million outbound trips in 2012, compared to 10 million in 2000, and are still the fastest-growing tourism source market in the following years. The compound annual growth rate from 2012 to 2030 is expected to be 11 percent, according to a study by Boston Consulting Group. According to multiple research reports, 50 percent of the sales in Chinese domestic travel retail are of destination-specific products. These destination-specific products provide a clue to retailers and brands first to recognize the need to better construct their product offering, and second to enhance the link between the travelers' willingness to purchase and their traveling destinations.

Strategic Decisions in Geographic Expansion

The decision to expand geographically is a strategic one. During the initial years, luxury companies were flush with cash. They decided on the go where to expand without much analysis. It was on instinct, on demand, and on intuition. Things have changed over time. With so many options and destinations in which to expand, the decision can no longer be based solely on gut feeling. For example, in the case of Singapore, how many stores of a particular brand can the island nation sustain? Each year new malls are being constructed, each bigger and more beautiful than the last. Which one to go to? What will happen to the previous one? On the other extreme, there are China and India. Which city to expand to next? There are not many options. Will the shop be in a five-star hotel or a luxury mall that has just been built? Is it just for securing a presence for the future or for an immediate business purpose? For example, the Chanel store in Delhi in the Intercontinental Hotel is the only store in the hotel. The Hermès store in Mumbai is the only free-standing store in the whole western part of India. Does the free-standing store make any business sense?

For example, Bottega Veneta of the Kering Group went on an expansion spree in 2011–2013. It had been doing extremely well in both mature and emerging markets. Established in 1966, Bottega Veneta (literally translated to "Venetian atelier") was conceived by Michele Taddei and Renzo Zengiaro. Started primarily as a company producing artisan leather goods, Bottega Veneta developed a technique coined as the *intrecciato* weave that is now the brand's signature and most unique identifier. At a time when fashion centered on trends, and the logo-mania craze was rampant, Bottega Veneta personified the notion of unassuming opulence. In the 1970s, the company unveiled the campaign, "When your own initials are enough," and continues to create pieces that stand on the pillars of high design and quality, devoid of obvious branding elements. Bottega Veneta's current portfolio extends from premium leather accessories to fragrances.

We became the segment that was growing the fastest during the crisis as consumers started preferring high craftsmanship rather than ... fashion logos or celebrity trends.... When the crisis happened, customers changed completely the way they were shopping. It was Coco Chanel who said when there is a crisis, people outgrow fashion and look for timelessness. They buy less but buy better.... The momentum was behind labels that were craftsman-led, so much so it suddenly became quite crowded as all brands tried to move into this. But we were the first to launch it.... Bottega Veneta was already positioned in a particular way. What changed was consumer behavior. It's clear to me that companies that are consistent and coherent with their brands will continue to be relevant.... It means to be relevant in the moment you are in. We have been able to link all products under an umbrella and with a consistent theme.... That is not by chance and we do not license everything. And even on those we do license we have full control of image, the creative process and distribution. All our contracts are crystal-clear on this and there is no compromise. In today's world, you buy into the world of a brand and the lifestyle it promises. We create products that are relevant to our customers across multiple touch points. If you look at fragrances, it is consistent with our brand values.

—Marco Bizzarri, CEO of Bottega Veneta

Bottega Veneta had achieved sales growth consistently in high double-digits and is proving a stellar performer for its parent company, Kering. Its expansion plan in China has been consistent. Bottega Veneta in 2013 opened its fourth store in Shanghai, a store that doubles as gallery space for up-and-coming Chinese photographers. It is the label's twenty-second store in China. Bottega Veneta's CEO Marco Bizzarri said he felt particularly confident about China and the Asian market. "If you look at our business, over 55 percent of our business is in Asia, 45 percent is in the United States and Europe. That is completely the reverse of the industry."

While most of the success in Asia comes from its performance in Japan, Bizzarri is optimistic about China. "China is a super-important market and it is growing very fast. The fact that the Chinese customers are approaching our brand quicker than any other emerging country is due to the speed of the maturity of the market."

Another brand that is doubling its expansion year-on-year is Michael Kors. New York–based Michael Kors is rewriting history in its retail distribution strategy. It has found a niche as an accessible luxury brand with the look and feel of a higher-end label. By producing goods at lower prices with a mix of American novelty, the label has appealed to recession-stricken, cost-conscious European consumers who still want high style. It emerged as one of the leading high-fashion maisons in brand strategy and retail and distribution initiatives in 2013. Michael Kors grew from US$38 million in 2011 to US$109 million in 2012 to US$221 million in 2013 in European sales. Comparing this growth to industry figures, Europe's luxury goods industry grew just 2 percent in 2013, slowing from a 5 percent rate in 2012, according to Bain. Michael Kors grew at a break-neck speed, opening stores across countries, cities, airports, duty-free zones, and within new and old malls. Kors has 76 European stores selling handbags, watches, shoes, and apparel, and added more than 36 in 2014. Michael Kors's CEO John Idol says Europe can support 200 locations and generate revenue in excess of $1 billion. The stores, in Europe's luxury retail strongholds, from New Bond Street in London to Via della Spiga in Milan, are doing well, he says, and the merchandise is selling out. Coach, another more-affordable luxury brand and an archrival in the United States, has also opened stores in Europe, though it has about a third as many as Kors. In 2014, Michael Kors was not only the best-performing luxury brand in the market, but may be the most impressive of the last decade. It had a 28 percent increase in comparable-store sales quarter-to-quarter in 2013 and was able to produce overall revenue growth of 57 percent while having a very impressive operating margin of 30.7 percent.

"As a company, we believe that this dynamic and integrated approach to marketing will better inform, engage, educate, and inspire our customers as we continue to grow our brand awareness globally . . . . It's very exciting to see our efforts succeed and our successes acknowledged. I'm extremely proud of the teams that we have in place—we set high targets for 2013 and we achieved our goals. Now, we're looking forward to keeping our momentum going," said John Idol.

According to Google's Zeitgeist 2013 report, Michael Kors is the second most searched for high-fashion brand of the year. It has climbed up two spots from its number four spot on the same list in 2012. It is also one of only two maisons that remained on the list of top-searched high-fashion brands from 2012. Michael Kors has also been named as the top fashion brand on social media for 2013 by social media analyst, Starcount. Michael Kors came up tops amid competitors like Chanel, Louis Vuitton, and Burberry. Starcount highlighted Michael Kors's partnership with Instagram in the innovative launch of Instagram ads, and noted the expansion of the brand's total social media audience across all platforms by nearly seven million followers.

Online Distribution and E-Commerce

Internet retailing is a growth story in the luxury sector, with North America and Western Europe vying for the title of top Internet consumption markets. The original idea of e-tailing was to sell a large range of brands and to liquidate old or surplus stock at discounted and often cheap prices. Thus luxury and e-tailing create an interesting paradox.

An ensuing debate that rages within the luxury industry is the notion of online distribution. Historically, the luxury brands were successful in their delivery of elegance and exclusivity in their stores, the retail space. Luxury goods and services have been reluctant to embrace e-tail, fearing that it will cheapen their brand's image in the eyes of affluent customers. The Internet, after all, is synonymous with no-frills "accessibility" and bargain hunting, which clash with the discriminating nature of luxury. But it may be a lucrative option. As a thriving medium, used by an estimated 95 percent of luxury buyers, more savvy luxury brands are seeing it as an opportunity to engage in efficient niche marketing, while harnessing the Internet's incredible reach. Slick production websites are an opportunity to extend the exclusive service experience of luxury purchasing online, while websites are ideal backdrops for customization and could never be understocked. Moreover, it may be that an online retail presence is a way to stop counterfeiters from "filling in the gaps."

E-tail has its advantages and disadvantages. The key challenges in e-tail are the following. How to tell the story of the brand? How to provide in some way the touch and feel of the brand? How to convey the brand DNA? How to live in the ecosystem and transfer a unique interpretation of service that would not only listen but would also act as an effective sales driver?

The experience factor: Those in favor of e-tail propound that design and concept are also the key in e-tail. The believers put forth that although online and offline experiences aren't the same, the goal is the same. The main purpose of the boutique and the website is to bring a unique, memorable experience to the affluent customer. The moment they land on the doorstep or the homepage, the exclusiveness of the brand needs to be reflected to entice customers in a world filled with aspirations. It is possible to make purchasing online a sophisticated, unique process.

The sites though very different from brand to brand often have many of the same features in common: high-quality images, multimedia, an element of surprise, and an appeal to the imagination of the user in order to enter a typically bland homepage. The storytelling is celebrated through brand rituals and ceremonials and can be integrated by videos, short movies, and pictures. This provides a scope for consumer interpretation, consumer musing, and consumer dreaming, especially in markets where consumers are still being educated. Embedded video features enable customers to view an item from multiple angles, which helps overcome the disadvantages of not being able to feel the cloth. For example, Chanel's podcasts and videos of catwalks and fashion shows add story elements to the mix. Gucci takes a bold step at capturing the sensation of the in-store experience on their website. Instead of providing search and navigation like most e-commerce sites, the brand instead displays handbags and watches on shelves just as in their offline shops. By displaying the product in this light, the designers are able to evoke some of the emotion that one might get from shopping in the store. Gucci has online sales for consumers in France, Germany, Austria, Belgium, the Netherlands, and Ireland, as well as the United Kingdom and the United States.

The accessibility factor: The sites can be accessed by one-and-all and provide instant reach to customers in far-off places, especially in large emerging markets where any number of physical stores is not enough. Among the most visible international brands providing access are Net-a-Porter, Guilt Group, and Yoox. Yoox, for instance, is a virtual boutique, with about three million visitors a month. It sells Armani, Roberto Cavalli, and other top designers from their website. It has developed some very clever features, including the zoom-in functionality offering visitors a good "feel" for the fabric. Designer Marc Jacobs launched his ecommerce site to generate new revenue opportunities via online and mobile with a playful, unique, and innovative feel combined with whimsical illustrations, photography, and video to bring the experience to life as in his own retail location. When the online shop first loads, shoppers view a colorfully illustrated storefront, and click the front door to enter the main site.

The analytical factor: Instead of a physical store, the consumer experiences a virtual store with much more information to process, compare, and decide at their leisure from home. Potential customers will spend significant time dreaming of a luxury product and should have ways to talk with the brand online. The purchase decision is much more analytical in that sense as the decision has been processed. For example, the Apple site provides the cue. Its homepage and e-commerce sections consistently benefit from luscious photography and design. It provides the consumers all the details and provides them with an option to buy online or visit the Apple stores with all the information beforehand.

Thus, most luxury brands stand by their in-store experience rather than fully integrate their offering by combining it with e-shopping convenience for their niche market. The inherent risk associated with leveraging e-commerce platforms to generate sales is in a way the cannibalization of sales from the brick-and-mortar stores. But this is not such an important issue. The discount-oriented stigma in the e-commerce space is the more important issue that may in turn dilute the prestige associated with the brand. In addition to this, one also has to acknowledge that Internet and mobile Internet are the fastest growing channels of retailing. Any web search will reveal that many luxury brands have their own websites with information on products, and even a catalogue and retailer/dealer locations but stop short of selling their products online. For example, Burberry is one such brand that has been raising the bar on how to fuse brick-and-mortar retailing with digital technology. Its strategy revolved around tightening its supply chain and logistics, as well as heavy investments in its own retail network. Burberry opened around 15 mainline stores in 2013 and is looking to expand its retail footprint by around 12–15 percent per year. Its focus on larger format stores targeted toward the emerging markets and flagship stores in high tourist inflow city markets gives insights into its business growth strategy. While moving toward digital sophistication, by integrating its brick-and-mortar stores with its online platform, Burberry is looking to promote a more egalitarian retail environment than is normally associated with luxury stores. Burberry's focus on the "come and hang out" ethos in its new store exemplifies the highly successful retail model of the latest luxury shopping developments.

The Internet may be used to entice consumers to visit the store. It is used by brands to increase brand awareness, as well as to educate clients about the products and the brand universe. With the availability of improved technology, brands are trying to recreate a complete experience online. For example, in the luxury jewelry and fashion sector, the Internet is being used as a tool for providing information, raising brand awareness, and increasing consumer interaction using social media. For emerging markets, an integrated social media strategy is a way to penetrate deeper. This is primarily because of the limited technology and high prices of the products, which hinder sales online. Lower price-point items, such as those in cosmetics and apparel, are easy to use for e-commerce. For example, Ralph Lauren has been 10 years ahead of its competitors in e-tailing. The company has launched an online shopping service beginning in the United States, then gradually in Europe and the United Kingdom. Now it ships to 13 countries, including Australia, Japan, and Korea. It has also been known for the integration of digital innovations. Ralph Lauren provided the world its first four-dimensional experience: an integrated experience of 3D imagery, digital sound effects, and Ralph Lauren fragrances, now available in the brand's iconic flagship store on New Bond Street in London and on Madison Avenue in New York City. The brand is active in online digital marketing too, being among the first brands to stage virtual runway shows online.

Luxury online sales can benefit significantly from cross-channel marketing, which has become a crucial part of the Internet world. The Internet has advanced capabilities to track where and how customers find a homepage; these activities can be directly measured to offline and online campaigns. This allows a brand to better understand customer behavior and marketing efforts of all kinds. Online sales overcome one of the limitations of luxury real world shopping—the fact that the location of the shop is not always convenient for the affluent or super-affluent customer. Custom personalization options online improve the overall consumer experience and add familiarity.

Conclusion

The relationship between luxury retail and distribution with e-commerce is still in its growth phase. Very little is known about consumers' preoccupations and their perceptions of the risks associated with e-commerce. While innovation in retail and distribution continues, success will depend on adapting diverse strategies that address the new behaviors of the modern, highly educated consumer online. It means that the presence of luxury brands on the web has to be as luxurious as in their retail stores. Data suggests that 75 percent of wealthy consumers on the Internet use social media. The data obtained by the wealthy consumers are used categorically to know the history and the heritage of the product and the brand. This knowledge adds in some way to the buying decision.

Contrary to the above, in the past the consumer was empowered through tightly controlled media channels such as direct marketing, print, events and others. The consumers made their decisions within their peer group. With online data and social media, however, access to information is no longer a barrier to taking part in the discussion. As the information is available to all, an urban teenager in Vietnam can comment on a product to a socialite in Paris. Over time, a host of unknowns can make or break the brand image. The dilemma rests on the degree of accessibility.

A case in point was the rise of Chinese overseas retail agents. In 2013, when visible impact was seen in the Chinese luxury market due to decelerating economic growth and the government's anticorruption drive, the Chinese customer could understand clearly that the high import tax on foreign luxury goods made the products anywhere between 30 and 60 percent more expensive in Beijing or Shanghai than in Paris, London, or New York. As a result, some clients were tempted to buy knockoffs, sourced online or at locations like Shanghai's Nanjing Xi Lu market. This market and similar markets have become notorious for selling fake

luxury goods. Others simply purchase their luxury goods while traveling abroad. Data suggests that more than US$54 billion purchases out of
US$80 billion in purchases of personal luxury goods by Chinese con-
sumers in 2013 were made outside China. To circumvent steep import
duties and get their hands on authentic luxury goods at lower prices, the
Chinese were employing overseas retail agents.

It was reported that nearly 60 percent of consumers have made at
least some luxury purchases through parallel channels known as *daigou*
(via overseas contacts, Taobao, or other professional buying agencies and
e-commerce websites) rather than from brands or department stores,
according to a study by Bain & Company, a global consulting firm.
A consumer on OnlyLady, a daigou website, explains how it works: "In
simple terms, I remit you some money, you buy a product for me, and
then mail it or give it to me. You can buy what I cannot find, or must pay
a much higher price for, in my region. I should pay you for your time or
labor, according to a percentage we have negotiated. Among the most
popular brands requested by clients are Chanel, Prada, and Louis Vuitton.
Daigou agents operate in Hong Kong, Guangdong, New York, London,
Paris, Tokyo, Seoul, and elsewhere. The daigou market was worth ¥74.4
billion (about $12 billion) in 2013 and was to exceed ¥100 billion in
2014. There are thought to be over 20,000 daigou operating between
Hong Kong and China alone, although about a thousand were arrested
last year.*

---

*http://www.businessoffashion.com/2014/04/daigou-agents-help-chinese-consumers-get-
luxury-goods-less.html

Chapter 12

Intellectual Property Rights and Counterfeiting

E thics are not morals. Morals are external, a matter of duty, whereas ethics are internal, a matter of personal responsibility toward others.

For all the great fashion, crafts, and wine companies, in high-class restaurants and among major manufacturers, ethics is a life purpose, a way of organizing one's conduct and working toward the realization of goals and dreams.

The ethics of true luxury is first and foremost a kind of solidarity in support of creation, in support of the subcontractors, those who work to put the product together, solidarity in the challenges, in achieving success, and over time.

Ethics in luxury means protecting one's culture and roots to preserve that which forms the DNA of a brand name.

A certain ethics must be imposed. A company that simply makes money would be poor indeed, but a company in the field of luxury that only loses money would be useless, because ethics also means longevity, and compensating one's staff and partners for their contributions.

Ethics in luxury is defined by the pleasure taken in a job well done, be it in manufacturing or sales, in the importance given to creation, true creation, the kind that is expressed in total freedom, the kind that provokes and disturbs.

As such, ethics lies at the core of the definition of luxury, a refusal to sell an imperfect product or one not consistent with the brand, the possibility of having to start over and therefore spend even more . . . . An opportunity is given to those who do not always succeed.

There are no ethics without sharing, and luxury can show the way. Without ethics, audacity is unguided, like a disjointed puppet. Without ethics cynicism rules the day, and cynicism is the evil genius of luxury. But with defined ethics and a firm will to apply its rules, luxury earns its stripes, the company gains its recognition, and the brand name achieves high esteem.

Undoubtedly, the two key problem areas confronting luxury goods companies as of today are counterfeiting and gray marketing. The gray market has arisen due to the license manufacturing system that exists in Europe coupled with the increased globalization of luxury goods, which has given rise to arbitrage opportunities. Yet the most insidious of the two problems remains the counterfeiting of goods, which not only damages companies financially but can also have a deleterious effect on a company's image, particularly companies with iconic recognition such as Louis Vuitton and Burberry. Dior, Chanel, and Giorgio Armani are touted to be amongst the most copied brands on the market, with LVMH's Murakami bag being the most popular.

In response to this problem, luxury goods companies are tightening both distribution and manufacturing through the repurchase of licensees. LVMH in particular was proactive in taking action against counterfeiting operations by hiring a bevy of lawyers and counterfeiting experts to take court action against vendors of fake Louis Vuitton handbags. Yves Carcelle, Vice President of the Fondation d'Entreprise Louis Vuitton pour la Création and a member of the LVMH executive committee, who passed away in September 2014, was quoted as saying, "The problem with counterfeiting is that it destroys your image. In every study we do, it shows that brand lovers are always at risk one day to see somebody carrying an ugly counterfeit and then say 'I don't love them anymore. They betrayed me.' "[1]

Stemming the illicit production of fake branded goods has proven to be a lengthy and difficult task for luxury houses: launching complains, employing a battery of lawyers, and creating awareness of the counterfeit goods have met with some success with the increasing number of seizures.

In the luxury and fashion industry, intellectual property rights (IPR) define a company's range of ownership over creative ideas and unique designs, textiles, and patterns. It is sometimes a complex issue to define what is possible to be copyrighted and what must be left within the general domain. The fashion designers, who rightly have ownership over their creations, do not have any valid legal recourse, because their original designs are not registered. For example, it is not possible to put a copyright on items such as the cut of a dress, a type of garment or its color, whereas one can copyright a specific textile pattern. The retailers and ready-to-wear apparel makers, however, can come out with inexpensive and affordable knock-offs or similar designs that consumers are happy to buy at affordable prices. The infatuation with designs, especially of clothes and accessories, has led to an insatiable urge to possess the latest in fashion trends.

This is a reason IPR and counterfeiting are an important recurring concern for luxury and fashion goods manufacturers. Not only is this an issue for the luxury industry directly concerning the companies themselves, but it also holds implications for others involved, including manufacturers, distributors, retailers, and consumers. Historically, the illegal practice of manufacturing goods that impersonate other branded goods and are sold as registered legal goods has been considered a serious threat since 1970s. By conservative estimate, the presence of counterfeit goods in the world market has grown more than 10,000 percent in the past two decades. Recently, it has been estimated that counterfeits account for 6 to 10 percent of world trade, according to different sources, with Asia

---

[1]Elliott, 2010.

being the market that incurred about a third of the losses. This continues to become more complex when goods are sold through more diverse
outlets, including over the Internet or through third-party stores such as
discount stores. It is estimated that about $30 million are lost annually
by the French luxury goods industry, where luxury goods account for
more than 5 percent of the counterfeiting market.

The counterfeiting market affects the luxury industry in several
ways, and can be analyzed from the perspectives of production, distribution, consumption, or purchasing. The facts that are relevant for
decision making include a loss of profit for the brand through missed
sales, through spending on lawsuits, and due to damage to the brand
image, which could indirectly lead to loss of profit if the normal luxury
consumers of the brand flee from the brand after seeing products owned
by less desirable consumers, therefore eroding the brand's exclusivity
and high-end image of quality for the elite. The problems faced in this
situation and thus the managerial challenge for the luxury companies
would be how to control brand image and maintain brand authority and
heritage, along with top-quality products, when imitations are being
produced and distributed.

Counterfeiting: Issues for Luxury Brands

*With time, the new emerging countries are going to produce and
become competitors. They began with copies, but nothing is
stopping them from upgrading the quality of products.*

—Hubert Vedrine, LVMH

In order to be irreplaceable, one must always be different.

—Coco Chanel

Issues with counterfeiting are relevant for the luxury industry, as
its products are based on creativity, uniqueness, and originality that
have been built through wealth of craftsmanship spanning decades.
They are also closely tied to brand heritage and brand DNA, with each

product representing the "house" as a whole and acting as a reflection of brand values and positioning. Uniqueness allows for exploitation of the dream factor, inspiring consumers to dream of objects that are not necessary for daily living, whose costs are higher than other products that could be considered comparable but that are not meant for the wealthy consumer. Due to this issue, intellectual property rights are meant to protect creative ideas, the knowledge created by the craftsmen, and therefore in some way protect the products in order to maintain their exclusivity, product authenticity, image, and their power to evoke the dream factor in the minds of consumers. An easy way to access this dream is to create counterfeits.

Counterfeit goods appear in all shapes, sizes, and industries. The most rampant are in software, apparels, movies, music, luxury goods, pharmaceuticals, software, and so forth. CDs and clothing are the largest categories targeted by counterfeiters, followed by fragrances and cosmetics products. In sectors such as the music or film industries, illegal copies have a dramatic effects on the sales and even threaten the very subsistence of the artists (singers' main revenues come no longer from CD sales but from tours). In sectors such as cosmetic or fragrances, customers may buy a counterfeit without knowing it and be deceived by the quality. Counterfeit business can also undermine customers' trust in the quality and safety of the genuine brands, and prevent them from buying those brands again.

Counterfeiting is one of the most profitable businesses. It has become as profitable as trading illegal narcotics, and is lot less risky as it does not entail any research and development, marketing, and advertising costs, nor heavy investments, only a cheap labor force. For example, a fake handbag that sells for $100 or more costs $1.25 to make in China. It is reported that U.S. companies lose between $200 billion and $250 billion each year to counterfeiting. Also, it is a cause for job losses in different industries. For example, the auto industry estimated that it could hire 210,000 more workers if the fake auto parts trade disappeared, not to mention losses in tax revenues for governments.

The counterfeit business has been witnessing a booming period. It is a global industry that is starting to rival the multinationals in speed, reach, and sophistication. Counterfeiters are skilled at duplicating holograms, "smart" chips, and other security devices intended to distinguish fakes from the genuine article. Most of the counterfeit financing comes from a variety of sources, including local entrepreneurs and organized crime.

> *We've had sophisticated technology that took years to develop knocked off in a matter of months. The counterfeiters are building sophisticated organizations with diversified nature of business from their sourcing and manufacturing units across borders. Their global nature and their customers worldwide make them increasingly hard to eradicate*
>
> **—A spokesperson from Unilever**

The global counterfeit goods market is worth about $540 billion, which represents 7–10 percent of the global merchandise trade. Seventy-five percent of counterfeit luxury goods in Europe and the world originate mainly from China or Hong Kong. Luxury goods account for about 5 percent of the counterfeiting market, about $27 billion. It was reported that China was the main country where the counterfeit business originated. It produced nearly two-thirds of all the fake and pirated goods worldwide. For years, Chinese authorities turned a blind eye to the problem, largely because most of the harm was inflicted on foreign brand owners, and furthermore, most counterfeiting was seen as a victimless offence. Every year, more than 3,500 cases involving intellectual property rights (IPR) were reported in China. The only time China got tough on counterfeiters was when there was a clear danger to Chinese products. In 2013, Richemont Group disabled more than 2,700 "rogue" websites that sold counterfeit watches, jewelry, sunglasses, and handbags bearing a number of Richemont's brands, including Cartier, A. Lange & Söhne, Panerai, Roger Dubuis, and Alfred Dunhill. Many counterfeiters have ties to local officials, who see counterfeit operations as a major source of employment for the local economy. In 2013, Cartier was awarded almost $30,000 in compensation by a Shanghai court in a trademark infringement case.

To fend off the threat from counterfeit products, many multinationals have integrated an anticounterfeit department in their organizational structure. For example, LV, perhaps, holds the record as the most counterfeited brand in the world. It is reported that only one-odd percent of all Vuitton bags are genuine. It is thus logical that within LVMH group, 60 employees are dedicated to fighting counterfeit-related issues within different brands of the Group. LVMH spends around $16 million a year in investigations, arrests, and legal fees. And their greatest challenge is getting cooperation from China. Different luxury brands have teamed up to fight piracy and counterfeits. Twenty-two luxury brand manufacturers, including Louis Vuitton, Burberry, Calvin Klein, Chanel, and Gucci, have hired law firm Baker & McKenzie to fight trademark piracy in wholesale and retail markets in Shenzhen and three other major Chinese cities. It was reported that staff members from the law firm will visit wholesale and retail markets as ordinary customers, and if evidence of counterfeiting is found, legal actions will be taken.

Recently it was reported that the Chinese government has started to take counterfeiting issues more seriously because of unprecedented pressure from the U.S., Europe, and Japan, combined. A Chinese court recently handed out prison sentences and heavy fines to two men who were found guilty of exporting illegal copies of perfumes that are patented by LVMH. The move is unusual and it could be a sign that, after years of lobbying by the luxury goods industry, the authorities are starting to make moves toward clamping down on the practice.*

On one hand, counterfeit goods are a menace that can harm a brand's image, tradition, identity, and reputation in diverse ways. It can tarnish the image because of low quality and cause loss of brand loyalty (genuine consumers may shy away as they do not perceive the exclusivity anymore), it can saturate the market (for example, the adoption of Lacoste counterfeit products in France by the youth of Paris suburbs had disastrous effects on the brand, its sales, and image for several years), and it can decrease profit and activity, both in the domestic and the international market space. In case of counterfeit medicines, customers may be ill and complain to the companies whom they believe have manufactured the product. In case of luxury goods, such as LV bags, it is difficult to refuse after-sales services to a customer who believes she has a genuine bag. Nations can lose sales tax and employment.

On the other hand, some argue that luxury manufacturers do not lose sales or profitability, because customers buying counterfeit products generally cannot afford the genuine ones. They also argue that the more counterfeiting occurs, the greater is the brand power. And most consumers do not understand the legal implications of IPR issues and the use of counterfeit products.

---

*Som, A (2006). Technical Note (C). Issues of Luxury Industry in Emerging Market. Case Centre Reference No. 306-513-6

The Issue of Legality

There are some very basic legal connotations of IPR issues and counterfeit goods. First and foremost, any garment designed by a person does not fall under the purview of the Copyright Act and shall not be entitled to protection under the same. Copyright under the Copyright Act, 1957, and the Designs Act, 2003, have different relevance. The Designs Act of 2003 is applicable to articles of clothing, husbandry, textile piece goods, artificial and natural sheet material, and furnishing, unlike the Copyright Act, 1957, which is applicable to artistic works, literary works, dramatic works, musical works, photographs, cinematograph film, and software. From the spectrum of tools for the protection of intellectual property, the most closely relevant to the fashion industry is that of the protection of industrial designs, simply referred to as designs. Designer clothes and accessories are entitled to protection under the Design Act of 2003, provided such designs are registered under the said act. The registration is available for a total period of 15 years. This means that a designer shall not be, ipso facto, entitled to protection for his work until and unless the same is registered under the Design Act of 2003. Only on such design or work, which is registered, can the creator bring an action against the infringers. The design can be registered when it is new and distinctive, compared to the prior art base for the design, as it existed before the priority date of the design.

Counterfeiting is an illicit business, in which criminal networks thrive. It is larger than the national gross domestic products of 150 economies and affects nearly all product sectors. One of the daunting challenges that luxury brands face with counterfeiting is loss of business in terms of revenue. Given new technology, it is quite easy to manufacture knock-offs nowadays, and it is increasingly difficult to control the distribution of products from illicit vendors. At stake is the most important asset of the luxury brand—its reputation. Counterfeiting is only possible when the brand has reached a significant awareness threshold (characteristic and universally recognized logo—LV; or a shape—Rolex), and is highly desirable; we may even say that if there are no counterfeits of a brand (apart from those cases in which it is technically impossible, such as cars), it is because the brand is not luxury. For example, the scale of affairs has grown so much that governments and regulatory bodies are now directly involved in the discourse and action. The International Anti-Counterfeiting Coalition (IACC) based in the United States has information available online on "How to Spot a Fake" and "How to Report a Fake." This information is helpful for educating consumers on the types of goods that are counterfeited, and what they might look like. However, the examples on "How to Spot a Fake" are not exhaustive, and only cover a few iconic items that consumers might be aware of. The IACC describes its mission as "the world's largest nonprofit organization devoted solely to protecting intellectual property and deterring counterfeiting." The U.S. federal government is also directly involved in the crackdown against counterfeiting, and conducts its investigations through Homeland Security. Since 2010, 350 domain names have been shut down.

In France, the Comité Colbert started an anticounterfeiting education campaign that included online information, explaining that "counterfeit products can have bad consequences: It can be hazardous to your health. It helps finance organized crime. It undermines our industry." Consumers are lured by low prices and the appearance of high-status goods, as many counterfeit websites promise in their domain names. For example, consider websites that have been shut down, including "discount-louisvuitton-handbag.com," "louisvuitton-bags -forcheap.com," and "replicaoakleysale.com." It has been observed that more often than not, some ill-informed consumers may actually believe they are buying real products produced by the luxury brand, at a special discount rate offered on the Internet. The campaign was meant to spread awareness to mostly educated consumers that they need to purchase products in authorized outlets in order to be sure they are purchasing authentic goods.

As luxury companies go global, the challenge of fighting counterfeit goods will require working with various governments (both of their own country and the countries where products are produced and sold) to gain additional support within the legal framework. For example, in 2011, Silvia Fendi, creative director of Italian luxury brand Fendi, was directly involved with the European Commission, and directly appealed to them at their Innovation Convention in Brussels to support a strong Europe-wide intellectual property framework be put in place to protect all European luxury products. As Fendi stressed, it was in the interest of governments to protect the authentic industry, as it supported jobs within these countries where the luxury companies are based. Help from government translated into many benefits such as helping their own people, creating income for the country through taxes, protecting traditions for the past, present, and future.

Is It an Emerging Market Phenomenon?

There have been discussions whether IPR and counterfeit issues are an emerging market phenomenon. Counterfeit issues and IPR awareness are a challenge in emerging economies due to high illiteracy rates, low purchasing power, increasing unemployment rates, ineffective law enforcement, and the nexus between counterfeiters and law enforcers. Although most of the counterfeits are manufactured in developing countries, the consumers are not restricted to emerging market clientele. For example, many European tourists shop for counterfeits in China, and it has recently become a trend. Certain counterfeits are so well made that even experienced sales staff can hardly tell the difference.

Multiple studies show that counterfeit and pirated products are being produced and consumed in virtually all economies, with Asia emerging as the single largest producing region. It is also due to weak infrastructure and corruptible public officials and countries that have low-cost producing facilities and poor IP enforcement, and are close to large markets. They play a significant role in driving counterfeiting activity. One of the examples is China, where there are known loopholes and flaws in its copyright and intellectual property legislation, and due to the lack of effective law enforcement and absence of serious penalties, counterfeiters continue to sell illegal goods in the market.*

The growth of Chinese manufacturing has been one of the key drivers of the twenty-first-century global economy. Much of this growth is the result of outsourcing by overseas companies, looking to take advantage of China's high productivity and low costs. Most of the retail value of these products accrues to the companies doing the

---

*Som, A (2006). Technical Note (C). Issues of Luxury Industry in Emerging Market. Case Centre Reference No. 306-513-6

outsourcing, while the Chinese manufacturing firms retain a relatively small share. This mutually beneficial arrangement is only possible because most Chinese firms respect the intellectual property rights of the outsourcing companies. Unfortunately, this situation—in which the designers and manufacturers of a product often live on different continents—has fostered the growth of counterfeiting. Counterfeiting is an attractive alternative to licit commerce because costs are reduced to manufacturing, transport, and distribution.

The costs involved in research, design, and marketing are all avoided. Because counterfeiters are essentially unaccountable and have no interest in building a brand reputation, costs can be additionally reduced by cutting corners in the production phase, such as employing sweatshop labor, engaging in environmentally unsound manufacturing processes, and using inferior-grade materials. Avoiding taxes can further maximize profits: Import duties are evaded through customs fraud or outright smuggling, and sales taxes are avoided though informal retailing, which itself often makes use of illegal migrants working for low compensation. The end result is a product that can look very much like the original, but that can be sold for much less while still generating a large profit. The problem is perhaps more pervasive in China because counterfeit operations are secretive, resilient, and geographically dispersed.

Both the scale and the nature of Chinese manufacturing—which often involves a large number of small firms collaborating to produce a single product—leave the country vulnerable to this abuse. The situation is similar to that found around Naples, where a large number of cottage industries have traditionally produced the world's haute couture alongside the world's best counterfeits.

Effect on a Brand

The illicit goods might not take a substantial part of the market share of original luxury brands, for the simple reason that nondeceptive counterfeiting mostly occurs when people cannot afford a real luxury product, but they do undermine innovation and negatively affect economic growth for numerous reasons. Counterfeiting partially shifts demand from legitimate manufacturers to counterfeiters. Counterfeiting not only reduces sales of original goods, but also adversely affects the brand equity and consumer confidence and damages channel loyalty, which directly or indirectly affects the brand-customer relationship. Legitimate manufacturers incur the costs of protecting the brand and enforcing intellectual property rights, and costs are associated with legal remedies. Counterfeit products negatively affect the process of innovation, reduce the sales share of legitimate businesses, damage the brand reputation, and undermine the ability of luxury brands to benefit from breakthrough products.

As far as challenges that counterfeiting poses for brand customer relationship are concerned, it is a double-edged sword for consumers who desire genuine items—even if they mistakenly buy counterfeits or they firmly restrict themselves to the originals, they are at loss. The buyers of original luxury goods are affected when they buy fake goods due to deceptive counterfeiting as well as when others buy counterfeited luxury goods through nondeceptive counterfeiting. If the counterfeit product did not fulfill the expectations of the consumer, he would blame the original brand owner for the poor quality. Even "vanity" counterfeits—products of low intrinsic and low perceived quality—even if they initially do not damage the brand's reputation because of the obvious difference in quality, they raise serious questions regarding how legitimate manufacturers can distinguish the originals from counterfeits to avoid nondeceptive counterfeiting.

There might not be a noticeable difference in the quality, since nondeceptive counterfeits are low-priced alternatives of much more expensive original luxury goods. Sales of conterfeits would eventually result in the erosion of the equity of the genuine luxury brand, as well as decreasing the perception of luxury associated with the brand. The presence of counterfeits reduces the willingness of a number of potential buyers to buy the original products when they expect to be deceived, though actual deception takes place on a very small scale. Some of the main attributes of a luxury brand—exclusivity, quality, and timelessness—are negatively affected by the presence of counterfeits in the long term, if not in the short run. It still affects some customers of the same brand who buy originals, even when counterfeiters claim that all of their customers know that they are buying counterfeited goods.

Since the special characteristic of luxury brands are prestige and rarity, and luxury brands are supposed to be widely popular but not widely accessible, counterfeiters make use of such disparity and break an important rule of luxury brand management. An important element of luxury brands is exclusivity, which is negatively affected by the presence of counterfeit items.

In preserving brand–customer relationships, understanding the effects that counterfeiting has on consumers is a vital first step for luxury brands. The manufacturers of genuine items need to pay attention to the factors generating demand of counterfeits to curtail the negative effects due to counterfeits. To reduce nondeceptive counterfeiting, necessary actions should be taken to make it simple for buyers of original goods to distinguish between the originals and counterfeits. Changes in the packaging and protective elements of the products themselves can be made to achieve this objective.*

While government authorities are concerned that a proportion of profits from counterfeit goods goes to organized crime, companies are busy assessing the extent to which counterfeiting is undermining their brand value. Ultimately, despite the opportunities created by emerging markets like China, India, and Russia, luxury brands are fighting battles on multiple fronts, fighting to hold on to their own identity.

Most international luxury brands have experienced some problems with counterfeiting. Yet for many it is only during the past few years that they have formulated any systematic anticounterfeiting policies. Strategies are now discussed in wider groups and most conferences on product counterfeiting will have at least one company sharing its experiences of combating counterfeiting. Anticounterfeiting work is regarded as raising good will among companies, and more and more companies are seeing the advantages of publicizing their efforts.

Despite their vehemence, most luxury brands are reluctant to talk about the forgeries. Richemont Group, the world's second-biggest luxury goods producer by sales, refers callers to industry associations. LVMH, its bigger rival, gives the subject just a tiny space on its website. Such silence stems from fear that public discussion draws attention to fakes and provides legitimacy. Since the information on the subject is not easily available and highly fragmented, the next section showcases some examples. Figure 12.1 provides a summary of the effect that counterfeits have on a brand.

---

*Som, A (2006). Technical Note (C). Issues of Luxury Industry in Emerging Market. Case Centre Reference No. 306-513-6

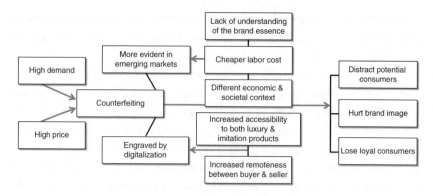

Figure 12.1   Effects of Counterfeiting on Brands

Examples of Responses to Counterfeiting

Louis Vuitton is one of the most counterfeited brands in the luxury world due to its image as a status symbol. Only a small fraction of products bearing the LV initials in the general population are authentic. Ironically, the signature Monogram Canvas was initially created to prevent counterfeiting. The company takes counterfeiting seriously, and employs a team of lawyers and special investigation agencies, actively pursuing offenders through the courts worldwide, and allocating about half of its budget of communications to counteract piracy of its goods. LVMH in recent years has become increasingly aggressive about fighting counterfeiting of its brands, which range from Vuitton and Christian Dior to Fendi leather goods and Guerlain perfumes. LVMH says its 60-person anticounterfeiting team and the collaborating network of 250 agents, investigators, and lawyers conducts on average about 6,000 raids worldwide, resulting sometimes in more than 1,000 arrests. As part of its proactive brand protection strategy, LVMH also pursues a policy to raise public awareness of the counterfeiting problem, while also developing relations with authorities in different countries and worldwide organizations.

In terms of marketing strategy, the product, one of the 4Ps, is directly affected by counterfeiting. The Louis Vuitton handbag offers a "product of distinguished quality" and "attention to detail," as well as "one with a story behind it." Furthermore, while general marketing places importance on "relative quality," for Louis Vuitton the concept seems to be "absolute quality," which prompts consumers to insist on "Louis Vuitton or nothing," rendering comparisons of Louis Vuitton bags with competing products meaningless. Many of the principles for products originated with the particular preferences and policies of the House of Louis Vuitton, as well as the creativity of Marc Jacobs, the artistic director of Louis Vuitton since 1997, and have been shared and carried on by the business corporation.

Regarding the product, Louis Vuitton observed the following steps to eliminate counterfeiting. First is the enlightenment campaign LV is carrying on in the fight against increasingly sophisticated imitations. For instance, in Japan, its largest market, by way of education campaigns aimed at the general public, the LV Japan Group has conducted seminars and symposiums related to intellectual property from time to time.

Second is the distribution of warning notices. Warning notices dated April 2000 were distributed to the major Internet-related firm of Rakuten. Even today companies from all over the world undoubtedly take it seriously when receiving a warning notice for using a "mock monogram." The mock monogram usually is a combined dark brown color with the characters L and V, as well as the company logo, flowers, and stars without permission of the company with the registered trademarks and designs.

Third is the creation of original lines. LV creates highly original lines that are difficult to imitate and then registers the trademarks and designs. It would not be an exaggeration to say that the design of LV travel bags, particularly their arrangement, has evolved in order to do away with counterfeits. The history of the complex and distinctive patterns for the Monogram Canvas bag resembles that of the evolution of currencies of countries around the world that have been designed to prevent forgery. Fourth, LV initiates activities through the Union Des Fabricants, a French public-interest incorporated association, which carries out trademark protection activities. In addition, the association also operates the Musee de la Contrefacon (Museum of Fakes) located near the woods of Boulogne on the outskirts of Paris.

Fifth is initiating appraisal of authentic, second-hand products in stores. It is simplistic to think that counterfeits are flourishing because appraisals of authenticity are not performed; rather, the opposite is true. It concerns who verified the genuine articles. None other than LV's officially sanctioned stores verify whether an article is genuine or not. As imitations are a violation of the Trademark Law and cannot be purchased or sold, dubious goods are rooted out and ultimately the phrase, "We cannot handle this at this store," comes into use.

Sixth is to prohibit licenses. This is a management technique, which is common to all of the LVMH brands, in which the distribution is controlled wholly by LVMH without distributing by licenses. On account of this, Kenzo has also stopped its licensing business. LV has so far not participated in licensed production a single time in its history. It is of the opinion that licensing produces gains for brand value over the short term, but lowers brand value over the long term.

Seventh is the prohibition of the use of the L and V monogram in a misaligned form. In terms of the principle for monogrammed products, it is stated that the products must be made so that the LV design winds up on the front and center of the product without fail. In the event that structurally the LV cannot be placed in the center, it is to be positioned so that it is bilaterally symmetrical. This holds true for bags, trunks, and accessories as well. The LV monogram is the soul of the brand, and this soul absolutely cannot become disjointed or fall out of alignment. Great lengths have been gone to in order to ensure this commitment.

Eighth is their rule of independent manufacturing and prohibiting production for outlet products. LV exercises immensely tight control from production to sales and does not produce outlet products. This is because artisans who have been cultivated on their own account are creating them in the company's workshops. If one is able to attain a structure of not buying and not letting others buy its products in stores other than officially sanctioned stores, then performing independent manufacture and independent distribution will increase costs. Even so, this still pays off if it is considered as the cost of maintaining and controlling brand value.

Ninth is the ostentation principle. First, to put it boldly, novices cannot tell whether an item, especially a luxury product, is good or bad. This is where innovation happens. Changing this concept around, it is important to make items that even novices can recognize for their ostentation and good quality. The motif used for for the padlock triggers a concatenation of notions to the effect that the product is always solid and robust.

What to Do to Prevent Counterfeiting?

Do Nothing

One recent study conducted on Chinese counterfeits noted an interesting finding that a large percentage of people who buy counterfeit goods end up buying the real product later (this was the case mainly in China). If this is the case, then counterfeit products can be seen as beneficial for a luxury brand, as an initial form of inculcation for potential customers and as a form of marketing. Therefore, in this option, the luxury brand being imitated should do nothing, and consider counterfeiting to be a form of free advertising for the brand.

Educate (on Website)   Luxury brands could try to educate consumers directly as to what makes an authentic product and where to purchase it. An example of this approach is Coach, which dedicates space on its website to "Counterfeit Education." On this page, Coach speaks to its own consumers through through topics such as What is Counterfeiting? What does Coach do? Where to Buy Coach Products? Here Coach indicates the only authorized purchasing locations for its products (Coach Stores, Coach Factory Stores, Authorized Department Stores, found on the "store locator" feature on Coach's website, www.coach.com) and gives indications of where Coach does *not* sell its products (through individuals, street vendors, Internet auctions, independent boutiques, flea markets, and house parties). This is helpful information for educating the consumer who is looking to purchase authentic Coach products. It also warns against being tricked online, and indicates that fake sites often use the word "Coach" in their URL, and have a content and layout similar to the authentic Coach website. Finally, Coach lists contact information to on how and where to report fakes, which can be done anonymously. LVMH also has a page under its FAQs section on its website, where for "Brand Protection" the company discusses "What steps does LVMH take to deal with the growing problem of the counterfeiting of luxury goods?" Consumers can find useful information in this section of the website in order to be more informed about guaranteeing they are purchasing authentic products from the group's brands.

Stop

An option can be for governments and regulatory bodies to step in and try to stop counterfeits. This could take place at any of the points throughout the chain: shutting down manufacturing places for counterfeit items, or at the point of distribution or sales, or even the sales of goods online. It can be difficult to try to stop counterfeit manufacturers, as many counterfeit goods are produced in factories in China, where the Chinese government is not necessarily interested in cooperating to work to protect intellectual property rights and to stop counterfeit producers.

Control Distribution Channels

Distribution plays a key role in luxury management. In luxury goods, retail directly operated stores (DOS) have been growing much faster than other forms of distribution over the past five years. The reason for that is because there is a perceived need for better control of the brand. In the 1980s and 1990s, when companies delegated the sale to third parties, the priority of these parties was to make the luxury goods available to a wide customer base. To achieve this, they offered often uncontrolled discounts. The discounts, combined with a broader availability of the product, diluted the brand image and reduced the willingness of customers to pay a premium for the products. This led to the need to control the brand and thus to integrate the distribution channels. To regain control of the distribution, many brands have started to acquire franchises and reduce wholesale and duty-free sales. Companies that have historically been manufacturers only (like Montblanc) have started developing both directly operated stores and franchises. For example, Burberry Group has announced its license with Mitsui will end in 2015. This license included Sanyo Shokai as the main apparel licensee. It will end five years ahead of the end of the original license contract in 2020. The licensing of Burberry Blue Label and Black Label in Japan has brought the brand many counterfeit issues, and the retail growth in Asia market has gone out of the brand's control. Therefore, in 2009, Burberry Group decided to end its license of apparel lines in Japan earlier in 2015, and to regain control over its retail in Asia.

Distribution of counterfeits could take place at the street level, in stores in areas such as Chinatowns, or on sidewalks of large urban cities, or more indirectly through legitimate stores, selling their "own" designs "inspired by" designer brands' specific products. Chanel brought a suit against websites selling fake goods, implicating 600 sites. A U.S. judge ruled in Chanel's favor and not only shut down the sites but also ordered large websites, including Google, Yahoo!, Twitter, and Facebook, to remove any links to these sites or listings for fake goods from these firms.

The existence of counterfeits often indicates that distribution may be too selective, that not enough points of sale are available, that clients do not have easy access to the real product and thus cannot differentiate between genuine and fake, and the value of the product may not be enough to justify the journey to the existing shops. This is often the case in emerging markets where the customer is not "sophisticated" enough, but aspires to own luxury brand products (an example being the Russian and the Indian consumer in Moscow and Delhi 10 years ago).

In contrast, the complete absence of counterfeiting in a country may signify the absence of desire for the brand, and therefore, the effectiveness of opening a sales point. In that case, a brand should concentrate efforts on the previous step of its value chain—marketing and communications—to raise awareness and create desire to buy the product. If the distribution is too large, it might happen that fakes will be sold with real goods.

Louis Vuitton believes in almost full control of the distribution of the products. Until the 1980s, Vuitton products were widely sold in department stores (e.g., Neiman Marcus and Saks Fifth Avenue). Since then, LV worked on the long-awaited retail stores while increasing its ready fire-power in the form of in-shop placement in department stores. Transforming its distribution network, Vuitton products are now primarily available at authentic Louis Vuitton boutiques, with very few exceptions. These boutiques are commonly found in upscale shopping districts or inside luxury department stores. The boutiques within department stores operate independently from the department and have their own LV managers and employees. LV has recently launched an online store, through its main website, as an authorized channel to market its products.

General marketing seeks to create "broad distribution channels," opening more stores or selling through nondepartment store outlets, such as mail order and volume retailers. On the other hand, Louis Vuitton bags are offered only through limited distribution channels—directly operated stores 100 percent controlled by the brand. One might go so far as to say Louis Vuitton innovated a method of selling that amounts to "controlling place" and "not using channels that cannot be controlled." As in the case of pricing, many of the principles for distribution were innovations that subsequently were implemented by other luxury brands.

Brands are attracted to urban areas that are suited to their brand image and establish stores. This in turn creates a virtuous paradoxical cycle whereby the area's image improves further and the establishment of stores accelerates. Brands do not establish stores in prime locations because they have made a profit or attempt to open stores in such locations when they do make a profit. They establish stores in prime locations in order to make a profit. For example, the establishment of large-scale flagship stores endows LV with bases from which to transmit a more prestigious and clear image. This ensures a sense of high added value. This acts as a measure to further enhance LV's image as a top brand. If LV is to attempt to cover an even greater number of customers through a smaller number of stores while avoiding tarnishing the image through excessive exposure, then it would necessarily have to make every single one of the stores into flagship stores. This is a tried-and-true tactic for luxury brands, with LV's global flagship store strategy serving as an excellent example.

What constitutes the importance of the role of flagship stores is their purpose as bases for transmitting the image in order to elevate the brand's added value. The growth of the brand stores to enormous proportions has powerful implications for the image policy more so than it does for the sales. It is because the flagship store is the best place to transmit the brand identity and heritage of the brand to its customers. It is the place to portray and control both the significance of and effects that are consistent to the mission, image, and brand identity, thereby reinforcing a consistent service policy for the brand.* This enables LV to be in control of the full value chain and life cycle of its products, thereby reducing substantially chances of counterfeiting at any stage of the process. For example, LV's repair service has often been used as an example. Over the decades, it has won the trust of customers and provides a sense of stability to the brand

---

*Som, A (2006). Technical Note (C). Issues of Luxury Industry in Emerging Market. Case Centre Reference No. 306-513-6

strength. The repair service could only be controlled through its own stores. As LV customers experience the service quality and, if needed, free repair service for life, it leads to repeat sales, thereby making the customer more exacting in their demand. This level of service provides customer satisfaction and makes the customer use the products over a long time period, which in turn results in raising brand loyalty.

On the other hand, Gucci implements the Italian model of controlling its value chain to curb counterfeiting. It involves a network of a handful of suppliers for its manufacturing. Although it requires more quality supervision and coordination, not owning the production in-house provides more flexibility to Gucci, without restraining its capacity to develop manufacturing synergies with its suppliers. Additionally it frees up cash that can be put to better use for the firm in brand promotion and distribution. However, with growth and expansion, Gucci also feels that taking the route to backward vertical integration may have more advantages than disadvantages. To keep tight control on its value chain, Gucci has realized in its history that both forward and backward integration is perhaps a better strategy to control the value of the brand in the long term. To save its brand from counterfeit products, it has replaced its distribution channels with directly operated stores (DOS) that is has either bought back from former franchises or created from scratch.

Growth in the emerging countries is vital for luxury groups that have used this opportunity to vertically integrate sales and distribution processes. This has resulted in the acquisition and direct control of their distribution networks and the extension of their own-brand retail network. The method proved effective for market leaders, for example, Hermès, Chanel, and Louis Vuitton. They have created a product palette large enough to ensure profitability for its retail networks and deployed substantial financial resources to undertake heavy investments.

Nevertheless, the in-house distribution strategy also has its limits. The implementation of integrated retail networks has proven to be expensive, though it restricts counterfeiting to a large extent. Moreover, market changes have been underestimated and distribution has absorbed resources that could otherwise have been invested in product innovation. The recent government crackdown on corruption and gifting in China combined with a growing penchant for traveling and shopping overseas to circumvent Chinese consumption taxes on luxury goods as high as 40 percent resulted in dramatic decreases in mainland China sales in 2013. The shrinking ranks of wealthy residents in China has also reduced luxury spending. One in three so-called high-net-worth individuals have already left China, or are planning to leave, mostly to seek better opportunities for their children's education. The main challenge for leading luxury brands may therefore be to optimize and better control their distribution networks (corners, through duty-free shopping, boutiques) in order to increase the impact of luxury-specific environments and optimize profitability.

Collaborate

Brands can try to work directly with the offending parties. For example, in 2011, the American handbag and accessories brand Coach signed a memorandum of understanding with the largest Chinese Internet shopping site, www.taobao.com, to prevent the sale of fake Coach products on this Chinese website. This is important, as China is a large market for both producing and selling counterfeit goods. For example, L'Oréal recently won a case in the courts of the European Union against the online seller eBay, where the Court of Justice ruled that eBay had the responsibility to play an active role in stopping their sellers from trading in counterfeit L'Oréal goods. The court said websites such as eBay might be liable for trademark infringements and that they were in fact playing an active role in the promotion of counterfeit goods by allowing them to remain on the site. If one goes to eBay now, one can find tutorials on how to tell authentic items from fakes, for example, when purchasing a Louis Vuitton bag.

Formal Programs Addressing Counterfeiting

Global luxury brands have started using formal programs to address counterfeiting. Trying to protect their intellectual property, they have started anticounterfeiting initiatives to coordinate efforts with law enforcement, government, and industry. They also build a strong in-house response, police retail websites, and conduct regular enforcement. They take professional advice and sue external counsel to possibly enter into federal court litigation.

For example, Burberry, like Hermès and Chanel, has in-house legal counsel. Burberry was not afraid to enter into federal court litigation at the prospect of $2 million damages when it filed, along with Louis

Vuitton, a lawsuit against Canadian firms selling fake goods. In an effort to stop widespread proliferation of Louis Vuitton counterfeits online, the company successfully sued auction site eBay, claiming that up to 90 percent of the Louis Vuitton products sold on the site were fakes. The company was awarded more than $60 million in the lawsuit, though eBay decided to reappeal. Gucci had in-house legal counsel as of 2010. A number of outside law firms, including Arnold & Porter LLP and Gorodisky and Partners, have represented YSL.

Gucci and YSL also participated in the "Special Covert Anti-Counterfeit Operation" announced by Taobao, a leading retail website in China, aiming to remove the sales of counterfeit products from the e-commerce websites (a total of 89 participants, including Apple, Louis Vuitton, Chanel, Estée Lauder, Samsung, Panasonic, and Swarovski). Furthermore, Giorgio Gucci, heir to the fortune, had testified before Congress on the need to stop counterfeiting.

Kering, along with LVMH, Chanel, and Hermès as members of the Comité Colbert, launched in 2009 an anticounterfeiting initiative with French national anticounterfeiting committee. It aimed to remind the public that defending intellectual property means protecting imagination, creativity, and intelligence, and to inform the public about the risks associated with the purchase of counterfeit goods.

Ralph Lauren certainly hasn't shied away from protecting their IP, filing lawsuits to pursue online counterfeits and suing Jordache and the United States Polo Association (USPA), for instance. In the lawsuit of 2000, Ralph Lauren said that the use of the name "polo" and the symbol of a polo player on a horse on clothes infringes on the Polo Ralph Lauren trademark by confusing consumers. Most items on record are of Ralph Lauren Company suing companies or fighting to shut down online counterfeit websites.

Labels like Coach and Kate Spade have information set up on their websites for customers to report anyone who is selling knockoffs of their goods; these sites also have more detailed ways for people to spot fakes of their labels.

Counterfeiting in the Digital Era

The past decade has witnessed luxury fashion brands embracing online exposure and simultaneously has also seen a sharp rise in counterfeiters.

The Internet has enabled the brands to expand their reach, create a more direct relationship with their consumers, and receive instant online orders.

According to ACG Statistics on Counterfeiting and Piracy, in 2008, 0.15 percent of a total 2.7 billion listings on eBay were identified as potentially counterfeit using an anticounterfeit program, which includes proprietary tools for online prevention, detection, and enforcement in close cooperation with brand owners and law enforcement. In 2004, Tiffany purchased 186 random items from eBay and found that only 5 percent of the items were genuine. Out of 300,000 Dior products and 150,000 Louis Vuitton items offered on eBay during the first six months of 2006, 90 percent were found to be counterfeits. In tests conducted by Microsoft on 115 copies of physical media purchased on eBay, 39 percent were found to be counterfeit and 12 percent contained software that was either counterfeit or had been tampered with. Internet auction fraud is the most commonly reported Internet offense, comprising 62.7 percent of all complaints, according to the Internet Crime Complaint Center's 2005 report.

Clearly, the advent of the digital age has changed the rules of the game, shifting the dynamics of buying fakes and widening the frauds' reach. This has chiefly been the result of increased accessibility to both luxury and imitation products. Many fashion houses have managed to successfully balance being online and preserving an aura of mystery. There is no doubt that embracing digital exposure has brought luxury to a much broader audience. Desirability coupled with the high price point have created a disparity between demand-and-supply; and once the Internet let luxury goods into our households, counterfeit luxury goods weren't far behind.

Second, with globalization and expansion, the remoteness between buyer and seller has increased. The Internet creates transactional remoteness, and in practice this impacts the buyer and seller in different ways. On one hand, transactional remoteness ensures anonymity for the buyer, meaning that she escapes the social and moral opprobrium that comes from buying fakes. On the other hand, it protects fraudulent sellers by making it harder for law enforcement to shut down the offending websites. This is largely due to counterfeiters operating across several nations and often out of countries that take a lax approach to IP protection. Moreover, the social acceptability of the imitation of luxury goods has played a significant role in the growth of these websites. Despite countless articles exposing the high correlation between counterfeiting and organized crime or child labor, feigned luxury goods are still regarded by many as harmless, comparable to finding a bargain. Interestingly, studies in recent years have highlighted that people who buy fakes are statistically already spending more on luxury goods than nonbuyers. Further, they suggest that these people benefit from personal satisfaction associated with the purchasing and consuming of counterfeit luxury goods—they feel smart about having saved money and get a kick out of fooling others and not being discovered.

Third, what anticounterfeiting methods can be used by luxury brands? Stifling online supply is a must. Several luxury fashion brands take a proactive approach to eradicating the supply of counterfeit goods. Christian Louboutin is a brand that invests significant resources towards eliminating feigning of its own products, with particular attention to the online channel. Among other activities in antifraud, the company monitors Internet auction websites, helping to remove listings of counterfeit merchandise. They also work closely with law enforcement and search engines to remove sites selling imitations and if necessary, shut down their web-hosting service providers. The company maintains constant training and dialogue with international customs offices around the world, and most recently started monitoring "fake blogs" that purport to share information about Christian Louboutin products, but in reality are just ways to lead users to fraudulent sellers' sites. Indeed, the company has identified over a thousand unauthorized sites selling counterfeit Louboutin shoes, including multiple instances of cyber-squatting (defined by the U.S. Anti-Cyber Squatting Consumer Protection Act as "registering, trafficking in, or using a domain name with bad faith intent to profit from the goodwill of a trademark belonging to someone else"). This has become an increasingly insidious problem. According to the latest press release from the World Intellectual Property Organization (or WIPO, the specialized agency of the United Nations whose mission statement is "the promotion of creativity through a balanced and effective international intellectual property system"), cases involving cyber-squatting in 2010 increased by 28 percent—a new record high. While the increase of website registrations may certainly be a contributing factor, it demonstrates how the Internet can be a fertile breeding ground for counterfeiters.

However, to successfully abolish the supply of fraudulent luxury goods, one needs to also tackle demand. Several organizations—such as the International Anti-Counterfeiting Coalition—are tackling the demand-side by raising public awareness campaigns, which are designed to educate consumers in the dangers of buying fakes. Within the luxury fashion industry, counterfeiting remains an important topic that regularly receives coverage in the fashion press. Of particular note is *Harper's Bazaar*'s yearly groundbreaking investigative report into frauds and their permanence.

In addition, it touts its online initiative "Fakes Are Never in Fashion," which promotes awareness of the developments in the fight against fakes year-round, offering tips in recognizing feigned goods and providing links to useful resources in combating international counterfeiting.

Similarly, developments in online marketing could prove to be useful tools in counteracting the pervasive and harmful presence of fraudulent goods on the web. For instance, SEO techniques can at once help users find what they want and help brands ensure users find what the brands want—thus optimizing the visibility of the brands' legitimate website and authentic merchandise.

Next, a strategic approach to web content management allows luxury fashion brands to convey both the tangible as well as the intangible value of their product range, educating consumers regarding their superior craftsmanship, manufacturing excellence, heritage, and know-how. Moreover, in creating valuable content that users will organically want to share and talk about, brands can ensure their message reaches wider communities. Finally, a strong social media strategy enables brands to bridge the gap further, helping to build and nurture real relationships with their customers, thus drawing them in and further excluding the possibility of them purchasing counterfeits.[*]

Gray Market

The gray market (or parallel market) refers to the flow of goods through distribution channels other than those authorized or intended

---

[*]Som, A (2006). Technical Note (C). Issues of Luxury Industry in Emerging Market. Case Centre Reference No. 306-513-6

by the manufacturer or producer. It is a market where a product is bought and sold outside the manufacturer's authorized trading channels. For example, if a store owner is an unauthorized dealer of a certain high-end electronics brand, the product is considered to be sold in the gray market. If the product is illegal, it would be selling on the black market.

Unlike those on the black market, gray market goods are not illegal. Instead, the trade happens with companies that may have no relationship with the producer of the goods. Frequently this occurs when there is an opportunity to arbitrage on price. This situation is widely practiced with cigarettes and electronic equipment such as cameras, and at the high end with luxury watches. Entrepreneurs will buy the product where it is available cheap, often at retail but sometimes at wholesale, import it legally to the target market, and sell it at a price that provides a profit but which is below the normal market price there.

Importing certain legally restricted items such as prescription drugs or firearms would be categorized as black market, as would smuggling the goods into the target country to avoid import duties. A related concept is bootlegging, which normally implies the making or distribution of counterfeit goods but also describes the illegal distribution of highly regulated goods, especially alcoholic beverages.

Because of the nature of gray market economics, it is generally difficult or even impossible to track and verify the precise numbers of gray market sales. When gray market products are advertised on Google, eBay, or other legitimate websites, it is possible to petition for removal of any advertisements that violate trademark or copyright laws. This can be done directly, without the involvement of legal professionals. eBay for example, will remove listings of such products even in countries where their purchase and use is not against the law (for example, in the cases of U.S. jeweler Tiffany & Co. and eBay).

The gray market is a booming business in the luxury sector, especially in watches and bags. One of the reasons is that big brands like LVMH, Chanel, Hermès, and Richemont practice differential pricing in different markets. Private companies based in cities like Singapore, Hong Kong, Miami, and Tokyo can buy and sell volumes of luxury goods through this channel, especially sourcing from duty-free shops and airports.

Conclusion

Counterfeiting that grows from strength to strength poses threats to luxury brands. The customer loses interest in a brand that is widely counterfeited. The growth in the supply of counterfeits is due to the high demand of those counterfeits from consumers. Consumers gain the same experience in some aspects, at a lower price. Counterfeits are manufactured and consumed in all economies—emerging economies being developing countries that provide favorable conditions for counterfeit businesses.

The longstanding problem of counterfeiting poses challenges for legitimate manufactures of luxury brands in developing brand equity and maximizing benefits from the resources utilized in developing brands. The presence of counterfeits not only affects the potential customers of brands negatively, but also makes it arduous for legitimate manufacturers to retain their existing customers.

The losses incurred due to counterfeiting businesses are enormous. Counterfeits undermine the phenomenon of innovation and negative affect the brands, economies, and consumers of legitimate goods.

Safeguards against counterfeiting within private organizations have three main ingredients: anticounterfeiting policy, technologies, and legal enforcement. Increased cooperation between governments and industry would be beneficial, as would be better data collection. Since counterfeiting of luxury goods does not present any physical danger for the consumer (compared to pharmaceutical counterfeiting, for instance), and the client dream is sometimes viewed as snobbish, it is often difficult for a copied brand to obtain genuine support from the authorities in their struggle against counterfeiting. It means that to protect themselves from counterfeiting, luxury brands have to demonstrate efficient performance and use managerial guidelines all along their value chain. Presence of counterfeited products not only proves the strong dream factor of a certain brand, but also can be a checkpoint of the brand's strategy. At the moment, there is very little social stigma attached to buying/wearing a counterfeit garment. To change this situation, acclaimed luxury brands should use their image to initiate campaigns raising public awareness. Consumers need to step back and think of where the money they spend on knock-offs could be going. Just as selling knock-offs is a crime, a connection is drawn between counterfeit goods and funding for other crimes involving drugs and weapons. Now law enforcement is worried about a link between counterfeit goods and terrorism, which means that since September 11, authorities have stepped up their pursuit of those knocking off fashion brands. Although the whole issue may first appear to be a simple yet rampant case of copycatting, in fact it demonstrates that there is a real need for stricter protection of luxury fashion brands, enforcement of those laws, and harsher punishments for merchants and makers of counterfeit goods. But as far as eliminating counterfeiting completely, as with any type of crime, it will never be completely gone, and brands need to view counterfeit products just like any other competition.

Law firms specializing in intellectual property rights related to fashion and the luxury industry work on specific issues for the industry, and will know where to look out for issues of counterfeiting in a proactive manner. It will be worth the investment for the company to make sure they are up-to-date on what is happening not only in the authentic sales market but also in the underground counterfeit market. For example, LVMH indicates that for their luxury group of companies.

Experts suggest that there are some ways to get out of the counterfeiting trap, though it may be costly, time consuming, and not foolproof. Some of them are:

- Maintaining a database of customers
- Limiting the number of articles sold to each person (as practiced by LV in France for foreigners)
- Price discrimination for higher profits (for example, Louis Vuitton handbags, which cost 40 percent more in Japan than in Europe)
- Continue innovating, differentiating, and upgrading while focusing on services
- Reinforcing controls at the airport, especially from France, Italy, and Switzerland, and from China, Thailand, Malaysia, Indonesia, Singapore, and other nations.
- Limiting point-of-sales or strictly controlled (LV, Chanel, and Hermès have only their exclusive stores)
- Concentrate on a few brands to keep tight control on the portfolio (for example, TAG Heuer and Dior in India, Vuitton and Dior in Japan)

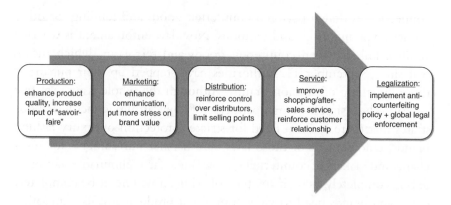

Figure 12.2   Interventions in the Value Chain to Prevent Counterfeiting

- Have some brands developed in the local culture (for example, Shanghai Tang [Richemont Group], which is now exported to Europe)
- Enhance cooperation with national and foreign authorities, including lobbying with governments, customs' administration, and police (for example, Taiwan's Intellectual Property Rights Police since 2004 or cyber-crime units on the Internet)
- Invest in anticounterfeit measures within the organization to be able to bring counterfeiters to the court effectively (for example, the recent lawsuit won by LVMH against Carrefour in China)
- Conduct a global campaign against counterfeiting to raise awareness, educating the consumers to be more sensitive (for example, the exhibition in April 2006 on China IPR) and that buying counterfeit products is illegal (some European airports, such as Charles de Gaulle, Paris, now confiscate counterfeit products and impose fines that can amount to the value of the genuine product)

Figure 12.2 provides a snapshot of the interventions that need to be done in the value chain.

Chapter 13

Emerging Markets and Emerging Market Luxury Brands

A s the twenty-first century approached, the luxury industry was experiencing a transition. Shunning its traditional
family-oriented business model, luxury businesses were
reinventing themselves as corporate houses, keen on spreading their
tentacles to the rest of the untapped globe. The race for increasing profit
margins became more and more competitive. Creativity was ushered
in to boost profitability. Access products were pushed to attract those
with lower reservation prices. In short, the luxury industry underwent
democratization. As the desire to accumulate more brands was growing
in the hearts of the luxury conglomerates, a similar desire was growing
in the hearts of prosperous Asians. This new generation of Asians had
stopped feeling guilty about spending their parents' hard-earned money.

Also, as traditional haute couture ran out of steam, it was no news to anyone that the new consumers of luxury were younger. They neither had the excess cash to spend on haute couture, nor was it in line with their fashion requirements. Thus, large luxury houses began providing youth with accessible products, which included ready-to-wear items and accessories. Licensing was the new way of entering untapped markets. Many brands, such as Pierre Cardin, lent their name to items ranging from chocolate bars to frying pans. However, many licensees did not invest enough in marketing, thereby diluting their brand name. Thus, these brands had to call back their licenses and take things into their own hands. This is when the luxury explosion started.

The luxury conglomerates and the family houses understood very quickly that the growth of the luxury goods market may no longer be fueled only from mature markets such as Europe, but more and more from the emerging markets. In a certain sense, mature markets such as United States have for a long time being emerging for the luxury goods sector. To win these markets, efforts made by luxury brands included an image makeover toward a logo-centric approach to attract those who wanted to use luxury items as a way to boost their social standing. They set up luxury mansions to house their collections and tried to include anything and everything that a human being could possibly ask for. Their products ranged from swimming gear to horseback-riding paraphernalia, from hats to stilettos, from iPod cases to ballerina shoes, from mittens to baby suits.

This was also accompanied with the setting up of malls in Asian markets. From Japan to Hong Kong, representatives of the luxury brands started visiting these shopping malls to understand buying behaviors, such as which brands were considered to yield high social status, and which brand was considered to be a mass brand.

Needless to say, the efforts put forth by the luxury brands did not go to waste. The Asian markets now constitute a healthy 40 percent of the global luxury consumption. If one takes into account the purchases that Asians make abroad, the figure may be more than 50 percent. Within Asia, the Chinese are the fastest-growing group of luxury consumers.

China's meteoric rise as a luxury market was slowly followed by the markets of Brazil, Russia, and India, which were considered to be the main engine of growth over the next decade. Of these countries, China still remains the most significant market. Due to global recession growth has slowed in mature markets such as the Americas and Europe, while the growth was hindered due to Japan's earthquake in March 2010. Still the mature markets remain significant for the industry. Japan surprisingly continued to be the third most relevant luxury goods market, with an expected growth rate of 8 percent in 2014.

The following section deals with the individual emerging markets, some of their nuances, and the emerging market luxury brands from those markets. Table 13.1 provides a snapshot of the BRIC countries in the luxury sector.

Brazil

Brazil has rediscovered itself, and this rediscovery is being expressed in its people's enthusiasm and their desire to mobilize to face the huge problems that lie ahead of us.

—Luiz Inacio Lula da Silva

Brazil, with its vast natural resources, substantial development boom, premier cosmopolitan center, and the incredible rise of its rapidly expanding middle class (which will account for 60 percent of the country's populace by 2014, from 38.8 percent in 2002) is considered by many to be the powerhouse behind South America's growth. With increased purchasing power and the democratization of knowledge through new media, Brazilians' appetite for luxury goods is surging along with its soaring economy. According to the 2010 World Wealth Report, Brazil was ahead of both India and Russia in terms of the number of millionaires residing in the country. It was the eleventh country for the number of high-net-worth individuals (HNWIs). The report stated that Brazil was home to more billionaires than Saudi Arabia, France, and Italy. The predictions stated that by 2015, São Paulo would have more people with higher income levels than London and Paris. Brazilians value fashion, as evident from the higher levels of disposable income they spend on fashion. There are a large number of consumers who aspire to own luxury products. These are the characteristics of a market that is ready for luxury.

Table 13.1 Characteristics of the BRIC Countries with Respect to the Luxury Industry

	Brazil	Russia	India	China
Government policies and actions (including legal)	Vibrant democracy, bureaucracy is rampant, pockets of corruption	Centralized elected government, coexisting with some regional freedom, oppressive bureaucracy, corruption at all levels	World's largest democracy, high level of bureaucracy, corruption at all levels	Communist Party, local governments make economic policy, joined WTO, officials may abuse power
Economic, market structure and competitive conduct	GDP per capita $10,800, average GDP growth 6–8 percent, overall luxury market growing at 20 percent to reach about $3 billion in 2012, luxury stores growing at 33 percent, high tax on luxury goods, starting phase in luxury goods.	GDP per capita of $15,900, average GDP growth 3–5 percent, overall luxury market reduced by half to $4 billion during the financial crisis, luxury stores growing at 42 percent, high tax on luxury goods, starting phase in luxury goods consumption.	GDP per capita $3,500, average GDP growth 5–8 percent, overall luxury market from $5.8 billion, estimated to be $15.6 billion by 2015, luxury stores growing at 56 percent, high tax on luxury goods, stagnating stage due to policy breaks.	GDP per capita $7,600, average GDP growth 7–9 percent, luxury spending reached $9.7 billion in 2011—more than 27 percent of the global market, luxury stores growing at 58 percent, high tax on luxury goods, advanced growth stage in the luxury sector.
Modes of Entry	Joint Ventures are possible in the luxury sector and companies prefer to team up with local partners, mainly retailers, to gain local expertise.	Joint Ventures are only possible in the luxury sector from alliances to gain access to government and local inputs.	Restrictions on greenfield investments and acquisitions in the luxury sector make joint ventures necessary, with 51 percent ownership in case on monobrands and 49 percent ownership in case of multibrands.	Restrictions on greenfield investments and acquisitions in the luxury sector make joint ventures necessary.

Social forces workforce	About 400,000 millionaires (with assets of $3,960 billion), Very high income inequality exists (about 5 percent of the population control 85 percent of the wealth), rich concentrated in mainly São Paulo and Rio, Trade unions are strong and pragmatic. Pool of management talent with some degree of proficiency in English. Preference for mix between expats and local in the luxury industry.	About 290,000 millionaires (with assets of $2810 billion), Very high income inequality exists, rich concentrated in mainly Moscow and St. Petersburg, Trade unions are present but less influential. Pool of management talent with some degree of proficiency in English. Preference for mix between expats and locals in the luxury industry.	About 370,000 millionaires (with assets of $3560 billion), High income inequality exists, should reap demographic dividend with rich people spread across the nation, trade union is active and volatile with political connections. Large pool of English-speaking talent fueled by engineering, technical, and business schools. Preference to local hires.	About 1,015,000 millionaires (with assets $9810 billion), income inequality exists, one-child policy, wealthy people mainly on the coast, workers can join the government-controlled all-China Federation of Trade Unions. Negligible number of locals speak English and have the competencies to work in the luxury sector, prevalence of large number of expats and foreign-educated Chinese nationals.
Technological, Infrastructure, and system changes	Good network of highways, airports, and ports exists. Luxury malls are being built.	European region has decent logistics. Recent major construction and opening of high-profile luxury malls in Moscow.	Road network not well maintained. Ports and airports are being developed. Most luxury stores are in five-star hotels. Four luxury malls built in 2012.	Road network is well developed. Excellent port facilities. Numerous malls and luxury stores.

(continued)

Table 13.1 (*Continued*)

	Brazil	Russia	India	China
Product development and IPR	Local design capability exists, IPR disputes also exists.	Strong local design capability, ambivalent attitude about IPR.	Strong local design capability, IPR rules put in place with monitoring from regulatory authorities.	IPR laws misguided. Imitation and piracy abound. Punishment for IPR theft varies across provinces and by level of corruption
Brand perception	Consumers accept local and international brands	Global brands are preferred for automobiles and luxury. Local brands for food and beverage.	Consumers accept local and international brands	Consumers prefer European, Japanese, and American luxury logos.

Source: Adapted from Ashok Som, *International Management: Managing the Global Corporation* (New York: McGraw-Hill, 2009).

The luxury market, characterized by increasing access to disposable income among the majority of Brazilian consumers, in addition to rising interest in what Brazilians call "pleasure consumption," is a growth market. Moreover, the average Brazilian millionaire is younger than those in other countries, with one-third of its high-net-worth individuals aged 35 or younger. Carlos Jereissati Filho, President and Chief Executive of Iguatemi, commented that, "Every part of the world has to give something. Brazil's heritage to the world is Youth. Luxury in Brazil is seductive by nature, creativity, intimacy, sense of belonging."[1] Brazilians of all ages love spending money and if they have it, they are not ashamed to flaunt it. Older people don't save because they remember the 1980s, when hyperinflation made planning impossible. Vanity, conspicuous consumption, a growing and solid economy, steep markups, and an infectious desire to live for the moment—these are just some of the things that set Brazilians apart from other emerging markets in the luxury goods market. And the young believe in living for the moment. Brazil is also unique, as many luxury brands such as Dior and Tiffany allow their consumers to pay in installments ("parcelas") for their purchases.

In Brazil, unlike in other emerging markets, female consumption of luxury goods represents about 75 percent of the total spending. Brazil is the third largest personal and beauty market in the world after Japan and the United States. For example, an average Brazilian woman uses as much conditioner as two Americans, 10 Russians, or 20 Chinese women. For this reason, Diane von Furstenberg commented, "Brazilian women know what they want to be. They take care of their body, have good legs and they love to show it off. They exemplify seduction, youth." That explains why the amount spent on luxury cosmetics and fragrances accounted for more than 60 percent of the total market. "Fragrance is the secret of antiquity. The seduction power is in the bottle. Brazilians are obsessed with coherence and the mission is to empower women. When one wants to tell children something, they don't say 'Do it'. They travel together; they give hints so that they can learn by

---

[1] Carlos Jereissati Filho, president and chief executive, Iguatemi, at the "Hot Luxury" Conference, November 10–11, 2011, Hotel Unique, São Paulo.

themselves. Brazilians should put their enthusiasm in a bottle, it will be bigger than Coca-Cola."[2]

Hard luxury, and especially semiprecious jewels, is the second largest category for luxury products in Brazil. High-end food items, beverages, and designer clothing are the third largest category. Brazilians are said to have a keen interest in all divisions of the luxury market, including perfumes, cosmetics, fashion accessories, and shoes. Furthermore, with the recent growth of the ultra-rich, there is also a market for ultra-luxury items such as luxury cars, cruises, real estate, yachts, and private jets.

The opportunities in this market have lured international luxury brands that entered the Brazilian market between 1995 and 2010 and have focused their openings in the city of São Paulo (which holds 70 percent of the domestic luxury market) and the city of Rio de Janeiro (25 percent of the domestic luxury market), for a total of more than 80 stores in these two cities. There are already 60 international brands in the country, including Louis Vuitton, Burberry, Gucci, Armani, Emilio Pucci, Jimmy Choo, and Chanel. The recent construction of new luxury malls by Iguatemi[3] has also helped luxury brands such as Gucci, Burberry, and Chanel gain access to wealthy Brazilians. There is also a growing demand for luxury items in tier 2 cities. The majority of the

---

[2]Diane von Furstenberg in conversation with Suzy Menkes at the "Hot Luxury" Conference, 2011.

[3]Iguatemi, with its 45th anniversary in 2011, is one of the major pioneering portals to access luxury in Brazil. It currently manages 13 strategically placed shopping centers in Brazil, located in Rio de Janeiro, Brasilia, Campinas, Sorocaba, São Carlos, Florianopolis, Porto Alegre, Caxias do Sul, and its flagship in São Paulo—which attracts over 1.6 million visitors a month and includes Brazil's largest number of luxury stores. Iguatemi is known for providing its clientele with a comprehensive shopping experience that brings together the world's luxury brands, Brazilian designers, dining, entertainment, and art. Iguatemi has been a pioneer of indoor shopping in Latin America, Iguatemi opened its flagship Iguatemi São Paulo in 1966, making it the first shopping center in Brazil. Iguatemi opened in May 2012 its new luxurious shopping center, Iguatemi JK, in São Paulo. International brands who chose Iguatemi as their first Latin American location were Burberry, Christian Louboutin, Diane von Frustenberg, Emenegildo Zegna, Gucci, Kiehl's, Mac, Missoni, Salvatore Ferragamo, Tiffany & Co., and Vilebrequin. Other international brands present are Armani, Bang & Olufsen, Bulgari, Chanel, Lacoste, Louis Vuitton, and Marc Jacobs. International Brazilian brands include Carlos Miele, H. Stern, Jack Vartanian, Jo De Mer, Osklen, and Track and Field.

market still remains in São Paulo, but with the recent rise in wealth among other cities in Brazil, plans are underway to remodel shopping centers elsewhere to attract more high-end brands.

Perhaps more promising than the fashion industry is Brazil's luxury tourism market. The cost of construction, land, and labor are significantly lower than in North America and Europe, therefore requiring less investment for setting up new businesses. The tourism luxury boom is already happening in some areas. The 2014 World Cup in Brazil added to the tourism boom, but the result won't be fully felt until 2015, when the region will be booming with new properties being built and demand growing higher than ever before.

In the past, many luxury groups stayed away from Brazil due to high import duties, complex bureaucracy, and nontariff barriers, and a lack of retail space.[4] For example, Brazilians are taxed at upward of 34 percent, and luxury goods in particular carry a whopping 25-percent tax. For this reason, 45 percent of Brazilian purchases are made outside the country, mainly in New York (36 percent), Paris (21 percent), Miami (15 percent), Buenos Aires (6 percent), and Milan (6 percent). Over and above, Brazilian distributors and luxury company–owned importing entities have to add the cost of distribution, which generate a price escalation of up to 75 percent over the same item in the United States or Europe. However, as a result of rising commodity prices and a stronger currency in recent years, Brazil's middle class has grown at a rapid rate and many luxury brands see the great potential Brazil poses for growth.

Long the underdog of the BRIC markets, Brazil will probably remain a mix of opportunity and obstacles for some time to come. Consequently, luxury firms need to gauge their approach according to the capacity of the country's main urban market to accommodate them, as well as the pace at which the middle classes might become a formidable segment to target.

Aside from the operational challenges, the unique characteristics of local consumers are striking in Brazil. There is a collective memory that luxury is European at heart, but also a strong sense of national identity and the idea that Brazil can build its own luxury sector from scratch. At the moment, the focus in on the homegrown brands.

---

[4]"Brazil on Way to Luxury Growth, Execs Say," reuters.com, May 26, 2011.

H. Stern

H. Stern is a Brazilian nonlisted company, the largest jewelry maker and jewelry store in its home country with 65 percent colored precious and semiprecious stones that gives "the look from outside." The company was founded in 1945 by German refugee Hans Stern at age 22. It is currently owned by the founder's four sons: Roberto, Ronaldo, Ricardo, and Rafael.[5] The company is known for turning its colored gemstones into beautiful jewelry, able to compete with other luxury jewelry companies worldwide. The company is also world renowned for its innovative and modern designs. Roberto Stern is the president and creative director of the company, and he believes in the combination of creativity, innovation, and product development. Currently, H. Stern is a vertically integrated company that creates its own designs and content to the minutest details.

From the beginning of the 1950s, with beautiful jewels and an audacious marketing strategy for that time, the company was poised to revolutionize the traditional jewelry industry. Stern and his company trained a large number of young Brazilian jewelers as H. Stern gained customers and market credibility. The company's designs could be linked with Brazil if the bright gemstones and use of gold is considered. The designers who are based in Rio still take inspiration from Brazilian cultural elements, such as a line of jewelry inspired by the cobblestone streets of Buzios. But for the most part, the jewelry designs don't just stick to Brazilian cultural elements, and the style of the jewelry is ever evolving. The design team on one hand is very much focused and structured but also extremely flexible. Stern's work propelled the Brazilian jewelery industry to meet international standards. Stern was also the first to create a worldwide warranty certificate and to offer tours of his workshops to present the creative and production process with integrity and transparency. In 1964, while Hans was preparing to cross the Atlantic to expand his business in Europe and the Middle East, *Time* magazine called him the "king of diamonds and colored gems, capable of unveiling the personality hidden in every precious stone." The first international boutiques appeared in Frankfurt, Lisbon, and New York in the 1970s.

---

[5]H. Stern Com. & Ind., S.A. Company Information, hoovers.com. www.hoovers.com /h.-stern/--ID__132451--/freeuk-co-factsheet.xhtml.

For many decades the company focused its creations on Hans's beloved colored gems, although Stern also won several Diamonds International Awards and other prizes for his avant garde diamond designs.

Its popularity with Hollywood stars has propelled the brand on to the international scene. Its product offering includes bracelets, earrings, necklaces, pendants, rings, watches, and other high-end jewelry. Although it is a Brazilian company, the headquarters are based in New York, but the design team has remained in the company's founding city, Rio de Janeiro. The company has 165 stores in more than 15 countries and 170 retail partners in Europe, the Middle East, and the United States. It has stores in Argentina, Brazil, Canada, Colombia, France, Germany, Israel, Mexico, Panama, Peru, Portugal, Russia, the United Kingdom, the United States, and the Virgin Islands, and is said to be rapidly expanding in Eastern Europe and the Middle East, where its designs and style are in line with local tastes. H. Stern Jewelers, Inc. operates as a subsidiary of H. Stern Comercio e Indústria S.A.[6]

Today, H. Stern appears prominently in the editorial texts and photographs of the world's most respected fashion magazines, including *Elle, Marie Claire, Vogue, Harper's Bazaar, W*, and *InStyle*. The company focuses on generic advertising with no link to its Brazilian roots, featuring models such as Kate Moss, who poses for many other fashion and jewelry luxury brands, such as American competitor David Yurman. The company also partners with other designers for limited edition collections, such as American-German Diane Von Furstenberg (DVF).[7] This has helped the brand increase its presence and credibility in international markets, given that DVF is a well-known designer and brand across the world.

Carlos Miele

Carlos Miele is a multidisciplinary Brazilian fashion designer with Italian origins who "looks to traditional Brazilian artisan techniques like

---

[6]Company Overview of H. Stern Jewelers, Inc., Bloomberg Businessweek. http://investing .businessweek.com/research/stocks/private/snapshot.asp?privcapId=4667429.
[7]Diane von Furstenberg by H. Stern collection, H. Stern Virtual Store. www.hstern.net/site /loja_virtual/produtos.asp?codigo_area=12&codigo_categoria=281.

patchwork, stitching, crochet, and leatherwork in his exuberant and insanely sexy designs. The red-carpet-ready looks tend toward the highly structured and the busy, with bold color combinations, clingy silhouettes, plunging necklines, and jagged hemlines open to the thigh."[8] He combines various frontiers and different languages as art performances, videos, installations, fashion, and architecture. His designs transcend the influences of his Brazilian roots, reconstructing them for new audiences. The designer also distills a variety of urban environments, drawing inspiration from very distinct groups of women: cosmopolitan, sophisticated, and independent. His work, which manages to mesh a strong fashion vision and a social conscience, has allowed him to develop important partnerships with artisan cooperatives from several regions of his native country. In his words, "I am inspired by the exuberance of Brazilian popular culture, the special beauty of our natural landscapes, biodiversity, and the mixing of races among the Brazilian people."[9]

Due to the Brazilian-Italian connection, the brand brings Brazil's beautiful handcrafted techniques, which were slowly being lost and forgotten, to fashion along with Italy's modern "la bella figura" concept, creating a connection between two worlds that would normally never find each other. The label focuses on high-end women's ready-to-wear. The brand was established in 2002 and is based in his hometown of São Paulo, Brazil. In June of 2003, Miele opened his first flagship store in the Meatpacking District of New York City, which received many awards as the "Store of the Year" and became one of the city's references of contemporary architecture as published in several architectural publications. In 2006, he launched a lower-priced brand called Miele. In November 2007, Miele opened a store at Rue Fauborg Saint-Honoré in Paris that was designed by Hani Rashid. The space takes inspiration from a combination of influences, including Brazilian masters Oscar Niemeyer and Roberto Burle Marx and their interest in abstract figurative affinities, the French Baroque and Parisian Art Nouveau. In Brazil, Miele designed his São Paulo flagship store, a space with nearly 800 square meters that opened in November 2011, much like he designs his signature dresses,

---

[8]"Carlos Miele: Label Overview," the Cut, *New York Magazine*. http://nymag.com/fashion/fashionshows/designers/bios/carlosmiele.
[9]Michault, November 9, 2011.

as a three-dimensional figure. The store's architecture is directly related to the proportions of the human body, space, and time.

Although brand awareness is not extremely high, given that it is a fairly new luxury brand on the fashion scene, the style is directly associated with Brazil, all while maintaining legitimacy from the designer's Italian roots. The brand is sold in more than 30 countries, and it operates its stores through its directly owned stores in São Paulo, New York, and Paris. Its Paris store is located on the Rue du Faubourg Saint-Honoré alongside other French and Italian luxury brands.

Daslu

Daslu is Brazil's world-renowned multibrand and boutique/department store in São Paulo, Brazil. It is a boutique of fashion apparel for women, men, and children. The boutique is known as the "fashion designers' mecca" of Brazil, as it houses more than 60 labels plus 30 store-in-stores and is the place where Brazilian socialites, ranging from multimillionaire soccer players to conglomerate bigwigs, shop for the latest accessories and clothing. It is a renowned shopping institution in South America for being a purveyor of chic and exclusive couture. It also offers décor and luxury items, such as jewelry, watches, cosmetics, food and drink, and gifts. The company exports its products to the Americas, Europe, Africa, the Middle East, Asia, and Oceania.

The history of Daslu began in 1958 when it was opened by businesswoman Lúcia Piva de Albuquerque Tranchesi. Using a classical mansion as its first retail location, the boutique's clientele base was made up of São Paulo's elite. The store evolved in 1996 when Brazil opened its economy to foreign products and Eliana Tranchesi, business owner at the time and daughter of the founder, brought Chanel and other international luxury brands, such as Jimmy Choo, Louis Vuitton, and Valentino to Brazil under exclusive contracts, and established them as shop-in-shops in the Daslu department store.[10] The boutique recently moved into its new and larger location in Vila Olímpia, a district in São Paulo. The store represents a landmark for Brazilians, as it was the first establishment of

---

[10]Benson, July 16, 2005.

international luxury brands. The store is also known for its impeccable service, and therefore represents a true luxurious offering.

The store has attracted significant controversy since its opening for a number of reasons. First, the store is one of the most public and unapologetic displays of São Paulo's immense economic inequality: the four-story behemoth of a store is located right next to Coliseu, one of the city's many favelas, or shanty-towns. Since the beginning of the store's construction, much has been made of this geographical juxtaposition in the media. While Daslu has made an effort to launch a number of social programs in this neighborhood, it is uncertain what impact they have made.

Daslu now has its own brand of clothing which is exported to American department stores such as Bergdorf Goodman's and New York City's Scoop,[11] and operates three stores in Brazil, two in São Paulo and one in Rio de Janeiro.[12]

Lenny Niemeyer

Lenny Niemeyer arrived in Rio de Janeiro in 1980. As she began her search for sophisticated bikinis with the sensual allure of the Carioca, she ended up finding not only a new talent but also a new career. She gave up trying to find bikinis that suited her style, hired a seamstress, and purchased small amounts of lycra to design precisely the swimsuits she imagined. Niemeyer, previously a landscape architect, became a swimwear designer and worked with a variety of swimwear brands for more than 10 years. In 1993, after 10 years designing and manufacturing bikinis for famous Brazilian brands, Niemeyer decided to create her own brand, opening her first store in Ipanema, a wealthy neighborhood in Rio. In the beginning, she rented additional rooms in her apartment building to have enough space for her designs. Later, she converted a shed into her very first factory. Niemeyer has since transformed into a true fashion legend in Brazil. Ever since her runway debut in 1996,

---

[11] Todd Benson, "An Oasis of Indulgence Amid Brazil's Poverty," *New York Times*, July 16, 2005. www.nytimes.com/2005/07/16/business/worldbusiness/16daslu.html?adxnnl=1&adxnnlx=1323864495-7FmVtQbxuyQ1Wfuobi9XSw.

[12] Daslu Call Center Stores. www.daslu.com.br/institucional/lojas.

the name Lenny has been synonymous with high-fashion swimwear, a charming label that is now sold in more than 300 locations. Her shows have been supported by famous names of the fashion world.

Russia

Tsarist Russia was a major market for Western luxury goods during the 1700s. Tsar Alexander I was one of Breguet's first and most influential Russian aficionados. Russians were well known for their love of expensive luxury goods. Moscow is frequently referred to as the fifth fashion capital of the world, following Paris, Milan, London, and New York.

After the Bolshevik Revolution, the luxury goods industry lost its charm during the Communist era. Thus, the Russian luxury goods market is rather young, due to the recreation of Russian wealth among the new elite. The first luxury shop opened in Moscow in 1993. At that time, the Torgovy Dom Moskva retail company offered goods from Chanel, Gucci, and Jil Sander.

The Russian luxury goods market includes fashion, cosmetics, cars and yachts, jewelry and watches, food and wine, furniture and accessories, and many other products of exceptional quality and considerable price. There are no official statistics about the volume of this market, but some say that in 2008 it was worth between $7 and 9 billion with an annual growth of 20–25 percent. According to an estimate made by the Strategic Investment Group in 2006, the size of the market was $9.2 billion for local transactions and $12.5 billion for off-shore purchasing by Russians. During the recent global financial crisis of 2009, the Russian luxury goods market almost shrank by half to $4 billion. Ultra-luxury goods such as high-class real estate, yachts, business aircrafts, rare and expensive cars, objects of art, and jewelry are usually consumed by the upper-class consumers. A conservative estimate of Russian high-net-worth individuals could be close to 100,000 people. By 2012, overall sales volumes for luxury items probably exceeded $100 billion. It is not uncommon for affluent Russians to spend 13 percent of their household budgets on clothes and shoes, which is more than double that of well-off Japanese and British. This certainly makes Russia, and especially Moscow, where 80 percent of the market is concentrated, a promising country in the eye of high-end goods producers and retailers.

Social psychology can explain the consumption pattern or the purchase habit of elite goods or services. It is always a question of prestige, of special status as well as a sign of the social "elitism" of its owner. Unlike any other consumer, the Russian consumer of luxury goods is the most glaring example of the concept of conspicuous consumption and status seeking. There are a number of explanations for such behavior. First, it is historical. Russian nobles were among the first consumers of luxury goods worldwide since the early 1900s, especially in high-end jewelry. Second, the wealth has been acquired during the last 10–15 years and is therefore quite young, and in Russia there are absolutely no traditions for the financial management of such million-dollar fortunes. Such traditions are usually formed over centuries. The third important factor influencing people in the average age category is backlog demand. The generation of today's successful 35- to 45-year-old businessmen grew up in the period of total deficiency in the country and was denied free access to information available to the rest of the world. In this consumer group, the exaggerated consumption and desire to show off is a natural psychological response to the current rise in financial status and an awareness of global fashion trends. Essentially, Russian consumers are easily influenced by public opinion, and it is therefore important to them that the product they choose be recognized by others. Thus, in order to determine the current fashion trends in clothing, cosmetics, vacations, and so forth, interviews with prominent personalities, who express their consumer preferences, are frequently used.

The Russian luxury market is currently shaped by its retail space. Most, if not all, luxury goods store in Russia sell merchandise from one brand only. The three main distributors, Mercury,[13] Bosco di Ciliegi,[14] and Jamilco,[15] have led the import of luxury goods since the early 1990s and are the owners of TSUM and GUM department stores. Luxury retailers such as Mercury and Bosco have direct access to clients and

---

[13] Mercury has tie-ups with Prada, Armani, Dolce & Gabbana, Tiffany, Tods, Ermenegildo Zegna, Gucci, Chanel, Brioni, Jil Sander, John Galliano, Bulgari, and Fendi.

[14] Bosco de Ciliegi is in tie-ups with Givenchy, Mariana Rinaldi, Max Mara, Nina Ricci, Kenzo, Mandarin Duck, and Pomellato.

[15] Jamilco is in tie-ups with Christian Dior, Cerruti, Yohji Yamamoto, Escada, Wolford, Jean Paul Gaultier, Paul Smith, and Burburry.

leverage this to put pressure on the luxury companies. In fact, it has become rather difficult to get Russians interested in new brands because they are "spoiled" by the world-famous brands that can be promoted without any significant effort. If a new brand is launched, it takes time, money, and energy to reach a certain level of acknowledgement from the target group. This is why, in order to attract the attention of a major Russian luxury retailer, one has to offer either an outstandingly interesting product or service, or very special conditions of cooperation. Also there is an exodus of Russians who prefer to shop abroad. Yet this situation is also changing.

Valentin Yudashkin

Valentin Yudashkin is Russia's most famous fashion designer and the only Russian designer to be honored with membership in the Syndicate of High Fashion in Paris. He is also a decorated member of the Academy of Arts of the Russian Federation and a National Artist of Russia.

In 1991, the Valentin Yudashkin brand and first haute couture collection were created. The brand was named Fabergé and was inspired by the famous work of art. The most popular items of that collection were dresses made in the shape of an egg and decorated in the Fabergé style. He took the dresses to fashion week in Paris, and they became an instant success, impressing even such renowned couturiers as Pierre Cardin and Paco Rabanne. His Fabergé dresses traveled the world; some of them were purchased by the Louvres Dress Museum, and a few other items went to the California Museum of Fashion and the New York Metropolitan Museum of Art. In 1994 and 1996, Yudashkin dressed Russia's Olympic team. He also designed the uniforms for the Russian air company Aeroflot and the staff of the Hotel Ukraine in Moscow. In 2010, Yudashkin created new uniforms for the Russian Army. By 1997, Yudashkin had so many ideas that haute couture could no longer contain them and he launched the production of prêt-à-porter line. Interestingly enough, he began with a practical jean collection, which was sold in his first boutique, opened in central Moscow. Yudashkin expanded his designer talent to accessories, shoes, perfume, jewelry, and even silverware. In 2003 he came out with his biographical album entitled "Valentin Yudashkin" and an exhibition of his clothing was held in the prestigious

State Historical Museum in Moscow. Since 2003 Valentin Yudashkin has been a member of Camera Nazionale della moda Italiana. The Valentin Yudashkin's House of Fashion has existed since 1988. Today, his clothing collections comprise both haute couture and prêt-à-porter, and accessories, jewelry, porcelain, and sunglasses.

It is worthy of note that the company is famous not only in Russia but also abroad. At present the Valentin Yudashkin brand can be found in his boutiques in many Russian and foreign cities and interest is increasing rapidly. Valentin Yudashkin's collections have been shown during the weeks of haute couture and prêt-à-porter in Paris, Milan, New York, and other cities.

Concern Kalina

Concern Kalina is Russia's largest local personal care player with leading positions in skin and hair care. With an expected 2011 turnover of around RUB 13 billion (€303 million), 82 percent of the company was acquired by Unilever in December 2011. Concern Kalina is headquartered in Ekaterinburg, where its manufacturing facility is situated. The company has a strong, extensive distribution network and sells its products primarily in Russia, Ukraine, and Kazakhstan. It employs around 1,900 people.

With the mission of building the leading brands in personal care and cosmetics, the company's values lie in leadership and honesty with a focus on results. The company's strategy consists of three parts: successful marketing that is customercentric; successful products; leadership in distribution, and international human resource practices.

Concern Kalina developed strong brands in the key segments of the Russian cosmetics market. In October 2011, Unilever acquired 82 percent of this leading Russian beauty company.

Andrei Ananov

Andrei Ananov has become famous as a contemporary jeweler in Russia. His jewelry has, in recent decades, become a social phenomenon that symbolizes the Russian lifestyle. His work could almost be compared to that of fiction—his biography incorporates experience of theatrical direction and underground jewelry work, and in his character one can sense both the drive of a young capitalist and the confidence of nouveau Russian affluence.

Following Perestroika, Ananov opened his first officially registered jewelry-making business in Russia. He started reviving the ideas of the unforgettable Peter Carl Fabergé, the world-famous jewelry supplier of the Russian Royal Court. Ananov's ideas and design became very successful and his jewelry pieces found their way to the private collections of the Boris Yeltsin family; Queen Elizabeth of England; Alexis, the head of the Russian Church; Queen Sophia of Spain; Renie III, Prince of Monaco; Montserrat Cabalie; Placido Domingo; Stevie Wonder; and many others.

With time Ananov's style and his craftsmanship acquired the aspects of the modern design, without surrendering the heritage of his celebrated predecessors. The new designs gave a fresh, less orthodox, and more purely decorative quality to even traditional Easter eggs, unlike Fabergé famous Easter eggs of the turn of the century. Mosques, crescents, and Arabic legends appeared among egg themes. More and more Ananov's ideas represented a shift from the universal symbol of life to the celebration of life itself.

Raketa

Raketa watches have been manufactured since 1962 by the Petrodvorets Watch Factory in Saint Petersburg. It is Russia's oldest factory and was founded by Peter the Great in 1721 as the Peterhof Lapidary Works to make hardstone carvings. Raketa watches were produced for the Red Army, the Soviet Navy, and North Pole expeditions, as well as for civilians.

In April 12, 1961, Yuri Gagarin made the first flight in the history of mankind in outer space on the rocket Vostok 1. In honor of Yuri Gagarin, the Petrodvorets Watch Factory named its watches Raketa, or "rocket" in Russian. At the height of the Cold War, however, the name Raketa was perceived negatively in the West, as the word was associated with the latest generation of Soviet intercontinental ballistic missiles, the R-16.

Before the Petrodvorets Watch Factory began to produce watches, it produced objects made of precious and semiprecious stones for the tsar and his family. Later, it began to produce goods for military manufacturers as well as jewels for the watch industry. In 1949, the factory released the first watches under the names Zvezda ("Звезда," star) and Pobeda ("Победа," victory). The factory's own watches, sold under the brand name Raketa, first appeared in 1961 and the factory also began to manufacture its own movements (internal mechanism of a watch), like the Raketa–2609N. Over the years, the Petrodvorets Watch Factory produced more than two dozen versions of watch movements. Some were equipped with features such as automatic winding, calendars, 24-hour models for polar explorers, antimagnetic watches (for use in case of a nuclear attack), as well as watches for the military. Mechanical Raketa watches produced in Petrodvorets were exported to many Eastern Bloc and communist countries and are considered one of the most durable and reliable movements in the world, and by the 1980s, Raketa was producing 4.5 million watches a year. Unlike most watchmakers around the world, Raketa produces every piece of its mechanisms on site, making these product 100 percent Russian made. In June 2010, the factory announced that the super model Natalia Vodianova offered to design a new model. Vodianova's model was based on an old Raketa design from 1974.

Jacques von Polier, an alumnus of the ESSEC Business School and a French designer and businessman based in Russia, is currently heading the creative and design department of the Petrodvorets Watch Factory for the production of Raketa watches. With David Henderson-Stewart, his business partner, they are the keystone of restructuring and rebranding of Russia's historical watch brand Raketa.

India

> ... the land of dreams and romance, of fabulous wealth and fabulous poverty, of splendor and rags, of palaces and hovels, of famine and pestilence, of genii and giants and Aladdin lamps, of tigers and elephants, the cobra and the jungle, the country of hundred nations and a hundred tongues, of a thousand religions and two million gods, cradle of the human race, birthplace of human speech, mother of history, grandmother of legend, great-grandmother of traditions, whose yesterdays bear date

with the mouldering antiquities for the rest of the nations—the one sole country under the sun that is endowed with an imperishable interest for alien prince and alien peasant, for lettered and ignorant, wise and fool, rich and poor, bond and free, the one land that all men desire to see, and having seen once, by even a glimpse, would not give that glimpse for the shows of all the rest of the globe combined.[16]

India has historically been a country rich in culture and outstanding heritage, but a majority of the population has lived in desperate poverty due to the colonial regime of Great Britain. However, currently the country is going through a significant transformation in terms of the amount of wealth that is being created. According to a survey by the Confederation of India Industry and A.T. Kearney Ltd.,[17] the luxury market in India grew 20 percent to $5.8 billion in 2010, and will triple to $15.6 billion by 2015. Research from the McKinsey Global Institute (MGI) shows that within a generation, the country will become a nation of upwardly mobile middle-class households, consuming goods ranging from high-end cars to designer clothing. It is believed that this growth will persist into the future as well, given the overall growth of the economy and the fact that India is the home to the world's third largest population of millionaires (200,000) trailing only the United States and China. But despite such affluence, the region accounts for only half a percent of the global luxury market ($846 million). Greater China accounts for 10 percent of the same pie ($17 billion).

Following two years of intense political debate, in December 2012, India's union cabinet passed a bill allowing 51 percent foreign direct investment (FDI) in multibrand and 100 percent FDI in monobrand retail for single-brand retailers like IKEA, Adidas, Louis Vuitton, and Gucci. However, those opting for taking FDI beyond 51 percent will have to source at least 30 percent of their merchandise from the domestic micro and small enterprises. This decision will remove one of the major obstacles for Western companies, and luxury brands will finally be able to open directly owned, operated, and controlled boutiques. The true

---

[16]Mark Twain, *Following the Equator: A Journey around the World*, *Vol. II.* 1887/1889.
[17]DeMarco, 2011.

benefits of the FDI legislation have yet to be determined due to the complexity of operating stores in India. Following the positive outlook, the jewelry, electronics, fine dining, and cars sectors have registered the strongest momentum, growing between 30 percent and 40 percent in the past year. Apparel, accessories, and wine and spirits have continued a constant increase of about 25 percent to 30 percent. For example, Jean Christophe Babin, CEO of TAG Heuer, reiterated in 2012, that "TAG Heuer is third largest luxury watchmaker in India. We want to triple our business in the next 10 years. I cannot pretend that I will do the same in America or Europe, they are big or mature, I can only grow at 5 or 10 percent a year. In India, I can grow at least 30 percent annually. We are today present in 93 outlets (seven of them exclusive boutiques) and want to add two to four boutiques and two to five multibrand outlets a year. It is not just the quantity of locations, but the quality of the mall and its location. So maybe in five years this number will be 140, but it won't be 300."[18]

The drivers of recent growth in the luxury industry in India have been attributed to the use of cash or black money, which is extensively used to provide gifts. Coupled with this, the use of Bollywood, with more than 1,000 movies, and sports such as cricket as marketing tools, has proven to be effective beyond all means.

Despite these positive figures, India remains one of the toughest luxury markets in the world, mainly because of the lack of suitable luxury retail spaces. There are multiple drawbacks to opening luxury store in India. India's largest cities lack proper street retail locations or the ability to create shopping districts within an appropriate environment. Luxury retail development is impeded by less-than-desirable surrounding neighborhoods, cleanliness, and security, which don't show signs of improvement in the near term. One of the reasons that organized retail has not taken off is due to the previous regulations on retail ownership, which has considerably delayed the penetration of luxury companies in India. For example, Tiffany & Co. still does not have a store in India, and Louis Vuitton—the first entrant in this market and an arguable benchmark in the case of luxury retail—has six points of sale that are not even located at street level but within upscale hotels or luxury malls. As a

---

[18]Sachitanand, 2012.

matter of fact, Hermès is currently the only luxury brand in the country to have a stand-alone store at street level, following its 2011 opening in Horniman Circle, Mumbai.

The complexity of India's luxury retail landscape makes it difficult to predict whether or not this change in ownership legislation will have a rapid impact on store openings. This explains why many companies are still reluctant to invest money in India. For example, Lew Frankfort, chairman and ex-CEO of Coach, commented that, "India is not yet on our radar screen. I don't think it will be for a long time. Wealth is very broadly distributed geographically. That is, the affluence is not concentrated in small enough areas that can support, we believe, any meaningful business for Coach, at least not now."[19]

Patrizio Bertelli, Chairman and CEO of Prada Group, commented, "India is potentially interesting for us, not now, but in the long term. You need to look 50 or 100 years into the future."[20]

A majority of the wealthy Indians purchase their luxury goods abroad, mainly because there is a wider selection of products available at a significantly lower price. This only adds to the reasons why luxury brands may think twice before putting time and money into establishing retail stores in India.

Product import duties in India hover at 30 percent, real estate is heavily regulated, existing retail infrastructure is nonexistent, and potential street-level environments are often disorganized. The creation of luxury retail precincts and street-level destinations—driven by a potential alliance of luxury brands entering the market independently—could help to solve problems associated with a lack of ecosystem and help to create the correct environment in which Indians can experience true luxury.[21]

If a luxury brand decides to embark on significantly increasing its brand exposure in India, one of the keys to success will be to properly understand the consumers' needs and how they differ from those in developed countries. It is common knowledge that there is wide disparity in style between the Indian community and that of developed nations. For example, it is widely known that Indian women wear saris

[19] At Piper Jaffray Consumer Conference 2005, Final, June 7, 2005.
[20] International Herald Tribune Conference, November 20, 2004.
[21] Sachitanand, 2012.

to formal events, and therefore the luxury ready-to-wear market has yet to be developed. Another peculiarity that sets India apart from other emerging markets is its huge cultural legacy in clothing, jewelry, and accessories, which dates back centuries. More and more luxury brands have recognized the importance of creating Indian-inspired items, such as limited collections to show connectivity with the taste and lifestyle of the locals. To cater to such local tastes and preferences, Hermès has created a limited edition collection of saris made in France that was exclusively available in India. Bottega Veneta launched its limited edition "Knot India" clutch, which blends conventional embroidery with a signature Bottega weave and has "India" embossed on a sterling plate inside, just below "Made in Italy." Italian luxury men's fashion brand Canali has designed a *bandhgala* (closed-neck) jacket specifically for the Indian market, inspired by jackets worn by India's first Prime Minister, Jawaharlal Nehru. However, this may change in the future with the influence of Western culture.

Showing respect and understanding of the local culture is important also for those foreign luxury jewelry brands that want to succeed in this country. India has a long tradition in high-end jewelry, especially gold and diamonds, and emphasizing the use of local precious metals and stones could be an additional factor to break through in this market. There is no doubt that India has its own set of unique challenges. However, given the country's rapid growth in the luxury market, the inflection point is not far off, and chances are that the initial time and effort required to establish a brand will pay off in the future. Can such a strong heritage in so many luxury product categories contribute to the beginning of an era of homegrown Indian luxury brands?

Ganjam

Indian luxury jewelry brand Ganjam is among the few jewelry brands in the world that has a house (workshop) of artisans and remains in the hands of the original family. With a heritage stretching back over a hundred years, Ganjam has carved a niche for itself as a master of jewelry design and production (crafting). The company was established in 1889 and can be traced back to the Vijayanagar Empire. Ganjam Nagappa founded the company in Bangalore in 1889 and was appointed jeweler to the Maharaja of Mysore, and by the early 1900s he was invited by the King of Nepal to train his goldsmiths. The jewelry crafted by Ganjam has been desired and worn by Maharajas and Maharanis and continues to grace the men and women of modern India and countries beyond. Inspired by the South Indian temple architecture, these pieces with sheer intricacies of design and flawless craftsmanship are true to their traditional roots. Carnatic jewelry is not merely gems and gold crafted into ornaments, but a symbol of human spirituality over the centuries. This is what drives Ganjam to preserve and continue the extraordinary tradition.*

This legacy of exquisite craftsmanship has sustained the excellence with which Ganjam is associated today. Expertise in diamonds, precious gems, and traditional carnatic jewelry has made Ganjam a cultural reference for Indian jewelry design. In creating these refined and elegant pieces, Ganjam has ventured into new terrains: not just in the use of precious gemstones, where it is one of the very few Indian jewelers to use only hand-selected "f" color diamonds in all its jewelry, but also in the introduction of new weaves and techniques to India. The emphasis on innovation, design, quality, craftsmanship, and heritage has made Ganjam jewelry not only fascinating but also highly desirable, as it combines the best in international trends with the richness of traditional Indian craft.

Ganjam's flagship location is in Bangalore where it was founded. The company operates through directly operated stores in New Delhi and in Mumbai's Taj Mahal Palace, a popular destination for luxury tourists. The brand also promotes itself internationally. A private exhibition of handmade and heritage jewelry was held in London in June 2011. The company launched a line of jewelry to appeal to the Japanese market in 2010. Although the collection retained the "Indian essence," the line was modified to meet customer expectations in Japan and to have a contemporary treatment. The company planned to use this venture, pursued in collaboration with Japanese Citizen Jewelry, to enhance its brand awareness and presence in the Japanese market. Ganjam also expanded its reach to the United States.

The challenge for the brand has been to handle the paradox of maintaining a balance between the classic and the contemporary in terms of designing—from creating jewelry with deep historical and religious

---

*http://www.thejewelleryeditor.com/2012/03/ganjam-a-living-tradition-of-indian-jewellery/

significance to crafting cultural pieces with references to the contemporary world of today. With the tagline "Heighten your senses," the brand aims at creating an exclusive image among high-end consumers, but has yet to face the test of time of being globally accepted compared with brands like Cartier and Van Cleef & Arpels.

The Leela Palaces, Hotels, and Resorts

The Leela Palaces, Hotels, and Resorts were established in 1987 when the company's first hotel opened in Mumbai. Over more than 25 years, the Leela has become a highly reputable, award-winning luxury hospitality organization. In the past decade, the hotel group has grown from four hotels to nine with the opening of the Chennai and Jaipur hotels in December 2012. Furthermore, the group announced it would increase its portfolio to 14 hotels by the end of 2017.

The Leela stands for "the Dynamism of New India," a sensory and energizing emotional experience. The Leela is about Indian expression without guilt, celebrating and bringing alive the richness of a new, rising India, proud of its heritage and looking forward to inventing a greater future. The brand is at its best when providing its guests an overwhelming sense of warmth and welcome.

Brand recall for the Leela among guests and consumers in India is very positive, but outside the country, the brand is virtually unknown. Dramatic changes in design (notably a blend of traditional aesthetics and contemporary styling in Bangalore, Udaipur, New Delhi, and Chennai) are elevating the perception of the brand. The Leela Palace in New Delhi, for example, is located in the heart of Chanakyapuri, near the capital's prestigious Diplomatic Enclave. It is the first new hotel to be built from the ground up in New Delhi in 30 years and the most expensive hotel ever built in India, at an estimated cost of $400 million. It is also the first hotel in New Delhi to receive LEED Platinum certification. The Leela aims to create a buzz about the brand nationally and to also positively position the group globally as the "brand on the move" in the Indian hospitality sector.

After the company celebrated its twenty-fifth year of owning and operating luxury hotels in 2012, the family ownership determined it was time for a thorough brand reevaluation and possible repositioning.

The Leela reached out to Paris-based Landor to redevelop a brand identity strategy that included the creation of the company's first design and style manual.

The challenge that the Leela faces in the future is to differentiate itself from its competitors and balance luxury with value in an ever-changing luxury environment. It has engaged in identifying and actively communicating with key audience segments for the discerning affluent market, from the baby boomer with the means to indulge in the very best life has to offer to the younger, moneyed "next generation" who aspire to the same standard of living. The goal is to harness the power of the Leela by managing and controlling the corporate and brand identity of the group, and heightening awareness of and interest in target domestic and international markets. Along the corporate identity journey, milestones include a call-out in four "ownable" brand territories: Indian, luxurious, in harmony with nature, and graceful.

Manish Arora

Manish Arora is one of the most contemporary designers of the fashion world. This star has flashed the light of his talents in many parts of the world and has, hence, made a mark and created his own style of working. The designs of Manish Arora are different, unique, and colorful. He always tries to choose a theme or a character before designing for a show. Bright colors are the main feature of his designs.

From the catwalks of New Delhi to some of the most coveted ones in Paris, his career trajectory is envied by every designer today. The Mumbai-born, New Delhi–educated designer, who has been a mainstay on the Indian design scene for many years, made his international debut at London Fashion Week in 2005. It's been a roller-coaster ride ever since, with acclaimed shows in Paris and a host of successful new lines, including the diffusion label Fish Fry and Indian by Manish Arora, as well as his eponymous label, Manish Arora.

Known for his richly ornamental style and eye-popping palette, Arora often digs deep into his heritage for inspiration. His biggest validation came in early 2011 when he was named the creative director of the iconic Franco-Spanish label Paco Rabanne, becoming the first Indian to head a major international fashion house. Arora currently

splits his time between New Delhi and Paris. The challenge is to
focus on Manish Arora the brand and not the designer and to be
internationally known both as a designer and as a brand along with the
likes of Tom Ford.

His work is regularly worn by Lady Gaga, Katy Perry, and Nicki
Minaj, and the list of Arora-ites continues to grow. Manish Arora stands
for innovation, craftsmanship, and unconventionality.

Forest Essentials

The investment of international luxury companies represents an emerging trend in India. In the same vein, in 2008, Estée Lauder acquired a
minority stake in the Ayurvedic[22] cosmetic company Forest Essentials.
Forest Essentials is a unique Indian luxury Ayurvedic cosmetic brand
that was launched in 2000. The unique selling point of the brand is
that it combines the traditional aspects of cosmetics made according to
Ayurvedic principles with a modern element: lighter textures and pure
essential oils as opposed to regular Ayurvedic products, which are messy
and uncomfortable. This makes the use of these products light, pleasurable, and utilitarian. The brand has 18 stand-alone stores across eight
cities around the country. Their products can also be found in leading
five-star hotels, including the Taj, Hyatt, ITC, and Intercontinental.

The idea behind Forest Essentials is to build a niche, prestige brand
that advocates the use of luxurious Ayurvedic products. Even though it
is tied to the culture of India, the brand aspires for a global appeal and
therefore the product packaging and store design are not ethnic Indian.

The collaboration with Estée Lauder has given Forest Essentials
access to sophisticated technology and the highest standards of quality.
Additionally, the company can utilize Estée Lauder's network of research
and development centers around the world. In our opinion, Forest
Essentials has carved a place for itself in the market as a distinctive luxury
cosmetic brand, but is still at the implementation stage. Therefore, many
efforts can be made to increase its impact on the cosmetics industry in
India and internationally as well.

---

[22]Ayurveda or Ayurvedic medicine is a system of traditional medicine native to the Indian
subcontinent and a form of alternative medicine.

The success of luxury brands is mainly determined by their ability to innovate and provide affluent consumers with a unique and bespoke brand experience. Currently, the company largely supplies to hotel chains and spas, which makes up about 60 percent of its revenue. In the short-to-medium term, the company must gradually move its focus toward retail. This will help to penetrate the growing Indian retail market and enhance the product credibility among consumers in an affluent, younger group. There are now more layers of luxury than ever before to match new levels of affluence. Generally speaking, buying power in developed economies as well as in emerging economies has been on the rise.

The developed strength of the brand will thereby act as a strong foundation to propel it into the relatively more mature international market. More and more consumers around the world are interested in beauty products with a natural heritage, and Forest Essentials has the opportunity to be among the first from India to be launched internationally in this segment.

China

The world has used China as a cheap manufacturing land. This has been the defining thing for the past 10, 20, 30 years. The time has come to move on from this idea. I'm not sure whether future generations will still value the international designer brands available today, but they will appreciate these things because this cultural link is timeless.

—Shu Shu Chen, Communication Director of Shang Xia

China is one of the most alluring markets for luxury goods. The next consumers of luxury goods will be Chinese—they will be young and successful and will live in cities with more than 10 million people. China is the new Eldorado for luxury products, but Shanghai and Beijing will not be the only cities participating; another 95 or 100 cities will participate in the staggering growth story.

While pre-1978 China saw an annual GDP growth of 6 percent per year (with some extreme highs and lows), post-1978 China saw average

real growth of more than 9 percent per year, which was relatively stable. In peak years, the economy grew more than 13 percent. Per capita
income has nearly quadrupled in the past 15 years. China's GDP grew
at 7.5 percent in 2013.[23]

As the rest of the world struggles through these tough economic
times, overall the luxury goods industry in China continues to thrive.
China is already a winner for a number of foreign brands and for Chinese
brands tomorrow. As the world's fourth largest population of wealthy
households, the Chinese market remains immensely attractive. When the
rest of the world was reeling from the effects of the subprime mortgage
crisis, housing bubble, and collapse of the banking system, China resisted
and emerged. In 2009 every market showed a decrease in spending for
luxury goods: spending in Japan dropped by 20 percent, the United
States showed a decline of 15 percent, and Europe declined by 4 percent.
China, to the contrary, grew by 20 percent. In 2010, when all the markets turned positive, China moved forward more strongly than any other
market with a growth of 50 percent and in 2011 became the leader, the
driver of global growth for the luxury industry. When one factors in
both luxury goods purchases in mainland China and by Chinese tourists
abroad, the Chinese represent more than 20 percent of the worldwide
luxury market. Also in 2010, luxury consumer goods sales across categories such as jewelry, leather goods, and up-market, ready-to-wear
clothing rose by 20 percent to reach $12.4 billion. Furthermore, at the
end of 2012 Chinese consumers accounted for 25 percent of the global
luxury spending, which only added to their influence on the industry.
By 2015, luxury goods sales are predicted to reach $27 billion—around
20 percent of global sales—which would make China the world's largest
luxury market.

To tap this Eldorado of the luxury industry, which previously was
located only in China's largest cities, retail outlets for brands such as
Armani, Hugo Boss, Dunhill, and Ermenegildo Zegna are now opening
all over the country. In total, there are nearly 600 luxury brand stores
across China. Many of these brands have an equal presence in China and
the United States. Burberry, for example, has around 44 stores in the

---

[23]Source: news.xinhuanet.com.

United States and 39 stores in China. Gucci plans to open 100 stores by 2020, up from 32 in 2011. Louis Vuitton, Rolex, Chanel, Christian Dior, Giorgio Armani, and Dunhill all plan to open at least one store in each of the main Chinese cities over the next 10 years.

This was inconceivable just 10 years before, especially if one takes into consideration the fact that the country had been closed under the communist regime. But with a revolution it was liberalized, and like a flower in spring, it opened its arms and said, "Get rich, get rich. Do business and learn politics on the side. As long as you concentrate your efforts on your wealth, it is fine for us."

Who in the business community knew the existence of Huizhou, Huoyang, Chonqqing, Chengdu, Wuhan, Hefei, Harbin, Zhenghou, Nanchang in 1990? Who could have predicted in 2000 that in 2012 Gucci, Montblanc, Burberry, and Hermès would each have succeeded in establishing 20 to 50 stores in China? However, some luxury brands such as Patek Philippe take the Chinese miracle with a pinch of salt. Thierry Stern, chairman of Patek Philippe, commented that Swiss watchmakers are making a mistake by overinvesting in China as the market will eventually slow down. "I'm not putting all my eggs in the same basket. It's a big mistake I think that a few brands are doing by going only in China. They focus everything on China and it's dangerous."

First, with the increasing competition, it will become more and more difficult to be successful in China in the future. Only those companies that in the past years managed to acquire the bigger market shares and a deep knowledge of the Chinese market's competitive dynamics and cultural aspects will be profitable. In fact, the potential will be so spread that to operate in China in 2020 and 2050 will require an investment capacity that will narrow the market. Brands that are large and financially strong will be capable of operating in the global market. It may close the market for small or weak brands that do not have the financial prowess. On this issue, multibrand conglomerate LVMH is ahead with its financial capacity, its advance with store openings and its control over its business and the industry. In the watch sector, Rolex tends to dominate.

The slowdown in sales that was observed in China and other markets may herald a red flag for tomorrow. Compared to the annual complex growth rate of 27 percent for foreign luxury brands in China from 2008 to 2012, the growth rate in 2013, which is only around 3 percent.

Statistics released by Bain & Company show that the number of newly opening outlets of luxury brands in China dropped from around 150 in 2012 to around 100 in 2013.

To put this all in perspective with the consumer, first China is still in the primary stage of luxury consumption and has shown many characteristics—both in terms of challenges and opportunities—that are different from the traditional luxury consumption market in Europe and the United States. In regards to the structure of consumer demand, Chinese luxury consumers showed a characteristic of being younger. About 73 percent of Chinese luxury consumers are under the age of 45 years, and 45 percent of Chinese luxury consumers are between 18 to 34 years old. A comparable ratio in Japan and Britain for consumers under the age of 45 years was 37 percent, and more than 45 years was 28 percent, respectively.

Second, more and more Chinese luxury goods purchases are made abroad. It is estimated that 83 million Chinese traveled abroad in 2013, and this number is projected to increase to 120 million in 2015. Going by the statistics, Chinese consumers bought 47 percent of world's total luxury goods in 2013, which translated to $102 billion's worth of luxury goods, with some $28 billion in the domestic market and some $74 billion in the overseas market. This is because of the tariffs, which make prices of luxury goods 40 percent more in mainland China than in Europe. In addition, the euro dropped about 16 percent against the yuan in 2012, making the price differential worse. For example, for one of Louis Vuitton's most iconic accessories, the popular Speedy 30 bag, customers at stores in Beijing or Shanghai will pay 6,100 yuan (US$964), while the price tag in Europe is €500, or about US $619. Likewise, Chanel's Timeless Classic Flap bag, which in France retails at €3,100, or US $3,839, sells for ¥37,000, or about US $5,850, in China. Thus, in 2012, Chinese luxury shopping in foreign countries reached $7.2 billion, an increase of 28.57 percent over 2011, which translated to about 44 percent of Chinese luxury goods purchases made in mainland China. Still, luxury brands continue to open new stores in China at a rapid pace to satisfy the second largest market (after Japan). Margins have also been reduced to offset the price gaps between other markets due to the Chinese luxury goods tax, but this may not be the case much longer, and luxury goods companies such as LV and Prada are expected to increase prices in Europe to boost their top line.

Third, with the Internet and a growing importance of online platforms, Chinese consumers are becoming more familiar with and sophisticated about various luxury brands and are therefore demanding better service and a better overall shopping experience. The advent of the Internet has armed Chinese consumers with knowledge and relevant information about the brands and its products, its launches, and their availability. The Chinese consumers have instant information about new products and services offered by the luxury companies in Japan, Europe, or the United States. With this trend the Chinese consumers, who now represent 20 percent of the entire luxury industry, are more demanding and would like companies to meet their specific needs and wants. For example, Chloé's GM from China commented that "Mainland women are extremely well-educated and trendy. Women come into the stores not knowing the brand, but are still opinionated and know what they want, which is trendy, classy, and fitting into the market." Also the CEO of Burberry reflected, "Men's wear and outerwear were big growth accelerators in China. Also, children's wear has heavy potential despite the one-child-per-family policy of China. There is so much money—spent by parents and multiple grandparents—on these only children."

The three major trends identified above seem to lead toward the same conclusion. The rapid growth of the luxury goods industry in China will not be simple and will be even less simple with local Chinese brands on the rise. According to Zhang Zhifeng of NE-Tiger, "Foreign brands are always offered considerable discounts, the best locations, extended rent exemptions for a couple of years ... all of these contribute to their rapid expansion in China ... in contrast, most new-born Chinese luxury brands are not treated fairly here and have to operate under considerable restrictions,"[24] which means the government may need to step in if it wants to help promote local luxury brands.

NE-Tiger

NE-Tiger was founded in 1992 by Chinese designer Zhang Zhifeng. It is considered to be the oldest Chinese luxury brand.[25] According

---

[24]Silverstein, 2011.
[25]Fan, 2011.

to Zhang, "The history of luxury goods in China dates back a very long time," with the examples of Chinese silks being brought to Europe in 193 B.C.; the fashion consciousness of the Tang Dynasty (618–907); and coveted luxury items produced at the time of the Ming Dynasty (1368–1644), such as Chinese silk, jade, china, tea, and Yun brocade. In 1998, NE-Tiger became the largest specialized fur shop in Asia.[26] In 2001, the brand launched its own luxury brand of clothing and introduced an evening dress line called "Lady NE-Tiger" in 2003. In 2004, the brand was receiving international recognition and appeared in several international fashion shows and finally, in 2007, NE-Tiger was invited to attend both the English and the Dutch Luxury Exhibitions.[27] The brand began by extending into these various product lines, and now seeks to increase its retail presence. Following its first stores in Beijing, NE-Tiger's next move was to open a store on Libao Square in Shanghai, an area usually reserved for Western luxury brands such as Louis Vuitton, Tiffany & Co., Cartier, and Ermenegildo Zegna.

The brand focuses on mixing traditional Chinese design and cultural elements with a modern twist. This sounds similar to Shanghai Tang, however, NE-Tiger is perceived to be of higher quality and to have more tasteful designs. The brand was associated with a different period in Chinese history. The brand participated in China Fashion Week in October 2011, with its first haute couture collection. This sent a clear message to the world that a Chinese luxury brand was entering the couture arena, which had before been meant only for French and Italian craftsmanship, heritage, and creativity.

Headquartered in Beijing, NE-Tiger operates multiple stores throughout China, including Shanghai, Tianjin, Jinan, Harbin, and Qindao. It has extended its product offering to custom wedding and special event outfits, as well as it launched its Hua Fu collection—a collection of traditional Chinese dresses.

Shang Xia

Shang Xia was founded in 2008 by Chinese designer Jiang Qiong Er and the Hermès Group, which owns 75 percent of the company. "Shang"

---

[26] Silverstein, 2011.
[27] Silverstein, 2011.

means "up," and "xia" means "down." The name reflects the "flow of energy from the past through to the future, transmitting the essence of a culture and its aesthetics."[28] Its first store was opened in Shanghai in September 2010 and focused on bringing "the excellence of Chinese and other Asian craftsmanship into contemporary lifestyle through the encounter of heritage and innovation."[29] The brand is considered a lifestyle brand and its product offerings are based on home collections, which include furniture, decorative objects, accessories, garments, and an exotic experience of tea drinking.[30] The products are primarily created from traditional Asian materials such as bamboo, porcelain, and jade using Chinese handwork and craftsmanship traditions.

The financial viability of this new model of creating a local luxury brand with the expertise of a traditional luxury brand from France is yet to be proved. Shang Xia claims that sales have exceeded expectations, but the brand is said to be unprofitable so far. Artistic director and founder Jiang Qiong Er has time to develop Shang Xia into a strong international brand with the support from Hermès, which is looking for sustainable local luxury brands to grow and prosper. It seems that the philosophy and core values of both brands fit perfectly together, as both brands are focused on heritage, quality, craftsmanship, and "the search for excellence"[31] above all else. The brand expanded into additional product lines such as handbags. It expanded internationally with store openings in Paris and in Beijing.

Shang Xia is a purely Chinese brand that is designed for Chinese consumers. The brand is therefore trying to avoid, rather than benefit from, perceptions of foreignness. The brand allows itself to be priced quite high, given its association with the Hermès brand; however it is currently perceived as overpriced by the local consumer. But in a country where foreign brands are still widely regarded as higher quality than domestic brands, Hermès' support could act as a double-edged sword, buttressing the brand's reputation as luxurious and well-made while hurting its chances of being perceived as Chinese. This balancing act of how best to weigh local relevance against the prestige that may

---

[28] Shang Xia website. www.shang-xia.com
[29] Shang Xia ibid
[30] Shang Xia ibid
[31] Shang Xia ibid

come with foreign provenance has been a critical factor for any foreign brand doing business in China. Brands doing business internationally must also acknowledge the strategic importance of staying true to their core idea and promise.

Shanghai VIVE

State-owned Shanghai Jahwa Group is China's largest cosmetics company and owner of Herborist, a natural-ingredient cosmetics line that has recently exported products to Europe and the United States.

In 1898, Shanghai distributors launched a line called "Shuang Mei" for the local upper class. Shuang Mei offered both perfume and beauty products. Over time, the brand expanded, and around 1930, it was launched in Parisian stores under the name Vive. After three years of marketing brainstorming, Jahwa relaunched Shuang Mei under the name "Shanghai VIVE," harking back to the 1930s, and using the original ads with the two sisters. Not wanting to mess with success, Jahwa tapped French creative firm Cent Degres for a marketing strategy blending the "wild 1930s" tradition with a contemporary design feel. Shanghai's history is marked by a tradition of cultural collaboration and emulation between East and West. During the summer of 2010, the group relaunched one of its iconic legacy brands, previously known as Shuang Mei (双妹), established in 1898. The brand has a new name, Shanghai VIVE, but everything else about it looks nostalgic and retro. Shanghai VIVE's logo, packaging, advertising, and scents—even the location of its first store in the newly renovated Peace Hotel—are all reminiscent of Shanghai's 1930s glory days. With premium pricing and plans for more than 20 new stores by 2013, the resurrected brand's soaps and perfumes want to compete directly with dominant foreign brands in this category, such as Estée Lauder, Dior, Lancôme, Chanel, Guerlain, and Clarins. According to Shiseido, the number of Chinese women purchasing cosmetics was about 100 million, and is expected to grow to 210 million by 2015 and 400 million by 2020. In 2010, L'Oréal planned to post sales growth of 16.1 percent in China. Witnessing this trend, Sephora has also invested in China in a big way.

Shanghai Jahwa Group is not the only company bringing back old Chinese brands, however. Other recent examples include Warrior and Feiyue sneakers, Red Flag limousines, and Forever bicycles. These throwbacks represent a growing desire to revive old Chinese brands, some of which lost out to foreign brands during China's opening up in the 1990s. Now, as Chinese entrepreneurs and consumers are increasingly empowered, both figuratively and literally, a continuing resurgence of fallen-but-not-forgotten Chinese brands can be expected.

Chow Tai Fook

Chow Tai Fook is considered to be one of the most famous luxury jewelry brands in China. The company was founded in 1929 in Canton, with a heritage of more than 80 years. Acquired by Hong Kong entrepreneur Mr. Chen Yu Tung in 1956, it combines luxury with fashion and high quality products, such as high jewelry that appeals to wealthy customers. Chow Tai Fook made 56 percent of its revenue in 2014 in mainland China, with the rest coming from Hong Kong, according to data compiled by Bloomberg. Thus, in 2014 the Hong Kong-based retailer was relatively unknown to most Western consumers.

Chow Tai Fook has an extensive retail network with 1,421 jewelry points of sale (POS), mostly in China, Hong Kong, Macau, and Taiwan, and 85 watch points of sales as of 2011. Chow Tai Fook caters specifically to Chinese tastes, both with its line of products and customer service. There is less of the silver and white-gold jewelry popular in Europe and the United States, but plenty of the high-karat yellow gold used to make traditional Chinese wedding jewelry and the vivid green jade pendants that many Chinese believe offer health benefits to the wearer. Diamonds are also a big part of their business. In 2011, the company purchased the world's most expensive rough diamond for a record-breaking US $35.3 million (£23.2 million; €26million). Its self-operated and franchised stores are strategically located in densely populated areas and prime shopping districts, efficiently maximizing brand exposure and recognition. In 2012, its net income was more than that of Tiffany & Co. It has announced ambitious plans to have 2,000 stores by 2015.

Chow Tai Fook has an effective vertically integrated business model that provides a centralized, tight control over its processes from raw material procurement, design, production, marketing, and sales through its extensive retail network.

Jewelry sales have been growing at 40 percent a year in China since 2008 and are a key part of the luxury goods market in that country, which is expected to be worth US $100 billion (£64billion; €74 billion) by 2020, according to brokerage group CLSA. Chow Tai Fook is certainly a rare example. A study by CLSA of the most searched-for luxury brands on the Chinese search engine Baidu in the first week of November placed Chow Tai Fook fifth after Louis Vuitton, Chanel, Gucci, and Coach. U.S. and European jewelers Tiffany & Co. and Cartier ranked eleventh and twelfth, respectively. There was only one other non-Western brand in the top 25, another Hong Kong jewelry chain, Chow Sang Sang.

Strategic Actions

Good business leaders create a vision, articulate the vision, passionately own the vision, and relentlessly drive it to completion.

—Jack Welch

The above list of emerging market luxury brands is far from exhaustive; there are several other brands born in emerging countries that aspire to be luxury brands of the future. These brands now face a double challenge: to defend their positions in their domestic environments and, if possible, to conquer market shares abroad.

Unlike markets in the United States and Europe, where customers have reached a certain level of understanding and sophistication, the emerging markets still demonstrate branding infancy. On one hand the information asymmetry, misguided political regulations, inefficient judicial systems, lack of proper IPR rules, and complex labor laws make it difficult for them to thrive, innovate and create. On the other hand the mindset, the complexity of business structures, the diversity of demographic composition, and the geographic spread require a certain unique branding philosophy. Within this context, what are the conditions and the competencies that can help homegrown luxury companies in emerging economies to achieve their goals?

Heritage of the Brand

The heritage and story of a brand is usually the starting point for emerging market luxury brands. Brazil's Daslu, for example, has the potential to expand into other South American markets such as Argentina or Chile given that it is very well-established and well-known in its home market and is more than 50 years old. It is also considered a landmark for luxury for Brazilian consumers, since it was the first point of sale for many luxury goods brands in Brazil. Expanding into other international markets such as North America, Europe, or Asia, however, would take more time and resources for the brand to cement its position in the Latin American market as has been done by H. Stern.

Building the heritage of the brand is important in general for all aforementioned emerging market luxury brands, given the high expected growth rates of each of the countries and the slowdown of today's economic leaders such as the United States. It is important for these countries to have established their luxury brands so they are able to reap the benefits of having a luxury brand with a heritage by the time they become a leading economy.

Historical Association

Emerging market luxury brands might be successful outside of their home markets if they are associated with a time that was considered "glamorous." The example of Shanghai Tang is relevant here, as it was perceived as a "kitschy touristy brand" that had nothing luxurious about it, as perceived by Western customers. Westerners picked up a souvenir but for the most part, the product offering was not considered authentic or luxurious. This was because the brand's designs were associated with Shanghai of the 1920s and 1930s, which was not considered a glamorous part of China's heritage. On the other hand, NE-Tiger has the potential, given its association with and inspiration from the Tang dynasty, a dynasty considered very fashionable and also a time when China was thriving and considered a world power. The same can be said for India's Ganjam jewelry brand. The brand is associated with what is perceived to be a beautiful period of India's history, when the Maharajas were very opulent and wore jewelry specially ordered not only from local craftsmen but also from brands such as Cartier and Chaumet.

Country of Origin

To be successful internationally, it is almost mandatory that an emerging market brand needs to be successful in its home market. To be successful in its home market it needs to be associated with the traditional technique and craftsmanship that are unmistakably associated with its country of origin. Examples would be the uses of Indian design used by Manish Arora, silks used by Kimaya, or leather used by Hidesign. Another example would be the techniques used by Shang Xia, again associating itself with China's heritage and going back to the time when China was considered a world leader.

Country Association

Some general country associations can be leveraged to a great extent to build the brand's reputation. The best example would be Carlos Miele or Lenny from Brazil. The brands are associated with what is perceived by the West as a very glamorous part of Brazilian lifestyle. The ads with the Ipanema Beach in the background evoke the idea that Brazil is a colorful place with beautiful women who are familiar with this beach lifestyle and who like to have fun and party—hence the colorful designs. This is also part of the reason that Brazil's Havaianas brand did so well and became the world leader in flip-flops.

No Association

Finally, some emerging market brands may opt for no association, or barely any, with its emerging country of origin, as with H. Stern. The brand is not known to be Brazilian by most consumers, and its designs are comparable to other luxury jewelry companies worldwide. Of course there is a Brazilian influence in some pieces; however, the company does not openly associate itself with Brazilian culture, similar to its American competitor, David Yurman.

International Expansion, Growth, and Way Forward

Most of the emerging market luxury brands are still family-owned and/or privately owned, with the exception of a few, such as Shanghai Tang (owned by Richemont), or Hidesign (20 percent owned by LVMH). It is therefore difficult to determine how successful these brands really are, given the limited information about earnings and other financial data.

Opportunity for Conglomerates

Usually, conglomerates wait until brands prove to be profitable by themselves before acquiring the brand. Emerging market luxury brands present a huge opportunity for conglomerates. Purchasing an emerging market luxury brand allows a conglomerate to increase its competition and presence in emerging markets. It would be able to develop and grow these emerging market luxury brands in Western markets, where it may already possess distribution networks and influence with retail space opportunities. Finally, the conglomerate would be able to increase distribution and manufacturing capabilities in these emerging markets, as well as create synergies between businesses. The conglomerate would also gain knowledge and expertise about doing business in these emerging markets.

Some luxury conglomerates such as Richemont or private equity (PE) investors like L Capital (the PE arm of Group Arnault) have already invested in or bought some emerging market luxury brands and are at the forefront of this upcoming trend and will certainly reap the benefits of this fast growth.

Expanding into International Markets as Private Companies

The other option for expansion for the brand is to expand into international markets by itself. This is a difficult process given the amount of resource, network, and franchise value required to start from scratch in a new market. There are three key steps to this process.

First is to make sure the brand has recognized excellence, is differentiated from similar products within the same category, and portrays a set of distinct and unique value propositions both in its product and service offerings in its home market. For example, LV proposes its roots are in travel bags, whereas Hermès proposes that its roots are in its craftsmanship in leather goods and accessories. The emerging market brands not only need to capture the unique spirit of the respective region, their country-and-place-of-origin, but they also need to lead the way by creating that spirit. An example of this type of expansion route was followed by Shiseido. The emerging market brands have to overcome their liability of foreignness. For example, the negative perception of the "Made in China" tag and the associated link to problems with intellectual property rights and counterfeit market remains a challenge and are detrimental to China's aspirations to become a branded giant.

Second, the emerging market brands need the know-how and legitimacy in Western markets, especially from France and Italy where the industry was born, while balancing local specificity. Thus, a way to be legitimate is either to acquire a luxury brand from those nations or to be integrated into a conglomerate. For example, to be considered a luxury watch brand, association with the Swiss watchmaking industry is a must and the brand has to build an affinity for the host culture.

Third, the emerging brands need to be positioned in the mind of the consumers. There may be more than one way to do this. Due to the geographic spread of emerging market countries, a critical parameter is the distribution strategy. This requires a considerable investment and will also need a heavy investment in directly operated stores in order to establish themselves as legitimate brands abroad. For example, Coach, being an American brand, grew by the power of association of its stores with the main luxury brands in the United States, Japan, and Asia. Until early 2011, it was not present in Europe, but it launched its Paris store in Printemps, adjacent to Dior and LV.

Fourth, brand awareness and a clear communication of the DNA of the brand are key. A stated long-term and shared strategic vision that moves from fragmented marketing activities to totally aligned branding activities is mandatory. Brand awareness and brand building are perhaps the most critical elements for a new emerging market luxury brand. The right marketing mix is almost mandatory. Companies should tap into these specific details and incorporate them into their brand personalities and identities so that customers can be offered an authentic experience.

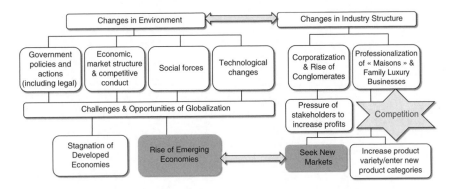

Figure 13.1 Globalization and the Luxury Industry

Conclusion

In conclusion, it is difficult to precisely predict the future of emerging markets. Today China is maturing, Russia and Brazil are emerging, and India is a long-time promising market for European brands. Although it might seem surprising, even the United States can be considered an emerging market for luxury brands, as a great number of American consumers represent a large untapped potential for personal luxury goods.

It is beyond doubt that China will continue to be a key market for luxury brands, especially as the development of the Internet allows an increasing part of the population to gain access to luxury brands online. Studies are predicting that based on how fast the region is growing, Asia Pacific will be the biggest region in the world for luxury goods by 2018. India was the most dynamic luxury market over the 2008 to 2013 period.

Moreover, it is assumed that luxury brands will discover the potential of Iran, Nigeria and South Africa, followed by several other African countries. In Asia, Vietnam and Mongolia will soon join the club of fast-growing South East Asian countries such as Indonesia, Thailand, Cambodia, and Malaysia. Thus, the emerging market story is here to stay in the long term, though it may shift to other locations in the future.

Figure 13.1 shows an overview of how globalization affects the market strategy of luxury companies.

Chapter 14

The Future and Questions to Ponder

L uxury has been a golden business since 1995, with big groups showing double-digit growth year after year. Only the sky seemed to be the limit. In 1996, Hermès was a small company with sales of €600 million; in 2014 it was worth more than €4 billion. Who could have anticipated the stock market success of Prada, LVMH, Kering, and Richemont?

Even during the years of recession in 2010, 2011, and 2012, most luxury companies realized an annual growth between 10 percent and 20 percent, and sometimes even more. However, these figures declined overall in 2013 due to a strong euro and a decrease in real consumption. Some resisted decline more than others.

Is it a new reality for luxury companies? In addition to the situation in Europe, China, one of the key markets, is showing signs of decreasing demand.

Other emerging markets are also suffering: Thailand is in turmoil, the Brazilian economy is not doing as well as expected, the political situation in Ukraine is unstable, and Russia is struggling with a very low ruble. At the same time, the Japanese yen continues to devaluate against the euro and the dollar, losing 20 percent to 30 percent in two years, which is very costly for luxury firms doing business in Japan.

These changes in the economic and political context of 2013–2014 have immediate consequences for the luxury tycoons. The future still remains optimistic, though not as before. Buoyed by a burgeoning middle class in emerging markets across Latin America, Asia Pacific, and Africa, in 2013 luxury goods sales were close to $320 billion worldwide, representing a year-on-year real value gain of 3 percent (compared to a year-on-year real value gain of more than 4 percent the previous year), according to Euromonitor 2014 report. The spending is projected to increase by more than 35 percent over the next five years.

This trend was witnessed at Kering Group with Gucci, Pomellato, Brioni, and Bottega Veneta showing an increase of 4.2 percent in sales in 2013 compared to 2012. Gucci, like Louis Vuitton, is pushing for sales of no-logo products while accelerating the sales of expensive leather bags—in four years the price of a Gucci bag has gone up 40 percent. It is remarkable that both Louis Vuitton and Gucci are now moving toward a new direction with more expensive products, especially accessories, and upgrading their quality to place themselves at the top of the luxury market.

This is in line with the policy of extremely high quality and a staggering price tag that for many years has proven successful for brands such as Hermès, Chanel, and Bottega Veneta. Bottega Veneta is a particularly good example that illustrates this strategy. In 2001 sales were €35 million, while sales in 2014 were expected to reach more than €1 billion with an impressive net result of around 35 percent on sales.

LVMH has also explained that 2013 was not a good year as their sales increased by only 4 percent and the profit remained stable compared to 2012. The main problem is Louis Vuitton. Since Yves Carcelle left the company, sales have been disappointing. The sales of its fashion and leather goods unit show a minus 0.4 percent for the first time in years. Is this a direct consequence of the Chinese authorities fighting against corruption? Is this the end of the logo policy that reached its limits in

2013? Many customers already have a Louis Vuitton LV monogram bag; are they getting tired of it? Are the stores too big, are there too many and are they just too much "everywhere," so that the customers can no have a sense of exclusivity and luxury?

If one analyzes the strategy of Hermès and Chanel in China, it is evident that they have fewer stores than their main competitors. Hermès has only 22 stores and Chanel does not even have 10, whereas Louis Vuitton and Gucci have around 50–60 stores. Dunhill has more than 100.

When Hermès showed an increase of 8 percent in sales in 2013, it was certainly a consequence of a stringent strategy with no compromise in quality and a limited number of stores.

Chanel's success can be attributed to extremely high standards for each product, high quality of service and store experience, and scarcity everywhere—Chanel only has two stores in India.

In 2013, Prada was the industry leader in front of Hermès, LV, Gucci, and the other brands of the LVMH, Kering, and Richemont groups. With an increase in sales of 9 percent in 2013 compared to 2012, Prada's impressive innovation in products, style, and service has proven to be a grand success in Asia.

We estimate Prada, Hermès, and Chanel to be the most successful trio in 2014, but brands like Moncler are showing even better signs of growth. Nonetheless, even Richemont, with brands like Cartier, Van Cleef & Arpels, Lancel, Dunhill, Chloé, and Montblanc that were suffering in 2012, showed a small 4 percent increase in sales in 2013, thus demonstrating that 2014 will be a turning point in the world of luxury.

Business "as usual" does not exist anymore. The game is becoming tough, forcing many brands to scrutinize their businesses and ask themselves questions, such as why consumers who used to be satisfied are now disappointed.

The years of 2013 and 2014 show that the luxury industry is not immune to the effects of external factors. The world—and the business of luxury—has changed because the crisis is everywhere, the political landscape is unstable, the currencies are uncontrollable, and the patterns of tourism are changing.

The luxury industry is also concerned with and affected by its own weak points: slow-paced innovation, too little effort in research and development, and a naïve belief in infinite success. Some brands opened too many and too large stores, forgetting the sayings that "small is often happiness," "a dream should be an obsession," "*surprise* is a slogan, *detail* is a must."

In fact, 2015 and 2016 will be the years when brands will go back to the basics and ask themselves what luxury is now and what luxury will be in 2020. What are the ingredients necessary to be a luxury brand in the future? Brands will be forced to renew their communication with and their way of serving the clients.

How will luxury brands use new technologies? Is the Internet compatible with the essence of a luxury brand, and how? Luxury and digital will have to find equilibrium where they support each other by reinforcing the dream factor of the luxury brand and helping consumers to buy the right products instead of diluting the brand. It will be a challenge.

Just as too much CRM can affect a luxury brand negatively, too much digital threatens to kill the desire for the brand—one of the ultimately most important aspects when discussing luxury.

Thus, the most important question remains: How does one stay unique when all brands use the same technologies, the same method for CRM, and the same training program for salespeople?

On top of this, more questions arise: How to be exceptional? How to find the stars of tomorrow? How to define the new level of services that ensure that luxury is fancied and recognized by consumers?

2014–2020 will be the beginning of a new era for tourism, the rise of the nomads, which will help to redefine the luxury industry. Until now the patterns of tourism have been relatively stable, with the Japanese being the main group buying luxury when abroad. Now this pattern is changing and new tourists are coming from Brazil, India, Russia, and China.

In 2014 more than 100 million Chinese traveled abroad; in 2020 this number is estimated to be 220 million or more. Data shows that Chinese consumers bought 47 percent of world's total luxury goods in 2013,[1] which translated to US$102 billion worth of luxury goods, with

---

[1] Statistics released by Fortune Character Institute, Bain & Company, in conjunction with the Italian luxury goods trade organization, Altagamma.

some US$28 billion in the domestic market and about US$74 billion in the overseas market. But the purchasing behavior of Chinese consumers is difficult to predict as they shop for luxury goods in countries with a favorable currency.

To attract tourists, even the United States is making more of an effort. To promote Miami as a luxury shopping destination and to attract tourists from South America, the United States is issuing visas valid for 24 hours. Europe still remains the most popular destination of luxury consumers, accounting for 35 percent of all global luxury sales, followed by the United States at 31 percent. Like the Chinese, Brazil's growing affluent class now makes up about 80 percent of its luxury buys abroad, identifying Miami, New York, and Paris as their go-to shopping hubs of choice.

In Europe, France and Italy are expected to be the two top countries benefiting from the tourist industry. Nonetheless, the strong euro can be an obstacle for European countries, turning clients and tourists toward the United States due to the weaker dollar. To attract these tourists, consistent efforts have to be made in areas such as visa regulations: multiple entry visas, quicker dispensing of visas, better and more efficient security, and new ways of welcoming the tourists.

Despite the hostile economic environment, the luxury industry should take advantage of the growing Chinese tourist in flux. In 2015, 1.5 million Chinese tourists are expected to visit France. This boom can, if well managed, have a real impact on the French economy and in particular on luxury brands. Paris-based department stores such as Galeries Lafayette and Printemps depend on tourists, since 60 percent of Galeries Lafayette's sales in 2013 were from tourists and 80 percent of these tourists were Chinese.

Furthermore, it is no secret that the American market is an emerging market for luxury brands. The potential is promising, with more and more rich women both buying luxury goods from the Internet and visiting luxury brand stores. The challenge of expanding in the American market is similar to the one in China—to have enough capital to invest in a market of that size. America is becoming the number-one target for the luxury industry.

Only rich and powerful brands that are strong enough to resist problems and drastic changes will be able to survive in the business of luxury.

As the key markets in the near future (2015–2020) are China and the United States, brands need to be able to overcome the challenges that these two markets impose.

Are the "big five" animals from the Kenyan savannah emerging on the luxury market? Four of the most powerful animals in the luxury landscape are Prada, Hermès, Chanel, and Cartier, but who will be the last one? Louis Vuitton, Gucci, Bottega Veneta, Dior, or Armani?

Obviously, the luxury landscape is large, and many other brands will survive and prosper, but which of the younger brands will be part of the next "big five"?

It is impossible to predict, as the business of luxury is changing, markets are unstable, big brands are suffering, and no one is protected.

In China, as well as in India, funds and creators like Shang Xia from Beijing—now with a presence in Shanghai and Paris—are thinking about the concept of luxury brands. Why should the French, Italians, English, and Americans have a monopoly on luxury brands? Why shouldn't an Indian brand be a competitor to the Western brands in the future? Luxury brands are not in a safe haven anymore. The country of origin, such as "Made in France" or "Made in Italy," is no longer a strong barrier. Tomorrow luxury brands can be made in India as well as in China and be as credible as the European counterparts. As the labels "Made in France "and "Made in Italy" lose their meaning, brands should push toward more innovative products and great improvements in the service level. Innovation is key at the product level, but it is crucial in terms of service. Not to take it into account would be a very big mistake.

It is an illusion to believe that luxury will keep meaning "foreign" and will be only for mature customers from developed nations. Take Ralph Lauren as an example. The brand represents an American success story. Coach offers a similar success story. They are affordable luxury and lifestyle brands, showing that the market is open to foreign luxury brands coming from many countries. The new trend suggests that affordable luxury brands such as Michael Kors and Black Box Wines (from the United States), Uniqlo (from Japan), Top Shop (from the UK), Havaianas (from Brazil), and others have consistently shown high growth and have successfully captured the generous spending of young affluents. The young affluents who are under 45 years of age are reported to repeatedly spend about 50 percent more than mature affluents on luxury. These young affluents are turning away from brands that primarily use "made-in" marks as status symbols. Instead, the young affluents want brands that reward them with pride of ownership and give them the appearance of being smart shoppers.

The "Made in France" or "Made in Italy" tag should be understood as a means to connect with the consumers and to become a love mark in different ways, including new technologies. However, it is important to stress that it is not an asset that guarantees a lasting credibility and advantage over other brands; it would indeed be arrogant and foolish to believe this. Before, the luxury brand was the privilege of fashion families and their wealthy customers and it was either French or Italian. Now it is open to millions of consumers in the middle class, there are only a few families left in charge of their brands, and the business is now "financial"—requiring both managerial skills and creative genius. All these factors combined generate a highly complex business model.

Luxury has a mission. It is to be part of a new sustainable development policy, which would give more nobility to this very profitable business. Luxury enjoys continuous growth, and the limit of the growth is not clear; it seems impossible to say where the end may be, so enormous are the market potentials. Europe will remain a stable market, full of tourists from everywhere—China, India, Africa, and South America. Crowds of tourists will make Europe a paradise for shopping in luxury shops. Japan is, for example, a country for growth in luxury foods; China and America will continue to show signs of good health, for Americans and also for herds of tourist from around the world. China, Brazil, Africa, and all Asiatic countries have not yet revealed how they will contribute to the growth.

Luxury as a territory seems unlimited. This is why luxury has obligations, to contribute to the sustainable development of the planet. Luxury brands should develop and train and re-train artisans of underdeveloped countries in Africa, Asia, and elsewhere, where so many talents have not emerged. A huge program must be put in place to support craftsmanship and to find a way to include new talent in the process of creation.

The development of craftsmanship around the globe will help brands to be more creative and enable artisans to escape from poverty. Luxury brands have an obligation to share their excess with others, to protect the planet, and to develop education programs. They can be leaders to preserve important resources worldwide and to renew expert regional industries, such as textiles in India, lacquer in Vietnam, porcelain in China, silver craft in Africa, and jewelrymaking in Africa and other nations.

The luxury industry is sometimes guilty of being too successful, and anyone can understand the occasional negative reactions. This is why the future of luxury is so closely linked to its willingness and ability to join the club of sustainable actions leaders.

- LVMH has many programs: Save the Children in Japan, *pont neuf* in France, *fondation Claude Pompidou*, Institut Pasteur, and others. LVMH also sponsors many artistic events like the Richard Serra exhibition in New York and Paris, Anselm Kieffer, and others.
- Hermès has created Fondation Hermès to help young talents all over the world.
- L'Oréal is very socially active, Gucci partners with UNICEF, and
- Kering is perhaps at the forefront of the movement of sustainable luxury, and particularly concerned about the leadership potential of women.

Sustainable development forces luxury brands to show their utility, to explain what they do, and show how they contribute to and promote beauty, innovation, and creation. Luxury is a business model that is successful due to its innovative capacity. It opens doors for others, as innovation is today the most important means to succeed. Luxury has obligations to consider how to employ people, how to recruit new talents, how to go further in creativity, how to innovate, how to find new usage of raw materials, how to better treat animals, and have a better usage of skins. Luxury is obliged to see the world with new eyes, to contribute more, to open the doors for the rest of the world to be part it its universe.

The consequence for luxury brands is to modify governance. More and more creators will have to travel, see the planet, get ideas everywhere, and they will work from all parts of the world, in house, outside, with others. The challenge will be to communicate, to grasp their ideas and transform them into products and services. Managers will learn to work differently to share views with travelers and to put together talent, some being "nomads," some being stable and some remote.

A management by community without hierarchical orders will replace the classical type of governance; each problem, each idea will be discussed through digital tools by interested citizens of the world who will bring their own experiences, ideas, and history to the subject. It will mean that to develop a luxury brand, classical management rules will not be able to fulfill the request for more innovation, as innovation will become the key element of differentiation. The questions will be how to be leaders in innovation while keeping hands-on with the strategy, or how to create more to surprise consumers, keeping the brand DNA alive, without compromise? Luxury has a huge future, but not for all brands: Some will emerge, some will continue to grow, and some will disappear.

Most of those that will emerge are unknown today, like Iran or Nigeria, but a lot of them are already open for business, like India, Brazil, Qatar, and South Africa. Why mention Africa when referring to luxury? Africa remains a land to be conquered by a certain type of luxury, based on authenticity and genuine quality. The combination of rapidly growing economies and youthful populations shows promise. Oil- and gas-rich countries have the potential to breed a new generation of high-net-worth individuals (HNWIs) within a short period of time. Countries showing promise are Nigeria, Angola, Ghana, Mozambique, Kenya, and Tanzania.

In fact, luxury usually sets in as soon as a middle class starts to emerge, as has been the case in Asia in countries such as Vietnam, the Philippines, Indonesia, and Latin America. However, why open a store in Mongolia's Ulan Bator and not in Dakar? That's probably for Louis Vuitton to find out.

Some questions that luxury companies should ponder include: Which will be the next growth markets? Will it be the young nations, or the nations where the middle-class is fast expanding? What type of products and goods will these markets like? How far should luxury brands extend in search of new markets or rejuvenate existing markets? How many stores should one open? Where? What needs to be the footprint for success? As markets will shift in the next 15 years, should luxury brands try local tastes and preferences or stick to global products? Will they follow the nomads? What would be the characteristics of the nomad of tomorrow? Should the creator anticipate the consumer's demands, their choices, and their preferences, or should they create only the best and let the nomads chose? How should brands renew the trust and loyalty from old customers while remaining relevant to the new generation? How does one transfer the values and the savoir-faire to the new generation? How does one know what the millennial will dream about and aspire to? Should luxury companies follow the demographic dividend route, or should they promote European roots while delivering global products? What is the future of affordable luxury? What about lifestyle? Is affordable luxury here to stay? With the digital age, what about time as a function to build a brand? How does one reconcile the past and the future? What about European leadership in the luxury goods business?

European brands will definitely have to face new competitors; the future of luxury will show new faces, new survivors, and new talents, we hope. The future is open. It can be bright, but it will be difficult, and one thing is sure: it needs new priorities and talented people, and includes risky decisions and high profits or losses.

It is a new frontier for luxury: The easy times are now behind us.

Research Design, Methodology, and Data Collection

The aim of this book was to examine the evolution of the luxury industry from the lens of management principles without losing the focus on business reality. It aimed to analyze the luxury phenomenon through several academic frameworks as applied to numerous practical examples. This book attempted to look at what the luxury industry had been, is, and will be.

Given the primary objective of the present study to examine the relevance and applicability of time-tested management principles within an evolving and constant change in the industry, exploratory research was conducted. Qualitative research is usually recommended for studying such process-related issues and also when the phenomenon being studied is not to be de-linked from its context.

Qualitative research, that is, case studies, gave a thorough grounding and a feel for real-life situations, especially where theory development

Figure R.1   Research Design

and research are in early stages. To develop a clear understanding of the interlinked phenomena in an ever-changing industry landscape, there was a need to look at varied data from multiple sources and study the phenomenon in its own context. The case method permitted a holistic analysis of a wide range of variables, open-ended and descriptive data, and multiple data sources and data collection techniques within the research setting. Figure R.1 shows the research design.

Methodology

The methodology of the study that was the basis for this book involved focusing on a wide number of organizations covering different sectors of the luxury business, documenting their creation, their historical evolution, and the processes that these organizations followed. A deliberate choice was made to focus on breadth, keeping in mind that it is unrealistic to try to attempt both detailed, in-depth analyses of organizations and also look at a large sample of firms at the same time.

In order to understand the contingent effects of the environment, both archival and primary data were collected through interviews. Longitudinal data was necessary to capture changes in the context and to observe the process of evolution, if any.

The method used in writing this book included three distinct phases. First, an in-depth analysis of archival data was undertaken, analyzing articles and documents concerning each organization, including analysts' and consultants' reports, changes in organization structure, annual reports (when available), industry reports, and others. Second, longitudinal case studies were written about the organizations. Third, primary data were collected from interviews, discussions, and by participation at luxury conferences.

Data Collection and Analysis

The data required during this study called for top management involvement and the opinions of industry experts. That was because the information needed involved strategic decisions taken by the family houses and the multibrand conglomerates. This data was available by attending industry conferences such as the New York Times Luxury Conference and Financial Times Luxury Conference over a period of five years, taking notes while CEOs spoke and interacting with top management on a one-to-one basis. The data required were mostly post hoc. To reconstruct an accurate account of the strategies, the informant also needed to have knowledge of events and should have observed it closely. Interviewing a range of informants enabled cross-checking of the data and identified multiple perspectives and differences of opinions within the business houses and family-held firms.

Constant effort was undertaken to increase the reliability and validity of the study. Multiple respondents provided reliability and validity. They provided insights into the evolution of the industry and the business houses. The interview data was cross-checked with the press reports. The study undertook several measures, such as informal solicitation, personal viewpoints, alumni feedback, and others in getting accurate and actual information. Before starting the fieldwork, an interview protocol was prepared that was improved and revised after discussion with experienced professionals. The interview protocol consisted of various questions broadly related to different categories of variables, such as the changing dynamics of luxury environment, the logic of the business, the global financial crisis and its effect on luxury, marketing vis-à-vis branding, the nature of people, their management styles, the skills of luxury brands working in this industry, distribution, and others. The data was collected over a 10-year period from 2004 onward.

The open-ended nature of questions gave the informants leeway in giving their responses. The interview protocol was strictly followed at all times and no constraints were imposed on the choice of responses.

Multiple respondents enabled cross-checking of the data. Use of multiple informants also helped in identifying multiple perspectives and any differences of opinions within the organization. The notes resulting from these interviews were transcribed into categories and used as raw data. Multiple case studies were written.

The data were analyzed through a variety of measures. The case analysis of each firm summarized the formal aspects of each organization. Results were compared and contrasted across multiple correspondents and functions. Emergent themes were further pursued to extract leads to understand in-depth the evolution process of the industry.

These are some of the important questions that were asked during the interview process:

- How do you define today "the logic of luxury"? What does "luxury" mean for you?
- Does the global financial crisis affect luxury, and how? Is the crisis positive or negative for luxury? What is the impact?
- Going by this trend, do you think that family businesses (focused and reactive) are more equipped to succeed vis-à-vis financial corporate groups? Or not?
- What is the definition of the classic sense of "marketing" in the luxury world? Does it exist or not?
- Who is the typical luxury consumer today? Describe. What is your assessment of the elasticity of the prices in the luxury world? Does it exist?
- How would you define the characteristics of the leadership and leaders in the luxury world?
- Do you think that the fact that the role of the *chefs des maisons* has been replaced by managers has changed the way the luxury groups are managed today? For example, has the business changed from being based on craftsmanship to being shareholder-value driven?
- How do you assess the potential or the feasibility of newcomers in the luxury world? Is it feasible or not? And where will they come from? The United States, India, Japan, China, Africa, or Europe? Some people say that China will represent 50 percent of the luxury market by 2025. Do you think this makes sense and how do you react to that?

- We are talking about innovation in products. What is the role of innovation in service and what type of innovations in services are you thinking of?
- What is the role of Internet in the distribution of luxury goods? Will it be an important distribution channel or not? Or do you think selective distribution will remain a vital element in the futures? Or do you think that luxury products will be in food and department stores?
- Do you think that counterfeiting will be a major obstacle to luxury sales? And how do you think luxury firms can fight against it in the future?

Bibliography

Ageorges, Dominique. "Champagne Corks Popping again in Luxury Business." PlushAsia.com. www.plushasia.com/article/10139.

Ainamo, A., and M.-L. Djelic. "The Coevolution of New Organizational Forms in the Fashion Industry: A Historical and Comparative Study of France, Italy, and the United States" (September–October 1999). *Organization Science.*

Benson, Todd. "An Oasis of Indulgence Amid Brazil's Poverty," *New York Times,* July 16, 2005. www.nytimes.com/2005/07/16/business/worldbusiness/16daslu .html?adxnnl=1&adxnnlx=1323864495-7FmVtQbxuyQ1Wfuobi9XSw.

Berry, C. J. *The Idea of Luxury: A Conceptual and Historical Investigation.* Cambridge, UK: Cambridge University Press, 1994.

Berry, Leonard L., Lewis P. Carbone, and Stephan H. Haeckel. "Managing the Total Customer Experience." *MIT Sloan Management Review* (2002).

Berthon, P., P. Leyland, M. Parent, and J.-P. Berthon. "Aesthetics and Ephemerality: Observing and Preserving the Luxury Brand." California Management Review 52 no. 1 (2009): 45–66.

Boroian, Michael, and Alix De Poix. *India by Design: The Pursuit of Luxury and Fashion.* Hoboken, NJ: John Wiley & Sons, 2009.

Blake, Robert Rogers and Jane Srygley Mouton. *The Managerial Grid: Key Orientations for Achieving Production Through People.* Gulf Publishing Company, 1972.

"Brazil on Way to Luxury Growth, Execs Say," reuters.com, May 26, 2011. http://in.reuters.com/article/2011/05/26/idINN2517159020110526.

Chadha, Radha, and Paul Husband. *The Cult of the Luxury Brand: Inside Asia's Love Affair with Luxury*. Boston: Nicholas Brealey, 2007.

Chevalier, Michel, and Gerald Mazzalovo. *Luxury Brand Management: A World of Privilege*. Hoboken, NJ: John Wiley & Sons, 2013.

Chevalier, Michel, and P. X. Lu. *Luxury China: Market Opportunities and Potential*. Hoboken, NJ: John Wiley & Sons, 2009.

Chitrakorn, Kati. "'Daigou' Agents Help Chinese Get Luxury Goods for Less." businessoffashion.com (April 9, 2014). www.businessoffashion.com/2014/04/daigou-agents-help-chinese-consumers-get-luxury-goods-less.html.

Danziger, P. "Let Them Eat Cake: Marketing Luxury to the Masses—As Well as the Classes." Fort Lauderdale: Kaplan Business, 2005.

DeMarco, Anthony. "India's Luxury Market Up 20% in 2010." Forbes.com (October 17, 2011). www.forbes.com/sites/anthonydemarco/2011/10/17/indias-luxury-market-up-20-in-2010.

DeMarco, Anthony. "Swatch Group Comples $1 Billion Harry Winston Acquisition." Forbes.com (March 26, 2013). www.forbes.com/sites/anthonydemarco/2013/03/26/swatch-group-completes-1-billion-harry-winston-acquisition.

Economist. "LVMH in the Recession: The Substance of Style." *The Economist* (September 17, 2009).

Eicher, B. *Selling and Managing for a Luxury Experience: Sales Training for Professionals*. Charlestown, SC: BookSurge, 2009.

Elliott, H. "How to Spot a Fake Louis Vuitton." Forbes (November 11, 2010). www.forbes.com/sites/hannahelliott/2010/11/11/how-to-spot-a-fake-louis-vuitton.

Fan, Haze. "Traditional, Ancient Accents at China Fashion Week." Reuters (October 27, 2011). www.reuters.com/article/2011/10/27/uk-china-fashion-idUSLNE79Q02720111027.

Fionda, A. M., and Moore, C. M. "The Anatomy of the Luxury Fashion Brand." Journal of Brand Management 16 (2009), 347–363.

Forbes. "Economy Is in Crisis, Yet Luxury Brands, Tiffany's, LVHM Still Report Sales Growth." Forbes.com (August 5, 2011).

Frank, R. H. *Luxury Fever*. Princeton: Princeton University Press, 2000.

Friedman, Vanessa. "Bernard Arnault: How to Manage Transition into Quality." *Financial Times* (June 15, 2009).

Kapferer, Jean-Noel, and Vincent Bastian. "The Specificity of Luxury Management: Turning Marketing Upside Down." Journal of Brand Management 16 (March-May 2009).

Kapferer, Jean-Noel, and Vincent Bastian. *The Luxury Strategy: Break the Rules of Marketing to Build Luxury Brands*. London: Kogan Page, 2012.

Kapferer, Jean-Noel, and Olivier Tabatoni. *Is the Luxury Industry Really a Financier's Dream?* Paris: Groupe HEC, 2010.

Koschate-Fischer, N., Diamantopoulos, A., and Oldenkotte, K. "Are Consumers Really Willing to Pay More for a Favorable Country Image? A Study of Country-of-Origin Effects on Willingness to Pay." *Journal of International Marketing* 20 (2012): 19–41.

Lent, Robert W., Genevieve Tour, and Alain-Dominique Perrin. *Selling Luxury: Connect with Affluent Customers, Create Unique Experiences through Impeccable Service, and Close the Sale.* Hoboken, NJ: John Wiley & Sons, 2009.

Lu, P. X. *Elite China: Luxury Consumer Behavior in China.* Hoboken, NJ: John Wiley & Sons, 2008; illustrated edition.

Luxury Society. "Exploiting Risk, Change and Creativity." luxurysociety.com, August 2, 2010. http://luxurysociety.com/articles/2010/08/exploiting-risk-change-creativity.

Matlack, C. "Handbags at the Barricades." *Bloomberg Businessweek* (March 28–April 3, 2011).

Menkes, Suzy. "Suzy Menkes: A Jewel of a Fairy Tale." *Vogue* (July 1, 2014). www.vogue.co.uk/news/2014/07/01/suzy-menkes-vogue-column-van-cleef -arpels.

Miller, Matthew G. and Peter Newcomb. "The World's 200 Richest People." Bloomberg.com (November 8, 2012).

Michault, Jessica. "Carlos Miele—Fashion and Art," *New York Times*, November 9, 2011. www.nytimes.com/2011/11/10/fashion/10iht-rcarlos.html?_r=1.

Neimark, I. *Crossing Fifth Avenue to Bergdorf Goodman: An Insider's Account on the Rise of Luxury Retail.* New York: S.P.I. Books, 2006.

Nissanoff, D. *FutureShop: How to Trade Up to a Luxury Lifestyle Today.* New York: Penguin, 2007.

Oechsli, M. *The Art of Selling to the Affluent: How to Attract, Service, and Retain Wealthy Customers & Clients for Life.* Hoboken, NJ: John Wiley & Sons, 2004.

Okonkwo, U. *Luxury Fashion Branding: Trends, Tactics, Techniques.* New York: Palgrave Macmillan, 2007.

Okonkwo, U. *Luxury Online: Styles, Systems, Strategies.* New York: Palgrave Macmillan, 2010.

Michman, Ronald D., and Edward W. Mazze. *The Affluent Consumer: Marketing and Selling the Luxury Lifestyle.* Westport, CT: Praeger, 2006.

Parr, M. *Martin Parr: Luxury.* London: Chris Boot, 2009.

Passariello, Christina, and Stacy Meichtry. "Gucci Chief Peddles 'Power of the Dream': How Polet Went from Popsicles to Purses." *Wall Street Journal*, September 24, 2007.

Reddy, M., N. Terblanche, L. Pitt, and M. Parent. "How Far Can Luxury Brands Travel? Avoiding the Pitfalls of Luxury Brand Extension." *Business Horizons* 52 (2009): 187—197

Roberts, Andrew and Vinicy Chan. "PPR Aims to Buy More Chinese Brands after Adding Jeweler Qeelin." *Washington Post* with Bloomberg, December 10, 2012.

Sachitanand, Rahul. "India Will Drive Growth in Global Luxury Watches Market: Jean Christophe Babin, CEO of TAG Heuer." *Economic Times*, May 16, 2012. http://luxurysociety.com/articles/2011/11/a-new-wave-of-opportunity-for -luxury-brands-in-india.

Silverstein, Barry. "NE-TIGER: Clawing Its Way Through China's Luxury Ranks." Brandchannel.com (July 22, 2011). www.brandchannel.com/features _profile.asp?pr_id=542.

Silverstein, Michael J., Neil Fiske, and John Butman. *Trading Up: Why Consumers Want New Luxury Goods—and How Companies Create Them*. New York: Portfolio Trade, 2008.

Swatchgroup.com. www.swatchgroup.com/en/brands_and_companies /distribution.

Taylor, D. H. Jim. *The New Elite: Inside the Minds of the Truly Wealthy*. New York: AMACOM, 2008.

Thomas, D. *Deluxe: How Luxury Lost Its Luster*. New York: Penguin, 2008.

Topham, James. "Japanese Retailers Give First Taste of Quake Profit Impact." Reuters (April 7, 2011).

Tungate, M. *Luxury World: The Past, Present and Future of Luxury Brands*. London: Kogan Page, 2009.

Twitchell, James B. *Living It Up: America's Love Affair with Luxury*. New York: Simon & Schuster, 2003.

Wathieu, L., and M. Bertini. "Price as a Stimulus to Think: The Case for Willful Overpricing." *Marketing Science* 26(1) (2007): 118–129.

Wetherille, Kelly. "Japanese Industry Assessing Damage." *Women's Wear Daily* (March 29, 2011).

Wetlaufer, S. "The Perfect Paradox of Star Brands: An Interview with Bernard Arnault." *Harvard Business Review* (October 2001): 116–123.

White, Belinda. "Cartier Debut Short Film 'L'Odyssée de Cartier' to Celebrate Their Rich History." Telegraph.co.uk (March 5, 2012). http://fashion.telegraph .co.uk/news-features/tmg9123145/Cartier-debut-short-film-LOdyssee-de -Cartier-to-celebrate-their-rich-history.html.

Winston, G. *Opting for Opulence: 14 Proven Strategies to Master Selling in the Luxury Market*. Garden City, NY: Morgan James, 2009.

World Luxury Index China 2013, second edition. Digital Luxury Group.

Online Resources

www.wwd.com

www.luxury-society.com

www.businessoffashion.com

www.inyt.com

www.ft.com

www.wsj.com

www.forbes.com

Index

Page numbers followed by *f* and *t* refer to figures and tables, respectively.

Advertising, 319
Africa, 18, 409, 419
After-sales service, 273, 274
Agache-Williot-Boussac-Saint-Frères, 244
Ahrendts, Angela, 82, 205, 262
Airbus A380, 99
Airports:
  duty-free shops/shoppers, 307–309, 324–328
  L'Oréal and, 74
  Swatch and, 69
Air travel, 49
Alexander I, tsar, 381
Alexander McQueen, 57, 61, 169
Altagamma (Italian Association of Industries of Alta Gamma), 13, 40
Alta Moda, 174
Ananov, 385
Ananov, Andrei, 384–385
Ansoff's grid, 111
Apple, 262, 333

Armani, 10, 47, 185
  brand extension, 110, 112
  and brand identity, 139–140
  digital marketing, 127
  in Europe, 16
  as family business, 172–173
  and financial crisis of 2007, 20, 22, 25
  and Italian management style, 222–223
  licensing, 318
  management style at, 222–223
  supply chain management, 292
Armani, Georgio, 172–173, 185, 222–223
Armani Collezioni, 223
Arnault, Antoine, 278
Arnault, Bernard, 6, 11, 21, 22, 55, 186, 209
  business strategy of, 196
  corporate strategy of, 39
  and French management style, 211–214
  on growth strategy for LVMH, 252–253
  and Gucci, 169, 319, 320
  and Hermès, 54
  and LVMH, 51, 53, 54

Arnault, Bernard (*Continued*)
  management style of, 55, 211–214
  and Marc Jacobs, 188
  on marketing, 92
  pricing strategy, 96
  and professional management, 244
  Henri Racamier and, 200
  on star brands, 30
Arnault, Delphine, 96
Arora, Manish, 393–394
ArteCad, 55
Artémis, 60
Art of the Trench campaign, 124, 205
Arts de la table sector, 19, 20
Asia Pacific region, 44, 65, 77, 419
Aspirational consumers, 145, 309
ASUAG, 65
Attali, Jacques, 99
Automobile industry, 89, 149
Aveillan, Bruno, 125
Aviation, 89

Babin, Jean Christophe, 388
Baccarat, 20
Bailey, Christopher, 118–119, 205, 262
Bain & Company, 12, 13
Balenciaga, 57, 61
Balmain, Pierre, 43
Bastien, Vincent, 139
Bauer, Henri-Louis, 216
BCE (brand—customer—employee) triangle,
  138f
Bearman, Erika, 127
Beauté, 71
Benefit, 54
Benetton, 165
Bensoussan, Robert, 178, 179
Bergé, Pierre, 142, 144
Berluti, 111–112, 278
Bertelli, Patrizio, 170, 171, 224–225, 322,
  389
Bettencourt family, 72
Bianchi, Luisa, 169–170
Biennale des Antiquaires, 118
Biollot, Laurent, 203
Birkin, Jane, 215
Birkin bag, 291

Bizzarri, Marco, 329–330
Blackstone, 177
Blogs, 120–121, 126
Blush, 189
BME (Burberry Middle East), 83
BMW, 7, 109, 317
Bogart, Humphrey, 79
Bonpoint, 30
Bootlegging, 363
Bosco di Ciliegi, 382
Boston Consulting Group, 30
Bottega Veneta, 30, 40, 224, 237
  corporate culture, 243–244
  CRM at, 300
  and financial crisis of 2007, 23, 24
  geographic expansion, 328–329
  Gucci Group's acquisition of, 57
  in India, 390
  in Japan, 15
  and Kering revenue, 57
  market positioning, 412
  and PPR, 61
  pricing, 113
Boucheron, 61
Boussac, 51
Brand(s):
  counterfeiting's effect on, 347–349, 350f
  star, 31, 39
Brand—customer—employee (BCE) triangle,
  138f
Brand DNA circle, 140, 141f
Brand extension, 109–112
Brand identity, 134–140
Branding. *See also* Marketing
  co-, 107, 109
  and ethos, 140–144
  and persona, 103–104
  premium vs. luxury, 131f
  and publicity, 105–106
Brand nirvana, 138–139
Brand positioning, 94
Bravo, Rose Marie, 79, 81, 82
Brazil, 369, 370t–372t, 373–381
  Carlos Miele, 377–379
  Daslu, 379–380
  digital marketing in, 120
  H. Stern, 376–377

Lenny Niemeyer, 380–381
L'Oréal in, 73
Breguet, Abraham-Louis, 239, 381
Brennan, Ed, 49
Brioni, 24, 40, 48, 58, 169
British Tobacco, 62
Brunello Cucinelli, 180–182
Bulgari, 25, 40, 55
Bulgari, Gianni, 171
Burberry, 10, 47, 79–83, 86t–87t, 262
    anti-counterfeiting measures, 354, 358
    and brand identity, 134–135
    brand segmentation, 81
    in China, 118, 396–397, 399
    digital marketing, 121–122, 124, 204–205,
        302
    and financial crisis of 2007, 20–24
    footprint and international expansion, 81
    future outlook of, 83
    growth and mergers/acquisitions, 82–83
    in Japan, 15
    launch of brand, 35
    in North Africa, 18
    online retailing, 333–334
    organizational/financial structure, 80–81
    social media use by, 123
    strategy of, 81–82
Burberry, Thomas, 79
Burberry Middle East (BME), 83
Burle Marx, Roberto, 378

Calza Turificio Rossimoda S.P.A., 189
Canali, 390
Carcelle, Yves, 30, 31, 338–339, 412
Cardin, Pierre, 111
Carlos Miele, 377–379, 406
Car Shoe, 170, 321
Cartier, 10, 62, 111, 204, 317
    after-sales service, 274–275
    Biennale collection, 118
    in China, 63
    digital marketing, 124–125
    and financial crisis of 2007, 20, 25
    in Japan, 15
    in United States, 18
Cashmere, 181
Catroux, Betty, 142

Cayenne, 8
Céline, 18, 53, 55, 213, 324
Celts, 32
Cent Degres, 402
Central Asia, 33
Champs Elysees, Paris, 105
Chan Ch'ien, 33
Chanel, 7, 12, 39, 47, 83–85, 86t–87t, 88,
        102–103, 116, 162
    anti-counterfeiting measures, 355
    and brand identity, 136–139
    brand identity prism, 137f
    CRM at, 300
    customer services, 271
    digital marketing, 301
    in Europe, 16
    and financial crisis of 2007, 19, 24
    future outlook of, 88
    in Japan, 14, 15
    launch of brand, 35
    licensing, 318
    online retail, 332
    sales strategy, 413
    and storytelling, 116–117
    strategy of, 84
    success factors with, 84–85, 88
    in United States, 18
Chanel, Gabrielle "Coco," 5, 29, 84,
        102–103, 329
    on being irreplaceable, 340
    and brand identity, 136–139
    and branding, 92–93
    and Chanel, 83
    design philosophy, 233
    on luxury, 94
    and storytelling, 116, 117
    and United Artists, 232
Chanel No. 5, 83, 84, 97, 99, 116, 140–141
Charismatic legitimacy, 311
Chaumet, 54, 155–156
Chen, Shu Shu, 395
Chen Yu Tung, 403
Chevalier, Alain, 50, 51
China, 370t–372t, 395–404, 409
    Bottega Veneta in, 329–330
    Burberry in, 83, 118, 302
    Chanel in, 85, 88

China (*Continued*)
Chow Tai Fook, 403–404
Coach in, 358
counterfeiting in, 342–343, 353
decrease in demand for luxury goods, 252
decrease in sale of luxury goods, 357–358
demand for luxury goods in, 44
digital marketing in, 120–121, 128
as emerging luxury market, 415, 416
and financial crisis of 2007, 16–17
flagship stores in, 312, 314
Hermès in, 112, 208
imperial period, 33–34
L'Oréal in, 73
Louis Vuitton in, 312, 314
luxury market in, 414–415
luxury retail stores in, 123
Marc Jacobs in, 189
NE-Tiger, 399–400, 405
online retailing, 335–336
Ralph Lauren's retail strategy for, 315
Richemont Group management training in, 256–257
Richemont's expansion into, 63, 65
rise of luxury market in, 368–369
Shanghai Vive, 402–403
Shang Xia, 400–402
and travel retail, 327–328
world travel by citizens of, 100
Chinese Empire, 33–34
Chloé, 127, 213, 399
Choi, Sandra, 178, 179
Choo, Jimmy, 178, 180
Chopard, 19
Chow Tai Fook, 403–404
Christian Dior (brand), 22, 50, 99, 262.
See also Dior
Christian Dior Couture, 23
Christian Dior Haute Couture, 51
Christian Lacroix, 18, 54
Christian Louboutin, 361
Christopher Kane, 58
Chrysler, 7
Church and Co., 170, 321
Citizen, 391
Clarins, 19
Clinique, 117

Club des Créateurs de Beauté, 74
Coach, 126
anti-counterfeiting measures, 353, 358
brand nirvana, 138–139
CRM at, 275–276
European expansion strategy, 408
and evolution of luxury market, 416
and financial crisis of 2007, 22, 24
and Indian market, 389
and Italian management style, 225–227
in Japan, 14
management style at, 225–227
in United States, 18
Cobranding, 107, 109
Coca-Cola, 98
Coco Mademoiselle, 85
CollaGenex, 74
Colorama, 73
Comité Colbert, 39–40, 163, 164, 205, 345
Communication, 289, 313
Communications gap, 279
Community, 288
Compagnie Financière Richemont, 62
Computing, 288
Concern Kalina, 384
Conglomerates, 11, 11*f*, 12, 36, 192, 194, 210, 244, 407. *See also specific conglomerates, e.g.*: LVMH
and brand ethos, 142
family houses vs., 184*t*
Connex Consulting, 31, 93
Connoisseurs, 145, 147
"Constrained freedom," 39
Consumer(s), 48–50, 144–145, 146*f*, 147–149, 326–327. *See also* Customer(s)
Consumer electronics, 89, 90
Content, of luxury goods, 287
Convenience, of luxury goods, 287
Copyright Act (1957), 344
Copyright law, 344
Corporate culture, 262
Cosmetics sector, 20
Cost/time value of price, 287–288
Coty, Inc., 189

Counterfeiting, 335–366, 366*f*
  and consumer awareness, 345, 353
  in digital era, 359–362
  and distribution channels, 354–358
  education as response to, 353
  effect of, on brands, 347–349, 350*f*
  and emerging markets, 346–347
  extent of, 344–345
  and luxury industry, 340–343
  online sales of counterfeit goods,
    122
  responses to, 350–359
Countries, 6
Craftsmen, 235–236
Creator (management style), 197–198
Credit card companies, 273–274
Crisis, 8–10. *See also* Financial crisis
  and luxury industry, 10–12
  types of, 8–10
Cristalleries de Saint Louis, 20
CRM, *see* Customer relationship management
Cucinelli, Brunello, 180, 182
Culture, 149–150, 262
Cunanan, Andrew, 176
Customer(s), 99–102. *See also* Consumer(s)
Customer delight, 288, 289*f*
Customer engagement, 281–282, 281*f*
Customer expectation, management
    perception vs., 281*f*
Customer experience, 332
Customer franchise, 288
Customer happiness, elements of, 270*f*
Customer relationship management (CRM),
    124, 269–270, 275–276, 295–300
Customer service, 277–280, 281*f*
Customer value, 289–290
Customization, of luxury goods, 287
Cyber-squatting, 361
Cyprus, 8, 10

Daigou, 336
Daimaru, 15
Danzinger, Pam, 41
Daslu, 379–380, 405
Daum, 20
De Beers, 19
Dedar, 78

De La Bourdonnaye, Geoffroy, 203
Della Valle, 165
Della Valle, Diego, 19, 175
Della Valle, Dorino, 175
Demand, 49–50
Demand curve, 112, 150
Demand-driven pricing, 152–153
Democratization of luxury, 36
Deneuve, Catherine, 142
De Quercize, Stanislas, 204
De Seynes, Guillaume, 216
Designs Act (2003), 344
De Sole, Domenico, 59–60, 142, 168,
    186
  Bernard Arnault and, 319
  departure from Gucci, 230
  and Gucci Group, 169
  and Italian management style, 223–224
  licensing agreement buyouts, 319
  management style of, 222–223
  and Tom Ford brand, 320
DFS, 49, 54, 326
Diageo, 19–20, 25
Diane Von Furstenberg (DVF), 376
Diesel, 165
Digital marketing, 119–129
  and brick-and-click paradox, 122–123
  and e-commerce, 128–129
  and mobility paradox, 121–122
  and paradox between digitalization and
    luxury brands, 119–121
  and social media, 123–128
  traditional marketing vs., 204–205
Di Marco, Patrizio, 224
Dior, 55, 112, 148, 212. *See also* Christian
    Dior
  brand extension, 110
  brand identity, 141
  customer services, 272–273
  and financial crisis of 2007, 19, 22
  in United States, 17
Dior, Christian, 5, 35, 99
Dior Group, 39
Directly operated store (DOS), 42, 181,
    316–317, 322, 354, 357
Discounting, 323, 354
Disney, 203

Distribution channels, 95, 307–336, 310*f*
  anti-counterfeiting measures, 354–358
  case studies of innovation in, 319–322
  and geographic expansion, 328–331
  gray market, 362–363
  and licensing, 318–319
  online distribution and e-commerce,
    331–335
  outlet stores, 322–324
  pop-up stores, 317–318
  retail stores, 311–315
  travel retail and duty-free, 307–309,
    324–328
  and trinity stakeholders, 324–327, 325*f*
  wholesale, 315–317
DNA, *see* Brand DNA circle
Dolce, Domenico, 173, 174
Dolce & Gabbana, 18, 21, 23, 107, 173–174
Dom Pérignon, 106–107
Donna Karan, 53
DOS, *see* Directly operated store
Dot-com bubble, 8, 9
Dow Jones Average, 9
Ducasse, Alain, 270
Duffy, Robert, 187
Dumas, Axel, 209, 214–217
Dumas, Jean-Louis, 214–216
Dumas, Pierre-Alexis, 216
Dumas, Robert, 76–77
Dumas family, 39
Dunhill Holdings, 62
Duty-free shops/shoppers, 307–309, 324–328
DVF (Diane Von Furstenberg), 376

eBay, 358, 360
e-commerce, 128–129, 331–335
Economic crisis, *see* Financial crisis
Egypt, 18, 33
Egypt, ancient, 5
Egyptian revolution (2011), 18
Eight P's of marketing, 102–108, 108*f*, 266
Elbaz, Albert, 126
Electronics, 89, 90
Elizabeth II, Queen, 168
Emerging markets, 367–409
  Brazil, 369, 370*t*–372*t*, 373–381
  China, 370*t*–372*t*, 395–404

and counterfeiting, 346–347
  demand for luxury goods in, 44
  digital marketing in, 120–121
  and globalization, 409*f*
  India, 370*t*–372*t*, 386–395
  and POS issues, 268
  Russia, 370*t*–372*t*, 381–386
  strategic actions for, 404–408
Employees, 243–244. *See also* Talent
    management
Emporio Armani, 223
Equinox Luxury Holding, 178
Ermenegildo Zegna:
  in China, 17
  company origins, 242
  digital marketing, 301–302
  as family business, 174–175
  loyalty cards, 273
  origins, 242
  Tom Ford and, 187, 320
Escada, 18
ESSEC, 253, 254
Essie Cosmetics, 74
Essioux-Trujillo, Belén, 248
Estée Lauder, 12, 49
  customer services, 271
  financial crisis of 2007 and, 19, 20, 22,
    24
  Forest Essentials and, 394
  Tom Ford Beauty and, 187, 320
  value-added services, 273
e-tail, 331–335
Ethical consumers, 149
Ethics, 337–338
Ethos, brand, 140–144
Etro, 191
Eugenie, empress of France, 241
Europe. *See also specific countries*
  Chinese customers in, 314
  contemporary trade with Asia, 37,
    38
  and evolution of luxury market, 417
  and financial crisis of 2007, 15–16
  as luxury shopping destination, 415
  size of luxury goods market, 43
European Commission, 345
European Union (EU), 10

Evolution of luxury market, 29–45
  in ancient world, 32–34
  and industry trends, 40–44
  in recent times, 35–40, 35*f*
Excess (term), 32

Fabergé, 383
Fabergé, Peter Carl, 385
Facebook, 123–125, 128, 302
"Fakes Are Never in Fashion" initiative, 362
Falaise, Loulou de la, 142
Family houses and businesses, 155–194, 167*f*, 207–208, 228, 262
  characteristics of, 159–160, 161*f*, 162
  corporatization and future of, 178–186, 184*t*, 185*f*
  during crisis, 177–178
  development cycle of, 158, 159
  French fashion houses, 162–164
  Italian brands, 164–177
  management styles, 205, 207
  and new entrants, 186–190
  trends with, 190–193, 193*f*
FAY, 175
Fendi, Silvia, 345–346
Ferragamo, *see* Salvatore Ferragamo
Ferragamo, Fulvia Visconti, 238
Ferragamo, Salvatore, 171
Ferragamo, Wanda, 171
Ferrari, 10, 96
Ferraris, Gian Giacomo, 224
Ferre, Gianfranco, 262
Ferris Baker Watts, 226
Financial crisis (generally), 8, 9
Financial crisis of 2007, 10–27
  China's relative immunity to, 396
  effects of, on luxury industry, 10–12, 18–20, 369, 381
  and global markets, 12–18
  strategic response to, 20–25
Fish Fry, 393
Flagship stores, 312–315
Flash sale sites, 323
FNAC, 61
Fondation Louis Vuitton, 118

Ford, Tom, 60, 90, 142, 168, 186–187, 313
  corporate strategy at Gucci, 319–320
  departure from Gucci, 229, 230
  and Gucci Group, 169
  and Italian management style, 223–224
  licensing agreement buyouts, 319
  management style of, 222–223
  and Rive Gauche, 143
Ford Motor Co., 97
Foreign direct investment (FDI), 387–388
Forest Essentials, 394–395
Fossil, 189
Foundation Altagamma, 40
Four Seasons, 18
Foursquare, 128
Fragrances sector, 20
France, 5. *See also* Paris, France; *specific French companies*
  Comité Colbert, 39–40
  digital marketing in, 121
  fashion houses, 162–164
  and financial crisis of 2007, 15
  management style, 210–217
  share of world production of luxury goods, 47
  Swatch stores in, 69
  tourism industry, 415
Frankford, Lew, 225–227, 275, 276, 389
Fred, 54
Fred Segal, 17
Fresh, 54
Frey, Pierre, 207
Frisoni, Bruno, 175
Fukushima nuclear meltdown, 14, 15
Furstenberg, Diane von, 373–374
FuturA program, 254

Gabbana, Stefano, 173
Gaemperle, Chantal, 246, 257
Gagarin, Yuri, 385
Galeries Lafayette, 16
Galliano, John, 55, 212
Ganjam, 390–392, 405–406
Ganjam, Nagappa, 391
Gao, Feng, 30
Gaultier, Jean-Paul, 78, 134, 215
GDP (Gross domestic product), 9, 9*f*

Gehry, Frank, 118
Genesis Colours, 83
Geneva International Airport, 69
Germany, 150
Ghana, 18
Giannini, Frida, 60, 127, 224, 229, 313
Gianni Versace Couture, 24. *See also* Versace
Giorgio Armani, *see* Armani
Giorgio Armani Privé, 104
Giornetti, Massimiliano, 172
Givenchy, 53
Glenmorangie PLC, 54
Globalization, 34, 290–295, 409*f*
Global supply chain management, 290–295
Goldwyn, Samuel, 232
Google+, 128
Goyard, 19, 36
Gray market, 338, 362–363
Great Britain, 32
Great Universal Stores (GUS), 79
Grillo, Beppe, 10
Gross domestic product (GDP), 9, 9*f*
Gucci, 5–6, 10, 40, 58–61, 90
    anti-counterfeiting measures, 359
    Bernaud Arnault's attempt to acquire,
        54
    charitable ventures, 418
    in China, 397
    digital marketing, 121
    distribution channel control, 357
    as family business, 168–169
    and financial crisis of 2007, 19, 25
    Tom Ford and, 186, 319–320
    and Italian management style, 223–224
    in Japan, 14
    Kering and, 229
    licensing, 318
    licensing agreement buyouts, 319
    management style at, 223–224
    management talent identification, 255
    managers from other industries, 203
    in North Africa, 18
    online retail, 332
    pop-up stores, 318
    PPR's acquisition of, 56, 61
    recent sales growth, 412
    and smartphone apps, 127

Gucci, Aldo, 58, 59, 313
Gucci, Guccio, 35, 58, 59, 168
Gucci, Maurizio, 59
Gucci, Paolo, 168
Gucci, Rodolfo, 59
Gucci Beats, 127
Gucci Group, 61, 143
Gucci Women, 60
Guerlain, Jean-Jacques, 39, 90, 125, 163
Guerrand, Wilfried, 30
Guerrand family, 39
Gunex, 180
GUS (Great Universal Stores), 79

H. Stern, 376–377, 406
Han Dynasty, 33, 34
Hankyu, 15
Harlow, Shalom, 125
Harper's Bazaar, 362
Harrison Group LLC, 30
Harry Winston, 24, 70, 71
Haute Horlogerie (HH) group, 317
Hayek, Nicolas, 65, 66
Hayek, Nicolas, Jr., 66
Hefei, China, 314
Heiniger, André, 219–220
Heiniger, Patrick, 220
Helmut Lang, 170
Henderson-Stewart, David, 386
Heng Long International, 55
Hennessy, 50
HENRYs (high-earning, not rich yet), 41
Herborist, 402
Hermann, Válerie, 315
Hermè, Pierre, 277
Hermès, 10, 30, 37, 39, 47, 49, 76–78,
        86*t*–87*t*, 92, 103, 107, 111, 112, 183
    after-sales service, 273
    Bernaud Arnault's attempt to acquire, 54
    in Asia Pacific region, 16
    and Birkin bag, 291
    brand extension, 112
    and brand identity, 134, 135
    business model of, 207–209
    charitable ventures, 418
    company origins, 240–241
    and counterfeiting, 122

and customer service, 279
customer service at, 283–284
diversification, 164
in Europe, 16
and financial crisis of 2007, 19, 20, 23, 24
footprint and international expansion, 77
and French management style, 214–217
future outlook of, 78
growth, 1996–2014, 411
in India, 389, 390
in Japan, 14, 15
licensing, 318
management style at, 214–217, 227
mergers/acquisitions, 78
organizational/financial structure, 77
sales growth in 2013, 413
strategy of, 77–78
success factors with, 78
supply chain management, 292
travel retail, 326
in United States, 18
Hermès, Emile-Maurice, 76
Hermès, Thierry, 76, 240–241
Hermès Group, 400, 401
Hermès International SA, 76
HFS, 23
(Haute Horlogerie) group,D
    317
Hicks Muse Tate & Furst, 179
H&M, 7, 109
Hogan, 175
Holtmann, Franka, 30
Homoluxus, 195–196
Hong Kong, 171, 189, 315, 326, 403
Hotels, 18
House of Chaumet, 155–156
House of Lanvin, 205, 207
Hublot, 19, 326
Hugo Boss, 49, 204
Huguenots, 239–240
Hyatt, 18

IACC (International Anti-Counterfeiting
    Coalition), 345, 362
IBB (Idaho Barber and Beauty Supply), 74
Idaho Barber and Beauty Supply (IBB), 74
Idol, John, 330

Illegal sales:
    via counterfeiting, see Counterfeiting
    via gray market, 362–363
Imaginex Holdings, Ltd., 189
Impérial Champagne, 98
India, 370t–372t, 386–395
    Burberry in, 83
    and China-Mediterranean silk trade, 33
    demand for luxury goods in, 44
    Forest Essentials, 394–395
    Ganjam, 390–392, 405–406
    Leela Palaces, Hotels and Resorts, 392–393
    luxury branding in, 104
    LVMH in, 148
    Manish Arora, 393–394
Indian by Manish Arora, 393
Infinity, 7–8
Information technology, 301–302
Inneov, 74
Instagram, 127, 128
Intellectual property rights (IPR), 337–340,
    346–347. See also Counterfeiting
International Anti-Counterfeiting Coalition
    (IACC), 345, 362
International Olympic Committee (IOC), 69
Internet, 359–362. See also Digital marketing;
    e-commerce; Online sales
Intime Center (Hefei, China), 314
Inventory control, 299
Investcorp, 59, 168
IOC (International Olympic Committee), 69
IPR (intellectual property rights), 337–340,
    346–347. See also Counterfeiting
Iraq war, 43
Isabel Marant, 109
Isetan, 15
Italian Renaissance, 5
Italy:
    Altagamma, 40
    digital marketing in, 121
    early trade with China, 34
    evolution of luxury brands in, 164–167
    management style, 220–227
    share of world production of luxury goods,
        47
    tourism industry, 415
IWC, 23, 24

Jacobs, Marc, 55, 135, 187–188, 333, 351
Jacobs Duffy Designs, 187, 188
J'Adore, 141
Jaguar, 97
Jamilco, 382
Japan:
    Burberry in, 81–83, 354
    Dolce & Gabbana in, 174
    duty-free shops, 307–308
    and financial crisis of 2007, 14–15
    Leonard in, 209
    luxury goods market in, 43–44, 369
    perfume market, 150
    and watch industry, 65
Jardin d'Acclimatation, 53, 118
Jean-Paul Gaultier, 78, 215
Jereissati Filho, Carlos, 373
Jewelry, 150, 274
Jewelry sector, 19
Jiang Qiong Er, 400, 401
Jil Sander, 170, 225
Jimmy Choo, 178–180, 192
Johansson, Scarlett, 174
Jones, Owen, 75
Jordache, 359
Just-in-time, 299

Kapferer, Jean-Noel, 136, 139
Karen Millen, 123
Karr, Jean-Baptiste Alphonse, 38
Kashiyama USA, Inc., 188
Keepall, 295
Kelly, Grace, 77, 168
Kelly bag, 77, 216
Kempinski, 18
Kenzo, 53, 352
Kering, 11, 40, 47, 56–61, 86t–87t, 186.
        See also specific brands, e.g.: Gucci
    anti-counterfeiting measures, 359
    Bottega Veneta and, 329
    business strategy of, 196
    charitable ventures, 418
    in China, 17
    and financial crisis of 2007, 24
    footprint and international expansion, 57
    future outlook of, 61
    global market share, 210

group companies, 56–57
growth and mergers/acquisitions, 57–58
Gucci and, 54, 229
hiring/promotion practices, 204
in Japan, 14
management talent identification, 255
organizational/financial structure, 57
origins of, 169
recent sales growth, 412
skill-sets needed at, 248
strategy of, 57
success factors, 61
Kering University, 256
Khan, Shah Rukh, 104
Kirkwood, Nicholas, 318
Knightley, Keira, 85
Knockoffs, 335–336
Koh family, 55
Kors, Michael, 55, 229
Krakoff, Reed, 226, 227
Krug, 116
Kublai Khan, 34
Kuwait, 315

Labelux, 179, 180
Lady Gaga, 394
Lady NE-Tiger, 400
Lagerfeld, Karl, 8, 83, 85, 99, 116
La Légende de Shalimar (The Legend of Shalimar)
        (film), 125–126
Lalique, 20
Lambertson, Richard, 186
Lamer, David, 226
Lancaster Group US, LLC, 189
Lanciaux, Concetta, 252, 254, 258
Landlords, airports as, 325
Landor, 393
Land Rover, 97
Lanificio Zegna, 242
Lanvin, 126
Lanvin, Bernard, 207
Lanvin, Jeanne, 205, 207
La Samaritaine, 54
Lauren, Ralph, 136
Lean production, 293–294
Leather goods sector, 19
Le Bon Marché, 54

Leela Palaces, Hotels and Resorts, 392–393
Left brain/right brain, 202, 236–236, 243
Lehman Brothers, 8
Lelong, Lucien, 163
Le Meurice, 30
Lenny Niemeyer, 380–381, 406
Leonard Fashion, 18, 209–210
Le Parfum (film), 141
Le Weekend, 117
Lexus, 7–8
Licensing, 318–319, 352
Lignes d'horizon (Attali), 99
Limited-edition products, 291, 323–324
Lion Capital LLP, 179
Livestream, 205
Liz Claiborne, Inc., 82
L'Odysée de Cartier (film), 117, 124–125
Logistics, 301
Look, Inc., 188
L'Oréal, 47, 49, 71–76, 86*t*–87*t*
 anti-counterfeiting measures, 358
 brands of, 71, 72, 72*t*
 charitable ventures, 418
 and financial crisis of 2007, 19, 20
 footprint and international expansion, 73
 future outlook of, 76
 growth and mergers/acquisitions, 74–75
 organizational/financial structure, 72–73
 strategy of, 73–74
 success factors with, 75–76
L'Oréal USA, 74
Loro Piana, 40
Louis Vuitton (brand), 10, 18, 30, 31, 39, 43,
  48, 50, 55
 and brand identity, 135
 in China, 123, 312, 314
 cobranding with BMW, 109
 company origins, 241–242
 counterfeit products, 342, 355, 358–360
 and customer engagement, 282
 distribution channel control, 355–357
 ethos, 141–142
 in Europe, 16
 and financial crisis of 2007, 19, 20, 22, 25
 in India, 388–389
 in Japan, 14
 launch of brand, 35

market positioning, 412
merger with Moët-Hennessey, 164, 244
pop-up stores, 318
POS problems, 270
pricing, 114–115
sales growth in 2013, 412
and service, 270, 271
supply chain management, 292–295
vertical integration, 191–192
Louis Vuitton Mansion, 312
Louis Vuitton Moët Hennessey (LVMH),
  see LVMH
Louis XIV, King, 5, 31
Loyalty cards, 272
L.S.A. S.P.A., 188
Lula da Silva, Luiz Inacio, 369
Luxury:
 defining, 6–8, 29–31
 fashion vs., 7
 hard vs. soft, 10
Luxury credit cards, 274
Luxury experts, 145, 147
Luxury goods, 30
Luxury hedonists, 145
Luxury industry. *See also specific topics, e.g.:*
  Financial crisis of 2009
 crisis management strategies in, 26*f*
 evolution of, 29–45
 future of, 411–420
 revenues of main players in, 13*f*, 14*f*
 trends in, 40–44
Luxury market sectors *(métiers),* 19–20
Luxus, 32
LV, 18, 112
LV Japan Group, 351
LVMH (Louis Vuitton Moët Hennessey), 6,
  11, 12, 36–37, 40, 43, 47, 49–51, 52*t*,
  53–56
 anti-counterfeiting actions, 338–339,
   342–343, 349–353
 Bernard Arnault's strategy for, 39
 brands under, 52*t*, 86*t*–87*t*
 business strategy of, 196
 charitable ventures, 418
 in China, 397
 creation of, 164, 244
 development of management talent, 253

LVMH (Louis Vuitton Moët Hennessey)
(*Continued*)
and DFS, 326
and family businesses, 177–178, 182
and financial crisis of 2007, 19, 23, 25
footprint and international expansion, 51, 53
and French management style, 211–214, 243
future outlook of, 55–56
global market share, 210
group companies, 51
growth and mergers/acquisitions, 53–55
Gucci and, 60, 170, 319–320
Hermès and, 208, 209
hiring/promotion practices, 204
identification of management talent, 254–255
in India, 148
Marc Jacobs and, 188, 189
in Japan, 14, 15
licensing, 318
management performance appraisal, 257
management retention, 258
management style at, 211–214
management talent search, 252
management training, 255–256
managers from other industries, 203
organizational/financial structure, 51
professional environment at, 246
sales growth in 2013, 412
skill-sets needed at, 246
strategy of, 53
success factors with, 55
treatment of smaller affiliated companies, 229
in United States, 17
LVMH Experience, 255
LVMH House, 255

McElroy, Neil, 92
McKinsey & Co., 15
Macro-segmentation, 297
MAG (minimum annual guarantee), 326
Maier, Tomas, 237
Maison Chanel, 39
Maison Martin Margiela, 109

Maly's Midwest, 74
Management perception gap, 279, 281*f*
Management style(s), 195–233, 206*f*, 233*f*
ambidextrous, 202–205
and familial autonomy, 205, 207–210
French, 210–217
Italian, 220–227
Swiss, 217–220
Managers, professional, 244–245
Manish Arora, 393–394
Marc by Marc Jacobs, 188–190
Marc Jacobs, 187–190, 333
Marc Jacobs Collection, 190
Marc Jacobs International Company, LP, 188
Marc Jacobs Perfume, 189
Marcolin Group, 320
Marcus, Carrie, 274
Marcus, Stanley, 139
Marino, Peter, 312
Marketing, 92–115
and brand extension, 109–112
and cobranding, 107, 109
digital, 119–129
eight P's of, 102–107
people and, 99
and pricing, 95–96, 106–107, 112–115
and promotion, 96–97
and storytelling, 115–119
Marshall Salon Services, 74
Martens, Maxine, 203
Martens & Heads, 203
Martini, 107
Matsuzakaya, 15
Maybach, 7
Meier, Bruno, 220
Meier, Thomas, 224
Mello, Dawn, 186, 319
Mellon, Tamara, 178–180
Mercedes, 7
Mercury, 382
Miami, Florida, 415
Michael Kors, 123, 127, 330–331
Micro-blogging, 120–121
Micro-segmentation, 297
Microsoft, 360
Middle East, 65, 83
Miele (brand), 378

Miele, Carlos, 377–379
Milan, Italy, 315
Millenium, 15
Minaj, Nicki, 394
Minimum annual guarantee (MAG), 326
Mini-nurse, 73
Miss Dior, 99, 117
Missoni, 25
Mitsubishi Corporation, 188
Mitsui & Co., 81, 82, 354
Mitsukoshia, 15
Mitterand, Frederic, 215
Miu Miu, 170, 321
Mizani, 74
Mobile phone, purchases via, 25
Mock monogram, 351
Moët & Chandon, 19, 50, 98
Moët-Hennessey, 51, 164, 244. *See also*
    LVMH
Moncler, 98
Mongols, 34
Monobrands, 48*t*
Monroe, Marilyn, 85, 116, 140–141
Mont Blanc, 25
Moss, Kate, 82, 85, 376
Moss family, 70
MSN (Microsoft), 68
Multibrands, 48*t*
Mussard, Pascale, 214, 215
Mystique (Ritz Carlton CRM system), 25

Napoleon III, emperor of the French,
    241
Natural disasters, 10
Nehru, Jawaharlal, 390
Neiman Marcus, 16, 139, 274
Nestlé, 72, 74
NE-Tiger, 399–400, 405
New Markets, 73
New York City, 5, 315, 320
Nice Cote d'Azur Airport, 69
Nicholas Kirkwood, 318
Niemeyer, Lenny, 380–381
Niemeyer, Oscar, 378
Nirvana, brand, 138–139
Nissan, 7–8
Nomadism, 99–102

Nordstrom, 25
Norsa, Michele, 172

Oasi Zegna, 273
Odysée of Cartier (film), 117, 124–125
Okinawa, Japan, 307–308
Olympic Games, 69
Omega, 69
Online sales, 25, 331–335, 342
Operations, *see* Systems and operations
Oscar de La Renta, 127
Ostentatious individuals, 147
Outlet stores, 322–324

Paco Rabanne, 393
Paradoxes, in management, 202–205
Paralympic Games, 69
Parfum Chanel, 83
Parfums Christian Dior, 50, 51
Paris, France:
    Chinese customers in, 314
    luxury retail space in, 105
    Marc Jacobs in, 189
Parthian Empire, 33
Patek Philippe, 17, 24, 102, 317, 397
Paucity, 103
Pegase manufacturing system, 293
Performance, 102
Perfume, 150
Perfume sector, 19
Pernod Ricard, 19
Perry, Katy, 394
Perry Ellis, 188
Persona (of luxury brand), 103–104
Personage, 104
Peter the Great, 385
Petrodvorets Watch Factory, 385–386
Philo, Phoebe, 55, 213
Phoenix Equity Partners, 178
Pierre Cardin, 111
Pilati, Stefano, 143
Pinault, François, 11, 60, 164, 186
    and Bernaud Arnault's attempt to acquire
        Gucci, 54
    business strategy of, 196
    and Kering, 56
    and PPR, 169

Pinault, François-Henri, 24, 60
Pinault Bois et Matériaux, 58
Pinault-Printemps-Redoute, 58
Pinterest, 128
Pitt, Brad, 116
Piva de Albuquerque Tranchesi, Lúcia, 379
"Pocket multinationals," 166
Point-of-sale (POS), 265–284
  and CRM, 298
  customer dimension of, 269–277, 270f, 272f
  and customer happiness, 270f
  issues in, 268–269
Point of sale and service (POSS), 268–269
Polet, Robert, 60, 203, 255, 313
Polier, Jacques von, 386
Political crises, 10
Polo, Marco, 34
Polo Ralph Lauren, 204, 318
Ponsolle, Elisabeth, 205
Pop-up stores, 269, 317–318
Porsche, 8, 10, 273
POS, see Point-of-sale
Positioning, 94, 104–105
POSS (point of sale and service), 268–269
Poverty, 6
PPR, 56, 186. See also Kering; specific brands, e.g.: Gucci
  and consolidation, 244
  development of management talent, 253–254
  and Gucci Group, 56, 57, 60
  and LVMH's Gucci takeover bid, 319–320
  origins of, 169
Prada:
  in China, 123
  customer services, 272
  digital marketing, 126
  as family business, 169–171
  and financial crisis of 2007, 20, 22–24
  in India, 389
  and Italian management style, 224–225
  in Japan, 14, 15
  management style, 224–225, 228–229
  retail strategy, 321–322
  sales growth in 2013, 413

Prada, Luisa, 228
Prada, Mario, 169, 228, 321
Prada, Miuccia Bianchi, 170, 171, 224–225, 228, 321
Prada Epicenter, 322
Premiumization, 7
Price/pricing, 7–8, 95–96, 106–107, 112–115, 150–153, 153f
Price elasticity of demand, 113–114, 151
Privilege, 273
Process, 97
Procter & Gamble, 92, 204, 286
Productivity, 98
Professional managers, 244–245
Promotion, 96–97
Prorsum, 82
Provenance, 102–103
Publicity, 105–106
Puech family, 39
Puiforcat, 77, 215
Puma, 56, 58

Qeelin, 58
QR codes, 25
Quality specification gap, 279

Racamier, Henry, 39, 50, 51, 200
Raketa, 385–386
Rakuten, 351
Ralph Lauren, 10, 47, 136
  anti-counterfeiting measures, 359
  brand nirvana, 138
  and CRM, 301
  and customer service, 276
  digital marketing, 121, 301
  and evolution of luxury market, 416
  and financial crisis of 2007, 22, 25
  online retailing, 334
  retail strategy, 314–315
  in United States, 17, 18
Rashid, Hani, 378
Ready-to-wear sector, 19
Redcats, 61
Redcats USA, 58
Reggiani, Patrizia, 59
Rembrandt's, 62
Remy Martin, 19

Renaissance, 5, 33
Reputation, counterfeiting and, 344
Restoration, 33
Retail stores:
  flagship stores, 312–315
  and global distribution strategy, 311–315
  pop-up stores, 317–318
Return-on-net-assets (RONA), 291
Revlon, 20
Rexel, 58
RFM (recency, frequency, monetary value)
    data, 295, 296
Richemont, 11, 40, 47, 62–65, 64*t*, 86*t*–87*t*
  anti-counterfeiting measures, 342, 349
  in Asia Pacific region, 16
  business strategy of, 196
  in China, 17
  consolidation, 244
  and financial crisis of 2007, 19–21
  footprint and international expansion,
    63
  future outlook of, 65
  global market share, 210
  growth and mergers/acquisitions, 63–64
  hiring/promotion practices, 204
  in Japan, 14
  management performance appraisal,
    257–258
  management retention, 258–261
  management style at, 217–219
  management training, 256–257
  mergers and acquisitions, 63–64, 64*t*
  organizational/financial structure,
    62–63
  sales growth in 2013, 413
  skill-sets needed at, 246–247
  strategy of, 63
  success factors with, 64, 65
  Swatch and, 70
  and Swiss management style, 217–219
Richemont Retail Academy, 256–257
Right brain/left brain, 202, 236–236
Ritz Carlton, 23, 25
Rivamonti, 180
Rive Gauche, 142–143
Roger Vivier, 19, 175
Roitfeld, Carine, 186, 319

Rolex, 10, 12, 317
  after-sales service, 273
  and brand identity, 135
  in China, 397
  and financial crisis of 2007, 19
  management style at, 219–220
  and Swiss management style, 219–220
Rolls-Royce, 103
Roman Empire, 33
Rome, ancient, 32
RONA (return-on-net-assets), 291
Ronson, Mark, 318
Rothmans International, 62
Ruben Thomas, Inc., 187
Rupert, Anton, 62
Rupert, Johann, 11, 62, 196, 217–219
Rupert family, 62
Russia, 370*t*–372*t*, 381–386
  Andrei Ananov, 384–385
  Concern Kalina, 384
  demand for luxury goods in, 44
  early silk-fur trade, 34
  Raketa, 385–386
  Valentin Yudashkin, 383–384

Safilo SpA, 189
Saint Laurent, Yves, 35, 142, 144
Saint Laurent Paris, 143–144
Saint-Louis, 215
Saks Fifth Avenue, 79
Sales staff, 282
Sales team, 243–244
Sally Beauty, 20
Salvatore Ferragamo, 17, 18, 25, 171–172,
    300
Sälzer, Bruno E., 203–204
Sander, Jil, 225
Sang Xia, 112
Sanofi, 143
Sanofi Beauté, 60
Sanyo Shokai, 81–83, 354
Sara Lee, 275–276
Schiaparelli, 19
Schueller, Eugene, 71
Schulman, Josh, 179
Scotland, 32
Seibu, 15

Sensharma, Ashish, 93
Sephora, 20, 54, 271, 272, 402
September 11, 2001, terrorist attacks, 43, 166, 170
Sergio Rossi, 61
Service:
    and customer engagement, 281*f*
    and customer happiness, 270*f*
    importance of, 265–267
    at point-of-sale, 277–280
Service delivery gap, 279
Service quality gap, 279
Shalimar, 125–126
Shanghai Jahwa Group, 402
Shanghai Tang, 400, 405
Shanghai Vive, 402–403
Shang Xia, 395, 400–402, 416
Shiseido, 408
Shuang Mei, 402
Sidem, Emmanuelle, 31, 93
Silk, 33–34
Silk Road, 33, 34
Sina Weibo, 120–121
Skill(s), 235–264
    of entrepreneurial designers, 240–242
    evolution of, 263–264
    historical craftsmanship, 238–240
    requisite, 245–248, 249*t*–251*t*, 263*f*
    of sales team, 243–244
    talent management, 248, 252–261
Smart car, 7
Smartphones/smartphone apps, 126–127
SMH (Société Suisse de Microélectronique & d'Horlogerie), 65–66
Smith, Adam, 236
Socially conscious companies, 418
Socially conscious consumers, 149
Social media, 120–121
Sofitel, 18
Sogo, 15
Song Dynasty, 34
Sophia Coppola, 96
South East Asia, 409
South Korea, 120
Speed to market, 299–300
SSIH, 65
Star brands, 31, 39

Status-oriented individuals, 147, 382
Stella McCartney, 21, 57, 61, 169
Stern, Hans, 376
Stern, Roberto, 376
Stern, Thierry, 397
Store manager (management style), 198–200
Storytelling, 115–119
Subprime mortgage crisis, 8, 9
Suhl, Sebastian, 225
Sumimoto Corp., 189
Sumptuariae Leges, 32
Sunglasses, 112
Suppliers, 326
Supply chain management (SCM), 290–295
Supply-driven pricing, 152
Sustainable development, 418
Swanson, Gloria, 232
Swatch, 47, 65–71, 86*t*–87*t*, 217
    divisions/brands of, 66, 66*t*
    and financial crisis of 2007, 19, 22
    footprint and international expansion, 67
    future outlook of, 70–71
    growth and mergers/acquisitions, 69–70
    organizational/financial structure, 66, 67
    strategy of, 67–69
    success factors with, 70
Swatch Group (South Africa) (Pty) Ltd., 70
Swiss Precision Watches (Pty) Ltd., 70
Switzerland, 217–220, 239–240
Systems and operations, 285–305
    creating value with, 302–303, 304*f*, 305
    customer relationship management, 295–300
    globalization as challenge to, 286–287
    and information technology, 301–302
    supply chain management, 290–295
    10 Cs of, 287–290

Taddei, Michele, 328
Tag Heuer, 19, 54, 104, 148, 388
Takashimaya, 15
Talent management, 248, 252–261
    acquisition, 253–254
    cycle of, 259*f*
    development, 255–257
    exit, 259–261
    identification, 254–255

length of service, 260, 260*f*, 261
performance, 257–258
prospecting, 252–253
retention/integration, 258–259
Taobao, 358, 359
Tata Motors, 97
Taylor, James, 30
Tech-Airport Holding SAS, 69, 70
Technology, 89
10 Cs of luxury goods, 287
Testino, Mario, 186, 319
Thankran, Ravi, 153
Thomas, Patrick, 54, 208, 216
Thomas Burberry collection, 22
Tiffany & Co., 10, 47, 48
  counterfeit products on eBay, 360
  pricing, 115
  social media use by, 125
  Swatch and, 70
  travel retail, 326
  in United States, 17, 18
Timex, 171
Tod's Group, 19
Tod's S.p.A., 16, 175
Toga virilis, 32
Tom Ford, 187, 320
Tom Ford Beauty, 187, 320
Torgovy Dom Moskva, 381
Tourism, 415
Toussaint, Jeanne, 125
TowerBrook Capital Partners, 179, 180
Toyota, 7–8
Trading-down, 36
Trading-up, 7, 36, 115, 151, 323
Tranchesi, Eliana, 379
Travel retail, 324–328. *See also* Duty-free
  shops/shoppers
Tribouillard, Daniel, 209
Tribouillard, Nathalie, 209
"Trinity" stakeholders, 324–326, 325*f*
Trussardi, 25
Tsunami (Japan, 2011), 14, 15
Tumblr, 128
Twitter, 123, 127, 128

Ungaro, 43
Unilever, 203, 255, 286, 342

Union Des Fabricants, 351
United Retail Group, 58
United States:
  Dolce & Gabbana in, 174
  as emerging luxury market, 415–416
  and financial crisis of 2007, 17–18
  Marc Jacobs in, 189
  quarterly GDP growth in, 9, 9*f*
United States Polo Association (USPA), 359
Unity Marketing, 41
"Up-or-out," 259
Urban Decay, 75

Valentin Yudashkin, 383–384
Vallat, Eric, 30
Value-added services, 273
Van Cleef & Arpels, 15, 64, 105–106, 204
Veblen effect, 113, 114, 150, 151
Vedrine, Hubert, 340
Vendôme, 62
Versace, 24, 109, 176–177, 292
Versace, Allegra, 176
Versace, Donatella, 176
Versace, Gianni, 176
Versace, Santo, 176
Versace Couture, 176
Versace Jeans Couture, 176
Versace Sport, 176, 177
Vertical integration, 37, 191–192, 218, 357
Vilebrequin, 93
Viva Glam, 149
Vive, 402
Vlisco, 18
Vodianova, Natalia, 126, 386
Volcom, Inc., 58
Vuitton, Louis, 50, 241–242
Vuitton, Odile, 39

Warning notices, 351
Watches, 66*t*, 239–240
  after-sales service, 274–275
  and financial crisis of 2007, 19
  wholesale distribution, 315–317
Web 2.0, 126
WeChat (Weixin), 120–121
Weibo, 128
Welch, Jack, 404

Wertheimer, Alain, 39
Wertheimer, Gérard, 39
Wertheimer, Paul, 83
Wertheimer family, 39, 83
Western Asia, 34
Western Europe, 73
Wholesale business, 315–317
Wilsdorf, Hans, 219–220, 240
Wines and spirits sector, 19–20
Winfrey, Oprah, 279
Wolseley, 58
Worth, Charles Frederick, 5

Yamaha, 107
Yoox, 332–333
YouTube, 117, 123, 125, 126, 128, 302
YSL, *see* Yves Saint Laurent
YSL Beauté, 74
Yuan Dynasty, 34
Yudashkin, Valentin, 383–384

Yuesuai, 73
Yves Saint Laurent (YSL):
    anti-counterfeiting measures, 359
    in China, 17
    ethos of, 142–144
    Tom Ford and, 90
    and Gucci Group, 186, 320
    and Kering revenue, 57
    Pinault's acquisition of, 169
    and PPR, 61

Zara, 7, 99, 299–300
Zegna, *see* Ermenegildo Zegna
Zegna, Angelo, 242
Zegna, Ermenegildo, 175, 242
Zegna, Gildo, 174
Zengiaro, Renzo, 328
Zenith, 54
Zhang Zhifeng, 399, 400
Zvezda, 386